*To: Sharon
The quiet one*

D. Bice 8/23/03

Southern Smiles & Tears

By David A. Bice

Southern Smiles and Tears

Copyright © 2003 by David A. Bice

All rights reserved. No part of this book may be produced or transmitted in any form or by any means, electronic or mechanical, including photocopying, recording, or by any information storage and retrieval system, without permission in writing from the Publisher.

First published in the United States of America in 2003 by Heritage Publishing Consultants, Inc.

Library of Congress Control Number: 2003102922
ISBN 1-891647-75-X

Printed in the United States of America
First Printing

Southern Smiles and Tears

To: Alley

Southern Smiles and Tears

Southern Smiles and Tears

FOREWORD

Here I am, 62 years old and my memory seems to have kicked into high gear. Events hidden beneath the surface have suddenly risen to the fore. Though many events are separate threads, they now seem woven into a tapestry. I now see them more clearly as they relate to each other. Characters paraded through my life leaving indelible prints. Some meetings were brief, others occurred over the entire 50-plus-years.

Each is a part of whom I am.

These memories are mine. This is how I remember people and events. Others, identified herein, may have different recollections of the same events. That is what makes memories so great. They belong to one's self. Some of the people, of whom I have written, are identified explicitly. Others simply have a first name. A few of the people have names slightly altered. This was a conscious choice by me.

My observations and memories cover a rare time in history. The Cold War, the Civil Rights movement, an explosion in telecommunications, assassinations, an Interstate Highway system all became fragments of those living during the era. The time fell immediately after World War II. I did not live during the Great Depression or serve during the war but knew those who had. The greatest transition I experienced was the social changes occurring between the white and black races in America. Some of us accepted the changes. Some of us rejected them. Some of us hoped for a better future for all Americans. Some of us passed our biases and prejudices on to children and grandchildren.

My wife Alice, second if you want to keep track of such a thing, often asked me over the past 17 years about my early years. Alice Ruth Skidmore Bice is from a close family, which neither Patty, my first wife, nor I had. I need a scorecard to keep up with discussions about Alice's family. Cousins, first, second, third, and more distant, are not only identified by name in conversations but so are their children, parents, and grandparents.

Some things were evident. Five children: Penny Lynn, Cheryl Ann, Daniel Mark, Jeffrey Alan, and Richard Paul came from a marriage to Patty Adkins. I missed much of their growing years by working two and three jobs. We did, however, have good times. We played softball, traveled on vacations, and went to church together. I know their memories of those years are much different than I have, but I would not exchange mine, good or bad, for anything. Each has enriched, or educated me.

I believe my mother, Gunhild Olander Bice, would have wanted to be part of the Skidmore clan. She loved to relate stories of family. When I realized the importance of passing down events, I did it in an opposite manner than my mother. It was easier for me to do so by the written word than verbally.

When you read the following, remember the words reflect me. You can enjoy, dislike, or ignore the words. What you cannot do is take them away from me.

Southern Smiles and Tears

All persons are puzzles until at last we find in some word or act the key to the man, to the woman; straightway all their past words and actions lie in light before us.
Ralph Waldo Emerson, *Journals*

Southern Smiles and Tears
Table of Contents

Part One 1950-1954
1. Move to the Front of the Bus
2. First Day of School
3. Eleanor and the Fence
4. The Invisible Fence
5. The Catechism Versus a Revival
6. Mom and Eleanor Explain Salvation
7. "Honor thy Father…"
8. "…and thy Mother…"
9. The All White Summer
10. The Library
11. My First Gumbo
12. "Uncle" Graves
13. Delivering Bread
14. Goodbye Eleanor! Hello Johnny!
15. Pecans and Pop
16. Paper and Pop

Part Two 1954-1963
17. Oscar Moves With Me
18. Miss Delaney
19. To Play or Not to Play
20. The Atomic Bomb
21. Snow Boarding Is for Wimps
22. Hitching a Train Ride
23. Personal Gas Stations
24. When a Brother Dies
25. Kip and Helen
26. Chemistry and Physics
27. Do You Want a Root Beer Mug?
28. Sharecropping
29. West Virginia Department of Rehabilitation
30. A Fake High School Diploma
31. Drive-In Movies
32. Ignorance Is a Terrible Thing
33. What Was That?

Part Three 1963-1979
34. Two Kennedys
35. Rome Fell
36. Kroger Hires a Negro
37. A Foot Soldier for Civil Rights
38. Different War, Same Dates
39. The Beetle and the State Trooper
40. Demon Rum
41. Canonizing a Demagogue and Demonizing a Statesman
42. Selecting a Career
43. It Was Just a Statue
44. Which Is the Bomb?
45. Murderers Three
46. Station Wagon Vacation
47. Redcoat Mary
48. Sweet Alice Moore
49. A Career Change

Part Four 1979-2003
50. An Angel on My Shoulder
51. Boston Pops
52. Peanut Butter and Jelly
53. "Swave and Deboner"
54. The Peabody
55. A Christian and a Jew
56. Old Dogs Can Learn
57. The Blind Can See
58. Roots of an Activist
59. Cancer! Your Name Is Not Modesty
60. Celebration of Life
61. Invisible
62. Evil Still Exists
63. Grace
64. Y2K Southern Style
65. West Texas Etiquette
66. The Confederate Flag
67. What's in a Name
68. Religion Versus Faith
69. Fertilizer and Flour Sacks

Southern Smiles and Tears

Southern Smiles and Tears

Part One
1950-1954

Southern Smiles and Tears

Southern Smiles and Tears

Chapter 1
Move to the Front of the Bus

The Greyhound Bus stopped in Bristol, Virginia, right at the Tennessee State line. Until then, I had been enjoying the long back seat. Stretching out. Standing up. Bouncing around. I suppose acting as any 10-year-old boy would on a long bus trip. The bus driver stood up, and the seat gave a whoosh of relief. I thought that it must be another rest stop. Not this time.

My mom and I were on our way to Mobile, Alabama. Actually, nearby Prichard. For some reason, lost in my recollections, the other kids and my dad had already moved to Prichard, leaving mom and me to come afterwards. This was another location in our family odyssey of following our dad in the construction business. Dad had worked on the Empire State Building and Holland Tunnel in New York City, giving the reason for me having been born in Connecticut. He then took us to West Virginia where he helped supervise the construction of the first synthetic rubber plant in the

Southern Smiles and Tears

United States during World War II. Before heading for Alabama in 1950 to build docks, there had been an additional stop in Wichita, Kansas, to build Purina silos, and another in Somerset, Kentucky, to raise a dam.

None of my travels had prepared me for what was to happen to me that day in Bristol, a city lying straddle the Virginia and Tennessee borders. The driver hefted himself to the back of the bus.

"Son, y'all hafta move up to the front of the bus. Onliest coloreds are to sit back here."

I know I was too young to know what "flabbergasted" meant, but that is what I was!

"This is the seat I've been in since we left Charleston! Why should I have to move now?"

"Because coloreds can't sit in the front of the bus."

Thus began my life into a culture heretofore unknown to me. I knew of Negroes, having seen several in Charleston. There was one man in particular; he worked in the Fife Street Shoe Repair shining shoes. Whenever we went to town my dad would stop to have his shoes returned to their day of purchase splendor. Sometimes, I even got to sit in the elevated chair as John spread the sweet smelling wax on my Buster Browns. Then he would snap the cloth and vigorously make my shoes shine.

Now, I found out John was a "colored." Something in the bus driver's voice let me know that John held a lower status than white people did. I pondered this as the bus continued down Route 11 on its way to Birmingham. At each stop people stepped aboard, while others departed. Without fail, the boarding Negroes walked to the back and sat down. When the last six rows were filled, the Negroes coming aboard stood, hanging onto the silver rail above. This made no sense — there were empty seats in the front of the bus, and men and women were standing in the back. More surprising was that there had been no announcement requiring this. Everyone, excepting me, seemed to understand the rules of this peculiar way of traveling.

I had much to learn about "...the land of the free."

We entered the city of Birmingham to the glow of huge stacks belching fire and smoke. My mind flashed to Alloy, West Virginia, where the coke furnaces along Route 60 burned with a fury, obliterating the sun and sky at mid-day. Here the sun was an oval obscured by steel mill produced ash being pumped into the air. The driver pulled into the bus station, and my mother and I exited the bus to two different worlds. In front of us was a black and white sign. It was divided in half. On one side was an arrow pointing to

Southern Smiles and Tears

the left beside big, bold letters **WHITES**. The arrow on the right side of the sign pointed in the opposite direction and was firmly ensconced beside the word **COLOREDS**. The left arrow directed those of the proper hue into the terminal. Those of improper shading were directed to benches outside the terminal and snack bar.

My mom searched the schedule board and found that we would change buses and head for Mobile in an hour. I wandered around the terminal and came upon a familiar sight. Before me was a raised chair for shining shoes with a Negro dipping his fingers into a tin of shoe polish and rubbing it on a man's shoe. Bent with time and crowned with gray, he was the only dark person inside the terminal; all other Negroes were outside on the benches. It was several months before I understood that there existed an exemption to enter the havens of whites for Negroes who worked in subservient positions in jobs white people believed were beneath them.

Soon the announcement came to board the bus for Mobile. We rolled down the dark highway.

The Negroes in the back. The whites in the front, and me with my head on my mother's ample lap.

Southern Smiles and Tears

Chapter 2
First Day of School

Where were the shoes?

Every year, in August after my birthday on the 12th and before school started, mom gathered all of us up and we caught the Charleston Transit bus at Stop 16 and went to Charleston to buy "school" shoes. We would go into Thom McAn and be fitted for shoes by a clerk sitting on a stool. After selecting our shoes, always one size larger than need be so we could grow into them, we would put back on our "everyday" shoes. As each of us went out the door swinging the bag with the boxed shoes, mom would ask, "Does anyone want a donut from Woolworth's?" After a cacophony of positive responses we would all head up Capitol Street to the five and dime where the donuts were being deep-fried hourly. We all would order two warm cake donuts and then consume them with a milkshake. Satiated, we then caught the "St. Albans" bus to return home.

Now looking around me on the first day at Glendale School in

Southern Smiles and Tears

Prichard, hardly anyone had on shoes. They were barefoot! It was easy for everyone to notice, with my new shoes amongst the dusty feet, that I was out of place. A black-headed chunky boy looked at me and said, "Y'all ain't from around here, are ya?"

"No, I just moved here."

"Y'all sound like a Yankee."

"I am not. I'm from West Virginia."

"That's up North, ain't it?"

"Yeah! So what?"

"Well, that makes you a Yankee!"

Thus began my acquaintance with Johnny Baxter, who was to become my alter conscience.

Teachers herded us into the school auditorium. One by one teachers would call out names, gather up their new brood and lead the scholars off to a classroom. A grandmotherly lady named Mrs. Brantley called out "Baxter" and "Bice". Along with about 30 others, we trudged off to our fifth grade classroom. She seated us boy/girl/boy/girl, with the boys in alphabetical order beginning with "A" and the girls in reverse alphabetical order. Seated between Johnny and me was the most beautiful, redheaded girl I had ever been near. If I had to be separated from Johnny, Linda Southerner was worth the distance.

Mrs. Brantley tapped her desk with a pointer to bring us to attention. I could not believe my ears! This lady began talking about using the bathroom and what to do after you finished. Linda's hair may have been glorious red, but it paled to the crimson rising from my neck to my hair.

Our first lesson was to be about **HEALTH and HYGIENE**. There — right on the blackboard — she had spelled out the words.

What was she doing talking about private stuff?

First, she told us if we had to go to the bathroom, we were to raise our hands and say, "Lavatory, please." That was all right with me, but then she began telling us what we were to do when we got to the lavatory.

"If you boys make water, make sure your pants are buttoned or zipped afterwards. Girls, make positive your dress is down and not caught in your undergarments. Then never forget to flush the commode. I know some of you do not have a lavatory in your house and do not have to flush, but here you do so. You flush by pushing the handle downward. When you are finished, wash your hands before returning to class."

I hoped that was the end of the lesson, but no, it got worse.

She continued with, "If you have a bowel movement..." but was

Southern Smiles and Tears

interrupted by none other than my newly acquired friend Johnny.

His hand shot into the air as the words, "What's that?" left his mouth.

Without so much as a reprimand, Mrs. Brantley explained the process, and my face passed crimson headed for scarlet.

"A bowel movement is when you remove from your body all of the solids not used for nutrition."

Snickers began to cross the room but soon exploded into full-fledged laughter when Johnny brightened as he said, "Oh! Take a crap."

The pointer rapped loudly on the desk.

"You children are in the fifth grade and need to act grown up. There is nothing humorous, nor vulgar, about bodily functions. I will continue about having a bowel movement. Once you have finished, you are to take four panels of toilet tissue from the roll, fold the panels, and wipe yourself from the front to the back. You then repeat this until there is no more residue on the tissues."

Not only was the scarlet returning to my face, but also heat was building up inside my head.

"When you are clean, flush the commode! Make sure your attire is returned to a proper state, and then wash your hands well."

What was I going to tell mom, if she asked what I had learned in school today?

Chapter 3
Eleanor and the Fence

 Because of the probability of moving within a couple of years, my mom and dad did not purchase a house in Prichard but rented. It was a two-story house down an oyster-shell covered driveway, which intersected with 5th Avenue, a four-lane street that ran to downtown Prichard.
 When mom and I arrived in Prichard the house was already furnished and bedrooms assigned. I was to sleep with my older brother, Billy. That was no surprise, but one thing was. We had a maid/cook named Eleanor. I couldn't believe it. Only rich families had maids. People like the Rockefellers, not us. My dad introduced Eleanor and told us she would keep the house clean, wash and iron our clothes, and prepare all of our meals, except for Sunday.
 Eleanor seemed to take an immediate liking to me. Perhaps, because I was the youngest of the family and probably the skinniest person she had ever laid eyes on.

Southern Smiles and Tears

"Law, child! You need some meat on dem bones," were the first words she uttered to me. For the next year and a half, Eleanor did her best to fatten me up. It didn't work. Almost everyday she wore a blue dress, which was partially covered with a bright, white, starched apron. Below the dress were hose rolled down below the knees. Above her collar was a chestnut brown face topped with black hair.

Eleanor became part of the house; her presence dominated. Nothing negative, just that we became dependent upon her. Not only for clean clothes and subsistence but also for advice and consolations. She was a regular weather bureau letting us know what to, or not to, wear, whether we should not go swimming because of the probability of a thunderstorm, even though not one cloud graced the sky. When our dog, Blacky, was hit and killed by a car, it was Eleanor who gave me comfort. Being careful to sing toward my chest where my cigarette-lighter size hearing microphone was strapped, she held me closely while softly singing, *Swing Low, Sweet Chariot*. She never told me that everything would be all right, only that Blacky was a memory Jesus had given me to cherish.

Our family was "High Lutheran" and speaking out loud about Jesus was not done. The closest any family member came to that was when my dad spouted "Gee whiz" or "Jesus Christ!" at Billy or me when we spilled or broke something. Eleanor, in contrast, said Jesus in a beautiful, prayerful manner. She ate separately from us and always bowed her head giving thanks to Jesus for her "daily bread." We said a prayer over our meal on Thanksgiving Day.

Eleanor would tell me stories from the Bible and talk about her church, the AME Zion Church in Prichard. I asked her once if I could go with her to church, and she answered, "No chile, I don't think your momma and daddy would 'low that. Why don't you ask your friend Adair about going to the Baptist Church across the street? They preach Jesus there."

I told her, "Maybe some day. We're Lutherans, and I don't think Lutherans go to Baptist churches."

With an all knowing look, she told me, "Jesus don't care if you're Lutheran, Baptist, or Episcopalian, He'll lead you where He wants you to go."

I never knew where Eleanor lived, what her last name was, if she was married, or if she were a mother. As I said, she was part of the house. Sometimes, it was almost as if she was a piece of brown furniture like the coffee table as far as my mom and dad were concerned. They did not mistreat her, as far as I know, but acted toward her more in the manner of her being a necessity in their lives, but wishing there were some other way to accomplish the same end.

   I believe Eleanor may have lived across the fence that ran behind our house and all the neighbors' back yards. This finally struck me when I remembered one of the first admonishments given to me after arriving in Prichard.

   "Don't cross that fence in the backyard." came the word from on high from my dad.

   "Why not?" I asked.

   "Because that's where the niggers live."

   And that was that. Now I had learned that there were certain places coloreds, Negroes, and niggers were supposed to be, and I was not allowed to go to those places. However, under certain circumstances the above named classified people could cross out of the designated places, if they served the whites. I had also learned, in my short time in "The Heart of Dixie", as the license on our new Oldsmobile proudly declared, that there were different names for the same people. Sometimes these names were interchangeable, other times the words seemed to indicate some type of social declination.

   What a peculiar system.

Chapter 4
The Invisible Fence

At recess we played tackle football. It always seemed Johnny and I were the last chosen. I could understand about me; skinny, with a hearing aid, and most important a "Yankee" placed me at the bottom of the list for most favorite people of fifth grade boys. But, why Johnny? Apparently born and bred in Alabama, he should have fit in. He ate grits, went barefoot, knew what butter beans were, and always said, "I'll carry you to the store for an RC and peanuts." He said the latter, even though I had learned he meant that he would ride me there on his bike.

I was the only one in our class who would sit outside with Johnny at lunch, exchanging goodies from our respective paper bags. Johnny seemed oblivious to being snubbed. He was just happy we were friends. When the final bell rang to end school, Johnny would take off for his house, ignoring my requests for him to come over to my house. Every once in a while I would ride along with him to his

Southern Smiles and Tears

house, but I never was allowed inside. I couldn't understand any of this but would soon find out about another rung in the social ladder of the South.

One Saturday I asked my dad if I could go play with my friend Johnny. He said it was okay with him. Billy had our bike out riding with his friend, Terry Mayfield, so I took off running for Johnny's. He was outside playing in the yard, and I shouted the southern greeting, "Hey!" We had played for a while, when I needed to practice Mrs. Brantley's health and hygiene. I told Johnny and asked him if I could use the bathroom. He said, "Sure." But instead of us going into the house he led me around back to a little shed and pointed toward the door. That was the smelliest, spider web covered place I had ever been in my life. A board with a hole in it served as the sitting place. I did my business, came out, and we continued playing.

Later that evening, after arriving home and eating, I told my mom about Johnny's bathroom. A look crossed her face that was the same one when Blacky had made a mistake on the living room rug.

"Where were you?"

"Over at Johnny's. Dad said I could go."

"Ray!" she shouted as if he were in Mobile instead of in the same room. "Did you allow Davy to go play with a Johnny?"

Why would she ask that? I had just told her so.

Disturbed from his bottle of beer, he responded, "Yes, he asked me, and I told him he could go."

"They have an outhouse!"

"What?"

"I said they have an outhouse!"

Right then, I knew a situation had developed.

My mother grabbed me by the collar and shaking her finger in my face so close I could see the cuticle. "I never want to hear about you playing with that 'white trash' again."

Oh, no! I thought. *Here is a new social stratum to add to my growing list of those considered to be beneath our family.*

I knew better than to ask any question, with my mom on the verge of apoplexy, so I decided to investigate this new phenomenon on my own. Monday, at recess, I asked Buddy about this. Buddy was the meanest and toughest boy I had ever met, so I figured he would know what "white trash" was.

"You mean that nigger lovin', dirt eatin' Johnny Baxter?"

Well, that wasn't what I meant, but that's what I got.

"I wondered how long a Yankee like you would hang around that trash before you knew you shouldn't."

Immediately, I realized that Johnny was a *persona non grata,* and if I did not want to achieve that status, I had to do something. I erred on the side of character weakness, and later told Johnny I couldn't be his friend anymore. To my surprise, this was not a shock to Johnny. He accepted my pronouncement with the equanimity of a diplomat. Johnny understood his position in the South. His lot in life was to be in some no man's land existence between the top of the heap and the bottom. He also knew that I could be lowered to his position by associating with him, but that no mechanism existed for him to rise in the social structure by associating with me. I would like to be able to say that I stood up to Buddy and told him that Johnny was my friend and not trash.

I didn't.

Chapter 5
The Catechism Versus a Revival

Church in our family was schizophrenic. My mom was devoutly Lutheran, but I do not remember my dad ever entering through the portals of a church. My mom's idea of being devout, however, meant attending services on religious holidays; Palm Sunday, Easter, Christmas Eve, and New Year's Eve Watch Service were mandatory — all other services were optional. To my dad, church was something that other people needed. The children, including me, had more severe religious obligations. Mom required we attend Sunday School and Catechism Classes. Dad required we miss Sunday School during the summer because the Gulf of Mexico required his family's attention on weekends.

All the other kids in the family had passed Catechism Classes before we moved to Alabama. Now it was my turn to learn the history of Lutheranism, along with memorizing the Books of the Bible, the Apostle's Creed, and other high church structures before I could be confirmed, sprinkled, and be an acolyte. I did my duty. That is how it was presented to the seven of us who were at the proper age, to learn about being a Lutheran. Mostly though, I learned that the Reverend, I forget his name, at the Lutheran Church on Schillinger Road in Mobile had the biggest feet I had ever seen. I know this because throughout all of the Catechism classes, I focused on the floor where his number fourteens were firmly implanted.

Church services were organized with each week having a designated name and or number. There was the Fifth Sunday after Pentecost, Maunday Thursday, Second Week of Advent, and so forth. Each week the Reverend wore different colors on his robe to signify that particular Sunday. It was awe inspiring and formal. Whispers and low voices were expected in the sanctuary. Even the Reverend spoke in a soft voice. The hymns, accompanied by the pipe organ, were the loudest sound in the church. This adherence to low volumes made it difficult for my hearing aid and me to comprehend most of what was happening.

The sermons must have been excellent. Almost everyone congratulated the Reverend, in loud, boisterous voices, as they exited the church. I believe many were relieved at being able to speak in normal tones, and others thought that the Reverend would know they had paid attention because of their loud enthusiasm. As for me, I didn't know what he had said so congratulations seemed out of order. My body may have been in church, but my mind was elsewhere.

Then I had a tremendous shock. My friend Adair invited me, "...to attend a Revival." That sounded like fun. I asked my mom if I could go to church with Adair on Monday night.

"They have church on Monday night? What do they do?" She asked.

"I'm not sure, but I think its games and things," I replied.

She assented at that moment, but that would soon change.

I met Adair at the Baptist church, along with his mom and dad. We went in to a sanctuary where almost every seat was filled and extra chairs were down the aisles. I had never seen a full church before and was astounded, but that was the least of my epiphanies that night.

Everyone was talking as if they were out on the street. Babies were crying as they writhed in their mothers' arms. Not one was in an enclosed "cry room" that was in every good Lutheran Church. When a baby screamed, the mother simply talked above the din. Then the choir began singing, and the congregation began clapping in rhythm. Where was I? Surely not in church. Then a man in a

Southern Smiles and Tears

brown suit and striped tie walked up behind the pulpit, prayed, and began to read from the Bible.

"Who's that?" I asked Adair.

Adair looked at me as if I were stupid and said, "The Preacher."

"Where's his robe?"

"He don't wear no robe. Them's for the choir."

Something was seriously wrong. I was getting nervous.

This is not to be a night of games.

The preacher finished reading "The Scripture", paused for a breath and began shouting. I mean football game hollering. Then people in the congregation began shouting back at him.

"Amen!"

"You tell 'em, brother!"

"Glory, glory!"

I did not have any problem hearing what the preacher said. In fact, the decibels caused me to lower the volume on my hearing aid. I wasn't sure what was going on, but I knew it wasn't a Lutheran Church. The preacher shouted at us for two hours. I thought there was a law that sermons were not to be longer than 15 minutes. Obviously, this man was unaware of the rule. He shouted, cried, wiped sweat from his head with a hankey, and pointed his hand toward the ceiling as he declared us all sinners. He could not have been talking about me because I had just passed Catechism Class.

The sermon was about "The Good Samaritan." It centered on not disliking people because they were different. We were to treat everyone the same. If we did not stop and help our fellow man, it was a sin.

"You better confess your sins and be saved, or spend eternity in Hell!"

This man shouted, "Hell" more than my father said the word, and that was going some.

At the end of the two hours, the preacher told us it was time to walk down the aisle and be "saved" from our sins.

Rapidly, I began to run the Ten Commandments through my head trying to remember which ones I had broken. *Murder? Nope, not that one. Stealing? Just small stuff like my brother's ball glove, and I'll have to give that back when he finds out where it is. Coveting? I want a new bike, but not someone else's. Adultery? That has always confused me. I'm not sure if I've committed that one, or not. Honor thy father and mother? I'm safe there. Have no other God? That's easy, I don't know of any other God.* I couldn't remember the others right then, but six out of ten seemed enough to keep me out of the bad place.

Southern Smiles and Tears

My good feelings about myself began to weaken as the service entered the third hour. The choir started singing, the congregation clapping, and the preacher scaring the bejabbers out of me with all his talk about Hell. People began to go down the aisle to the preacher. Most of them hugged the preacher, and just as they let go, the preacher shouted, "Hallelujah!" I had no idea what was happening, only that I did not want to go to Hell. Then the preacher said, "You may die tonight and if you have never accepted Jesus Christ as your Savior you will spend eternity in the fiery furnace! Walk down this aisle and be saved!"

Now, I was scared. I walked out of the pew down to the preacher. He grabbed me asked me something. He was talking into my ears and not my chest.

I said, "Huh?"

He shouted, "Do you come by faith, or by letter?"

Now, I was scared plus confused. I had come by foot. He shouted at me again. I thought, *Well, I only have two choices, a fifty-percent chance of getting the right answer.* I responded, "By letter." It must've been the correct choice, because he shouted that the church had a new member. He asked the members if they accepted me into their fellowship, and a whole bunch of people shouted, "Yes!"

Later, I found out I had become a Baptist.

Adair's mother was so happy when I returned to my pew that she hugged me. It was not fifteen minutes later that I think she wished she could have withdrawn that hug. As the four of us stood outside the church talking about the service, I asked a question about the sermon.

"When the preacher talked about treating everyone right, did he mean Negroes too?"

Adair's mother looked at me as if I were the chief of sinners. "Niggers are different. They take care of themselves."

This was a surprise. Negroes were not only excluded from many areas and amenities of the South; they did not qualify under the Bible. *How could I explain that to Eleanor?* She believed Jesus loved everyone.

Apparently, the Southern Baptists knew better. I had no idea where the Lutherans stood on the issue.

Chapter 6
Mom and Eleanor Explain Salvation

Mom probably would have lived beyond Palm Sunday 1960, if I had not caused her so much stress. As I entered the door after my night at the revival, mom asked me where I had been so long.

"At church."

"For almost four hours?"

"Yes ma'am, and I got saved."

Sure enough, with one short statement from me, my mother's heart took another hit.

"You what?"

I proceeded to explain the evening's events, only to be interrupted when I reached the part about being a sinner.

"You are not a sinner!" my mom shouted. "You were confirmed

Southern Smiles and Tears

only just a month ago!"

It's a wonder the heart failure didn't occur at that precise moment. Her voice was louder than the "Amens" at the Baptist Church. Disturbed by the volume, and my mother bordering on having what she called a "hissy fit", my dad entered the fray.

"Gunnie! What in the hell is going on in there?"

"Those heathens at the Baptist Church are attacking the Lutheran church, and telling Davy fairy tales about him going to Hell!"

I guess in that one night I heard more about the bad place than I had in my entire ten and one-half years on earth.

"You better straighten him out, Gunnie." said my father, thereby absolving himself from becoming too involved in religious matters.

She did straighten me out. I was told in no uncertain terms that I was not to go around Adair and the Baptist Church anymore, for any reason. I wondered how the Baptists had become equal to the Negroes as with whom I could associate. It was a fitful night of sleep for me with Martin Luther explaining the Catechism, the Baptist preacher explaining Hell, Adair's mom explaining niggers, and my mom explaining that I better, "Straighten up."

I could hardly wait until school was out the next day. First, it had been hard avoiding Adair all day, especially at lunch. I spent some time in the lavatory. I wasn't practicing what Mrs. Brantley had taught us — just hiding.

Second, I needed to talk to Eleanor. If anyone could help me understand the events of the preceding evening, Eleanor could.

"Chile, there's too many people tryin' to make you be what they wants. How you feel about Jesus and salvation is your own business."

Somewhat comforted, I asked her a question that had long been on my mind. "Eleanor, are you a nigger?"

"Some people may think so, but I'm a child of God. Someday, I'll be asingin' in the same choir as all those white folks what been saved. All God's children goin' to go to heaven. You an' me goin' to sit at Jesus' feet an' praise him. They ain't goin' be no whites and coloreds there. Only God's children wearing robes and singing 'Hallelujah!'"

I wasn't clear on every point Eleanor made, but everything she said sure gave me comfort. I pledged to myself to keep my religious feeling between Jesus and me, and maybe Eleanor.

Since I would not be going back to the Baptist Church, and it was impossible to hear the Reverend in the Lutheran, I figured everything was going to be all right.

Southern Smiles and Tears

Chapter 7
"Honor Thy Father..."

My dad's religion may have had nothing to do with churches, but he did some things faithfully. Mostly, these things had some recreational or entertainment aspect. He loved college football games and the beach, but these soon paled in comparison to Mardi Gras. Not the one in New Orleans, but the original one, which was in Mobile. Dad's love of this pageant was infectious. Our whole family attended every parade the entire week the first year we lived in Prichard.

It was magnificent! Especially the night parades. Negro drivers handled the teams of mules, which pulled the floats down Government Street. On either side of the mules was a Negro man carrying a broomstick with a railroad flare; we called it a "fusee," attached to the end. The flares emitted a bright red flame that whooshed as the combustible material burned and dripped white residue on the street. The red glow reflected off the floats and

Southern Smiles and Tears

buildings creating a surreal effect.

Crowd control barriers were not needed. The mules and red-hot flares kept everyone back from the floats. The floats and bands would progress in a herky-jerky fashion, totally dependent upon the temperament of the mules. Should a pair of mules decide to stop, so did everything following. If the stoppage occurred with a band in front of where we stood, we got to hear the same march over and over. It was much more exciting when the mules caused a float to stop close to us. Candy, flowers, cheap jewelry, and sometimes, expensive gifts flew from the Krewe members on the floats. We all scrabbled about grabbing some things in the air, or recovering treasures from the street. Once in a while a brave party goer would dash out into the domain of the mules to pick up a trinket that had fallen just beyond arm's length. Occasionally, one of the gift throwers, overcome from imbibing too much, managed to throw himself from a float. The alcohol must have had some elasticity in it, for the dismounted rider usually managed to climb back aboard his trusty float and continue as the mules decided to proceed.

My dad, a steely-faced ironworker, regressed to childhood immediately as the first band of a parade approached. He was *non-pareil* in catching the missives leaving the floats. Large enough to encourage acquiescence, he would push his way forward in the crowd, shouting like a six-year old. "Here, here, throw it here!" His wavy black hair bobbing up and down, he would leap into the air, as if he were Joe DiMaggio going after a Duke Snider fly ball.

I wasn't embarrassed by his actions; at that time, it was more amazement and adulation. I knew who the recipient of his actions would be. Each piece of candy or bubble gum I managed to gather in was multiplied 10 times by my father's actions.

Dad also had his soft side. Simultaneous with the Mardi Gras was the bursting forth of Azaleas in Mobile. Huge green bushes 30 feet in diameter would transfigure themselves in to hemispheres of pink, scarlet, white, fuscia, and purple in the yards of the old mansions in Mobile. My dad drove us up and down the wide boulevards pointing out the beauty.

Nothing in Mobile's azaleas, however, touched the glory of Bellingrath Gardens on the Dog River, southwest of Mobile. Dad took us there innumerable times as different flowers burst to bloom, but azalea time was his favorite. Our family would spend February and March Sunday afternoons walking the grounds of Walter Bellingrath's estate absorbing the beauty.

Dad would tell us how Mr. Bellingrath made a fortune by investing early in Coca-Cola. The estate was his home, but he allowed

Southern Smiles and Tears

people to visit and enjoy it. Every year on Mr. Bellingrath's birthday in the summer, no admission was charged to visit the grounds. Coca-Colas by the thousands were iced down in #10 washtubs and dispensed free of charge in celebration of his birthday. Ninety degrees and a sweat covered Coke made an indelible memory for me. Once the old man, generous enough to share his bounty, appeared on the balcony of his house and waved to the crowd. The applause returned to him was deafening.

Then came the early summer of the South, and the beaches of South Alabama called us. Almost every weekend from April through October, Palm Sunday and Easter excepted, we were at Gulf Shores or Fort Morgan. Oftentimes, we would go down on Saturday morning and return Sunday evening. We would swim, collect shells, gig for flounder, net crabs, explore, and cookout. Then at night, each of us would dig a hole in the sand, crawl in and cover ourselves with blankets as the stars passed over us unimpeded by artificial light.

Our dad was a strong swimmer, but he was a floater *par excellence*. Early in the morning and late afternoon, he would swim out several hundred yards past the sand reefs, turn over onto his back and float for an hour or more. The best thing about this was when bottlenose dolphins would come and swim with him. The school of dolphins would often begin to nudge him, pushing him toward shore. We would watch from shore awestruck by the magic of it all.

When we went to the beach at Fort Morgan, long before houses, condominiums, and politicians assaulted it, we would go over and wander about the Civil War structure. Here we would hear the story of how our Grandfather Olander, and his ship's crew had been jailed overnight at the fort after having participated in overzealous revelry while docked in Mobile.

Life had an idyllic quality.

Then I saw a side to my dad that hurt. Not only did Mobile have Mardi Gras parades, but Davis City did also. I do not remember whether Davis City was part of Mobile in the early 1950's, or not, but it was where the Negroes lived. It must have been a short cut to go through Davis City from Prichard to Mobile because when my dad was in a hurry that was the route he drove.

Sunday afternoon, in the middle of the Mardi Gras, my dad announced we were going over to Davis City to watch "...the coloreds strut." Brown faces were predominant along the main street. But even here in their own haven, the Negroes stepped aside for the sprinkling of whites who had come.

Dad was right. The band members and majorettes did strut.

Southern Smiles and Tears

They also played music with a fervor that made the bands in the Mobile parades sound like tea-party string quartets. Wonderful barely described it.

Interspersed between bands were floats. The riders began throwing candy to the crowd, not as elaborate fare as in Mobile, but candy none the less. As the third float passed, a piece of candy came flying down, hit a small brown hand, and fell to the street. As the brown hand reached down for the missed prize, a foot landed on the hand. Aghast, I looked up and saw my father grinning, as he reached down and snatched the piece of candy.

I never saw that man in the same light again.

Chapter 8
"...and thy Mother..."

Mom was quite opposite from our dad. He was a rough-talking, hard drinking, charismatic, handsome, construction worker born to what my Grandfather Olander considered the "lower class." Uneducated, but smart, he bullied those below him and finessed those above him as a way of life. She, on the other hand, had the blood of European royalty in her veins. No matter how her station in life rose or fell, she had class. She wasn't above letting a curse word fling from her mouth, or enjoying her daily Miller High Life, but this gentle lady suffered the slings and arrows of Ray Bice as if they never had occurred.

She had a streak of superiority in her that was not restricted to one group. Mom had gone to normal school and had taught school. She could speak German fluently and knew which fork went where. Dad could eat everything with a spoon. The Negroes of the

Southern Smiles and Tears

South were no different to her than anyone else without the proper bloodlines. They simply were there to serve. Dad knew that if the driver in front of him were going too slowly it was "...probably a dumb, black bastard!"

Once on the way back from Gulf Shores, we were behind one of these people, who was according to my father of dubious parentage and improper color. Dad cursed, swerved in and out of his lane looking for an opening, and finally passed the slow miscreant with a puff of smoke and a mighty round of swearing.

It is fairly obvious to me now that, if perchance an Alabama law officer had observed this scene, the passee would have been stopped and the passer given a nod. If I had been the southern black man in the 1950's, I would have made certain that my vehicle did not even come close to exceeding the speed limit. My dad saw the man as a nigger impeding him, my mother saw him as a servant on the way to work, and I saw him as a man who knew the rules and fickleness of unequal justice. I just did not say it.

Gunhild Christina Olander was born in Texas, in 1897, the year of the Galveston Island hurricane and flood. Her father was a merchant marine captain of impeccable genealogy. Gustav Olander was part of the Swedish royal family when, at age 12, he stowed away on a ship with two friends and headed for America.

In the evenings, mom would sit in her chair and tell us stories about Grandfather Olander. You could see the glow of pride in her face as she recounted his story.

"Your grandfather killed a man." She would begin. "It was years after he had stowed away and came to America. When the three boys were found aboard ship, they were too far out to sea to return to shore, so the ship's Captain assigned them to work. Your grandfather became a cabin boy, taking care of the ship's officers. One boy, I don't remember the name of the other two, was given to the cook to work in the galley, and the third became a sail maker.

"Several weeks out in the Atlantic, the galley boy did something to make the cook mad. He beat the boy to death. About 20 years later, your grandfather saw the man in a bar in San Francisco. He waited until the cook left the bar, caught him in an alley, told him who he was and stabbed the murderer."

All of us kids, but especially Martha, Billy, and I would sit around mom spellbound. She would continue, riveting us in the adventures. I never could picture Grandfather Olander other than as old and having snow-white hair, so that is how he was in the alley, or in jail in Fort Morgan.

"Your grandfather sailed for the United States Merchant Marines

Southern Smiles and Tears

in the Spanish-American War, in the Philippine Insurrection, and World War I. When World War II began, he volunteered and was rejected because of his age. He wrote a letter to President Roosevelt, and when rejected again, took his rifle and patrolled the Jersey shore looking for German saboteurs." Mom proudly related to us.

Then came the high moment. We all knew it was the time for "The Question?"

"Mom, you speak German, how come you never have taught us any Swedish?"

Swelled with pride, she always answered, "When your grandfather became an American citizen, he vowed never again to say anything in Swedish, because he was '...now an American.' I never heard, or was allowed to say, another Swedish word."

It was mom who introduced me to opera music. One of the two movie theaters in Prichard charged 10 cents admission, and the other 15 cents. Mom took me to see the opera singer Melba in a movie, and then to a truly wonderful experience. Yma Sumac was a singer of Incan descent from Peru who could hit five octaves. The movie with her singing was wonderful, even through the imperfect sound of a hearing aid microphone. My love of this music has lasted a lifetime. Alice gave me the most exquisite present when she bought tickets for us to see The Three Tenors perform in Los Angeles, California. I only wish my mom could have lived to hear Luciano Pavoratti hit his high "C" that night.

Mom always believed "her ship would come in" and she would achieve what she believed to be her proper status in society.

It never docked.

Southern Smiles and Tears

Chapter 9
The All White Summer

It was the best summer ever. Johnny was forgotten in the wake of my joining up with three new schoolmates. Joe Tom Summers, his brother Eddie, and Carlisle Singleball all lived within rock throwing distance of our house. Monday through Friday, when our family was not at the beach, the four of us were inseparable. Prichard City Park was our main lair. All day swimming in the pool for a nickel, a free zoo, swings and hoisting bars, and even a Ferris wheel placated the energy needs of our gang of 11-year olds.

Nowhere do I remember seeing a sign declaring the park to be **Whites Only**. But it was. I asked Eleanor if she had ever ridden the Ferris wheel at the park. She told me she had not.

"I see it all lit up and turnin' at night when I goes home from my other job. But I ain't never rode it. Coloreds can't go in there."

It is surprising how much you could learn from a few, short

Southern Smiles and Tears

statements. Eleanor had another job besides working for our family. At that time, I thought, She must have a bunch of money. Now I realize that even with two full time jobs, Eleanor probably made less than $20.00 a week total. She had also let me know, without stating it, how fortunate I was to be able to go to the park. Supposedly a public park, it all depended upon whom was declared to be part of the public.

Even though it was not expensive to me, not once did I see Johnny enjoying the facilities. It would be later before I was able to comprehend that a nickel to poor Southerners was not something to be spent on something as frivolous as swimming in a pool. Somewhere deep in my conscience, these things may have bothered me but did not stop me from enjoying my all white summer. Memories abounded. Almost all of them connected to the park.

One July day the four of us were in the pool when the lifeguard told us to get out because a thunderstorm was coming. We had seen the darkening skies but hoped he had not heard any rumbles. No such luck. We got out, dried off and pulled on our pants sans shirts. It was important to pull your pants over your wet trunks, so that everyone would see the dark band encircling you. Everyone would then know you had been in the pool, plus there was an added benefit.

The four of us ran over to the playground and begin sliding down the slicky slide. Now the wet pants became utilitarian. The water from our pants soon made the metal slide wet and faster. As we were playing, it began to sprinkle. Then rain. We sought shelter under a picnic canopy. The lifeguard, who was also in charge of the small zoo, came out of the poolhouse at a dead run. There were four alligators in a concrete pool and hutch. They were less than three feet long, but alligators nonetheless. One cage had several monkeys, another had two raccoons, and the one nearest us contained a red fox kit.

The lifeguard/zoo keeper ran through the large drops of rain to check on the animals as the thunder crashed and lightening scorched the sky. All of the animals had retreated to shelter with the exception of the fox. Fur plastered down from the rain, the frightened animal ran about banging into the fence, which surrounded him. The lifeguard opened the cage, went in and caught the kit. Just as he picked up the bedraggled animal a bolt of lightning struck the ground. The fox planted all four feet and multiple claws into the rescuer's chest. The lifeguard screamed, went stiff, fell backwards and splashed into a mud puddle. The fox, determining everything had gone far enough, ran into his personal den.

Southern Smiles and Tears

We were awestruck. There was a dead man in front of us. Carlisle was the first to come to his senses. He ran toward the pool house shouting.

"He's 'lectrocuted! He's 'lectrocuted!"

Several people hearing the ruckus came running. Carlisle turned and ran back to the fox cage. As they arrived, the lifeguard began to stir. He sat up, blood running down his chest, and uttered that famous word, "Wow!"

We had witnessed a resurrection that was more exciting then the biblical ones. Over the next few days, our renditions of the event became more and more embellished. This continued until people began to tell us to quit bragging. I think that happened after, some how or another, I had become a hero by rescuing the downed lifeguard by dragging him to safety after the bear had attacked and almost killed him.

The four of us usually had enough money to buy an RC Cola and peanuts to put in the bottles. This would quench our thirsts after a hard day at the park. One fatal day, however, we all were nickelless. Carlisle, who lived nearest the park, suggested that we go over to his house for some ice tea or lemonade. Off we ran, our bare feet making small puffs of smoke in the dust. Carlisle's mother gave us each a big glass of refreshment as we sat on the front porch. When she came out and asked us if we wanted another drink, I politely said, "No thank you, Mrs. Singleball."

It was one of those innocent statements with immense repercussions. Carlisle's mother looked at me and asked in a strained voice, "What did you say?" Joe Tom and Eddie almost fell off the porch laughing, and Carlisle's eyes opened as wide as possible.

I answered her with, "I just said, 'No thank you, ma'am.'"

She looked at me half in anger and half in astonishment and strained out, "You're welcome."

Carlisle shouted urgently, "C'mon, let's go back to the park."

We ran back to the park. As soon as we got there, Carlisle hit me in the shoulder and shouted, "What's wrong with you? Ya' dumb Yankee!"

"Wha'd I do?"

"My last name ain't Singleball. It's Matthews."

I had been tripped up by Southern names, and the tradition of calling each other by last names. The three of them called me "Bice," and more and more I had begun to refer to them as "Summers," "Summers," and "Singleball." I thought that was what was happening with Carlisle.

Wrong.

Southern Smiles and Tears

Everyone called Carlisle "Single Ball" because he had gone down a slicky slide that had a piece of metal upturned and ripped off one of his signs of masculinity. Kids nicknamed him right after the tragic accident.

Mrs. Matthews never gave me lemonade again.

Chapter 10
The Library

    One place that the four of us did not go as a group was to the library. Joe Tom, Eddie, and Carlisle were not interested in anything to do with education during the May to September school hiatus. They did not ride me about going to the library but classified it as another peculiarity of a "Yankee."
    Planted firmly at the end of Fifth Avenue, Prichard City Library was a brick building sheltered by Live Oak and Pecan trees. Azalea bushes bordered the sidewalk leading to the front door. Squirrels kept busy chasing each other and cracking pecans. Mockingbirds zipped about chattering to one another. The grounds were sandy of a reddish hue spotted by green outbursts of grass, which had survived the foot traffic of strollers and ball players.
    It was a magnificent day in 1951 when I got my first library card. Here was my passage to worlds unknown. That summer I read *Tap Roots, Two Years Before the Mast*, a book about King Carol of

Southern Smiles and Tears

Romania, *Kon-Tiki*, by Thor Heyerdahl, and countless others. Beside novels, I located the encyclopedias. Anything a person wanted to know was contained in those beautiful volumes. I would spend hours reading about different cultures, various geographies, and multiple climates. To this day, those encyclopedias provided me with more excitement than any other medium I have known.

Taps Roots was one book, which almost caused me to change my reading habits. Quite thick, I needed to renew the book after the two-week rental period in order to complete my reading. Not only did I want to finish the book, it was imperative. There was a passage, as I now remember, where one of the young characters referred to a female adult as having "...tits as big as cabbages." That was enough for a young boy entering puberty, although that word was never spoken in the early 1950's, to cause extreme urgency in my reading more of the narrative. Renewal was the undoing. When I approached the librarian tome in hand, you would have thought I had handed her a cotton mouth water moccasin.

"What are you doing with that book!"

"Reading it."

"That is from the adult section. Children are to get books over there!"

Her index finger pointed to the dreaded Children's Section, as she shoved my precious *Tap Roots* aside with her left hand. I had visited that area of the library on my first visit and concluded that I had read many of those books by the age of eight. What I had not read appeared as palatable as mashed potatoes without gravy. Now, she was banishing me to pabulum for the mind while I needed substantial nutrition.

She refused to allow me to renew the book. What was I to do?

I went over to the children's section and fiddled around with the Hardy Boys and Uncle Remus and Br'er Rabbit, trying to look innocent. In reality, I was G. K. Chesterton's Father Brown watching the librarian's every move. She stood behind the book check out counter whacking books with her date stamp, as if tenderizing a steak. Finished with a lady, who had several books, she turned to an assistant and said, "Carol, I have to make a telephone call. Will you watch the front?"

That was when I struck.

I grabbed a book from the shelf, fairly flew to the desk, and plopped the book down. "Would you check this out for me please?" I said with all the innocence that a devious 11-year old could muster.

"Surely," came the reply.

33

Southern Smiles and Tears

After the book was dutifully stamped, I picked it up and turned to leave.

"Oh, no!" I exclaimed. "I forgot to renew my mother's book. Is *Tap Roots* still here?"

The assistant looked around, saw the book and asked, "This one?"

I nodded my head. She stamped book as she said, "This will be due in two weeks."

Each visit to the library, thereafter, I had a piece of paper on which was written the name of a book I wanted to read. I would meander over to the Children's Section, grab something, return to the desk, give the note to the librarian, and ask for help finding the book my mother wanted. I then had the book I wanted to read.

Right then, though, I rushed home to find out more about cabbages.

Chapter 11
My First Gumbo

It is now fairly evident to me that I served as a tactical diversion on my first trip to MacIntosh, Alabama. Ostensibly, my dad was going up to Washington County for a fall weekend to hunt on some politician's place. He really needed a cover so my mom would not know he was going to drink and gamble.

The politician apparently had quite bit of political clout as my father referred to him as "...a bigwig." We were to stay in a hunting cabin owned by one of the politician's relatives. It was the first night when I found out the true purpose of the trip. Ensconced in bed in a side room, I heard unintelligible mumbling in the next room. Curiosity overcame me. I inserted my earpiece, turned on my hearing aid, slipped out of bed, and crept to the door. I heard my father and others talking about who would be able to play cards the next day. The gurgling of whiskey being poured into glasses interspersed the discussion. After much negotiation, a sum of $1,000.00

Southern Smiles and Tears

was agreed upon, as the amount needed for a seat at the table.

A thousand dollars! My father gave mom $100.00 a week for all household expenses, and here he was glibly agreeing to put up 10 times that amount for one Saturday of card playing. I returned to bed thinking about spending that princely sum of money in one day.

The deer hunting was not entirely untrue. The three of us young people, children of the invitees, were awakened at 4:00 A.M. to watch the hunt. It was not an hour later that I found out the phrase "deer hunt" was an oxymoron. What it was, was a "deer sit." We all went out on the front porch. The adults sitting in rocking chairs with rifles resting across their laps. It reminded me of the movies where the sheriff, and the few brave people in town, sat waiting for the lynch mob to come and get the jailed prisoner. Only now, the lynch mob was frightened deer being driven toward the sitters.

Negroes had been sent out earlier to bang sticks against trees to drive the deer to the "hunters." Later I learned that a huge amount of acreage had been fenced off and the deer were there just to be hunted and killed by friends of the politician. We all heard the banging of sticks moments before the first of the running frightened deer came into the clearing surrounding the cabin. One of the men stood up, fired, and shouted as the hapless deer fell to the ground. The scene was repeated several times.

A thought crossed my mind of how glad I was to be on the porch and not behind the deer driving them toward men with rifles well fortified with sippin' whiskey. Here were men in various states of inebriation firing high-powered rifles at running deer with human beings right behind the deer. Of course, most of the people on the porch weren't positive those driving the deer qualified as real humans. This had to be true because only about half the bullets flying about hit the intended targets.

The carnage lasted about 15 minutes. Then came another surprise. The deer drivers now became deer gatherers. As soon as the firing stilled, the Negroes emerged from the pine trees and scrub brush. The "hunters" hollered at the gatherers telling them which of the animals belonged to whom. The Negroes then took the deer and hung them from low-lying limbs on the edge of the woods and began eviscerating them.

Amidst much bragging, the great hunt was over, and the men began discussing the true purpose of the migration to the area. Gambling.

I still do not know where the activity took place. We young peo-

Southern Smiles and Tears

ple were placed in the hands of Mary, an apron covered Negro who had an eating place nearby. She was to watch us as we played outside and feed us when the need arose. The men gathered into two cars and left the premises. We filled a third car, and a driver took us to Mary's Place.

Our play was not of enough consequence to be worth remembering. The lunch and dinner were. Mary prepared a concoction called "gumbo" for both meals. At first look, it did not appear edible. Once tasted, it was heavenly. A large bowl was filled with rice, and a brown soupy stuff. It was the brown soupy stuff that lighted my taste buds. Dispersed throughout the liquid were a multitude of things. Identifiable at first was shrimp. Unidentifiable, to me alone, was a sliced section of some type of green vegetable. It looked like a wagon wheel, except there were whitish seeds among the spokes. Okra. This particular vegetable was previously unknown to me, but it is probably the slimiest food God placed on earth. That is, unless cooked in gumbo. There it is a necessity. Gumbo without okra compares to spaghetti without sauce.

In 2001, I was holding a book development committee meeting in Chatom, the county seat of Washington County. Several of the attendees were surprised that I knew anything about the county. One woman, though, was astounded when I told my story about gumbo and mentioned Mary.

"I remember her. She used to have a place over near MacIntosh. I ate there many a time."

Fifty years after my encounter with Mary and gumbo, here was someone else who remembered her.

I know of no where in the Bible where it says that we will eat in heaven. I know I will sing with Eleanor, and I hope I get to eat with Mary.

No venison allowed.

Southern Smiles and Tears

Chapter 12
"Uncle" Graves

He may be the most principled person I have ever met. He introduced himself as "Mr. Graves." After a pause of several seconds, he continued with, "But you can call me 'Uncle.'"

I was already amazed because he was to be my first male teacher. Now, he was going to allow a level of familiarity heretofore unknown to me between students and a teacher. I knew that the seventh grade was going to be different, but this was a 180-degree move. I wasn't even positive teachers had families, let alone nicknames.

My dad had taken a short working assignment in Big Stone Gap, Virginia near the end of my sixth year in school. Eddie, my second oldest brother, had been drafted for the Korean War and was no longer at home. My sister Doris had left home on one of her traveling adventures, and Martha, my pretty sister, had married. Mom, Billy, and I had moved to Big Stone Gap and then returned to

Southern Smiles and Tears

Prichard in time for my seventh year in school to begin. The house on Fifth Avenue was rented during our absence, and with just four of us remaining, we moved into an apartment on the same street where Glendale School was located. Eleanor came back to the family but for only three days a week.

My classmates and I had Uncle Graves for homeroom and Social Studies. We had different teachers as we moved in a group from class to class. The only other teacher I remember from that year was Miss Peters. She had dark wavy hair surrounding a beautiful olive face, which hinted at her Greek heritage. Her father had come to the United States as a sponge diver in Ybor City, Florida. Uneducated, he had demanded his children go to school. She was the first in her family to go to college. She played the flute, violin, and piano for us as she explained how music was universal in its appeal and knew no barriers of language or culture. Her music class was the perfect complement to my mom in adding to my appreciation of classical music.

Miss Peters was my fantasy. Uncle was my reality. He had served in World War II, gone to college on the GI Bill, and taught the truth. His principles shone forth from an assignment he made.

"Does anyone know what the Nobel Peace Prize is?" he queried.

The lack of knowledge must have stunned him.

"Does anyone know who Alfred Nobel was?"

He must have enjoyed talking to himself.

"Perhaps, someone knows what dynamite is?"

Now he was in our realm of expertise. Every Saturday at the movies Johnny Mack Brown, Roy Rogers, or Gene Autry would throw a stick of dynamite to frighten those rascals in black hats. Uncle had more answers than he needed. However, with him being a teacher, he wasn't satisfied that we knew something. He wanted to pinpoint more of our lack of knowledge.

"It comes from the Greek word, *dunamis*. Does anyone have an idea of what that means?"

Well, as soon as he said Greek, my mind made a rapid jump from what's his name's prize to music class. Specifically, Miss Peters. I was in love with this "older woman."

"It means 'power!'" Uncle shouted me back into reality. I preferred fantasy.

"Alfred Nobel invented this powerful explosive intending it to be used for good. He was appalled when it was turned into a weapon of war. He then devoted the profits from his invention to promoting peace. He set up a trust fund awarding money to the person, or persons, who did the most to promote peace the previous year. What I

Southern Smiles and Tears

want is for you to find out who won the Nobel Peace Prize for 1950."

Uncle told us that he would give 50 extra points to the first 10 students with the correct answer. A murmur crossed the room. That many points could salvage many a poor grade. Alas, the assignment was given Friday afternoon right before music class and two days of freedom. The whole question of a peace prize evaporated from my mind.

The trouble with weekends during the school year is that they are followed by Mondays. As Fats Domino later sang, this was to be a *Blue Monday*. Most of us had forgotten about Alfred Nobel, but Uncle had not.

"Who won the Nobel Peace Prize in 1950?"

Only one person raised an arm with a piece of paper held tightly. This was followed by a name. "Ralph Bunche." There went my 50 points down the drain. But then came a reprieve.

"Why is it significant that this man won the prize and why did he win it?"

I did not realize it at that point, but Uncle had crossed a line he did not need to cross. He could have stopped right there. Granted, the lesson would not have stayed with me for 50 years, but he could have stopped.

"I will give another 50 points to the first 10 people who bring in the answers tomorrow."

Class began as normal the next day, but not 10 minutes into it, things changed. This time four of us had the answer written on paper. Uncle took the four sheets of paper, read the answers, and his mouth slowly broke into a grin. Uncle then asked one of the girls with the correct answers to tell what she had found out.

She stood saying, "Ralph Bunche was a Negro who helped with peace in the Middle East in 1950."

Uncle then "...crossed the Rubicon."

"It is significant in this world that a Negro can win the highest honor the world has to offer for promoting peace. This could not have happened a few years ago because Negroes were thought to be less intelligent than whites."

Silence sounded loudly across the room. It was not until we left class that one boy said, "I ain't goin' to be learnin' about no niggers." There was an almost unanimous assent to this rebellion that took place out of earshot of Uncle.

Uncle always gave us 25 questions on tests. The next day he told us he was going to give us a test on Wednesday with only one question, and it would be worth 100 points.

The next day he told us to get out a sheet of paper. He then asked

Southern Smiles and Tears

his question.

"Who is Ralph Bunche?" Again, he could have stopped. He did not.

"If anyone uses the words 'nigger' or 'colored' in his answer, he will get a zero!"

I am not positive as to what were the immediate consequences to Uncle because of this incident. I do, however, believe the circumstantial evidence leads to the conclusion that the principal and patrons of Glendale School were not pleased with the lesson about Ralph Bunche

When school began the next fall, another teacher was in Mr. Graves' room.

Southern Smiles and Tears

Chapter 13
Delivering Bread

Martha, my sister nearest in age to me, had married after we moved to Prichard. Hollis Wright was the man fortunate enough to whisk her out of our house but not our lives. Hollis was tall, blond, smooth talking, a great bowler, and by most standards good looking. Physically, a good catch, his work efforts were akin to a yo-yo. When he worked he worked hard. He just seemed to move from one position to another like mercury spilled on the floor.

The summer after the seventh grade, at age 12, I was thrust into the working world. Dad had been injured in a construction accident and had dollars dancing in his eyes as he contemplated and engaged in a lawsuit against whomever he thought had money. He had been guiding a steel beam, holding it with his right hand, when the crane operator dropped the beam. His shoulder was ripped from its proper place, necessitating surgery, a long hospital stay, and a longer period without wages.

Southern Smiles and Tears

Money was scarce.

Hollis, now the bread earner of the extended Alabama Bice/Wright families, offered me a job for $2.00 a day helping him with his Malbis Bread route. I leaped at the opportunity. It meant getting up at 3:30 A.M., eating breakfast, and hopping in Hollis' bread van at 4:00 A.M. He had two routes that summer. The first one was in north Mobile County and part of south Washington County. Later he got a route closer home in Mobile that included Davis City.

Much of the work was repetitious. We would arrive at a store, go in and check the bread rack for quantity sold, rotate the old bread to the front, place fresh loaves in the back, and bring in the new stock. We took the out-of-date loaves and placed them to one side of the van. Each day's bread had a code that let us know which day the bread had been delivered. The codes were supposed to be indecipherable to the public, and sometimes even store owners. Hollis worked on a straight commission based on loaves sold. Any returned out-of-date loaves were deducted from his commission.

He hated out-of-date bread.

How much Hollis disliked old bread came clear to me one morning about 10:00 in the backwoods of Washington County, Alabama. Once a week we serviced a Choctaw Indian store down a sandy road off Highway 43. These people, though predominantly Indian, had other blood mixed into their makeup. Hollis didn't exactly dislike them, but usually referred to them as, "dumb Cajuns." He was wrong on both counts. They were not the patois speaking Cajuns from Louisiana, but a remnant of Indians that Andrew Jackson's cronies had failed to round up and send to the West in the "Trail of Tears."

Hollis soon found out they were also far from dumb. He had developed a scheme to get rid of old bread and avoid the dreaded commission cut. The first weeks I went out to sell bread, we went out to the Choctaw store on Mondays. The fourth week in May, Hollis told the storeowner, who was also the tribal leader, that we would begin bringing bread to him on Friday. "That way." Hollis explained, "the store would have fresh bread for the weekend. As several naked little kids swarmed around him, the storeowner nodded his assent. We then left enough fresh bread to cover the extra four days of the following week.

As we headed for Washington County that fateful Friday, Hollis explained why he had changed the delivery day. He had not turned in any old bread that week but kept it on the side rack. He said, "Davy, you go in an take a count as to what that dumb Cajun needs.

Southern Smiles and Tears

I'm going to take the middle eight loaves out of the fresh bread trays and put in eight old loaves. Don't you say a word about the old codes on the bread we're selling him."

I didn't have to say a word.

The chief's daughter was in the store. I said, "Hey!" the proper Southern greeting I had acquired. She nodded back to me. I calculated the loaves needed and returned to the bread van.

"Hollis, they need 60 loaves."

"Okay. Let me get you five trays, and I'll calculate the bill."

He pushed five trays of the mixed date bread to the back doors. I started to take the top one to carry it in when a voice boomed behind me.

"Stop!"

I did.

Hollis stuck his head out and asked, "What's goin' on."

"You be given me your old bread."

Smooth talking Hollis did not say a word. Mostly, I believe, because the chief was using a shotgun as a walking stick. "You reach over there and give me fresh bread, now!" the chief emphasized as the shotgun changed from a walking implement to its manufactured purpose.

Hollis' tan disappeared and I peed my pants.

"Yes, sir! I'm sorry for the mistake, but the boy is new and didn't know what he was doing."

"That boy was in the store. You the one think you can give us your old bread," said the chief, "an if I catch you one more time, your family ain't never goin' see you again!"

Hollis took a big loss on his commission that week.

Later that summer, I'm not exactly sure of the month; Hollis and I witnessed a person being shot. We were on the Davis City run and had stopped at a store. Angle parked with the back doors of the van opened, we both had a view of the sidewalk across the street. I had already inventoried the store's needs, and the two of us were preparing to take the trays inside, when two loud cracks sounded. I looked up and there was a man standing with a pistol in his hand. In front of him was another man lying partially on the sidewalk with his head in the street. He was not moving.

"Hollis, he shot that guy!"

"Shut up!" Hollis shouted as he grabbed both doors and slammed them shut. He went to the front of the van, started the engine, and began backing out. I moved faster than I ever had before, and probably since, and leapt into my seat.

"Aren't you going to wait for the police?"

Southern Smiles and Tears

"Let them niggers take care of it." Hollis answered, reminding me of Adair's mother and the Southern Baptist philosophy about Negroes.

It seemed to be a common policy, even though I don't ever remember Hollis going to church to learn it.

Chapter 14
Goodbye Eleanor! Hello Johnny!

We always had money and to be without was a shock. My father was out of work, and it appeared that I was the one to get a job. Billy, my brother who was three and one-half years older than I, had returned to West Virginia. He was going to live with our sister Caroline and her husband Carlos. I was glad to see Billy get out of the torment of our dad but I missed him. Billy did not do well in school no matter how hard he tried. My guess, now, is that he was dyslexic at a time when the problem was not yet identified. A likable and generous boy, dad constantly called him stupid. Billy persevered; taking an extra half-year to be graduated from St. Albans High School. He then joined the Navy.

Then there were three. Mom, dad, and I remained in the garage apartment in Prichard. Mostly though, it was just mom and me. Dad was gone more often than not. He received a small Workman's Compensation check that changed to alcohol more often than food.

Southern Smiles and Tears

He did pay the rent on the apartment but little else. His belief that a monetary settlement would result from his injury led him to continue his lifestyle while mom's and mine sank lower and lower.

It was left up to mom to tell Eleanor that there was no money to pay her. I know this was an embarrassing moment for my mom. She had lost whatever status she believed she had in life. Eleanor took the dismissal without rancor or surprise. She knew more about us than my parents wished to admit, and the lack of money was a normal state for her.

"Ma'am, don't you worry about me. I be all right. I be praying for you and Davy."

Mom went into the bedroom as Eleanor began to gather up her cleaning supplies. I stood there trying to hold back tears. Eleanor walked over and hugged me. I didn't cry. I sobbed. Wiping my nose with her apron, Eleanor said, "You still the skinniest boy I know, but I love you." She walked out of my life but not out of my mind.

I could not continue to work with Hollis after school started so I began to look else where to make money. We still received *The Mobile Press* each day, and I read it voraciously cover to cover except the classified ads. Now that is where I went to find a job. First came disappointment. An ad appeared in the paper for Delchamps Grocery. I ran over to Joe Tom Summers' house to tell him about the opportunity. We walked the three blocks to the store, went inside, and found the manager. Enthusiastic we were but of age we were not. The manager told us we had to be sixteen to work there.

I thought, *That's four years away, mom and I could starve to death by then.*

Joe Tom said, "I don't need the job nohow."

Disappointment was followed by success. The next week the paper had two promising advertisements. One was for vendors at Ladd Stadium and another for pecan gatherers. Since the nut job was in Prichard and the football stadium job was in Mobile, I went to the closer one. No one brought up the age issue, and I found myself gainfully employed to gather pecans after they fell from the trees. The owner of the pecan grove told me I could work three hours each day after school. My income was to be five cents for each pound of pecans gathered. Hallelujah! I asked if any more people were needed. The owner said, "I could prob'ly use one more kid."

As I fairly floated home, I thought about telling Joe Tom about the opportunity. Something stopped me. *What about Johnny?* All the previous year we had passed each other at school with no more than a "Hey!" He had failed the seventh grade and was now a year

Southern Smiles and Tears

behind me but still ostracized by most people. Maybe it was because I had lost Eleanor, my first Alabama friend, that my conscience told me to recover my second. I turned and went to Johnny's. Shooting marbles with his sister, Johnny saw me coming to his yard. He acted as if I had been there the day before. I felt smaller than a Lilliputian.

"Hey, Johnny. I just got a job gatherin' pecans. Would you want one too?"

"Sure!"

"If I go get my marbles, can I play?"

"Sure!"

Everything seemed all right with the world.

Running home and back as fast as I could, the game was on. Johnny drew a large circle in the dirt with his bare big toe. As I knelt with cat's eye nestled between my index finger and thumb I said to Johnny, "Tomorrow's Saturday. Would you want to go to Ladd Stadium and try to get another job?"

"I ain't got no money for the bus."

"Me neither. Why don't we look for some coke bottles for the two cents' bottle deposit? We just need 10 bottles, and we'll have enough for both of us to get there and back."

"Okay."

We stopped playing marbles and went to find bus fare. After searching for a couple of hours, we had found only six bottles. Discouraged, I remembered something.

"Johnny! My next door neighbor gets two quarts of milk almost every day. She leaves the bottles on the front porch for the milkman. They're worth a nickel each."

"Watcha' gonna do? Steal 'em?"

"Of course not. I'll just borrow them until we make some money. Then I'll leave a dime on her porch."

"Okay!"

The next morning, I got up early, sneaked next door, and "borrowed" the two empty bottles. I told mom I was going to play with the Summers boys. Johnny and I, according to plan met at Delchamps to cash in the bottles. Twenty-two cents in hand, we caught the bus to Mobile. Success again. We both got jobs selling soft drinks for football games at Ladd Stadium.

I don't remember ever returning the 10 cents.

Southern Smiles and Tears

Chapter 15
Pecans and Pop

    Ladd Stadium had a high school football game every fall Friday night and college games on some Saturdays. Murphy and Vigor was the first high school game Johnny and I worked.
    We told our pecan boss about the football jobs, and he allowed us to gather pecans Monday through Thursday and on Saturday morning. Each gatherer had a gunnysack to throw nuts into as he picked them off the ground. Most of us used one of two methods to fill our sacks. One way was to "duck walk." This was efficient because of being close to the ground but created sore thighs. The "bend and pick" method seemed less of a strain until later in the evening when your back attacked you for the strain imposed on it. The first week I made $5.50 for pecans, but the "real" money was to be in soft drinks on college game days.
    Our first night at the stadium, Johnny and I found out just how heavy 24 bottles of pop, paper cups, a wood case, and bag of ice

Southern Smiles and Tears

weighed. A bunch. The six ounces of liquid in 24 bottles, not counting the glass, weighed over eight pounds. Altogether, we started out carrying over 20 pounds, walking up and down the 40,000 seat stadium steps. I weighed 95 pounds and was not another Charles Atlas.

People paid us a quarter a cup for a soft drink. We were to fill the cups with enough ice so that one bottle filled two cups. Johnny and I were to make five cents a cup, or $2.40 per trip.

A high school game, with the stadium packed with non-working students, usually allowed us to sell enough to make around $10.00 a game. College games were pure gold to us. We still made the nickel a cup, but three factors drove up our incomes. First was a stadium full of adults with money. Secondly, many of the fans did not want a cup filled with Coca-Cola. They wanted about one-half cup of ice and drink giving us more cups per bottle. Surreptitiously, these adults would slip a brown bag from under their seats and finish filling the cups with amber liquid. This substantially increased our profit margin. Thirdly, by the end of the third quarter many of those who had fortified their drinks became philanthropic. They would pay for their cup with a dollar bill and say, "Keep the change!"

Our best college game was Alabama and Maryland. Alabama fans were ecstatic and drinking heavily as the Crimson Tide poured it on the Terrapins 27 to 7. Late in the fourth quarter of that game, a man bought two drinks, gave me a twenty, and told me "keep it." Some weeks during football season, Johnny and I made over 50 dollars each.

Johnny and I had no expenses to deduct from pecan gathering because we could walk to the orchard. Ladd Stadium was different. The round trip on the bus cost each of us 10 cents. That was not the major problem. Sometimes at night it would take us a while to settle our accounts. Most of the buses had already left by the time we left the stadium, and we often had to wait on the midnight bus. This got us home after one o'clock in the morning. Mom did not like me coming in that late, so she asked my dad if he could pick us up in his car after night games. At first, that seemed to be a good idea.

My dad had an Oldsmobile 98 he had purchased right before his accident. Johnny had never ridden in such an automobile and was excited about being picked up after the night's work. It worked out fine the first time. My dad suggested that he take us to the stadium and pick us up afterwards. He said that since it cost him gasoline to do this, it would only be fair for us to pay him 25 cents for the round trip. Even at a nickel more, it seemed like a good deal to

Southern Smiles and Tears

Johnny and me. That is until the second Friday night. We gave the chauffeur our quarter and rode to the stadium. After cashing out our accounts we waited for our ride. We waited and we waited. My dad had not shown up, and it was well after the midnight bus had run. The two of us were getting nervous. Just then a Mobile policeman drove by, stopped, and asked us what we were doing out so late.

We explained our predicament.

"The last bus has run from here. I'll tell you what. I'll carry you downtown to the bus station and see if there's another Prichard bus."

We got home well after two o'clock that morning, worn out from walking the stadium steps and mad having to pay extra for the bus.

Johnny and I made our own travel arrangements from then on.

Southern Smiles and Tears

Chapter 16
Paper and Pop

The money I made from pecans and Ladd Stadium got mom and me through the fall. This largesse allowed us to eat fairly well, buy her insulin, and even attend a 10-cent movie each week on Saturday nights after the afternoon games.

Mom had had diabetes for four years. The disease had a dramatic appearance in our lives while we still lived in West Virginia. One evening about 8:00 mom and I were alone at the house. Dad was out of town working, and I have no idea where Doris, Martha, and Billy were. I was reading a book when mom staggered into our small living room screaming.

"Davy! I can't see!"

She then fell to the floor unconscious.

I ran over to her and tried to shake her awake. Nothing happened. We didn't have a telephone, so I ran about a quarter of a mile to the Wheeler's house. Mr. Wheeler and his wife lived in a small shack with his sister. All three were in their seventies. Mrs. Wheeler, the most ambulatory of the three, went in a back room and grabbed a can. The two of us went as fast as she could travel back to our house. Mom was still on the floor dazed and moaning

"Go get a tablespoon of sugar!" Mrs. Wheeler shouted at me. "She's had a spell."

Mrs. Wheeler then poured a little bit of liquid from the can over the sugar and forced my mother's lips apart and forced the concoction down her throat by covering mom's mouth and nose. By then Mr. Wheeler had reached our house and he told me to run down to Pettry's store and call the doctor.

There were two problems. One was that I did not know any doctor to call. Two, if I took out my earpiece, I could not hear anything through the phone. I ran to Pettry's anyhow. Red Pettry, with his flaming hair, listened to my plight and telephoned a doctor himself.

In no more than 30 minutes a tall, dark-haired man came to our door carrying a black satchel pinched together on top.

"I'm Dr. Jackson. What is the problem?"

Mrs. Wheeler explained that "Mistress Bice" had had a spell and had passed out. Mrs. Wheeler continued by telling the doctor that she had given her "a dose of turpentine and sugar."

"You what?"

"I gave her a dose to get her blood flowing."

"It's a wonder you didn't kill her. I think she is in a diabetic coma. Call an ambulance!"

Back to Pettry's I ran.

After the ambulance came and went, Billy came home. He told me we needed to call Caroline, our sister, and her husband Carlos Neal so they could come and take us to the hospital.

Yes! Back to Pettry's again.

Dr. Jackson was correct in his instant diagnosis. My mom did have "sugar." She would take injections of insulin the rest of her life. I administered the shots for many years, including our years in Alabama.

Now out of work, my dad paid our rent out of his worker's compensation check. He gave mom some money but my earnings supplied mom and me with most of our other needs. That is until the end of November. Football ended and pecans quit falling.

December was not to be one of sugarplums.

Mom had never been one to look to the future, but she had prepared for this time of penury. I did the grocery shopping at a "jot 'em down" store that allowed me to charge purchases each week. The last month of football season mom had added extra Mueller's Spaghetti and Hunt's Catsup to my shopping list. She also over bought canned Campbell's Tomato Soup, the cheapest flavor Campbell's had, and self-rising flour. December and January meals consisted of spaghetti with catsup as the sauce and soup and biscuits. Once I went to the store and bought a single fresh egg for our breakfast. When I returned home, mom looked at the egg and then me. Downcast, she told me I would have to return the five-cent egg to the store. It was then I knew for sure that we were poor. One egg would not supply the multiple meals, which spaghetti could provide.

Then our fortune took a turn for the better in February. This time it was Johnny who found us another employment opportunity,

Mardi Gras!

Johnny had heard about a man hiring boys to sell confetti during the two weeks of Mardi Gras in Mobile. He would sell a packet of paper confetti or serpentine to the young entrepreneurs for five cents per packet. These would resell for ten cents on the street.

We hitchhiked to Mobile. Johnny had a piece of paper in his hand with a Dauphin Street address on it. When we got to Bienville Square, with it's huge old trees and squirrels scampering about, we turned and walked down past Baker's Shoe Store. A couple of doors past the peanut shop was a doorway with steps leading to the second floor. A man sat behind a folding table, under a naked light bulb, and in front of boxes and boxes filled with Mardi Gras paraphernalia.

"Ya'll boys lookin' for a job?"

"Yes, sir."

"This here's how it works. Ya'll bring me five dollars each day and night of the parades, and I'll give you a tray with stuff to sell. When ya'll sell out, come back here and give me five dollars again, and I'll fill your tray for sellin' more. You keep the five dollars profit. The more you sell, the more you make."

"We'll be back tomorrow night."

We had a problem, though; neither one of us had five dollars.

Again my mother surprised me. When I told her of our dilemma, mom told me she had some money "put back" and would let Johnny and me have ten dollars.

The two of us worked every parade for two weeks. With all the kid's scurrying in and out between the floats trying to sell confetti and serpentine, Johnny and I considered it a good parade to sell

Southern Smiles and Tears

two trays each. We worked a total of 18 parades and made almost $200.00. Mom and I switched off our diet and indulged in real tomato sauce with meat and chicken noodle soup.

Our finances took a short dip into the negative in March but in April Johnny and I found another job selling pop. This was at the Mobile Bears baseball stadium. The two of us worked there until late mid-August.

Then my life took a change.

"Davy, we're moving back to West Virginia."

My dad and mom informed me that he had gotten a job with the West Virginia Road Commission and we would move right away. Not only was Eleanor gone, but now it appeared my best friend Johnny was leaving my life. The only two people outside my family who had ever accepted me without reservations were to be assigned to my fickle memory.

Sadness and heartbreak fell short of describing my emotions at that moment.

Southern Smiles and Tears

Part Two
1954-1963

Southern Smiles and Tears

Southern Smiles and Tears

Chapter 17
Oscar Moves With Me

    A pet, which was foreign to West Virginia, moved with us. This was Oscar my pet alligator.
    After Blacky had been killed, I did not get another pet for a while. Then one day Joe Tom, Eddie, and Carlisle wanted to go fishing and needed bait. They asked me if I wanted to go with them. I was not interested in that particular activity, but the idea of riding my bike down to the delta of the Mobile River and catching crickets seemed as if it would be fun.
    We had been walking around, bent over in the tall grass snatching and jarring crickets, when I spotted something moving in the grass. There right before my wide-opened eyes were three tiny lizard-like creatures. They were green and yellow with their eyes closed.
    Baby alligators!
    I hollered at the other three to come see. Joe Tom, the eldest and

Southern Smiles and Tears

surely most knowledgeable of the group, shouted with fear.

"Where's the momma?"

Apparently, this was a problem of some magnitude.

"Let's get outta here."

The three ran for their bikes. I stood there a moment fascinated by these strange creatures. Then for some reason, I grabbed one and ran for my bike. It was only about four inches long, but it sure was wriggling and protesting with a kind of hissing. When I reached the other three, I was once again subjected to the declarations of the mental deficiencies of Yankees.

All three let me know that the mother alligator was probably at that very moment coming after us to tear our legs off. I put the baby in my bike's basket, jumped on, and pedaled as if the Furies were after me.

Thus, Oscar came into my life. Surprisingly, mom did not object to my newly acquired companion, and my dad seemed to like him more than any other pet that had taken up residence in our various houses. Mom gave me the bottom half of her enameled, turkey-baking pan as a house for Oscar. Not positive as to the dietary requirements of alligators, I made an assumption. Oscar had lived where crickets abounded, so I figured he would eat crickets.

Bingo!

Oscar not only ate crickets, he devoured them. I made weekly trips out to the delta, sometimes solo, other times with the gang, to gather Oscar's dinners. Once fall came, and the crickets disappeared, small portions of cheap raw hamburger became his staple.

It was only a few days until Oscar's eyes opened and he viewed his surroundings. Not as large as the alligators in the Prichard zoo, he readily adapted to the non-alligator environment. I would take him out of his pan and let him wander around the house. He never objected to being held and even enjoyed a belly rub while lying on his back. My fingers stroking his whitish underside, Oscar would go into a sort of trance, as he became limp. He had sharp needle-like teeth, but as long as I had him he never once bit me.

It would seem that there would have been some hilarious occurrence where Oscar got loose and frightened my mother, or some other family member. It simply never happened. He was the most docile and laid-back pet I have ever had.

Almost every day I would take him out into the yard and let him walk around loose in the grass. As Oscar grew, so did my reputation with Joe Tom, Eddie, and Carlisle. Later, when I reacquainted with the normally inexpressive Johnny, he even seemed to hold me in higher esteem because of my pet. Joe Tom, Eddie, and Carlisle

Southern Smiles and Tears

took to telling people how they had helped to capture Oscar as his mother came running after us. I did not correct this version of Oscar's capture. Heck, it even made me less of a Yankee to have faced down an angry mother alligator.

As he and his teeth grew, I had to be more careful with Oscar as he took his daily walks. It became necessary to make him a harness and lead out of clothesline rope. The two of us were the talk of the block as we walked up and down Fifth Avenue. At 18 inches in length and standing four inches high while walking, the various dogs and cats gave him a wide berth.

My parents expressed some degree of surprise when I announced my intention of taking Oscar with me to West Virginia but did not deny him to me. It is a good thing we traveled by automobile back to the hills, because I am not sure where Oscar would have ridden on the segregated Greyhound buses of the South.

Oscar lived with me for two more years. I built him a house and a pond out of yellow bricks for his summer housing. In the winter, he lived inside by the open space gas heater. Two-foot long by now, Oscar had to curl around to sleep in his enamel pan. His food changed to small fish as his skin hardened and darkened. I could still hold him and rub his stomach, but he made a hissing-growling sound at others.

People in the neighborhood, especially J.R. and Timmy Abbot from across the street, came over often and looked at him in his pond. J.R., who was near my age, talked about how Oscar never seemed to do anything except sleep. Timmy, his aggravating younger brother, bragged about how he wasn't afraid of "...no alligator that small." For some reason though, Timmy never got closer than two or three feet to the pen. The most asked question by these two and others was, "Whatcha' gonna do with him when he gets bigger?"

I did not have to answer the question with any finality. One Saturday when I went out to give Oscar his fish, I saw that the mesh fence around his pond was torn down. Oscar was gone. I never found out who had torn the fence down or why. Nor did I ever find Oscar, even though I searched the neighborhood for several days.

With sadness, I returned the turkey pan to my mother's cabinet and vowed to myself never to have another pet.

Chapter 18
Miss Delaney

The Egg and I was my first encounter with book censorship. Perhaps, the Prichard librarian had exercised some type of censorship in her attempt to stop me from reading adult books but nothing like what I found in *The Egg and I*. Something peculiar had happened throughout the book. Certain short words were blackened out with ink. The marks were firm enough to leave rectangular pimples on the opposite side of the pages. Apparently, the librarian did not believe those words to be appropriate for ninth grade minds. That was okay with me. I just placed in mind a word I thought would fill in the inkblot. It was almost like a verbal Rorschach Test.

The books were an eclectic group. Most were leftovers from those the librarian at the new St. Albans High School did not want. The more advanced books had been moved along with the 10th, 11th,

Southern Smiles and Tears

and 12th graders transferred to the new building. Obviously, *The Egg and I* was a book our librarian would have preferred to have been relocated to be out of reach of impressionable 7th, 8th, and 9th grade scholars.

Miss Delaney was the librarian at St. Albans Junior High School. She had been left at the old school and a new and racier model installed at the new. Later when *The Beverly Hillbillies* became popular, Granny's stature and demeanor reminded me of Miss Delaney. The librarian was taller and much more articulate, but her temper was equal to that of Irene Dunn. I never remember seeing her more than a couple of steps outside the library.

I suspected she lived there.

Pity the poor scholar who dared to talk out loud in Miss Delaney's domain. In a total oxymoron, she would shout, "QUIET," somewhere near the 125-decibel level. She did know her library. In our Library Skills class, we learned the Dewey Decimal System, how to open and read books without breaking the spines, and the differences among fiction, non-fiction, and reference books.

At some point during that school year, several ninth-graders began to play a game with Miss Delaney. To them, it was a game. To Miss Delaney, it was war. The rules were simple. Whenever a member of the clandestine group obtained a hall pass from class that member was required to go to the second floor where the library was located. The now St. Albans Junior High had been built in the 1920's. A three-story, stone, high-ceilinged, non-air conditioned edifice, the school had recessed doors. These doors opened outward but did not extend into the hallway due to the recessed openings. This feature was an important part of the game/war. The player/enemy would approach the door of the library, knock loudly on the door, and run to the next door, skirt into the recess, and hide. Miss Delaney would go to the door, according to the captives inside, twist the knob, step outside, and inquire. "Who did that?" She never walked down the hall to look in the recesses for the culprit. She simply looked left and right before retreating into her lair.

It was fun for a while. Then it became mundane.

Until the day a game player upped the ante.

One of the group noticed what held the door up and allowed it to swivel. He probably learned this from a book in the library.

This particular event needed to be planned. It involved removing the pins from the hinges, in addition to the knocking. Four people had to synchronize their parts, or the ploy was doomed to failure. One person had to divert Miss Delaney's attention at a precise time. The plan was that exactly at 9:10 A.M., during second period,

Southern Smiles and Tears

the decoy was to go up to Miss Delaney's desk and asked her to help him use the card catalog. This was devious because it appealed to the basic instincts of any librarian to use "help" and "card catalog" in the same sentence. The next phase was more difficult because three students in three different classes had to request a hall pass for the bathroom at 9:05. This gave two of them time to go to their lockers, retrieve the screw drivers previously sequestered there, go to the second floor, and remove the pins. The key player was the knocker. As soon as the two pin removers left the library doorway, the knocker walked up to the door and pounded on it.

According to reports from those in the library, the perpetrators saw nothing from their hiding places in door recesses, the following actions occurred. Miss Delaney ran from the card catalog file to the door. She grabbed the knob to open the door.

Then it happened.

The door fell off the hinges with a bang. Miss Delaney stood there transfixed. She opened her mouth, but no sound was emitted. She turned, walked back into the library with aplomb, returned to the student at the card catalog files, and instructed her assistant to go get the janitor. The assistant was to tell the janitor that the library door was broken.

What a let down for the four of us. Our ploy had failed! We expected some huge reaction. What we got was a lady skilled at handling students. As long as the game was only a nuisance, she played. When it became obnoxious and dangerous, she took away all the thrill of the activity.

Years later, as a teacher, Miss Delaney's lesson served me well. I saw many a teacher paint himself into a corner by over reacting to the minor hijinks of students. Reaction had to fit the crime. It was necessary to "not see or hear" some of the things that occurred in school and class.

Besides, the knowledge about hinges came in handy in 2002. Bobbie Traywick, our text computer scanner, accidentally locked the bathroom door from the inside as she closed it. Later that afternoon, she could not open the door. Alice and I were traveling when she called us with her dilemma. My ninth grade knowledge of hinges and pins came rushing back. I told Bobbie how to detach the door and unlock it once it was down. She telephoned us 10 minutes later all excited because she had not only done as I had instructed but had also reattached the door.

Yes, you can learn things by hanging around a library.

Southern Smiles and Tears

Chapter 19
To Play or Not to Play

Brown v. The Board of Education had come to St. Albans, West Virginia. The newspapers headlined that in the fall of 1955 Kanawha County Schools would integrate all schools. The only real discussion I remember about "...coloreds coming to our school" concerned football.

One of the stars of the nascent St. Albans Junior High School Silver Eagles was a fullback named Jerry. He was short, probably four inches shorter than six feet, stocky, and strong. When we played basketball in phys ed, he thought it was football. I hated to be on the opposite team from him for dodge ball. He would unleash the ball with such velocity that it hurt if it barely touched you. Pity the poor soul who suffered a direct hit.

It was late May, after lunch and right before Mr. Gillespie's exciting science class, when a group conversation turned to "niggers." Here stood a group of 14-year old male students, most of whom had

Southern Smiles and Tears

had no contact whatsoever with people of color, discussing how to react to this catastrophic event. Many of us had been driven by but never entered "the colored section" of St. Albans, which was just across the Coal River Bridge and outside the city limits. It was several years before I realized we had been saying "Mandeeville", often in a derogatory tone, when the real name was the picturesque "Amandaville." Even when we walked toward Coal River Road to go swimming, we would walk on the far side of Old Route 60 to steer clear of "Mandeeville".

The discussion became lively, probably because it was based completely upon ignorance of facts. Comments came fast and furious.

"They better not try to date any of our girls."

"I ain't never goin' take a shower in the gym locker room again."

"My dad said not to worry because most of them were dumb and would quit school before high school."

"I don't want no nigger teachers."

Then Jerry dropped his bombshell.

"I'll quit football before I play with them."

Silence was oppressive. When it broke, it was mostly in alliance with Jerry's stand. Several other football players expressed their willingness to join his boycott. Those of us of the non-athletic bent mostly expressed sadness at the prospect of a poor football future for the mighty Red Dragons of St. Albans High School.

The discussion ended with the bell and Mr. Gillespie's lecture about the effect of the Doppler Effect on ambulance sirens.

Football practice began two weeks before school opened, and I do not know what had ensued during those two weeks. What I do know is that when the 1955 Red Dragons ran on the field for coach Sam LeRose there were black and white heads inside the helmets. Jerry was there as a member of the "B" team, and all was well in St. Albans.

That incident was in contrast to the beloved Crimson Tide of Alabama. The football team remained white for over 20 years. It wasn't until Southern California, with a fullback named Sam Baker embarrassed Alabama on the field, that "Bear" Bryant recruited blacks. In what may be true, or anecdotal, there is a story that Bryant actually contracted for the game knowing that the Southern Cal fullback Baker would run roughshod over Alabama white players. As the story goes, the loss would allow Bryant to grant football scholarships to blacks. Bryant had achieved a god-like stature to the alumni and followers of the University of Alabama football teams. If the story is true, Bryant was the person with a following within the state who could have pulled it off.

Southern Smiles and Tears

There have been many suppositions as to Bryant's thoughts about this. Many believe that recalcitrant segregationists in Alabama would subjugate their hate and disrespect for blacks to their love and fanatical desire for a winning football team. The loss did advance the integration of the state university where George Wallace said blacks would never attend, let alone play football.

Prejudicial thoughts about football players still surfaced in Alabama 25 years after Baker embarrassed the Crimson Tide. In the late 90's Alabama went through a period of less than stellar football performance. It was not uncommon to hear that the team would do better if "that colored" were replaced with "that outstanding white backup." Letters to the newspapers would begin with statements with prejudice underpinnings. Writers would insist they were not opposed to the black player, but that the white was just superior. Why then did many of the writers insist in saying it wasn't a black and white issue? If it were not, there was no reason to preface the missives with such statements. The whole "quarterback controversy" became moot when the white player, who was starting in place of the senior Andrew Zow, was injured. Zow took over the position he had held the previous year and led the Tide to a winning season as the fans cheered him. Perhaps, Bryant knew more about Alabamians than they knew about themselves.

The only question, which still haunts me is, *What if Alabama had won against Southern Cal?* Would Alabama's football be as all white as were the 2003 Greek fraternities and sororities in Tuscaloosa?

Southern Smiles and Tears

Chapter 20
The Atomic Bomb

    The opening lines of *A Tale of Two Cities* could well have explained the 1950's. Carefree on the surface, many of us as teenagers had a gnawing fear in the back of our minds. The Rosenblooms were executed for giving the design for the atomic bomb to the Russians, and the Communists were going to use it on us. Now, that thought will cause one to pause. Every member of the Highlawn gang had been born just before, or during World War II. Each weekend at the movies during *Movietone News* we saw the destructive capability of nuclear weapons in tests in New Mexico and on Pacific Ocean atolls, along with the repeating of film showing the destruction of Hiroshima and Nagasaki.
    It was frightening.
    At the same time, especially in the summer, there were girls, swimming, pick up ball games and other things to occupy our fertile minds.

Southern Smiles and Tears

Swimming at Upper and Lower Falls on the Coal River took up a great deal of time. Our gang, which consisted of boys in the 10th through the 12th grade who attended St. Albans High, spent many days at those two beaches and other locations on the river. There were two exceptions in the gang membership. Dave McGowan and I did not completely fit the profile. David was out of school and working for his father at the Mobil Oil Bulk Plant, but since he was a neighbor and friend of Booty Ball he qualified for *ex officio* membership. I lived north of the tracks to the east of Ordnance Park, which should have disqualified me, but my best friends Bill Nida and Jim Cottle lived on the proper side of the tracks. I also believe the mystique surrounding my brother Billy and his legendary appeal to girls helped. He was the only one in St. Albans with enough nerve to date Anna Lou Hall, the daughter of St. Albans Police Captain Crit Hall.

I believe some of the guys thought I had Billy's sway over females. Wrong, but somehow that factor, and my friends, allowed me to be full member.

Ordnance Park was a phenomenon of the war. The federal government had built these duplex apartments during World War II to house workers for the South Charleston Ordnance Plant. These hundreds of one-story duplex apartments had been built on bottomland along concrete paved streets named for members of Franklin Delano Roosevelt War Department. I have no idea why, but people from Highlawn, an undefined residential area south of the Chesapeake and Ohio Railroad tracks still with dirt streets, considered themselves superior to those living in the apartments of Ordnance Park. This was quite strange because the government had built several nice playgrounds for the residents there. After the war ended, the government began allowing park residents to purchase the duplexes. Slowly the sameness ordained by government officials began to change as the new owners painted the outsides with different colors. Some even purchased both sides and made one house. No matter the improvements, Ordnance Park people were still inferior to Highlawn ones.

During the summer of 1956, St. Albans town officials and the County Civil Defense decided our town had to prepare for an atomic attack. The word was that because Union Carbide, Dupont de NeMours, Monsanto, Westvaco, and several other smaller chemical plants concentrated in a 30 mile stretch through the Kanawha River Valley, our area was on a list of the 10 most likely places for the Russians to bomb. No one knew how the United States, or newspapers, had obtained this list, but it was the gospel according to gossip. In reality, I believe I was the target. I know this because when our family lived near Mobile that city was among the top 10 on the list because of Brookley Air Base and the harbor. That only left eight other places of any importance in the whole country.

A Sunday had been chosen for everyone in St. Albans to either leave town or stay indoors with the blinds and curtains pulled closed. I assume closed up houses were impervious to the effect of atomic weapons. My other assumption was that those who drove the seven miles to South Charleston to avoid the effects of the blast had never watched *Movietone News* and seen the square miles flattened in Japan. Besides that, the entire chemical area was in a long valley bisected by the Kanawha River. My assumption here was that all the radiation must have been going to rise straight up and be blown over the hills.

Anyway, on Friday our gang decided it was time to go swimming.

We began our trek out to Coal River around noon. We walked the three miles toward downtown St. Albans to the overpass crossing the railroad spur line going south to the coalfields. We stopped and discussed which of our two options we would take. The first route was longer. It took us to St. Albans proper, across Coal River Bridge, skirted Amandaville, and followed Coal River Road to the west side of the river. The second route was shorter by miles but had a particular obstacle. This route demanded we leave the road at the overpass, walk along the railroad track heading south, and through the railroad tunnel. It was an hour faster to the water to use that path.

Usually, the trip through the quarter-mile long tunnel was uneventful, as this one would proof to be. Other times it was a real experience. About every 25 feet along both walls of the tunnel were one-foot deep insets tall and deep enough for railroad workers to squeeze into if caught in the tunnel when a train came.

One day going out to the river Jim, Bill, and I were about halfway through the tunnel, when we as the song says, ...*heard that lonesome whistle blow*.... The only trouble was it wasn't lonesome, it was blowing to warn that a train was about to enter the tunnel. Each of us ran for an inset and made it before the train's headlight was visible. I was still skinny and fit nicely in the groove. Bill, somewhat heavier, fit also. Jim did not quite go in all the way.

We remained in our hutches, frightened as rabbits with a fox standing in front of us. The engine flew past followed by probably a hundred hoppers filled with coal. It was so close, if we had stuck an arm out straight it would have been ripped off. Coal cars were always filled with mounds rising above the edge of the cars. There

Southern Smiles and Tears

in the pitch-black darkness, coal projectiles flew off striking the edge of the tunnel. I had read of the bombings of London during the war, and that tunnel was as close to those descriptions as I ever wanted to be. None of us were attending church with any regularity, but I do believe prayers were offered up by all three of us. We probably would have even knelt, except that the cars would have decapitated us. The three of us survived, and in the best tradition of stupid teenagers, we often used the tunnel until the first one of us got a driver's license and car.

Penetrating and exiting the tunnel that day, we arrived on the other side safe and secure from any Russian attacks. We camped on McGraw's beach below Lower Falls. Friday and Saturday nights we all went skinny-dipping. During the day we dove from tree branches into the water and swung on a rope out over the river, diving or cannonballing into the cool water. I was good at diving, but Jim was the best cannonballer in the world. He also could swim the width of the river under water. No one else I ever knew could make it more than half way across without surfacing.

Summer days and nights ran together for a group of young boys between high school prison terms. We forgot about the attack. Additionally, we ran out of food and pop, even though on Saturday evening we had visited a local garden and borrowed a few warm, juicy, red tomatoes.

Casually, we began our trip back to St. Albans. For some reason, forgotten to my memory, we decided to take the long route back to town. It was eerie. As we approached town, not a soul was visible. The whole place was deserted. We were the only survivors of the attack.

Joking, pushing, and shoving, we made our way through town. When we reached Highlawn we decided to go over to the playgrounds in Ordnance Park to mess around. We crossed the tracks and passed the HiLawn Movie Theater. It really wasn't in Highlawn, but I suppose the owner knew no self-respecting Highlawn resident would go to an Ordnance Park movie theater.

Anyhow, in between the theater and the main playground was Salven's Drugstore. We were almost past the pharmacy, when Dr. Salven threw open the door and shouted, "What are you boys doing out during the air raid?"

He scared the bejabbers out of us.

"Get in here, or you will be exposed to radiation!"

We went inside. I suppose if you had to wait out an atomic attack, the place to be was in a pharmacy with medicine and a soda shop.

Dr. Salven did not release us until the all clear sounded at 5:00.

Southern Smiles and Tears

We decided to go our separate ways, tired from swimming, walking, and the possibility of having been radiated.

The next Wednesday, when the local newspaper came out, there was a photograph taken from downtown St. Albans. It showed how empty the town was along Main Street and across the Coal River Bridge. Those who looked closely saw something in the distance beyond the bridge.

Six tiny teenagers who had survived the blast.

Southern Smiles and Tears

Chapter 21
Snow Boarding Is for Wimps

The new Olympic sport of snowboarding may look dangerous, but it is tame compared to the 1950's sport of carhopping.

West Virginia is a peculiar state. Those living in New England or the Mid-Atlantic States consider it to be in the South. I base this on the story of the football player from northern New Jersey who signed with the West Virginia Mountaineers. He thought Morgantown, home of the university, was in the South. He wanted to play in warm weather. Imagine his surprise that first winter. Should he have bothered to look at a map he would have seen that part of the state is farther north than New York City. Those native to the real South, many of whom know more about the South's view of the Civil War than they do about current events, consider West Virginia inhabited with Yankee traitors. This stems from the fact that West Virginia turned its back on the South by separating from Virginia and supporting the Union cause.

Southern Smiles and Tears

Truth is that West Virginia is of mixed characteristics and weather. It can be hotter than much of the nation in the summer and have huge snowstorms during the winter. Other times the winters are mild with only a skiff of snow in much of the state.

The second winter after I returned from *The Heart of Dixie* was one of the cold winters with ample snow. The first day of snow came on as if God was defrosting his refrigerator and allowing the scrapings to fall to earth. My fellow scholars and I went to school without seeing a cloud in the sky. By lunchtime there were three inches of snow on the ground. More than six inches had accumulated by 3:00, and school was canceled for the next day.

Hallelujah!

"Let's go hop cars tonight!" Someone in our gang walking home suggested this over going sledding, a much more sedate winter activity than car hopping. We all agreed to meet at 7:00 in Ordnance Park. It would have been nice to be able to car hop in Highlawn, but the perfect grid of streets in Ordnance Park made for superb hopping.

Those unfamiliar with the sport may be a tad confused at this point, and a description of the activity and its rules are necessary for edification. The city of St. Albans, in the mid-1950's, did not salt the streets on level land when it snowed. That was reserved strictly for the steep inclines of the streets on the hills just south of Highlawn and the rest of St. Albans. The lack of salt made car hopping possible.

Car hopping was a real skill, entirely different from getting on a sled and pointing it downhill. A group of us would stand by one of the four-way stop signs that aligned the streets, which bisected the grid in the housing development. When a car began moving after stopping at a yellow and black stop sign, four of the group would run to the car, grab onto the rear bumper and crouch down using the boots on their feet as skis.

That first night was pure ecstasy. There was an ample supply of vehicles, and the streets were nicely covered with snow packed down by the cars the workers had driven home after work. It was quite a thrill riding behind a car going over 20 miles per hour. When the car slowed down, we would drop off and run before the driver screamed at us.

I only had one small problem that particular night. It happened because several in our group violated the four to a car rule. A '52 Mercury slid to a stop and began to accelerate. I started to run for the car at the same time as six other winter athletes. We all arrived at the bumper at approximately the same moment. There was

Southern Smiles and Tears

much pushing and shoving that resulted in me securing a hold on the outside of the right rear of the bumper. The driver was great! He swerved back and forth giving us a great ride. Apparently, he wasn't upset with teenagers grabbing on and using his car for an amusement ride.

At least that is what I was thinking. In reality, he was a demon in disguise.

I found out his devilish plan when he turned down Knox Avenue and began revving up the engine. He swerved to the left. He swerved to the right. He swerved to the left. He swerved to the right over a spot where a car had been parked during the snowstorm. The only problem was that the car had been moved and the concrete was in its natural state.

My position on the right outside of the car created a problem. A few years later in my aborted enrollment in Physics Class I was to learn about inertia. A moving object will continue to move until it is stopped by something. That something could be friction. Friction is what I got. My boots left the slick snow and encountered friction. The car continued to move while my feet stopped. That would not have been a disaster in itself, except I was still holding onto the bumper. It was a second or two before I became disengaged from the vehicle. At the moment of release, I no longer was foot skiing. I was body rolling. My body rolled and bounced across the curb accumulating snow for the next 15 feet. Dazed and dizzy, I sat up on the side of the street trying to figure out what had happened.

Mostly what had happened was that I was so sore the next day that I was unable to go carhopping that night. That, and because my mother wouldn't let me out because I had torn my coat and destroyed my new winter boots.

Southern Smiles and Tears

Chapter 22
Hitching a Train Ride

No matter how high the score teenage boys may achieve on an I.Q. test, they basically are not smart. Specifically, I refer to the stupid things boys do, and have done for ages, which place them in harm's way.

The aforementioned sport of car hopping, which did hold danger, was nothing compared to a form of transportation a few members of our group utilized — hitching rides on slow moving freight trains. Some mornings, usually when I overslept, I would opt to grab hold of one of the metal ladders located at each end of coal cars. This provided me a leisurely ride to St. Albans High School. Freight trains slowed down on the tracks behind our house as they entered the city limit of St. Albans and did not resume high speed until leaving the other side of the town. Fortunately for me, the high school was almost exactly in the center of the slow down section. It was a convenient mode for travel.

Southern Smiles and Tears

I did this so often that I became blasé to the danger inherent in this stupidity. I learned my lesson one unforgettable Friday evening. Several of our gang decided to go roller-skating on that almost fatal night. There was no skating rink in St. Albans, but one existed in Charleston. The only problem was that Charleston was located 15 miles due east.

Legally sane teenagers, that may be an oxymoron, would have used a red and white Charleston Transit bus for transportation. Not us.

A perfectly good transportation system awaited us, and it did not require 50 cents in change for a round trip. That was good because the rink required $1.00 in good folding money. Besides that a soft drink was 10 cents and popcorn a nickel. Then if one of us was lucky enough to make the acquaintance of one of the roller rink beauties, the cost of refreshments doubled immediately.

We had used the free system once before and were thrilled by our brilliance. An evening coal train went through town about 6:00. Another allowed us to make the return trip a little after 11:00 out of Charleston. The eastbound freight picked up speed as it left St. Albans, slowed down in South Charleston, sped up once more and then slowed as it passed by the Charleston train station. At least that is what it did the first time we hopped a ride.

Something happened that summer Friday evening. The train moved slowly through Highlawn, as six eager hands grabbed the metal ladders of the coal hopper. We gained speed, as we hung on for dear life. On schedule, the train slowed as it passed through South Charleston. Then it picked up speed, taking us to our evening of flirting and showing off by skating backwards or crouched with a leg stretched out in front while circling the rink on one skate.

Stupid engineer.

It only took a second to realize that the train was not slowing for its approach into Charleston. It actually was picking up speed. We could tell because our greased ducktails were all askew from the wind.

We flew by the train station, passed Marmet, barely saw Chelyan, and finally began to catch our collective breaths as the train slowed down as it approached Montgomery. We disengaged ourselves some 60 miles from home with neither skating rink nor fetching young lasses in sight.

It was not quite as bad as on Apollo 13 several years later when the immortal words of "Houston, we have a problem." were uttered, but our situation to us was approximately the same. Sixty miles from home and our mode of transportation had failed. Unlike the astronauts, we dared not call our home base for rescue. We may have been rescued but would have been grounded until we were able to collect social security checks.

We resorted to the tried and true method God intended when he gave humans an opposing thumb. We hitchhiked. It only took us six hours to reach St. Albans.

When I tried to sneak in the house at almost two o'clock in the morning, I was met with the glaring eyes of my mother.

"Where have you been? You were supposed to have been home by midnight."

I could have told her the truth, but a half-lie seemed more appropriate under the circumstances.

"We decided not to go skating and just rode around but lost track of time."

She didn't smack my behind too hard but may have been curious about my lack of interest in skating for the next few months.

Chapter 23
Personal Gas Stations

Perhaps the apogee of a teenager's right of passage is the securing of a license to drive a vehicle. The nadir has to be the realization that fuel costs money.

Even in the 1950's with gasoline costing around 15 cents a gallon, money for gas was scarce. Sometimes, as a group wanting to "cruise" around Highlawn, we would pool our coins and come up with a dollar. Other times we would pull into a filling station and spend the princely sum of 10 cents.

There were more economical gas stations, albeit with drawbacks. One drawback was that the economical stations were attached to other peoples' vehicles. Another problem was that these people got testy when certain teenagers tried to pump out fuel. The third hindrance was the imminent danger of swallowing the liquid when attempting to "prime the pump."

It only required a few accessories to obtain fuel from these per-

Southern Smiles and Tears

sonal stations: three feet of hose, a container, and someone to suck the air out of the hose once it was inserted into the personal gas station. Jim, with his large lung capacity, was our pump primer supreme. He not only had great suction; Jim did not seem to be adversely affected by getting a mouth full of gasoline.

We did not engage in this surreptitious method of obtaining fuel unless two conditions existed. First was that none of us had any money. This occurred with regularity. Second was when the opportunity arose. This also often happened.

Most of the time we used a sporadic method of finding the stations. It was important not to use the same ones with any regularity. People tended to get suspicious if they came home with a full tank and woke up to it half gone. The first occurrence could cause consternation. The second, suspicion. The third, retribution. The latter could be dangerous in a culture that accepted gun ownership and the right to protect one's own property.

Once in a while, though, an opportunity would arise that forced our group to take action. Each year there was a huge basketball tournament at dear old St. Albans High School. The Sportsman Basketball Tournament included the best college and professional basketball players in the nation. Each night large crowds of people attended, which meant many, many personal gas stations. The temptation for us to store up on fuel was akin to moth and flames.

Jim, Bill, and I looked forward to the 1956 tournament with excitement. Bill had his driver's license but not much money. His dad had died, and his mother worked in a drug store in South Charleston. She did have a 1952 Ford that Bill got to use, as long as he paid for gas.

Ha!

Why pay when gas was free?

We only had to make preparations for getting the gas. For several weeks before the event, the three of us scoured the neighborhood for containers with tight lids. Unbelievably, as I look back now, two of the containers we were already using were glass gallon vinegar bottles. We never thought about the possibility of blowing ourselves to smithereens if we happened to drop the gas filled glass containers.

The first night of the tournament, we were ready. We had two containers each to fill for each night of the Thursday, Friday, and Saturday games. This equaled 18 gallons of fun fuel just waiting for us.

Bill drove us down an unpaved back street beside the railroad track. He parked there, two blocks over from where most of the

Southern Smiles and Tears

tournament goers parked their cars. We wore dark clothes and had rubbed charcoal on our faces and hands. This was a major operation.

We had made one major mistake.

When planning something surreptitious, you shouldn't brag about it beforehand. We only told a few people of our plans. The trouble was that apparently those few told a few others. Word must have reached the one person at the high school, who had an allegiance other than to his fellow classmates. Corky. He was either an auxiliary policeman, a junior policeman, or a member of some other subversive organization. My memory does not give me the proper name, but what he was to us was a snitch, an old-fashioned tattletale.

Bill, Jim, and I were approaching the first vehicle in our clandestine operation, when a voice boomed out at us.

"What do you boys think your doin'?"

Standing behind us was a St. Albans City policeman, gun and all. Right beside the officer of the law, in his overfilled junior policeman getup, was a grinning Corky. He was having the time of his life. The only good thing about the situation was that the policeman was not the dreaded Captain Crit Hall. Rumor had it that the captain would take recalcitrant teenagers directly over to the Children's Home in Dunbar without even giving them a fair trial.

"Are you boys thinking of siphoning gas from these cars?"

Now in the list of stupid questions, that had to be number one. Three boys with six empty gallon jugs with screw-on lids, a five-foot piece of hose, dark clothes, and charcoal smeared on our faces. What was his first clue, other than that Corky had told him what was going to happen that night? Of course, we were going to siphon gas. He really didn't think we were going to put gas in all those vehicles, did he?

"Corky, you confiscate those jugs and hose, while I decide what to do with these three."

I'm glad that Corky wasn't deciding our fates. He probably would have shot us on the spot. Corky, his grin now a smirk, walked over and disarmed us of our precious equipment. He then did the unpardonable. He told the policeman, with glee, our names.

"That one's Jim Cottle," he said as he pointed to our chief inhaler. Jim was the first identified, I believe, because he not only had two jugs but the all-important hose in his hands. Rapidly, Corky went on pointing as he identified "Bill Nida" and "Dave Bice." I think he gave my name as that because he knew I hated the nickname.

I am not positive if I were more scared of the officer, or angry at

Southern Smiles and Tears

Corky. How could he be so low as to squeal on three classmates engaged in the act of siphoning gas? I guess some people just had no respect for this time-honored activity.

The officer wrote down our names in a notepad he was holding and revealed our fate.

"Whew!"

He told us to go on home with the warning that if he caught us again we would go to jail. Silly policeman. From then on, we kept our plans amongst the three of us.

Corky would have to become a better investigator, if he planned to ever rat on us again.

Chapter 24
When a Brother Dies

Taps played from behind a knoll by a trumpet for a dead relative has to be the most heart-wrenching tune that exists.

Eddie was dead. As much as I had tried to disbelieve this fact, the 21-gun salute and *Taps* had placed the final exclamation point on my hope. My hero was gone!

My 28 year-old brother was his own man. When mom whipped him for a misdeed, he would laugh heartily until she joined him as she forgot what he had done. Six weeks from being graduated, he quit high school.

Mom, my educated parent asked, "Why?"

"They aren't teaching me anything I don't already know." Eddie simply replied. "Besides, I'm going to be an ironworker. I can work six months in the spring and summer. I'll make enough money to see the world the other six months."

That is what he did. I would ask him where he had been when he returned home each spring.

"Cripple Creek."

Always Cripple Creek. It took me a while to understand that Cripple Creek was any place he had been. I missed him when he was gone but knew he would always return. Unannounced he would blow in as a March wind, hug and kiss mom, while whirling her around in a circle. As far as I can remember, Eddie was the only hugger in our family of reticent love. He then would grab me by my ankles, turn me topsy-turvy, and asked me if I had learned anything while he was gone. Eddie, more than anyone, understood that with my hearing loss, education was my key to the world. He would drill me over demanding I answer him out loud. He brought a variety of gifts for my siblings but for me only one thing. Books. He read incessantly, and wanted me to do the same.

Eddie's intelligence complemented his strength. I know he was smart from what happened to me my first day in Algebra I class in the 10th grade.

The teacher raised her eyebrows upon hearing my last name. "Are you related to Eddie Bice?"

"Yes ma'am, he's my brother."

"I went to school with Eddie. He helped me through math classes, and talked me into becoming a teacher. He surprised me when he left school."

I was taken aback when she used the word "left" instead of "quit." She understood Eddie. He had not quit anything, he simply moved on to another level of learning.

As to his strength, it amazed me. And others. He could take a 25-pound sledgehammer in his grip, stretch his arm out, lean the hammer head back toward his face, touch it to his nose, and return the tool to an upright position. Standard pushups were too simple for him. Eddie would do pushups on one arm, either the left or right one.

When our family moved to Mobile, Eddie continued to work constructing buildings. Then his life was interrupted. He received a notice from Selective Service, the dreaded draft board. The Korean War was to have a new soldier.

Just before he boarded the train to report to training camp, he told me not to worry, the army would surely use him in some type of construction. He was wrong. The army decided Eddie should be a medic. I believe his intelligence showed through in the battery of tests he wrote about taking.

Eddie never told us much about his two-year tour of duty in "The Forgotten War." He sent us photographs of him and his friends. His

Southern Smiles and Tears

smile always dominated the scenes. The only other tangible evidence of his time there was an expensive gold watch he gave me after his return home. He simply said he wanted no memories of that place. His letters were more of a travelogue about a picturesque country than a description of war torn battlefields. An historian relying on his letters as primary sources about the Korean War would fail to see much of a conflict. His one reference to actual fighting was more of a comment of human sensibility rather than that of inhumanity.

He wrote to us of a sniper. Eddie's company lived in trenches while the negotiators in Panmumjon were deciding how to end the conflict. One trench was on an incline, and the men had to sit and slide down the slope to get to the latrine. The only problem was that the inclined part of the trench was visible to the Chinese who had entered the war on the side of the North Koreans. Eddie told us that a Chinese soldier had tied his rifle to a tree branch and sighted it on the open trench. Every hour on the hour, during daylight, the Americans watched through binoculars as the enemy soldier climbed the tree and fired one round into the trench. He then left his perch and returned to the ground. Eddie said the bullets struck the same place so many times they made a hole in the middle of the trench. In some type of unspoken agreement the Americans did not shoot the Chinese soldier, and he never fired except at the proper time.

The only other thing we knew about his time in Korea also came through the mail after the conflict ended. A letter from the Pentagon informed Eddie that he had been awarded the Bronze Star. He was to go to the Army Reserve Headquarters in South Charleston for the formal presentation of the medal. Easy going, unflappable, Eddie's reaction shocked everyone in the family.

"I didn't volunteer to join the damn Army. I didn't ask to go to Korea, and I'm sure as hell not going to accept a medal for what went on over there!"

Case closed.

It was a warm September Saturday in 1957 while I was working at Kroger when the store manager called me to the office. My dad was in the office. This was strange because he and I were not on the best of terms and rarely saw each other. He told me Eddie had been in an accident, and I needed to go to the house with him. At home, mom was sitting on the couch moaning.

"Eddie's dead! Eddie's dead!"

Eddie had been working in Ravenswood, West Virginia building part of the huge, new Kaiser Aluminum plant. A steel beam being lifted several stories into the air began to swing wildly knocking Eddie and a fellow ironworker from the top of the building. Both fell from the building. Eddie died instantly. His coworker grabbed a beam on the way down, but his impact with the ground crippled him for life.

It was some weeks after my mother was handed the flag, which had draped Eddie's coffin, when she received a telephone call. The colonel at the Army reserve asked to come to our house to give mom Eddie's Bronze Star. He sat down in the living room and told us why Eddie had been awarded the medal. Two American soldiers had been wounded and were caught between the two lines of fire. Eddie had crawled out under fire and dragged one of the men back to safety. He then turned and ran across the field to the other man, picked him up, and carried him to the American lines.

He wasn't only my hero.

Chapter 25
Kip and Helen

Sometimes people are a great deal more intelligent and observant than what one believes. Case in point Kip Smith and Helen Treanor. Mr. Smith was the boy's counselor and Mrs. Treanor was the girl's counselor while I attended St. Albans High School.

My mom and dad were in the process of going their separate ways when I entered the 11th grade. He had become part owner of a drive-in restaurant, a euphemism for a beer joint, in North Charleston. The money came from part of Eddie's military death insurance. Because he was still working for the State Road Department, he convinced my mother to run the establishment. She agreed because that was the only place and time she would see him. They argued, spatted, and fought for a year with each one trying to get me to take sides. I figured, as the last child living at home, this was a no win situation.

So at the beginning of my 12th year of my education, I ran away

Southern Smiles and Tears

from home. It was probably more of a stroll away from home. I just kind of quit going home after school and work. It became easier for me to spend nights with friends rather than going home to an empty house. Besides, the food was better. Each week I would rotate among my friends' homes so their parents did not become suspicious of what was happening.

It had been my good fortune to get a job as a grocery clerk at the Kroger grocery store in South Charleston on June 6, 1957. The store, at that time, was open from 9:00 until 6:00 Monday through Wednesday and 9:00 to 9:00 on Thursday, Friday, and Saturday. I had been able to work 32 hours during the summer. When school began, such an inconvenience, I could only work five and one-half hours each on Thursday and Friday and nine hours on Saturday. This gave me 20 hours at the huge salary of $1.21 per hour. After deductions, my paychecks came to just right at $20.00 per week. The only exception was the weeks six-dollars were subtracted for union dues.

I needed a plan. How could I work nine hours on Friday to make up for part of the loss in income?

The answer seemed simple but would probably be frowned upon by Kip, as most of us called him behind his back. I told the store manager that I had permission to leave school early on Fridays and was able to begin work at noon. This was not quite the truth. The fourth Friday of September, two weeks after Eddie had died and during second period, I laid my head down on my desk and emitted a low moan. When this did not draw any attention, I increased the level of the moan. Finally, Miss Lynch asked me if I were ill.

"Yes ma'am, I think I need to go down to the clinic before I throw up."

Smiling broadly as I headed down to the clinic between Mr. Smith's and Mrs. Treanor's offices, I concocted my tale of an upset stomach, "...from something I must've ate."

Mrs. Treanor, who took care of those not feeling well, was sympathetic; probably thinking my illness had something to do with Eddie's death. She told me if I needed to, I could go home. She had no idea how badly I needed to go.

Looking pathetic, I left the school. A driver's license in my back pocket, but no car to drive, I headed for Old Route 60 and my bus to financial freedom. I got to South Charleston at 11:30 and was fully prepared for manning my cash register at 12:00 sharp. What a plan! I had totally put one over on the educational establishment.

Monday morning I took my written and signed excuse to Kip. He looked at it, failed to recognize that the signature resembled my

Southern Smiles and Tears

handwriting, and gave me my illness permission slip for admission to classes. I continued this process for several weeks, always rotating between first and second period as the time to become ill.

One Friday afternoon about 3:30 in the afternoon my subterfuge surfaced. I was at my check out counter in my crisp white apron when a serious situation arose. The third customer in the line-awaiting checkout was familiar. Too familiar. It was Mrs. Treanor. The old canard, "You can run but cannot hide," came to mind. The only problem was I could not even run. I was trapped. As I checked out Mrs. Treanor's groceries, I averted looking at her, and she never acknowledged that she recognized me.

She had.

Monday morning, with counterfeit excuse in hand, I walked into Kip's office. Lying there on the corner of his desk was my signed permission slip. It did not have "Illness" as the reason but "Personal." Each Monday for the rest of my senior year I simply went to the counselor's office and picked up the already signed slips. Mr. Smith never said anything to me when I arrived, and I said nothing to him. A couple of weeks later, I stopped going to school altogether on Fridays. My school year simply became a series of four-day weeks.

I never found out what discussions occurred between Mrs. Treanor and Mr. Smith about me. I don't know how they found out about my family situation, but they must have known. Some type of unwritten and unspoken agreement had been placed in effect. The two never harassed me about my attendance. For my part, I worked hard to keep my grades high.

I owe the two of them an unpayable debt.

Chapter 26
Chemistry and Physics

Mr. Reppert must have had some of my siblings in his chemistry or physics classes.

It was fifth period, right after lunch, when I entered chemistry class with visions of bombs and other wonderful concoctions in my head. Mr. Reppert began calling out our names and assigning seats. Not desks. Actual stools behind long black tables with faucets and sinks. Best of all were the gas jets. Wow! A class with gas jets. Wonderful things surely would happen here.

Mr. Reppert had seated several scholars when he flipped the next card. His countenance did not exactly show disgust but looked more as if his lunch had not settled well and the bile was attacking.

"David Bice!"

"Yes, sir."

"Don't you have several brothers and sisters who went to school

Southern Smiles and Tears

here?"

"Yes, sir."

"You will sit at the back table."

Thus began my tutelage for one and a half school years in chemistry and physics. That first day was the apogee of my relationship with Mr. Reppert. I was to learn later when I began teaching there existed an insidious system for stereotyping incoming students. This system had its home in the teachers' lounge. Many teachers, at the beginning of a school year, would gossip in the lounge about incoming students who had older siblings the teacher had taught. Traits of the older siblings were automatically placed upon the younger without any evidence of individual ability. This stereotyping was not only unprofessional, it was unethical.

Mr. Reppert had a grading system whereby he posted each student's accumulated weekly points from tests and work books on a side bulletin board. Every Monday you knew your exact standing in the class and grade at the particular point of the nine-week grading period. At least that is the way it was supposed to be.

Bob Farley was one of the smartest people in our class. Later, he became a pharmacist, so I know he understood chemistry. At the end of the first grading period, the breaking point between an "A" and "B" was 290. Bob and I both had 292 points. I was ecstatic. I had aced chemistry.

No!

Miss Lynch, behind her back called "Katy," my homeroom teacher handed out our report cards on a Friday. I looked. There was a mistake. My chemistry grade was a "B".

"Bob. What did Reppert give you?"

"A."

Obviously, there had been a mistake. When the bell rang I ran down the stairs to room 110.

"Mr. Reppert, I think you wrote the wrong grade on my report card. It should be an 'A' not the 'B' here."

"It's not the wrong grade. That is the grade you made."

I went over to the bulletin board and pointed to my 292 points. "Look here!" I demanded.

He looked at me and said, "When I factored in classroom participation, that is what you deserved."

"That's not what you said!"

"Young man, do not talk back to me or I will send you to see Mr. Smith."

He wanted classroom participation. Well, that is what he got. Surreptitious participation, but participation none the less.

Southern Smiles and Tears

I continued to maintain my level of work to receive the downgraded "A's" for the rest of the year. Behind the scenes I excelled at unauthorized class participation.

First, I made good use of the beakers and access to water. My first independent chemical experiment was in mixtures. I brought Kool-Aid packages and Domino sugar packets to class. When Reppert turned his back toward the class to write on the blackboard, I would run water into a beaker, stir in the other two ingredients. Voila! A chemical mixture of two solubles in water. I would pass the mixture down the row. With the exception of a couple of goody two-shoes, my fellow students would pour themselves drinks to test the quality of my experiment. I repeated the experiment until all, who wished to be, were satiated.

Next was an experiment in weights and measures. Being inquisitive, I noticed the sets of gram weights in the classroom had little knobs on top of each weight. It was possible to unscrew the knobs. This was great because inside each weight were beebee sized shot. I collected a few shot each day from the particular set of weights my partner, Jim Cottle, and I were using. This apparently did not help Mr. Reppert in his demonstrations requiring gram weights. It did, however, seem to make him move fast. I am not positive, but that may have occurred because once or twice a week I would unloose a beebee missile against the blackboard. He would whip around to face the class, his face bearing a most angry scowl. He never shouted or acknowledged that something had happened to cause the pirouette, but his eyes always seemed to alight on me. I always returned his gaze with an angelic smile.

I would like to believe that my innovative participation in the class led to Larry Thomas, another scholar, developing the "fireball." I know Larry excelled in chemistry because years later at a class reunion he revealed he worked for the chemical company giant, Union Carbide, at the company's headquarters in Connecticut. I was never able to perform the "fireball."

This was due to the abject fear of catching myself on fire.

Larry would lean over the gas jet used to fuel the Bunsen Burners. He would place his mouth over the jet, turn the valve, and fill his mouth with gas. He then would strike a match, hold the lighted match at arm's length, and blow out the gas. WHOOSH! He did this several times during the last nine weeks of that school year until he didn't blow out the gas high enough and singed most of the hair of his right arm.

My *coup de grace* of classroom participation came with my purchase of one of the newly developed small transistor radios with

Southern Smiles and Tears

earplugs. Didn't the earplug and cord for this type radio have the same appearance as my hearing aid cord and earplug? I believe they did. I placed a radio in the halter, which held my hearing aid microphone, and placed in the earplug. At the appropriate moment in a lecture or experiment by my esteemed chemistry teacher, I would pull the cord from the radio. A burst of Bill Haley's Rock Around the Clock or Elvis Presley's *Jailhouse Rock* would pierce the room. Quickly reinserting the cord and installing a shocked look, I would peruse the room searching for the culprit along with the harried Mr. Reppert. Would anyone with a hearing problem use the disability to create havoc? Of course he would!

Physics class in my senior year was my next encounter with Mr. Reppert. The two of us entered into a tenuous truce for almost the entire first semester. He had given me the grade I earned at the nine-weeks, and I had not engaged in harassment. This truce ended in of all places my English class. Mrs. Ellen Potter, my English teacher, asked me to wait after first period class. I had no idea what was coming. She had shocked me once by telling all the girls in the class to look at me and be jealous because, "David has the most beautiful brown eyes on earth."

Mrs. Potter closed the door as the last student exited, leaving the two of us behind.

"David, I am going to tell you something that you must keep secret but I believe you should know. Every teacher, with the exception of one, on the Honor Society committee voted for you to become a member. You need to know this before the assembly tomorrow, because I and the other teachers believe you not being selected is unfair."

She proceeded to tell me of the dark secret of the committee. If any one of the five teachers objected to a nominee, that person was eliminated.

"I cannot reveal the teacher's name but please accept my apology for this. The two of you must have some type of friction, which offended him."

Him? Reppert. It had to be.

No more than circumstantial evidence was there, but that was enough for me. I vaguely knew the Bible admonished that revenge belonged to the God, but this was personal. Reppert would get his comeuppance.

One week later my opportunity came during a lecture about buoyancy.

Mr. Reppert was detailing how weight versus displacement caused things to float on water. He explained that this allowed heavy ships to stay above water. If the object did not displace the water, it would sink to the bottom.

Innocently, I asked a question.

"You mean any object that sinks beneath the surface of water will descend to the bottom?"

"Yes."

"A water soaked log won't sink to a point where the pressure is equal, keeping it floating beneath the surface?" I asked.

Exasperated, Mr. Reppert replied, "Once an object sinks beneath the surface, it can no longer float. It will go to the bottom."

"Well, I think we better call the Navy because thousands of submariners are in trouble."

There was a pregnant pause. Then my fellow classmates broke into guffaws.

The next day at the beginning of physics class, I was sent to the counselor's office.

"David, Mr. Reppert does not want you in his class any longer. I am rescheduling you into mechanical drawing."

Everyone in my new class had a one-half year jump on my knowledge when I was enrolled halfway through the course, but I enjoyed the new class. It was the most interesting class, other than Spanish, I had during my final year of high school.

Besides that, not one sailor drowned!

Chapter 27
Do You Want a Root Beer Mug?

Our minds are wonderful and mysterious things.

For several years, I have driven by and sometimes eaten at Sonic Drive-Ins with hardly giving it a second thought. Then I began working on a book in Bay County, Florida, the home of the famous Panama City Beach. As I turned left off U.S. Route 231 on Harrison Avenue toward the Bay County Library in Panama City, there on my right was the Tally Ho Drive-In Restaurant.

Carhops were walking out of the building to parked vehicles with trays of food to be hung on lowered windows. *Déjà vu.* My mind flashed back to the 1950's and Smiley's Drive-In. That teenager's hangout was located beside U.S. Route 60 near the underpass in St. Albans.

Rumors abounded among teenagers about John Smiley, the owner of the aforesaid establishment. According to gossip, he was a notorious gambler, feared by local politicians, and carried a pis-

Southern Smiles and Tears

tol in his belt. Those things were enough to make it worthwhile for teenagers to eat at his drive-in. The only verifiable things I knew about John Smiley was that he owned places. Besides, the drive-in restaurant with curb service, I know that he had a golf driving range and a motel. Rumors, though, were much more exciting than facts.

The drive-in was his best establishment. At least to teenagers. It wasn't only a place to eat and hangout — it was a place to test your mettle.

Smiley's used frosted, glass mugs to serve root beer. Root beer in a mug was the Mountain Dew of the 1950's. You could drink every last drop and let out a belch that would turn girls' heads. Now in my golden years, I realize their heads probably turned in disgust and not admiration. But in 1956, it seemed like admiration.

It was necessary, in a manly way, to play a game with the carhops. These older women, probably all at least 21 years of age did not particularly like the game but played anyway. The rules were simple. See how may root beer mugs you could steal and not be caught by the carhop.

The game necessitated that there be at least four males in the vehicle, and that everyone ordered a root beer with their hot dog or hamburger. The trick was to order one extra root beer and empty it for the mandatory first belch. Then the drinker would slip the empty mug to the floorboard of the car. Everyone would then eat, drink, and be merry while showing off to any girls unlucky enough to have picked a contiguous parking space.

At time to leave with the purloined mug well hidden, the driver of the car would honk and wave for the carhop to come pick up the trash enshrouded tray. The four mugs had to be placed prominently on the outside of the tray. That way the carhop would know how honest the young men were in not trying to hide anything. Hope upon hope was that the carhop would not remember how many mugs she had brought to that particular car.

Here I must make fun of those people who have spent years studying the relative intelligence of males and females. What a waste of time and money.

Females are more intelligent. Hands down!

I simply do not recall one incident where the combined intelligence of four or more, teenage boys was higher than that of one female carhop. Those girls remembered everything and got downright nasty in retrieving the lost mugs. They also were somewhat smart alecky. They not only remembered cars of potential thieves, but facial features also. A group, with a different car, could go in to

Southern Smiles and Tears

eat and drink three weeks after losing the game and be met with, "You boys here to try to steal another mug?" That went beyond smart alecky — it was impertinent and an insult to our manhood!

Whenever I return to St. Albans, a wave of nostalgia passes over me like a warm shower as I pass the corner where Smiley's used to be. Horrors of horrors, a fast food restaurant of the national chain genre sits there. It is blight on the past.

The next time I am in Panama City, I think it will be necessary for me to go to the Tally Ho.

I wonder if they have any root beer mugs?

Chapter 28
Sharecropping

When slavery ended in the South after the Civil War a new insidious economic system replaced it. This system was called "sharecropping." It was predicated on the fact that whites had land and needed it farmed, while blacks and poor whites could farm but owned little land. What appeared to be a good idea for everyone was really a way of economically enslaving those at the bottom of the social structure.

Poor farmers were allowed to live in shacks on white-owned farms. Seed and mules, later tractors, were supplied to the farmers in exchange for labor and a share of the eventual crop. The problem arose when there were poor crops and a debt was incurred. The debt could be worked off, but more often than not, increased over the years. The debt tied the sharecropper to the land with little hope of escaping to a better life.

My sister, Doris, married into a sharecropping family from

Southern Smiles and Tears

Mississippi. J.W. Richardson, tall and lanky, epitomized a part of the South many have tried to hide. A proud, handsome man, J.W. was a victim of a society that did not see people such as him as any more than a mule. He was labor.

One summer before I entered the ninth grade Doris and J.W., along with their two small girls, came to visit the family in West Virginia. Doris had convinced him that job opportunities abounded at the many chemical companies dotting the Kanawha Valley. I was to be an important part of J.W.'s job search. My role was to go with him as a kind of guide. He had never been outside Mississippi and would need help.

The two of us left the house early one morning and caught the bus to Charleston. Doris had asked me to take J.W. to various places and help him apply for jobs. She gave him some money for the buses and food. What I thought was to be my role was not to be.

The first few places we went were not hiring. So I told J.W. we needed to head for South Charleston, the location of several chemical plants. My sister Caroline's husband, Carlos, worked at one of these plants. His background was somewhat parallel to that of J.W. He had been born and raised in the rural hills of Appalachia to a farming family. Carlos had fought in World War II and returned to West Virginia. He got a job at Carbide and later retired from there.

J.W. and I entered the personnel office, approached the glass behind which sat a woman receptionist, and J.W. asked, "Ya'll hirin'?"

A look of misunderstanding crossed the lady's face. Apparently, the heavy accent of J.W. did not immediately translate in her brain.

"Sir?"

"Ya'll hirin'?"

This time she deciphered the code.

"Oh! You wish to apply for a job."

"Yes ma'am."

She handed J.W. a sheet of paper and a ball point pen while telling him to "...fill this out completely and return it to me." He took the form, and we went over to the school desk like chairs. Sitting there, J.W. stared at the paper. After a few moments J.W. turned his head toward me.

"Davy, would you help me fill this out? I forgot my glasses and can't see what it says."

I was a little slow on the uptake. Halfway through writing J.W.'s

Southern Smiles and Tears

answers on the paper it struck me. He didn't wear glasses. J.W. could neither read nor write. That was why Doris wanted me to go on this quest. I was to complete any applications required. Here was a man in his late 20's reduced to having a smart-aleck 14-year old help him obtain a job. A result of a culture that devalued education and valued farm labor, J.W. sat there embarrassed. I suspect he knew that I knew. I completed the form, and we left. Three more times we stopped and applied for work. Each of the women took the forms and told us they would contact us. They never did.

Outside the last office, J.W. suggested we walk home instead of taking the bus. I told him it was seven miles, but he was insistent. I now realize he thought paying a quarter apiece for a bus ride was a waste of money when it was "...only a short walk."

J.W. and Doris soon returned to Yazoo City, Mississippi. I suspect, deep down, he was happy to get out of the foreign industrial society and return to the familiarity of the farm.

It was almost two years later before I encountered the Richardson family again. Mom had taken part of the insurance payment she received from Eddie's death and bought a car. Not any car. It was a red and black, St. Alban's High School colors, Pontiac. This purchase allowed mom to reply in the affirmative to an emergency telephone plea for help from Doris.

Doris had decided to leave J.W. and wanted mom to send her money for bus fare to West Virginia. Mom decided it would be more economical for me to drive her to Mississippi. Then we could bring back Doris along with her two daughters, Valinda and Racine. That sounded good to me. I would get to use my newly acquired driver's license and get to miss a week of school as a bonus.

Here I must confess that I was not quite 16, the age to legally obtain a license to drive in West Virginia. I had taken my brother's Billy's birth certificate as identification to the State Police headquarters to take the written test for a learner's permit. Once having passed the test and receiving the precious document to freedom, I had a problem. Now, two William Gustav Bices existed. This problem needed solving.

Two steps were needed to correct this duplication of persons. Meticulously, I erased "William Gustav" from the permit. Step two required a little more chicanery than step one. Boys in that era did not take typing, an 11th grade class designed for females. If boys had been in typing, I could have asked one of my older male friends to help me. Alas, that was not possible. Then an idea entered my devious mind.

I approached one of the girls, who had been "...in love with..."

Southern Smiles and Tears

Billy when he was still in high school. She was more than happy to help out "Bill's little brother." She carefully placed the altered document in her typewriter and carefully began striking the keys. **David Allan** miraculously appeared before the **Bice**. I now had a legal document to present to the state trooper riding with me when I went to take my actual driving test. People talk about having butterflies in their stomachs when nervously facing some unknown. When I was behind the wheel with the state trooper sitting beside me with a clipboard in his hand, I believe B-29s inhabited my digestive system. Somehow I passed the driving test with only one minor infraction.

Not quite sixteen, I placed the key in the ignition, turned over the engine, and took off for Mississippi with my mom. What power! Fifteen years old and steering a 3,000 pound car South. If I had only known of two future events, which were to punctuate our trip, my ecstatic mood would have been quite lessened.

The first incident to give me pause was in Mississippi, north of the state capital of Jackson. A Mississippi State Trooper, with his decaled patrol car parked side ways across the highway, was waving us to a stop. My first thought was that the West Virginia State Police had latched on to my chicanery and told their brothers in Mississippi to apprehend the lawbreaking, lying scoundrel. Whew! It was only a tornado. The officer informed my mom and me that there had been tornadoes spotted in the area and until the lightning storms passed, traffic was being stopped in the area. I once again breathed. That was until a funnel appeared in the distance zigzagging and dancing across a farm. Then when it should have zigged, it zagged right into a barn. The barn exploded as if Uncle Grave's dynamite had been inside. Then to the horror of the three of us, it zigged toward the highway, the patrol car, and my mom's brand new Pontiac.

The officer yelled, "Let's git outta here!" He jumped in his car, waved for us to follow, and tore off northward. I turned around and followed. Several miles up the rode he pulled into a gas station with me close behind. He got out of his car, looked at us and said, "Goldang!" My sentiments exactly.

My mom and I waited a while until the skies cleared and proceeded south toward our destination — Yazoo City, Mississippi. Another surprise awaited us. Not really a surprise — more like shock. We stopped in town and asked directions to the address given to us by my sister. Our requests were met with blank stares until one person asked us, "Who'ya lookin' for?"

"J.W. Richardson."

Southern Smiles and Tears

"J.W."

"Yes sir."

"He and his family live that way 'bout a mile. Y'all turn left and cross that there wooden bridge over the crik."

We followed the directions and received our shock. Doris, J.W., their children, and assorted relatives lived in a cave. A nice cave, but a cave nonetheless. To be fair, it was more a huge area dug out of the side of a hill with a wooden front built across the front with a door in the middle. We entered the cave. I was surprised at how cool it was inside. Doris was seated on a couch with my two nieces. Semblances of introductions were made in the tension filled earthen house.

My mom asked Doris if she were ready to go.

J.W.'s mom asked Doris if she really wanted to leave.

J.W. said nothing. He simply leaned against the side of the cave looking as if his world was coming apart, and he had no glue.

Doris gathered her brood and followed mom and me to the car. Everyone and everything loaded; I turned the car around.

Uh oh!

About a football field length ahead of us, right in the middle of the bridge, stood a group of bib overall covered men. The overalls didn't bother me, but the rifles and shotguns held in the crooks of their arms did.

To this day, I am not sure why I did what I did. Probably because teenagers have the idea they are invincible. Heck! I had a brand new Pontiac and had already been drag racing in Highlawn.

I floored the gas pedal, the car fishtailed in dirt, Doris screamed, and I headed for the crowd at the bridge. One of the men raised his weapon, I am not positive if it were a rifle or a shotgun, and pointed it toward us. Then in a scene to be reenacted years later on television in a program named *The Dukes of Hazard*, he tossed the weapon down and jumped sideways. His action had a domino effect as all his friends decided it was also time to take a swim. The car skidded as I turned to head toward town. I blew through town at 70 miles per hour, running two stoplights in the process. I didn't slow down until we had crossed the county line. We went about 200 miles before stopping to eat and rent a motel room.

Then love triumphed.

I now suspect that Doris and her fiery red hair had fought with J.W. In her pique, she had called mom and then reconsidered. Not one to admit she was wrong, Doris played out the second act with mom and me as supporting players. The third act is more definite. Doris decided it would be a good idea to take the two girls across

Southern Smiles and Tears

the street from the motel to get ice cream cones. When we volunteered to go with them, Doris told us that we could rest. She would bring us back two cones. She did get the ice cream, with mom's money, but she also went to a telephone booth and made a call. I know that to be true because I saw her when I looked out the window of our room.

The next morning it became evident to whom the call was made. J.W. was out front of the motel, leaning against a pickup truck. The driver of the truck was one of his friends whom I had encouraged to take a bath the previous day. Doris, acting as if it made perfect sense for J.W. to be there, simply told mom, "I've changed my mind and am going home with J.W.," and she did.

Mom was, to put it mildly, angry. She fumed all the way back to West Virginia, vowing to cut Doris out of her non-existent will. I believe Doris was disowned at least 100 times.

As for J.W. and Doris, I did not see much of them, except at our parents' funerals. Over 20-years later, my wife Alice told me that I needed to try to find Doris. We made a side trip from a business trip to New Orleans to go to Yazoo City. We went to the voter's registration office to try to locate where J.W. Richardson lived. The clerk told us that Doris had voted five years before and gave us the address. We went to the address only to find a vacant lot. The house had been torn down. It would be five years later that Alice, my sister Martha, her husband Jim, and I located J.W. and Doris in Vicksburg. We all went there and visited the two of them along with a multitude of nephews and nieces. J.W. spoke to me with fondness of our job-searching trip from years before.

Doris and J.W. had had 13 children. They are not all still living. Those who are would make any parent proud. Some are schoolteachers, some have their own businesses, and others have achieved success. I am glad Doris made that telephone call. Almost 50 years later, the two can look back on their lives and be content.

What I am not happy about is how many a follower of President Clinton classified them as "trailer trash." Yes, they live in a manufactured house, but I believe them to be far from trash. I doubt if that politician has ever met someone with the character of J.W. He raised a family despite lacking an education. He provided a home and encouraged his children to achieve more in life than he was able to do.

He also wanted a job so badly that he allowed a young kid to know he could neither read nor write. He ultimately put aside his pride to go and get his wife and children when he had been told he was no longer wanted.

That's a real man.

Chapter 29
West Virginia Department of Rehabilitation

Who is this woman? This thought kept running through my mind as she blathered on about my having to learn a skill.

I had been pulled out of my 12th grade Spanish II class and told to meet Mrs. So and So in the Counselor's Conference Room. She introduced herself. A name forever purged from my memory. She was from the Board of Education. Speaking as if the Board of Education were the anteroom to St. Peter's abode, the lady explained the purpose of our meeting.

"We have followed your needs since you enrolled in Kanawha County Schools. Even though you have done well for a handicapped boy, we believe you need to go to a special school after you graduate."

Southern Smiles and Tears

I started to tell her the proper use should be "are graduated" but held my tongue waiting to learn more about this "special school." Another thing I did not say to her was that I planned to go to college, teach school, and write books. Perhaps, that was the special school to which she was referring.

It wasn't!

"Three years ago I recommended that you be sent to the deaf school in Romney to continue your education."

Another remark crossed my mind about a school, which was deaf, certainly was special, but I held my tongue as she continued.

"The teachers at Romney could have taught you how to fit into society better, but your mother refused."

I knew I had untold reasons for loving my mom.

"But since you didn't go to Romney, I am recommending that you go across the river to the West Virginia Department of Rehabilitation in Institute." She spoke in a slow, over exaggerated manner that implied I was not only hard of hearing but also stupid. Years later when I was the liaison to the major textbook corporations for the American Printing House for the Blind in Louisville, Kentucky and later Chief Operating Officer for a California supplier of assistive computer technology for the blind, I noticed the same phenomenon. People would speak loudly and slowly to blind people as if the lack of sight affected brain capacity.

"Rehabilitation has classes that will teach you skills, which will allow you to get a job and support yourself. You will learn how to do something with your hands because your lack of hearing will prevent you from working at a normal job."

There it was. No matter how well I had done in school, the educational system believed I was incapable of surviving in the real world.

"I want to take you over there next week for some evaluation tests. Then we will know which classes to enroll you in this summer to begin your vocational training."

"I'm going to college."

A look of incredulity spread across her face.

"You can't seriously believe you can be successful in college? What do you plan to major in?"

"I am going to take history and Spanish and be a teacher."

The look this time was one of pity.

"It is always nice to have high goals, but you have to face reality. You have a handicap that prevents you from doing certain things. Believe me, you will be better off at Institute with other handicapped people than trying to fit into regular society. They even have a program where the school hires people to make things."

This woman, whom I had never met before, was planning my life. "Ma'am, I am not going to that school! I know what I want to be and do. I will go to college. I will teach, and then I am going to be an author."

Exasperation flooding the small room, she decided to call in the cavalry. "You wait here! I need to talk to the your counselor and principal."

A few minutes later, bespectacled and gray-headed Basil Liggett, St. Albans High School's venerable principal, entered the room with the board's representative. Mr. Liggett and I were not on the best of terms. A few weeks earlier he had caught me imitating him in the school hallways and had explained to me in no uncertain terms the impropriety of my actions. He had added what would happen if he caught me again.

"Mr. Bice, what is the problem here?" *Why does a principal always think there is a problem when asked to talk with someone?*

Miss Board of Education answered before I could open my mouth. "I'll tell you what the problem is. This young man does not understand that he is different and needs to learn a skill to live. He is incapable of being a success in college, and especially being a teacher. I am sure his teachers here have made allowances for him in school, but college is different. Please explain that to him."

As often occurs in situations such as these, there was a pregnant pause.

I looked at Mr. Liggett. He looked at me. He shook his head. I did not.

"I have been in education for a long time and principal for many, many years. Over these years many of David's," he actually knew my name, "brothers and sisters have been through St. Albans High School. Most have done well. One thing I can tell you is that they all have been stubborn. His sister Caroline quit school at 16 to get married. Now she is an elementary school teacher. Bill struggled, but stayed in school an extra half year to get his diploma as the first graduate of the new high school. Eddie quit school as a senior after telling me there was nothing else to learn. He may have been right. We all know that David wears a hearing aid and may have missed some of what he should have learned." I don't remember if the pause here was pregnant or poignant, but it was a long one. "But, young lady, no teacher in this school made allowances for him in his class work. It is my considered opinion that if this young man believes he can go to college than he should do so. I have not ever stood in the way of desire and will not do it now."

Southern Smiles and Tears

I had six more months of high school left after that particular meeting and I can tell you one thing — I never made fun of Mr. Liggett again.

Southern Smiles and Tears

Chapter 30
A Fake High School Diploma

Kanawha County Schools and St. Albans High School, in particular, owe James an apology.

These educational entities lied to him. They said he should be graduated with a High School Diploma. There was only one thing wrong. They failed to teach him how to read. James had attended the colored schools of Kanawha County until 1955 when all county schools integrated. Then in 1958 when our integrated class was to be graduated, James still could not read.

No one, as far as I knew, took time in James' three years of high school to fix the problem. In some type of unspoken agreement, James was simply given "D's" for his efforts and passed on to the next level.

James was not a problem in any of the classes we shared. These included homeroom, gym, study hall, biology, and one-half year of mechanical drawing. He actually helped me catch up in the latter.

Southern Smiles and Tears

In study hall, he showed me how to draw reverse images, which had been particularly difficult for me.

James could always make me smile, even in the saddest of times. When I returned to school after my brother was killed, James caused me to laugh once more. He approached me in study hall and said he was sorry to hear about my brother dying. He then related an incident in phys ed that happened while I was gone.

"You gonna love this, Bice. Coach Nida was so mad he made us run laps outside the rest of gym."

"What happened?"

"Well you know how the automatic divider separates the girls class from ours?"

"Yeh."

"Somehow, somebody got hold of his key and made a second one to operate the divider. We all agreed while dressing for gym to pass the key around. When coach wasn't looking, whoever had the key was to run over and start the curtain goin' back in so we could see the girls in shorts. The first time coach thought he must've not done the key right. He kinda laughed when we all hollered and whistled as the curtain opened. The second time it happened he looked at the curtain kinda funny. The third time the curtain started back in, and we began whistling, Coach Nida shouted for us all to line up against the wall. He went over and used his key to close the curtain. He was real quiet for a minute. Then he told us that if that curtain opened one more time we'd be sorry."

"That's all?" I asked. "That's not funny."

"No." James said cutting me off.

"We all started playin' basketball again. All of a sudden the passed around key fell on the court. Bice, everything got real quiet. Coach Nida looked at the key and then at us. He asked whose key that was. Somebody shouted, 'It must be yours.' He pulled out his key and said, 'This is mine. Whose is that.'"

"What happened then?"

"Somebody else, I think it was Booty Ball, shouted. 'Maybe, it's one of the girls. They been wantin' to see us in our shorts.' That was it. Coach told us to get outside, and it was rainin' hard. He told us to run laps around the softball field until we heard the bell. Someone else said, 'But coach that will make us late to our next class. We'll get in trouble.'"

"What did you all do?"

"We all went outside and ran in the mud and rain. When the bell rang we came back in and started to get dressed as fast as possible. Coach came in the locker room and told us we had to take our showers. We argued telling him that would make us later. He told us that if we could figure out how to make a key and open the curtain that we could think of an excuse for being late to our next classes and walked out."

"Was that it."

"No. We all tried to go to class but were all sent to Mr. Smith's office. There were over 50 of us lined up asking him for a tardy slip. He looked at us shakin' his head. He told us, 'Boys, I'm not going to excuse you, but there is something you can do to make Mr. Nida happy. Tomorrow during gym class the janitor will supply you with wax and cloths, and you will wax and buff the gymnasium.'"

"Bice we thought he meant the boys' side. But he didn't. The next day when we got to the gym the curtain was opened and the girls were sittin' in the bleachers. Coach Nida told us to get dressed in our shorts without shirts. When we came out the girls started shoutin' and whistlin' at us. He handed half of us cans of wax. The rest got rags to buff with. We started waxin' and buffin'. That wasn't the worst part. The girls started doin' cheers."

They named each of us as they cheered."

"James, James, he's our man. If he can't wax, nobody can."

I began laughing at the picture in my mind of all of them waxing and buffing in front of jeering girls. For a few moments I forgot about my brother.

A few days before graduation, right after our caps and gowns were distributed during homeroom, Miss Lynch was telling us how important our being graduated was. She told us how great it was that we were about to receive our diplomas. She continued telling us that a diploma was evidence we were educated.

Sometimes, you should just keep your mouth shut and let some things go unchallenged.

I didn't.

"Miss Lynch, that is not true for everyone."

She had not expected any retort to her congratulatory speech. "What do you mean?" came her sharp reply.

"There's at least one person graduating with us who can't read."

"That is not true."

I know Miss Lynch truly believed this. She taught geometry and trigonometry and had few occasions to interact with non-college bound students. She had a master's degree in mathematics from Duke University and believed that diplomas equated knowledge.

It would have been prudent of me to have allowed the back and forth to die at that point.

I didn't.

Southern Smiles and Tears

"It is. James can't read and he knows it. We have talked about it. He told me that as long as he is quiet and tries he gets 'D's' and passes. He will get a diploma that means he was stubborn enough to endure 12 years. Wouldn't it have been better to teach him to read?"

I couldn't believe what happened next. Miss Lynch began to cry. The problem was the tears represented anger at me, not sadness for James and humiliation for being part of the sham executed on James.

"You are a dishonor to this school!" she almost shouted. "There you are holding your cap and gown making fun of all those graduating with you. Get out of here!"

"Where do you want me to go?

"Go downstairs to Mr. Smith and tell him what you said." I did.

Mr. Smith looked at me as I entered his office and said, "David, what happened now?"

So I told him.

"David, David, David. You are going to have to begin choosing which cross you want hung on."

"Huh?" Maybe I would have understood his point better if I had continued religious activities after leaving Alabama.

"David, you are intelligent. More so than most people think. But you continually challenge authority. You are right about James, and several others, not getting a good education. You picked an argument with Miss Lynch, which will not change anything. She simply does not believe what you told her. All the argument did was get you sent down here.

"I am not going to punish you but for this last three days of school just sit in my waiting room and stay out of trouble. Think about this. It does no good to simply argue against injustice, you must be willing to do something about it. That is what I meant about the cross. Choose carefully those battles you wish to fight. Once you decide, fight hard."

I haven't seen James since we received our diplomas. Our paths were not tangential.

I do believe he probably has been successful in life, despite the bad hand dealt him. He was too stubborn to allow the system to defeat him.

Go, James.

Chapter 31
Drive-In Movies

A major loss for today's teenagers is the absence of drive-in movie theaters. These type of theaters became popular with the confluence of two things. Veteran's returning from World War II had been used to the military showing them films on outdoor screens. Second, automobiles became a necessity for most families in the late 1940's giving teenagers access to "wheels." These theaters usually showed two films an evening, a "double feature."

A few of these wonderful places still are in business, but most have been converted to other uses or torn down. St. Albans' drive-in theater was The Valley and is now a flea market. The one that was in Clanton, Alabama is the site of a manufactured housing dealership with kudzu growing up the side of the old screen. You can now shop at Walmart where the East Drive-In used to stand outside Huntington, West Virginia. The Moonlight near Bristol, Virginia still operates and shows first run films.

Southern Smiles and Tears

The Valley, located at the juncture of U. S. Routes 60 and 35, was surrounded by an eight-foot high fence and faced away from the highways. Each parking space for viewing was set on a slight incline with a speaker box located on the driver's side. The speaker boxes sat on top of poles that had long cords so the box could be brought inside the car and hung on the window. During the winter small electric heaters plugged into the base of the poles to help keep the movie aficionados warm.

Right in the center of the parking area was the projection booth, restrooms, and snack bar. Picnic tables were up front at the base of the screen in a grassy area, which also had swings and a slicky slide. Food items were limited to hot dogs, hamburgers, popcorn, candy bars, and soft drinks. Many people brought their own food to eat, but it was always a treat to be able to go to the snack bar. It was not a treat to have to go to the bathroom!

The price of admission was great for families and money deprived teenage boys trying to impress girls. The charge was 25 cents per person in a car. Once in a while there was a special of $1.00 per carload, which saved 25 cents with five people.

Therein was the challenge.

Why would a group of five male teenagers pay $1.25 to see a movie? It made much more sense to put two people in the car and three in the trunk and use the extra money for refreshments. That's right, in the trunk. It took particular skill and cooperation to fit three people inside the trunk. Always the smallest three of the group served as luggage. That meant I was destined to ride in the rear of the vehicle. I now realize the folly of these adventures. The drive-in was five miles from Highlawn. I cringe at the thought of what would have happened if another car had rear-ended us.

Nonetheless, we pursued the two in the front and three in the back tactic. Three things had to fall into place for the venture to be successful. First, the two in the front had to appear innocent when paying the entrance fee. That may have seemed simple, but the ticket sellers were more adept than Israeli airport security people in profiling security breaches. Much of the profiling was simple. It was not often that two teenage boys went to a drive-in movie together. Normal vehicles carried a couple with children, or a couple in heat. Everyone knew the best place "to make out" was at a drive-in.

The second part of the operation was even more critical. It was the point of release from the trunk. Owners of the drive-in looked down upon the two-three in a car tactic. They even went as far as to hire men to walk about the theater grounds watching for trunk openings. Sometimes the three in the back would miss half of the first movie. The trick for releasing those in the back was to observe the timing of the security people. Then it was essential that the person opening the trunk only allowed it to open about 10 inches and not allow the lid to pop up, thereby turning on the trunk light. A popped lid was a sure way to find the whole group outside the drive-in.

Once out of the back the three freeloaders did not go immediately to the back seat of the car. It was essential to head for the refreshment stand and restroom. Then one at a time the three would wander back to the vehicle.

We were successful more times than not, but I am not sure it was worth it. Five-mile trips in the trunk of a car with three teenagers, and one of them sure to have flatulence at least once per mile could not have been worth a quarter.

Chapter 32
"Ignorance Is a Terrible Thing"

"My name is Doctor Herman G. Canady."
He quickly followed with, "I am not your friend. I am not Herman. I am not Canady. I am Doctor Canady, and that is how you will address me. You are Mr. and Miss, and that is how I will address you. I am a full professor, and you will respect that. I do not care if you like me but respect is not negotiable. For those of you who may be curious, the 'G' stands for 'god' in this classroom. I know more than you do. I am smarter than most of you. I am more experienced than you. I have suffered more than you. I have achieved more than most of you will achieve. I am a Negro. Most of you are also. A few of you are Caucasians. I do not care what you are. I do not care about the terrible things that you may have suffered. I care that you learn. Knowledge will propel you to heights unknown. Football will not do that. Sex will not do that. Cheating and taking the easy way out will not do that."

Southern Smiles and Tears

All that was said without a tinge of ego. Dr. Canady was stating facts. If anything, there was a hint of sadness in his tone. He knew many of us in that "Introduction to College 100" course were destined to fail to meet the standards of what he considered to be a success in life and society.

He paused, breathed with a sigh, and continued his monologue.

"Look at the person to your left. Look to your right. Counting yourself that makes three people. One of you will not be here next year. Mostly because you will not take advantage of what you are being offered at this institution of higher learning. One other of the three will never be graduated from college. Mostly because it will not be easy, and your 'momma' isn't here to take care of you. The one of the three of you who survives will have achieved and will be successful in your endeavors."

What an introduction to college! I had made a decision to go to West Virginia State College instead of Marshall University. WVSC until 1954 had been a "Negro College" but with integration was now open to all. My decision to attend there was based on several factors. One it was economical. A semester, plus the cost of books was only $125.00. Second, it was close to where I lived, and I would not have to pay to stay in a dormitory. Third, one of my high school teachers wanted me to follow him to Marshall College and become a member of Tau Kappa Epsilon. He had even introduced me to the fraternity during the spring college recruitment. That introduction was a revelation. The group had a house with a fully stocked bar. One of the members, with a wink, said, "You all are 21 aren't you?" and poured drinks for everyone. Here I was fleeing a family of alcoholics only to be a prospective member of a fraternity full of them. Later I would go to graduate school there when Marshall became a university. That was to be after Marshall had been "restructured" somewhat by the Civil Rights movement.

Dr. Canady, rotund and ebony, was my introduction into the Negro *intelligencia*. Behind him on the chalkboard he had written in all capital letters a phrase that has guided me, and I hope my children, since I first saw it. After his opening volley, which had left many of us stunned, he turned to the chalkboard and shouted the words. "IGNORANCE IS A TERRIBLE THING!!!!"

"Some people are stupid. They cannot help that. Most of you are ignorant. That is fixable but only if you allow it to be fixed. Some of you came out of high school with high grades. Some with average grades. Some of you even had low grades, but this college wanted you because you could smell a football and knock down the person carrying it, or shoot a basketball well. I do not care which cat-

Southern Smiles and Tears

egory fits you. Should this institution in four years bestow upon you a degree, and you are still ignorant, it will be your fault. You can spend four years here and leave with knowledge, or you can spend four years here and leave ignorant. The choice is yours to make. Choose wisely."

He turned, walked to the door, and spun around.

"Class dismissed. Come back Thursday prepared to learn."

My first college class had lasted fewer than fifteen minutes. Slowly, my classmates and I arose and left the lecture room. Outside, I found myself beside Everette Knapper. Everette and I had attended St. Albans High School and were part of the 13 St. Albans students who had chosen WVSC for college.

I asked Everette if he had ever heard anyone talk like that. Everette, low spoken and pensive, thought for a few moments. "Never. I wonder if every professor here is like that?"

I was to find out that no one was like Dr. Canady. He was a singular scholar. I only had one other course from him because my bent toward history and Spanish led me away from his courses in psychology. Other professors were good. A few excellent. A smattering were poor. None though had the character of Dr. Canady. I would see him in the student lounge with a group of followers drawn by his aura. His booming voice extolling all never to accept mediocrity.

Years later on a fine Sunday in May hundreds of students were being herded into two lines. We were being readied to walk across the campus mall to sit in front of the library where Leon Sullivan, the first black to be a board of director of General Motors would deliver the commencement address. I read the names of graduates listed in the commencement program. Unbelievable! Of the 13 St. Albans students who had entered West Virginia State College that fall of 1958, only three were present to walk across the stage and shake hands with Dr. Wallace the president of the college. Dr. Canady had been correct.

Dr. Canady did not know me, remember me, or ever recognize me. I was simply one of thousands of freshmen who passed through his life. He did, however, affect me. Several years later, in the corner of one of the Charleston newspapers, I saw an article that shocked me. Dr. Herman G. Canady had been found on a railroad track dead. Apparently, it had not been an accident but a suicide. I will never comprehend or try to understand why such a brilliant man would take such an action.

I do know that his light lives on in many of us. We may have been formerly ignorant but have striven for years to fix that miserable

Southern Smiles and Tears

condition from which he pointed us away.

Chapter 33
What Was That?

Deafness is an invisible disability, unless the deaf person wears a hearing aid. There are also degrees of deafness. When I had my first hearing test in the first grade, the audiologist reported my hearing as 15 percent in one ear and 30 in the other. My hearing was depressed for the first 20 years of my life because I was born without eardrums. My mother being in her mid-forties when I was conceived may have contributed to that.

I have never considered my impaired hearing as a detriment. It was the way I was. How would I know I was different?

Well! That was not exactly the truth. When company came to the house I was shunted off to the bedroom. I later learned that some in the family considered me an embarrassment due to my speech, which reflected how I heard. Apparently, I spoke in a monotone, totally devoid of inflection. The bedroom became my sanctuary and classroom.

Southern Smiles and Tears

My mother, having been a teacher, believed in learning. She made sure dictionaries, newspapers, magazines, and an old set of encyclopedias were in the house. Fortunately, for me, the encyclopedias and dictionaries reposed in the bedroom with me. I spent hours alone looking at the written word and pictures in all of the above. I am not sure when I began to read the written word and other people's lips, except that both were before I was five years old. The mixture of what little I could hear and how people spoke words allowed me to begin understanding more than I heard. Another intrinsic fact in reading lips had nothing to do with their speaking. This now has been identified as body language. A multitude of emotions and words are relayed by the body actions and facial expressions of a speaker.

I know that one day right after the end of World War II; I was able to comprehend an insult to my intelligence. My brother Billy and I were playing croquet in our front yard. The Henley boys, from down the road, were playing with us. I was telling Billy about what had happened in the comic strip, *The Phantom*, in *The Daily Mail* newspaper the evening before. Older than I, Billy had difficulty reading, so I had begun telling him what the little balloons in the funny paper said.

"You can't read dummy! You ain't even in school." Charles Henley, about 10 years of age, shouted at me.

"Can too!" I monotoned back.

"Can not!"

"Can too!"

He should have let it go at that point but let loose with, "You're lying, because we all know you're stupid!"

Never insult a five-year old holding a blue-striped croquet mallet.

I whapped him in the head!

There was probably not much velocity in the swing of a five-year-old, but I did not need to interpret much body language to realize that Charles knew I was mad.

"Whatcha gone and done that for?" He shouted, as tears streamed down his face. "C'mon Timmy, we ain't goin' play with them no more."

They did play with us later but never croquet.

It was years after amplifying my lip reading skills and wearing a variety of hearing aids that the world of real hearing became a reality for me. I was in Dr. Harshbarger's second floor office in downtown St. Albans with one of my chronic ear infections. Peering through the cone shaped, lighted, ear inspector, Dr. Harshbarger

Southern Smiles and Tears

said to me, "David, there is new operation available in Charleston that may allow you to hear without a hearing aid. Dr. Reel at the Eye, Ear, and Nose Clinic may be able to help you. I'll make an appointment for you?

Twenty-years old, with a wife, one child, and two years of college behind me, my life was about to do a 180.

Dr. Reel said I was a perfect candidate for a tympanoplasty. He was going to give me an eardrum, specifically an eardrum in my right ear, the one through which I heard 30 percent. I entered the hospital the day in November when Richard Milhous Nixon and John Fitzgerald Kennedy were going to find out which one of them was to be the next President of the United States of America. Entering a pre-operation drugged world about 8:00 that evening, I would not know until three days later that Kennedy had won thanks to cemetery residents of Chicago.

The operation was a blast.

They did not put me totally to sleep, at first, but gave me enough drugs to take away all my cares. I was strapped down on my left side, a position I was to be kept in for three days, and my head draped with a white sheet. The plan was to cut a vein out of my left arm and graft it into my right ear. At some point during the operation, blood spurted onto the sheet just above my eyes. A nurse lifted the edge of the sheet and looked at me.

I giggled. She smiled. I lost consciousness. It was late Wednesday when I wakened, still strapped to a bed.

Dr. Reel wrote me a note telling me I was not to turn my head for the next couple of days. The graft had to grow together. On Friday, the doctor let me sit up as he removed the bandage from my right ear.

I couldn't hear in my right ear! The operation had failed.

"David, you will not be able to hear me very well. We packed your right ear to keep the graft in place. I am going to let you go home this weekend and come back Monday. I think we can remove the packing then. You will have to sleep on your side and not cough or blow your nose.

It was a long weekend.

Monday afternoon Dr. Reel began meticulously unpacking my ear. Then he shouted at me.

Not really.

He simply said, "How's that?" It was loud!

He grinned. I laughed.

That was nothing compared to my first night at home. I was as jumpy as the proverbial cat in a roomful of rocking chairs. Dr. Reel had given me an earplug for the ride home. He explained that a car horn could be frightening.

At first, I reveled in hearing Penny trying to talk. It was a blessed sound.

Years later, I could not understand the movement by deaf parents opposed to having their deaf children receive the cochlear implants. I did rejoice when Heather Whitehead, the former Miss America from Alabama, had an implant so she could hear her son.

That first evening with an eardrum was a series of revelations to me. A noise would be followed by a "What's that?" The refrigerator kicking on was a shock, but when the gas furnace ignited, it was frightening. I did not sleep at all that night. We lived beside a highway. Every time a car passed, my eyes flew open.

Surprisingly, within a few weeks hearing became natural. Twelve years later, I had another graft in my left ear. Slowly, I became aware that my ability to read lips slipped away. I learned to speak with inflection. That was a real surprise to my Spanish professors in college, who had become frustrated with a student unable to give proper accentuation its due.

It was not without a certain amount irony that it was in November 2000 that I became aware that once again I could not hear well. Over a period of almost 30 years there had been a substantial deterioration. That Thanksgiving four of our five children visited us in Alabama. Sometime during the visit, Danny took Alice aside.

"Alice, I don't think you realize it but you have begun almost shouting so dad can hear you. Also, every answer he gives you has 'Huh?' or 'What?' before it"

The two of them tried to convince me to go to a doctor. It's not that I was stubborn, but I refused. My fear was that my eardrums had failed. I did not want another operation.

Alice kept pressuring me, and Danny used quite a bit of sarcasm to push me to do what I knew I should do. It took a coincidence, you know one of the times when God wishes to remain anonymous, to place me in the office of Dr. Dabbs.

Jack Dabbs telephoned our office asking if we could do a reprint of a book written by his grandfather. He had seen one of our county books and wanted something similar. Alice and I have had a long time policy about helping people self-publish books. We always ask them, "If you publish this book and lose $5,000.00, will it substantially alter your financial situation?" If they answer "Yes" we tell them we cannot help them.

I asked that question of Dr. Dabbs.

Southern Smiles and Tears

"It won't hurt me. I'm an Eye, Ear, and Throat specialist and don't care if I lose the money or not. I want the book."

My response surprised Alice and myself. "You are just the person I need to talk with. I need an appointment about my hearing."

The upshot of all this was that he got his book, and I got two digital hearing aids. Danny was right. I could hardly hear. When the audiologist finished my test in Dr. Dabbs' office she told Alice, "I don't know how he can speak so clearly. Most people, with this severe of a hearing loss, slur words terribly. Although my eardrums were still intact, without hearing aids, I could only hear 35 percent in my left ear. My right ear was worse, only allowing me to hear 15 percent of the world around me.

Once more I learned to hear.

Do you realize how loud a coffee maker is?

Southern Smiles and Tears

Southern Smiles and Tears

Part Three
1963-1979

Southern Smiles and Tears

Southern Smiles and Tears

Chapter 34
Two Kennedys

It is a most remembered date. November 22, 1963. President John F. Kennedy died in Dallas, Texas at the hands of an assassin. Many of us as Americans can tell others where we were that infamous day. I was teaching my American History class at DuPont High School.

Suddenly, the school intercom came on with a crackling voice. At first, I did not process the information, but several students did. It was Walter Cronkite saying that the President of the United States had been shot as his motorcade drove past the Texas Textbook Depository warehouse. He had been pronounced dead in a Dallas hospital. Lyndon Baines Johnson was now President.

Silence enveloped the room.

I have no idea how long it was before a sob broke the hush. Carol Kennedy — slender, long naturally blonde hair, and blue-eyed shook as tears flowed.

Southern Smiles and Tears

I do not believe her tears were only for the fallen President. They had been left over from October earlier that year. Another Kennedy had died shortly before the President had. His family, not a nation, remembers him. He haunts my memory even though I never met the young man.

Each Friday I taught Current Events hoping to keep my American History students abreast of the world around them. One fateful Friday in October, I was pointing at the map of the world. My finger touched a small, Southeast Asian peninsula.

"Does anyone know about Viet Nam?"

A glazed look came over the faces of the majority of the students. The look must be practiced all over America because I have heard many other teachers speak of it.

I started to tell the class about Viet Nam and how the United States had a few troops there, but that it probably was an insignificant conflict. That was a comment I have forever wished I had not made. Insignificant the conflict may have been, at that point, to the world but important to those with a personal stake in it.

Carol had a stake in it.

Her voice came out in anger at me.

"It matters to me and my mom and dad!" she almost shouted as tears surged out taking her teenage mascara down her cheeks.

I was silent for a moment and then managed to ask, "What do you mean?"

"My brother was killed over there!"

There I was, a 23-year old college graduate standing in front of a 17-year old young lady who comprehended the sadness of the world better than I. I refocused and in an instance remembered a quote of Joseph Stalin that my Russian History professor had relayed about death. It was in response to someone saying how tragic was the death of a million Cossacks in the Soviet Union. Stalin had replied, "One death is a tragedy, one million deaths is a statistic."

Carol knew tragedy. I knew statistics.

A girl next to Carol took control of the situation, not me. She gave Carol a tissue to wipe her eyes, took her by the arm, and told me, "We're going to the bathroom."

The class remained silent. Most of the students had their heads down so as not to look at me in my embarrassment. I feebly said, "Let's listen to what is happening."

Carol and her friend returned to the room. I am not sure what I expected of Carol when she returned. What I received was a cold stare, which could have put an ice cap on the Sahara Desert. I thought that any statement from me to her would have sounded

Southern Smiles and Tears

insincere. I simply did not have the ability or experience to react properly to the situation. Perhaps, teachers should be in their 30's before being allowed to teach high school students, instead of those who are almost the student's peers. Short of experience and long on knowledge, I was completely unprepared to handle a serious situation.

Now 40 years later and in my early 60's, I can say what I should have said in 1963.

Carol, I'm sorry.

Southern Smiles and Tears

Chapter 35
Rome Fell

    Fresh out of college and knowledgeable beyond belief, I began my teaching career. My schedule included two World History classes, one American History class and three Spanish classes. Spanish was an elective course with most of the students intending to go to college. World History and American History were requirements with most students appreciating it as much as a dose of castor oil. I was going to change all that by making learning history so exciting that every student would become a scholar.
    Foolish me.
    Gerald was in my sixth period World History. He was one of those students, as I was to learn in my 17-year teaching career, who tolerated school and teachers. Both were simply obstacles in the way to getting a job and making money. Each day 50 minutes before the final bell of the day and release from prison, all six feet and four inches of Gerald would amble into my classroom. Shuffling to the

back row, he would emit a sigh as he struggled physically and emotionally to fit into the desk and history class.

It did not take a genius to figure out that Gerald had a following among those students whom teachers euphemistically titled "non-college bound." This sub class of students did not have the educational aspirations most teachers considered to be important. As college graduates, we saw post high school education as a norm, while the majority of our rural West Virginia students did not see education beyond high school as having value. Perhaps, this had something to do with the fact that as a first year teacher my salary was $4,100.00, while many of their coal-mining fathers made in excess of $30,000.00.

If Gerald ignored my great lectures in world history, his colleagues did the same. Disconcerting more than disruptive, this clique actually controlled my class for the first nine-week grading period. Obviously, these twelfth graders did not comprehend how fortunate they were to have me as a teacher. It actually appeared they believed their lives would continue on an even keel with, or without me.

Not wanting to face 27 more weeks of that type of class, I decided to discuss the situation with Gerald. I asked him to stay a few minutes after class at the end of the first grading period, in which Gerald had failed outstandingly.

"Gerald" I began, hoping my voice wasn't reflecting the turbulence in my stomach, " We need to have an understanding."

Gerald looked at me as if I were talking to someone who cared.

"You are not particularly interested in World History." Boy was that a revelation to the two of us. "But you need to pass the course to get your diploma. We need to figure a way for you to pass this class and for me to keep control of what goes on in class each day. How can we solve this?"

"Mr. Bice, you ain't a bad guy, but most of us have no idea what you are talking about. When we get bored, we talk, and you get mad. All them people and what they did just don't make sense. You talk like you know histr'y, and some is interestin', but you fly through the good stuff and then spend days on borin' dates and things. Like them 'Gyptians. I liked the part about discoverin' what was in the pyramids and that stone with writing that let people know how to read 'Gyption. And the flooding allowing people to live in the desert was good. But your test didn't ask anythin' about those. You asked somethin' about how the floods helped with math. I knew about that writin' stone but couldn't remember its name, so how could I pass your test. It was like a fore'n language."

Southern Smiles and Tears

There I sat, four years of college education and many hours of classes instructing me how to teach, and a 17-year old taught me more in those statements than every education course I had taken. These students weren't the problem. The textbook and I were. Both of us assumed the students came to class with a background of knowledge that did not exist. Then this huge amount of knowledge was dumped on them. The World History textbook was daunting. It contained over 500 pages that were to be covered in fewer than 140 hours of classroom instruction. These students were supposed to cover and understand the history of the entire world along with its many cultures in what amounted to 510 seconds for each year of history. How absurd!

"Gerald what if I pick out the interesting things, and we talk about those?"

"That sounds good to me!"

"Then, if I wander off into things you don't understand, just tell me."

Thus, I, a 23-year old teacher, reached my first major understanding of the learning process. Throw out the minutiae that seem important but concentrate on the larger ideas, which are important.

Gerald and I made it through the school year. He never became a history scholar but he did participate. This was particularly apparent with our studies and discussions about the Greek and Roman Empire. Gerald loved the stories of the elephants crossing the Alps and the spreading of salt onto the lands of conquered cities. I could see it in his face. His favorite, though, was the story of the fall of the Roman Empire. I know this because of an incident that shocked me.

Gerald raised his hand and answered a question.

We were reviewing the material on Friday for our unit test on Monday. The discussion covered how the Roman society deteriorated and weakened internally. Then, I asked the question.

"What ultimately caused the Roman Empire to fall?"

Gerald's hand shot into the air as if propelled by a Roman catapult. He didn't wait to be recognized but blurted out the answer.

"The Ballbearings invaded!"

Two years later I was driving in Charleston when a peculiar, grating noise began coming from somewhere under the hood of my car. I began looking for a garage because my knowledge of an automobile engine was that if you turned the key and nothing happened, the car was broken. About two blocks ahead was a garage that seemed to be pulling my car towards itself. I pulled in to the

Southern Smiles and Tears

bay and standing there was a grease stained, smiling Gerald.
"Well, lookee who's here. Hi, Mr. Bice. Gotta problem?"
I explained, as best I could, about the noise.
Gerald's grin got bigger.
He popped the hood, fidgeted around for a few minutes, closed the hood, and pronounced the patient well.
I asked him how much it was for fixing the car, and he waved it off as if a gnat were flying by his face. "It weren't nothin' much. I'll let you slide this time."
I opened the car door and was getting in when I heard a voice from behind me.
"Don't let those Ballbearings invade your car anymore Mr. B."

Southern Smiles and Tears

Chapter 36
Kroger Hires a Negro

Kroger, a chain of grocery stores, was good to me. I worked there for 20 years and 16 minutes from June 6, 1957 as a high school student until June 6, 1977 with a post graduate degree. The first year I taught school and worked at Kroger I made $400.00 more working at Kroger part time during the school year and full time in the summer than for teaching. It was five years and two children later before my teaching salary exceeded my grocery store wages.

I enjoyed the contact with the people who shopped in the store, but my fellow employees were the most memorable. Certain people left indelible impressions on me. One was a young man with whom I worked after I had begun my teaching career.

Something big was happening.

Mary Perry, the union shop steward, and Harry the store manager had both signed a notice and posted it on the store and union bulletin boards. Usually, notices were not done jointly by the com-

Southern Smiles and Tears

pany and union. All store employees, management and union members were to meet on Saturday morning at 8:00. Any persons not scheduled to work were to attend and would be paid for four hours.

Quite a buzz arose that morning when the Division Manager walked into the backroom of the store.

"This must be serious." I whispered to my friend Frye.

"Maybe they're closing the store." He opined.

He was totally wrong!

"I am sure you are all wondering why you are here. This division of the Kroger Company is about to make a major change in hiring practices. This store will be the first affected by the new policy. Next week a Negro will be hired to work here."

There was no gasp, nor other noise. Silence.

"I realize this is a change for many of you, and we wanted to talk to you before this young man shows up next Thursday. He will be part time and will go through the same 30-day probation period, as all of you did, before joining the union. We interviewed several Negroes, and it appears his employment will be less disruptive than hiring any other Negro. His name is Charles Boddy. It is important there be no trouble when he reports for work. Are there any questions?"

The first question came from an older meat cutter named Julian and was one of the dumbest and most prejudicial questions ever asked.

"Where's he goin' to go to the bathroom?"

"He will be treated as any other employee."

Murmurings and grumblings crept threw the group.

"Which department will he work in?"

"Until his 30-days are up, he will work in grocery. He will start on parcel pickup and then go to cash register training at Five Corners. If he passes checker training, he'll work up front checking people out and bagging groceries."

"Good. I don't want no nigger cutting meat."

Guess who tossed that into the melieu?

"That is another thing. No one, and I mean no one, is to call this young man by that term. Do you all remember when we had the last storewide meeting? That is when the company and the union agreed that anyone in the meat department discussing politics or religion would be suspended for a first offense and let go for a second. Well, we will have the same rule for the use of derogatory words directed at this young man."

I thought to myself that it was a good thing Charles wasn't going to start out working midnights stocking. Every time Ray Charles

Southern Smiles and Tears

came on the radio singing *I Can't Stop Loving You,* Frye would shout out, "Niggers ain't supposed to sing country songs!"

Charles came to work the following Thursday evening for his first 4:15 to 9:15 shift. During the next few weeks, I think he surprised many of his fellow employees. Charley, as everyone called him, was totally anti-stereotypical. He was a senior at South Charleston High School but did not play sports or sing. His grammar and syntax were better than 95 percent of those working in the store. Charley was going to go to college. This raised the hopes of some who thought he would be leaving in a few months. Surprise! He was already accepted at my alma mater, West Virginia State College, eight miles away. Most of all, he did not fit the image of *Amos and Andy* or *Steppin' Fetchin* that was ingrained in most of his fellow employees.

It did not take long before he was one of the fastest checkers on a cash register in the store. Customers migrated to his lane for good service. A couple of months after the big meeting, an opening came about in the produce department. Another shock! Richard, the produce manager, asked for Charley.

When Charley went to produce he began to get good hours. He and I worked the same hours on Saturday and often went to lunch together. I was the last teacher under a "grandfather" clause in the union contract that allowed a schoolteacher to keep seniority and not have to work Saturday nights as the rest of the part time people.

Despite the disparity of our ages, Charley and I spent the hour eating and discussing world issues and politics. His perspective of issues taught me quite a bit. Truths, well established in my mind, shattered in the face of Charley's insights. The best example was capital punishment. I had always accepted that the death penalty was justified for certain crimes. Charley disagreed. His reasoning was sound. Poor people, including but not restricted to many Negroes, suffered from inadequate legal representation. A poor person, indicted for murder, was often represented by an attorney who had barely passed the bar. On the opposite side was all the power of the state.

This revelation caused me to write a letter to a state senator, Mario Palumbo. He was a staunch opponent of the death penalty, and I asked him why. Mr. Palumbo was a Democrat. I thought I was a conservative Republican. When Goldwater ran for president, I had written *AuH_2O for President* on boxes in the stock room of the store just to aggravate some of the staunch Democrats. Mr. Palumbo answered my letter by telephone and as a lawyer virtual-

Southern Smiles and Tears

ly quoted Charley's reasoning. Mario and I began regular contact discussing this issue. When he ran for governor, I asked him if he would change his stand on capital punishment in order to garner votes from the pro-death majority Democrat voters in the coalfields. He responded that achieving an office was not worth violating his principles. Here was a statesman, who happened to be a politician.

He was never elected governor.

Charley probably never knew how he made me question my ideas. He may not even look back as fondly as I do on our Saturday lunch times together.

I was reminded of Charley Boddy and Mario Palumbo by an incident that began in Choctaw County, Alabama in 1999. What was to become a blight on the legal system of the county began rather simply. Victoria Bell Banks was in jail for a minor offense when she told Choctaw County Sheriff Donald Lolley that she was pregnant. A local doctor examined her and said he detected a fetal heartbeat. Lolley released her from jail for the supposed birth. If Banks had remained in jail, the county would have had to pay the medical bills.

Then trouble began for three black, poor, mentally impaired citizens of Choctaw County.

Several months after Lolley had released Banks, he saw the now slim woman on the street. Lolley asked Victoria to show him the child. She could not. Under pressure to produce the baby, the retarded Victoria told the sheriff that her estranged husband Medell Banks had killed the baby. District Attorney Robert Keahey jumped at the opportunity to convict a murderer. He eventually was able to get the Grand Jury to indict, not only Medell Banks, but also Victoria and her sister Diane Bell Tucker with capital murder. Two slight problems existed. No one had ever seen the alleged victim, and no body existed. That did not stop Keahey. He threatened the three with the death penalty or life in prison, if they did not plead guilty to manslaughter. All three entered guilty pleas and were sentenced to 15-year prison sentences. Lolley and Keahey placed three notches in their legal belts for ridding Choctaw County of three killers.

Rick Hutchinson, the lead defense attorney appointed by the courts, believed injustice had been served. He found out that Victoria Banks had had a tubal litigation in 1995 to keep her from becoming pregnant. Keahey retaliated that he knew she had been pregnant. Hutchinson brought in a noted fertility expert from the University of Alabama in Birmingham who confirmed Victoria

Southern Smiles and Tears

Banks' sterility. Keahey responded by calling the expert a "...paid whore..." for the defense.

The case wound its way through the Alabama Court system for three years. Keahey saw that the higher courts were not inclined to agree with the convictions and began to crawfish. The two women were freed but kept the felony manslaughter charges on their records.

Medell Banks proved to be a problem. He insisted on his innocence and refused an offer to be released unless his record was cleansed. Keahey tried to hide what was happening by persuading Choctaw County Circuit Judge Thomas Baxter to issue a "gag order" against the lawyers, witnesses, and investigators in the case. Lolley, Keahey, and Baxter had done exactly what Charley Boddy and Mario Palumbo knew to be true. The three had unleashed the full power of government on three people unable to fight back.

They did not foresee the possibility that some people believe in real justice.

Hutchinson, Medell Banks' lawyer, pursued justice with a furor. He had T-shirts and bumper stickers produced beseeching, "Free Medell." Two other lawyers joined the fray on Banks' side. James Evans, a former district attorney, and Jim Sears, a specialist in mental retardation. Perhaps, it was due to the pressure applied by that trio that Keahey asked for the "gag order." Keahey was incensed that what had been a duck shoot was now a tiger hunt.

The Alabama Court of Criminal Appeals allowed Medell Banks to withdraw his guilty plea during the summer of 2002 because a "manifest injustice" had occurred. Keahey, seemingly unaware of the embarrassing position in which he had placed himself, appeared on NBC network television in September 2002 to declare Banks a killer. "He is the one who killed that child. Make no mistake about it, Medell is the baby killer here."

Then Keahey slithered into the sanctity of his office. He delegated two assistants, Stephen Winters and John Thompson, to broker a deal under the watchful eye of Circuit Judge Harold Crow. An agreement was reached declaring Banks, "...not even remotely connected with causing the death, or participating in the death...," of the alleged baby. Alabama Bureau of Investigation agents and Sheriff Lolley admitted they had lied to Banks to get him to confess. It was obvious to most of those at the hearing that a man with an IQ between 57 and 70 had no comprehension of self-incrimination.

Then it fell apart.

Southern Smiles and Tears

Keahey interjected himself into the proceedings. In what may have been an attempt to preserve his political career and financial well being, Keahey requested a provision in any agreement that Medell agree not to pursue civil claims against authorities involved in the case. Keahey had been successful in having Diane Bell Tucker to agree to such a stipulation before being freed. Hutchinson could not have been more emphatic in rejecting Keahey's demand.

Judge Crow continued the process and within hours had an agreement. On Friday January 10, 2003, both sides entered the courtroom of Judge Thomas Baxter. Banks entered a "best interest" plea of tampering with physical evidence. Medell Banks walked out of the courtroom a free man with time served.

Charley's wisdom changed me. It allowed me to see the other side. Charley knew there were Medell Banks out there. I had never considered it. Mario Palumbo became a hero of mine. Though I was a devout Republican, Mario Palumbo received my vote for every office he sought as long as I remained in West Virginia.

Southern Smiles and Tears

Chapter 37
A Foot Soldier for Civil Rights

I didn't know Jean Peck in 1965. My loss, not hers.

While I was teaching about the Civil Rights events in 1965, Jean was living them. I was in Kanawha County, West Virginia. She was in the heart of the Black Belt in Lowndes County, Alabama. I lectured about equality. Jean fought for it.

Jean is the opposite of what my childhood friend Johnny had become. He would have been right at home with the segregation and poor sense of justice in Lowndes. She has spent a lifetime in Lowndes seeing someone like our maid Eleanor as an equal.

The people of Lowndes County do not have excess wealth. Many of them do not have an excess of anything except poverty. Sometimes it is difficult to understand poverty. In the spring of 2002, a bureaucrat in Hayneville, the County Seat, made a health decision. It had come to the attention of the County Health

Southern Smiles and Tears

Department that many residents within the county had neither sewer service nor septic tanks. With great intellectual forethought, the bureaucrat figured out how to solve the problem. Order every household in the county to install a septic tank, costing approximately $6,000.00, or face eviction. This order would have passed without notice in Marin County, California. It caused a problem in Lowndes. Most of the people affected did not have a spare $6,000.00 to install a septic tank. Many of them did not even make $6,000.00 per year.

Jean was one of the people who became incensed and helped get reversed such a stupid order. Then she helped to find a solution. That should not have surprised anyone who knew her at all. It doesn't surprise me.

I met Jean Peck at a book meeting. Several people attended the meeting. All except one told me Lowndes County was too poor to have a book like other counties in Alabama. One clear voice said, "That is exactly why we need a book."

Jean Peck's.

"We have important history here that the rest of the people in Alabama need to know about. We sit around talking about things we should do but always saying we're too poor to do it. We are going to have a book."

I immediately liked Jean. My respect for her grew as we became friends, and I learned more about her. She has had an active and valuable 75 years.

Jean is a lady with the impeccable ability to know right from wrong. Many people have that quality. Jean takes her ability an all-important step farther. She reminds me of Don Quixote. She tilts at the windmills of Lowndes County. As the lyrics state, she rights the unrightable wrongs.

The county neighbor of Lowndes is Dallas, known worldwide for its part in the Civil Rights movement. Lowndes' part in that era of American History, while not widely known, is no less important. Jean was part of the force of change.

Martin Luther King had put out a call for help in ending segregation and establishing voting rights for blacks in Lowndes. Jean proudly displays a photograph of the Reverend King and his colleagues walking down the street with her house in the background. Later, for our book, she made it a point to make sure that black families included their stories. She was adamant that Lowndes County's part in the Civil Rights movement be recorded. Many personal stories of courage exist in the county. One of them concerns a young seminarian, Jonathan Daniels.

Southern Smiles and Tears

Daniels had heard the call for equality in the South while at an Episcopalian Seminary in New Hampshire. He had been graduated from Virginia Military Institute in Virginia and obviously was aware of the double standard for voting rights in the South.

Several of the voting rights activists, including Daniels and a teenager named Ruby Sales, had been released from jail in Hayneville on August 20, 1965. They had been arrested in the nearby town of Fort Deposit for picketing without a permit. Ruby Sales was thirsty after her time spent in the hospitality of Lowndes County. She was also black.

Ruby didn't realize that being black and thirsty could be dangerous in Alabama. She and the group decided to go to a store for a cold drink. Little did they know, at the time, that this was a fatal decision. Tom Coleman, a highway department employee and volunteer sheriff's assistant, was standing at the store's front door with a shotgun when the group arrived to quench their thirst.

"If you don't leave, I'll blow your brains out." Coleman told Ruby Sales. Jonathan Daniels, in an act that would later lead him to be named a martyr by both the Episcopal and Roman Catholic churches, stepped in front of Sales. His body absorbed the full blast of the discharged 12-gauge shotgun. He died instantly. Coleman later was found not guilty by an all-white jury.

Jean never stepped into a shotgun blast. She simply continues to live in Lowndes with beliefs that do not always meet the standards of many others. Her presence probably causes consternation every time she sets foot inside a public meeting.

Should I ever decide to tilt at a windmill, Jean Peck is one of the people I would want at my side.

Southern Smiles and Tears

Chapter 38
Different War, Same Dates

A young girl in Georgia was doing homework for her American History class. One of the questions was about General William Tecumseh Sherman. She asked her dad, who had been born in Connecticut, what had Sherman done during the Civil War.

"He was a famous general who helped to end the war by splitting the South into two parts and destroying the South's major rail connections, especially in Atlanta."

The girl and dad continue discussing the general as their mother and wife, who had been born in Georgia, listened. At a lull in the conversation the daughter asked her mother, "Do you know anything about General Sherman?"

"He was an arsonist!"

That anecdotal story illustrates my studies of the Civil War, War Between the States, or War of Northern Aggression. As a senior at

Southern Smiles and Tears

West Virginia State College, the Dean of Students, Dr. Anderson, taught the Civil War class to eight history majors, of which I was one.

Dr. Anderson, a tall, thin, wavy-haired, imperious professor had obtained his doctorate at New York City University. His predilection toward the cause of the war was slavery. His view was that the writers of the United States Constitution made a pact with the devil by allowing the Southern delegates to the Constitutional Convention in Philadelphia to force a compromise about slavery. Thus, in his opinion, they endorsed this horrid labor practice. Dr. Anderson taught that State's Rights was a red herring when used in defense of the cause of the war. He opined that the Southern delegates knew that the federal government powers were to be superior to that of the states. State's Rights were no more than a way to defend an indefensible position about slavery.

As a senior, I had long ago learned the key to good grades. It was not to think or disagree with the professor, especially a Ph.D. My purpose as a student was to ingest the teaching, not digest, and regurgitate at exam time. Having become a world class regurgitator, I got an "A" from the good doctor.

Then came my surprise.

I enrolled at Marshall University to pursue a Master's Degree in History, with a minor in U.S. Geography. My assigned advisor was Doctor Moffatt; a short, overweight, cane needing Southerner educated at the University of Mississippi. He looked at my undergraduate credentials and classes and shocked me with his first observation.

"You will need to take a Civil War course."

Temporarily forgetting my creed not to dispute the word of any god of the Ph.D., I responded by telling Dr. Moffatt that I had taken a senior course and received an "A."

"I can see that, but you now need to be exposed to the opposite view of what you were taught at State."

Immediately, I realized this mixture would cause my stomach to have to endure something akin to the Jewish ban on mixing dairy and meat for a meal. Two things that were good as separate entities should not be consumed together. Here in the midst of my education I was to mix diametrically opposed views and digest them together. Then to make matters worse Doctor Moffatt told me he would be the teaching the class.

Was Dr. Moffatt's class different from Dr. Anderson's?

At the end of my first semester of graduate school, I not only was convinced that the North caused the war, but that the phrase "The

Southern Smiles and Tears

South will rise again." was not a mantra but a reality. Dr. Moffatt informed us that the South had lost the military conflict but in two later events won the political and economic ones. Out-gunned and under populated, the South had made a valiant, but futile, stand militarily, according to Dr. Moffatt.

However, owing because of superior political skills hewing back to the likes of Thomas Jefferson, George Washington, James Madison, James Monroe, and John C. Calhoun, the South was able to outmaneuver the North in 1877 and later during the presidency of another Southerner, Woodrow Wilson. He explained that in the disputed Tilden-Hayes election that the South had politically bested the North and gotten the post war military occupation troops withdrawn. Then, by electing Wilson, the South advanced economically by gaining several Federal Reserve Banks. Thus, Dr. Moffatt concluded, that the South in less than a century after the end of the great tragedy would be a leading force in the United States. His view of slavery was that if it had not been allowed at the formation of the new nation, the South would have outpaced the North earlier than the 20th Century.

Dr. Moffatt would enter the classroom, write an outline on the chalkboard, turn around and lecture to us for one and one-half hour, never once looking at the outline behind him. At exactly, 8:30 he would stop for a 10-minute break. We would talk in the hall during the break with Dr. Moffatt joining us once in a while. He always addressed us with Mr., Mrs., or Miss, never by our first names; even during the somewhat informal break time. Exactly, at 8:40, he would be at his station in front of the class, speaking once more. It only took one time of being late and having the Dr. ask, "Did you learn anything out there while I was teaching?" to stop any tardiness.

As I neared the end of my pursuit of a graduate degree, I saw how much Dr. Moffatt revered scholarship. Each of the six of us had finished our thesis and was preparing to take our oral exams. We were required to give Dr. Herschel Heath, the head of the History Department and French History scholar, a list of our classes and books we had read both in undergraduate and graduate school. As Dr. Moffatt was explaining what would happen during the oral exam, a fellow student asked him a question.

"Why do we have to take an oral exam to get a Master's when those in Education have a 100-question true or false test?"

Wrong question to the wrong person!

Dr. Moffatt's face turned red. His body swelled. He pointed his cane toward the offender.

Southern Smiles and Tears

"This DEPARTMENT believes in scholarship and knowledge. If you want a degree in sheep herding, then march yourself over there and take that test."

None of the rest of us had any questions.

I was scheduled to take my oral in August right after the Soviet Union sent tanks to Czechoslovakia and tried to suppress any thoughts of freedom the people might be harboring. At 3:00 on a Friday I faced Dr. Heath, Dr. Moffatt, and Dr. Clagg, the head of the Department of Geography. Questions came at me in a machine gun fashion. If I knew the answer to a lead question, there was no follow-up. If I paused, or gave a vague answer, the lead question was followed by deeper and deeper questions into the topic.

I had come to the inquisition with much trepidation. The day before the triumvirate had failed a student taking the oral. That in itself was frightening, because he was required to take six additional hours of class work and retake the oral the next semester. What caused reflux in me was that as a student he had made a 4.0 and had taught a year in a Delaware high school. Images flashed through my mind of Dr. Heath hauling Dr. Guillotine's machine into the room and telling me to place my head in the proper slot before he asked me questions.

After what seemed as if I had been in the room with the three for several hours, Dr. Heath asked Dr. Clagg if he had any more to ask. I said a silent prayer and God answered in my favor.

"No. I'm satisfied."

Dr. Heath then turned to Dr. Moffatt and asked the same question. I repeated my prayer. God must have been distracted because Dr. Moffatt responded differently.

"Well, I do have one more question."

"Is it your usual stumper?" Dr. Heath questioned with a smirk.

"Yes."

God must have really been busy handling a problem of immense importance, because He apparently had forgotten mine.

"Mr. Bice, what was *The Index?*"

My mind raced through every class and book I could remember. The first answer to surface was the list the Catholic Church published of books and movies Catholics should shun. Too easy. Dr. Moffatt would never come up with such a simple question.

God rejoined the fray, and He was on my side.

From somewhere deep in my mind remembrances of the Civil War class under Dr. Moffatt surfaced.

"*The Index* was the pro Southern newspaper published in England by Theodore Roosevelt's grandfather.

Southern Smiles and Tears

Dr. Moffatt grinned and said, "I have nothing else."

Then Dr. Heath told me to go out into the hall and wait. Once released from being held hostage by the three, I looked at my watch. The entire interrogation had taken 40 minutes. I waited outside the room. The event had taken place on the eighth floor, and thoughts of suicide flashed through my head.

The three professors came out of the room and looked at me sternly. I was about to throw up when Dr. Moffatt said, "Welcome to our club David." Each of the three then shook my hand.

I have no idea how I responded. Shocked at Dr. Moffatt's use of my given name and knowledge that I had survived left me speechless.

I never saw the three of them again, as I did not attend the graduation ceremony, but had my diploma mailed to me.

I was afraid they might have another question.

Southern Smiles and Tears

Chapter 39
The Beetle and the State Trooper

What an honor!

At least that is what I thought at first. My name had been sent in by the Kanawha County Foreign Language Supervisor nominating me to attend a National Defense Education Act Summer Spanish Institute at Washington and Lee University in Lexington, Virginia. It appeared to be an honor because the federal government was going to pay me a stipend, plus a subsidy for each of my dependents. The government was going to pay the tuition and housing also. W & L would award me with 12 hours of post graduate credits for making "B's", or better in the classes. All I had to do was give up a summer and promise to speak Spanish for nine weeks.

What a deal!

That was until it dawned on me that I had been accepted into the institute because I wasn't the best Spanish teacher in the county.

Southern Smiles and Tears

In fact, I was probably a member of the society of the two worst Spanish teachers. I know that because besides me one other Spanish teacher was selected from Kanawha County.

What the heck! I could swallow my pride for $150.00 per week, plus $50.00 for each dependent. This gave me a weekly check of $400.00. As a federal stipend, the money was tax-free. Imagine, I was used to making $113.00 a week teaching, plus my $80.00 per week for 16 hours at Kroger. Now, the government was going to give me more than twice that per week tax free and feed me to boot. I thought, *That's more money than God has.*

Why was the government being so free with its tax money? Congress, in reaction to the Soviet Union orbiting, Sputnik, the first non-God made Earth satellite, had decided American students were in need of better education, and teachers of science, math, and foreign languages. One way to accomplish this was to have better prepared teachers. The National Defense Education Act, NDEA, was established to insure that outcome. I was to benefit from this largesse.

I had never been "away to college", and W & L was an eye-opener for me. Males and females lived in separate dormitories but from my observations this in no way inhibited coitus. This was the beginning years of the "sexual revolution." However, the revolution had not yet appeared in much of the South. One teacher from California seemed to believe it was her duty to introduce the art of "free sex" to as many institute goers as possible. She pursued men at night with more fervor than Southerners pursued raccoons. She had no need of a flashlight, dog, and shotgun. She came equipped for the hunt and kill. Her major ploy was to ask for help in passing classes. Gossip around the male dorm was that while she was not a scholar in Spanish, she had a Ph.D. in sex.

The institute did have class work. The professors and teachers were of the highest quality and did not tolerate lackadaisical attitudes. We were even reprimanded if someone overheard us speaking English in our dorm rooms at night. I know because, Brother Brendan, my roommate and I were castigated several times for reverting to our native tongue. The good brother taught in a small college in Maryland. He and I hit it off from the beginning mostly because of our shared reverence for Roy Orbison and *Pretty Woman*. More than once Roy caused us grief because he refused to sing in Spanish. The brother was a revelation to me. He smoked cigars and drank beer. I had no idea that "religious people" did those things, at least not publicly.

We were allowed one weekend to go home if we wanted to do so.

Southern Smiles and Tears

That weekend was perhaps the most exciting and memorable of any 48 hour period in my life. We were allowed to leave at 5:00 P.M. on Friday and had to return by 5:00 P.M on Sunday. If we missed the meal on Sunday evening we were to be docked one day's stipend. Now that was an incentive to be on time.

I was going to catch a Greyhound bus, the way I had reached W&L for the trip to Malden, West Virginia. It was a 12-hour local bus run, but I would have almost one day at home. Then the god of transportation intervened. Dr. Fernando Guiterrez from Salamanca, Spain and his French wife, Monique, had become bored with Lexington and wanted to see more of the United States than the leeward side of the Appalachian Mountains. He offered to take me home and from there they would tour some before returning for his first class of the week on Tuesday afternoon. Great! I had a one-way no expense trip home. The trip by automobile would get me home faster, and it would only necessitate me riding the bus on the return trip. Then the transportation god intervened once more. Jim, my fellow Kanawha County teacher, had also ridden the bus to Lexington, now he knew he could have his car at the university for the last four weeks. He asked me if I would go to St. Albans, pick up his Volkswagen, and drive it back to Lexington. Now, I had a way back that would give me more time at home.

Was this too good to be true?

Fernando, as he insisted I call him now that we were traveling compadres, Monique, and I left promptly at 5:00. Those unfamiliar with the trip across the Appalachians were always deceived by what appeared to be a four-hour 180-mile trip but was actually a six-hour trip because of the terrain. U.S. Route 60 crossed two mountains, Sewell and Gauley, with more twists and turns than the inside of a Conch shell. Rising from near sea level to over 3,000 feet high, the highway had few passing zones once into the ascent and descent.

Fernando was blissfully unaware of the hairpin turns and switchbacks awaiting him. Several years later, when Alice and I were being moved to Missouri by a company truck, which had delivered books in Virginia, the flatlander driver asked us a question.

"Do you know why they have 15 MPH signs on Route 60?"

Perplexed, we both shook our heads.

"Because they don't make 5 MPH signs."

Fernando cruised across the remaining part of the Shenandoah Valley. Then as we approach the mountains his eyes brightened.

¡Cuervos.!

Southern Smiles and Tears

Excited he was. It was at this point that Fernando revealed to me that he loved to drive his sports car in European road races. He attacked Sewell as if it were the straightway on the backstretch of the Indianapolis 500. Double solid lines had no meaning. He drove in the right lane, the left lane, and with the double lines bisecting the hood. He slid sideways around curves, would stop in the middle of the highway to look at the views, and passed fuel trucks with no concern for approaching vehicles. No modern roller coaster comes close to what I experienced that day. We flew through Ansted, West Virginia with its mid-town narrow bridge, at 85 miles per hour. The car skidded off the road on to the thin, rock covered berm at the hairpin curve between Hawk's Nest and Chimney Corners. At Chimney Corners, we passed the stands selling handmade quilts.

Quel belle! Shouted Monique.

Fernando, in an extreme act of love for her and complete disregard for my life, slammed on the brakes, spun the steering wheel, and made a sliding 180 degree turn in the middle of the highway. Gunning the engine, he jumped forward and then screeched to a halt in front of the wide-eyed Appalachain entrepreneuers. Alighting from the vehicle, I realized the transportation god had played a horrific trick on me, and we still had to descend Gauley Mountain to the town of Gauley Bridge. Terror is too bland a word to describe the rapid descent. At the foot of the mountain Fernando made his customary deceleration into a restaurant parking lot. It was 8:15 P.M. Three hours and 15 minutes, including stops.

Fernando and Monique ordered a large meal, consuming it with gusto. I ordered a Coke to settle my stomach, hoping it would not visit my mouth a second time.

The trip on to Malden was fast but unevenful Once there, the two came in met Patty and the children. It was as if it were a United Nations confab. The same thing had occurred at the quilt stand. Monique spoke in French, Fernando translated into Spanish, and I translated into English. Then we would reverse the process when Penny or Cheryl asked a question of the two. Danny was old enough to talk but had stopped talking when we had to have braces and casts placed on his legs to correct curvatures at birth. Jeffrey was too young to talk. After a couple of hours, the international couple left on their mission to terrorize American drivers.

Saturday passed rapidly, with me having difficulty adjusting to thinking and speaking in English. Then came the return trip. Surely, it would be uneventful.

I left in the VW at 11:00 A.M. giving myself ample time to make

151

Southern Smiles and Tears

it to Lexington. Ambling across Gauley and Sewell, I was making good time. Then just past White Suphur Springs on the mountain dividing West Virginia and Virginia, I got behind a pickup truck being driven by Billy Bob and his wife Sue Ann. Behind me was a Cadillac with a Florida license plate. The couple in front was speeding at an excessive 20 miles per hour. The Cadillac wove back and forth behind me looking for a gap to pass. None existed. After crossing into Virginia and descending the mountain, miraculously a short, straight section of highway appeared. The Cadillac shot around the two impeding vehicles, and then I pushed the VW around the pickup. On a downhill slope the VW hit 65. I have no idea about the Caddy.

We both flew pass a county sheriff's car. I breathed a sigh of relief when he failed to pull out and follow us. He didn't have to. About a mile down the road, I caught up to the Caddy sitting by the road in front of a second police car. The deputy was standing beside the road signaling me over. I pulled off in front of the other offender. Watching in the mirror, I saw the Florida driver shaking his fist at the deputy. The shaking increased when Billy Bob and Sue Ann passed us by.

The deputy walked away from the Caddy and walked up to me. I showed him my driver's license and the registration for the VW.

"Why y'all in such a hurry?"

I wasn't being impertinent, mainly because the deputy looked to me as if he were seven feet tall and weighing 300 pounds, but I blurted out my answer.

"I'm going to be late for supper." Supper being the proper term for the third meal of the day in the South. Dinner was the third meal in the North. Speaking Southern seemed to have a calming effect on the behemoth.

"Where y'all goin' for supper?"

"I have to be at W&L by five, or I miss it."

I think he actually smiled. As he said, "I think y'all goin' to be late. Follow me to the JP."

Both the Caddy and the VW fell into line behind the bubble top.

The deputy pulled off the highway onto a side road and then to a dirt road. He stopped in front of an unpainted frame store erected on top of brick pedestals. Above the plank steps was a rusted Nehi Orange thermometer sign. The deputy opened the screen door. The Florida couple walked in, followed by me, and the deputy who allowed the spring to slam the screen door.

"Arthur! Y'all here?

A gray headed man rolled in from the back of the store in a wheel

Southern Smiles and Tears

chair.

"Arthur, I didn't see you and Aunt Jennie in church this morning."

Great! They're related.

"We were afeelin' poorly but we'll make tonight's meetin'. What'cha got here George?"

George, the deputy, walked across the room, bent over Arthur, and whispered to him. He then straightened up; announcing the Florida driver would be first. He then related the charge. Reckless driving by going 20 miles over the posted 55 MPH.

In a millisecond, Arthur announced the fine.

"One hundred seventy-five dollars plus $25.00 court costs."

I gulped. In my wallet were a ten-dollar bill and a blank check. Florida started to protest when Arthur interrupted.

"George, I think it was mighty nice of you not to press the resisting arrest charge."

Florida's mouth closed. He paid the fine, in cash, and left.

Arthur turned to me.

"Five dollars speeding, plus $25.00 court costs."

I know my mouth fell open. I had been going almost as fast as Florida. Only three things were different. I spoke Southern. I was attending W&L. I did not shake my fist at George. I was pretty sure he wasn't fond of the last one.

"Sir, I only have $10.00 cash. Can I write you a check?"

"Virginia don't 'low checks for fines." Arthur decreed.

Once more George bent down and whispered in Arthur's ear.

"Son," drawled George, "y'all go on to Lexington. Tomorrow morning you cash that check and go to the post office and send Arthur here a money order for $30.00. He's releasing you on my word, and if he don't have that money on Wednesday, I'm acomin' to W&L and gettin' you."

"Yes, sir."

"Now, get outta here and drive slow."

You better believe the next morning I was standing at the school finance office waiting for it to open at 9:00. By 9:10, the money order was in the mail.

Oh — I did make supper.

Southern Smiles and Tears

Chapter 40
Demon Rum

The South has no idea what to do about alcohol. Every Sunday in the Bible belt preachers attack demon rum. Then hundreds of thousands go home from church to watch stock car racing with roots in the transportation bootleg moonshine. Robert Mitchum and *Thunder Road* is now a multi-million dollar sport with Southern roots but spreading as far away as California.

Many things in the South are oxymorons. Bourbon County in Kentucky is dry while Christian County is wet. Chilton County, where Alice and I bought a house in Alabama, is dry. The county seat of Clanton is wet. It is strange that if one purchases wine or whiskey within Clanton it is legal. Try to purchase the items outside the city limits and the transaction becomes illegal. I am not positive about the legal status of alcoholic beverages purchased in Clanton, placed in a plastic bag, and carried into the county juris-

Southern Smiles and Tears

diction. It is clear where the preachers stand but a little fuzzy with the various governments.

Stories about moonshine and revenuers are part of the culture of the South. In the early 1960's just outside Marianna, Florida, Patrick Lawrence's father had a garage and filling station. Patrick, now tall, lanky, and addicted to cowboy garb, was just a splinter of his dad then. One afternoon the county sheriff's car pulled in to the gas station but not for fuel. The sheriff got out of the car, opened the trunk, and took out two five-gallon cans. Looking straight at Patrick's dad, he moved his head to the right, slightly upward, and a little to the rear in the universal unspoken sign of "Follow me." Patrick, barely reaching the waists of the two men, followed them around back unnoticed. The two of them stopped by the restrooms. One, with the paint peeling off the letters, was marked for men, One was for women, and a third carried the black letters identifying it as for COLORED. Patrick, small enough to go unnoticed but big enough to listen, stood behind the two.

"Whatcha' need sheriff?"

"I got me 10 gallons of whiskey here and I want you to sell it. When you run out just call and I'll bring you two more cans. The onliest thing is that once a year I have to come out here and arrest you. That way it'll be known I'm doin' my job."

"What'll happen when you arrest me?"

"Ya'll goin' hafta spend the night in my jail, but in the mornin' the JP will let you go."

Patrick's dad told the sheriff he would think on it, and the sheriff placed the cans inside the men's restroom. The three strolled to the front of the station where several loafers were drinking RC Colas from bottles and spitting tobacco into paper cups. The sheriff waved to them, got in his car, and drove off.

"Wha'd the sheriff want with you?" One of the idlers asked.

"He left me 10 gallons of whiskey back there and wants me to sell it for him."

"Gonna' do it?"

"Don't think so. I'd hafta spend a night in jail once'ta year and I don't think I want to do that."

"Whatcha' goin' do with the whiskey?"

"We'all gonna drink it, of course."

One of the most family oriented television shows in history was set in the South. The *Andy Griffith* show of mythical Mayberry, North Carolina was filled with wholesome characters and moral themes. Right in the midst of all this moral rectitude was Otis, the town drunk. He was a lovable character. Glossed over was that he drank while his wife went without necessities and that Otis was an alcoholic.

For me alcoholism long ago ceased to be humorous.

My father shunted back and forth from a medium drinker to an abject drunk. Alcohol was the reason the two of us were estranged in the last years of his life. I had asked him not to have been drinking when he came to see our two girls, Penny and Cheryl. He acquiesced to this request most of the time. Then alcohol became more important than his grand daughters. One terrible day, he came to our home in St. Albans, West Virginia with the odor of alcohol emanating from every breath. I was angry, but held my tongue. Until. He picked up Penny threw her into the air and almost missed her as gravity pulled her down.

I shouted. "Dad, I never want you to come back here if you can't stop drinking." I never saw him again until he lay in a casket.

Our family could be characterized in an off take of Cary Grant's description in *Arsenic and Old Lace* of "Mental illness doesn't run in my family. It fairly gallops." Alcohol wasn't a river in my family. It was a Noah type flood. My father would brag that, if he ever needed a blood transfusion, the doctor would have to go to the ABC state store. There were nine of us children issued from Ray and Gunhild Bice. One died before the age of one. Five of the others were alcoholics. Two died of liver failure. One killed two wives in automobile accidents before DUI became the acronym for drunken driving. One probably died in a construction accident with a hangover. One was surreptitious as to where the bottles were located.

I have a great fear it is true, as some doctors believe, that alcoholism is an illness able to flow through genes from parents to offspring. Did my bothers and sisters pass the evil gene on to their progeny? What about my grandchildren?

I can take a few sips of wine with a meal, but a quarter filled glass can cause my head to buzz and my speech to slur. Two ounces of grain alcohol would probably knock me on my keester.

The South may not know what to do about alcohol, but I know what alcohol can do to a family. Destroy it.

Southern Smiles and Tears

Chapter 41
Canonizing a Demagogue and Demonizing a Statesman

Many Southern politicians have used race and loud voices to drown out those of more temperate attitudes. Lester Mattox rode his bicycle backwards and tried to take Georgia with him. Cynthia McKinney tried to use race in Georgia to stay in Congress. Bob Barr tried to out shout any opposition he encountered. The voters decided to rid themselves of that group. Two Southern politicians somehow were able to be elected over and over even though their racial views were suspect.

I revere neither George Wallace nor Robert Byrd. Many people in Alabama and West Virginia appear to do so.

The name of George Wallace is ubiquitous in Alabama. From streets to junior colleges, you will find his name honored. The lat-

Southern Smiles and Tears

ter seems particularly ludicrous after his infamous stand in the doorway at the University of Alabama declaring that that particular institution would never be integrated. I am not impressed by the fact that he apologized for his actions as a segregationist long after his power to harm had declined. I do however, dislike him for what he did to Johnny. He provided the seed that changed a person, who had not seen a difference between himself and those of color, into a racist.

Johnny, my childhood friend in Prichard, had never believed himself to be above others until George Wallace, and many other politicians, saw a way to maintain power by playing poor whites against those of color. Wallace and those of his ilk played to the fears of poor whites by telling them that if schools were integrated their daughters would be marrying blacks and other such inventive bluster. These politicians repeatedly enforced that whites, any white no matter how much of a degenerate he may have been, was better than any colored. The word "nigger" rolled off the tongues of these demagogues as easily as sippin' whiskey slid down their throats.

Johnny changed. A poor white who had played and worked with persons of color all his life saw himself as being better than his former friends. I saw him in the mid-1970s on a visit to Mobile, and he told me George Wallace would "keep the niggers where they belonged." This seemed strange to me having come from someone who for over 20 years had been exactly in the same place that George Wallace wanted to keep "coloreds".

Johnny came to defend the inexcusable in my eyes. He found no fault with the fact that in 1956 Nat King Cole was driven from the stage at the Boutwell Auditorium in Birmingham and prevented from performing or that four little black girls were killed by Ku Klux Klan members in the 1963 Birmingham church bombing. I believe he would have thought it funny that an editor of a newspaper in Wilcox County helped push the county commission to cease operation of the Alabama River ferry crossing from the almost all black community of Gees Bend across the river to the county seat at Camden. A thirty-minute trip changed to a two-hour one. The newspaper editor then bought land that became devalued because of the lack of transportation. In 2000, he began pushing for a new ferry that would increase the value of his segregation days' purchases. He, as many politicians, seemed to have prospered because of racist policies

Almost diametrically opposite from George Wallace in his reaction to the United States Supreme Court decision finding segre-

Southern Smiles and Tears

gated schools to be inherently unequal was William Marland of West Virginia. Marland did not stand in any school house doors. He simply told his staff that if local boards of education defied the law of the land he would "put all of them in jails, until their feet stuck out the windows." It was not a popular political position to take. Marland, a Democrat, had a Democrat controlled legislature, and it would have appeared he could take an unpopular direction in regards to desegregation of schools. Not so. He found himself abandoned by his party and his power base gone.

Marland became a pariah within the Democrat Party. That occurred while Robert Byrd, a former member of the Ku Klux Klan, became an idol in West Virginia. Politicians, who had stood beside Marland on inauguration day, fled as if he held a skunk in each hand. Politicians in West Virginia may not have been as overt in using race to maintain power compared to those in Alabama, but they did not want to associate with anyone who would not. In one of the ironies of the times, Marland, who vowed to follow the law, ended up a disgraced and abandoned taxi cab driver in Chicago, while Wallace, an obstreperous segregationist, has his name etched in stone throughout Alabama. Robert Byrd, reformed from the Ku Klux Klan, still once in a while slips and speaks words from his segregationist past. It doesn't matter to most West Virginians. They delight in all the lucre he has brought to the state through Washington, DC. His name is as ubiquitous in West Virginia as that of George Wallace in Alabama. Most of all, though, George Wallace, and people like him, caused my former Alabama friend to head down a path of self destruction.

I cannot forgive him for that, even if Eleanor told me I should be willing to forgive everyone.

Chapter 42
Selecting a Career

Education supposedly prepares students for a career.

Educators define a career in the context of the lifetime of work one does to make a living. What one learns in school helps you find direction in choosing a career. Study math, become an accountant. Excel in chemistry, the world of science awaits you. Learn the rules of English, you may write a book. Revel in history, dig carefully as an archeologist. High school would point you in a direction, and college would refine it.

At least that is the way it is supposed to work. I had fallen into that trap.

Students, though, often have other concepts about a "career." I was shocked to find out what one particular student I had in class perceived as a career. It would be wrong to have said, "A student I was teaching," because it is now apparent I was not teaching her anything.

Southern Smiles and Tears

My first misconception, to which I have already confessed, was to believe college was essential in learning the skills to pursue a career. Many of the most successful, intelligent, and happiest people I have known never entered the hallowed halls of higher learning. Conversely, some of the saddest and boorish individuals to cross my path have excelled at education but not at life.

It has been almost 30 years since a conversation with Ella shocked me into understanding just how much I did not understand about real life. Homeroom that particular week was set aside for teachers to counsel students in selecting classes for the next year. Extra time was allotted so students could discuss their choices and goals.

The first three days had gone well, and I was swollen with pride about my powers of guidance in directing students to achieve greatness. That was until Ella approached my desk with her card filled with class choices. A raven-haired beauty of 15 years, whose body made Marilyn Monroe's pale in comparison, Ella had selected all non-academic classes.

It was my sworn duty as an all-knowing teacher to correct Ella's error in judgment.

"Ella, you need to take some type of math class."

"I don't want to."

"You will need math to succeed."

"No, I don't."

Apparently, there was some lack of communication occurring. I was saying things, but she was not hearing.

"Ella, maybe you need to explain to me what you plan to do after you are graduated."

The explanation I got was far from what I expected. Ella was intelligent, made excellent grades, and never caused one minute of trouble as a 10th grader. She had high-achiever written all over her.

"I'm not going to graduate. I'll be 16 in July, so I won't coming back here."

Now that took all the substance out of my course counseling.

"What?"

That was the most erudite reply I could muster for a few seconds.

"I'm quitting school."

Now she was talking, and I wasn't hearing.

"Why would you quit school?"

"I don't need to go to school anymore."

"What about your career?"

There. That ought to stop her from her foolish thoughts.

Southern Smiles and Tears

"I'm going to have a baby and go on ADC. The government pays so much for each baby. Joey and I think we will have six. We also can get food stamps. That will give us enough to get a trailer and live behind his momma's house."

"When are you and Joey getting married?"

"We can't get married. The government won't pay us if we're married."

I had no answer to her logic. I did not know enough about ADC to talk to her about it. She probably knew more about the rules and regulations for ADC and the Food Stamp Program than any bureaucrat administering the programs. The Aid to Dependent Children was to be her career. She would get so much per month for each child, as long as she did not marry. It is entirely possible that Ella's response to the largesse of the federal government was no different from my accepting the money I received the summer at Washington and Lee University. It is all in the point of view. I got more money than most of the other students because I had children. Ergo, Ella and I were the same in some respects.

Ella continued her formal education for the last month of that year. Her name was not on the list of 11th graders the next September. I was transferred the next year to a junior high school and never saw her again.

She still haunts my thoughts this many years later. In my mind I see her as the bright, pretty girl she was the last time I saw her. Then the image of that haunting photograph of an emaciated Depression-era Appalachian woman superimposes itself over my memory's image of Ella. The woman stands on an unpainted porch with a baby on her hip and three young children with patched clothing clinging to her skirt.

Maybe Ella is happy with her six children. I hope so. She may have achieved all of her goals, which places her ahead of many career-oriented people. Maybe she and Joey inherited his momma's house and have lived happily ever after. Maybe, with changes in welfare programs, the two have even been able to marry.

If she has not, my problem is that I do not know who failed Ella. Me? The educational system? A generous government? Herself? Probably all four.

Then I think. What was the difference between my taking federal dollars to have gone to Washington and Lee, and Ella taking money on which to live?

Probably, not much!

Southern Smiles and Tears

Chapter 43
It Was Just a Statue

Booker T. Washington never hurt anyone in Malden, West Virginia.

Yes, he did go to the Salinas Church where he sat in the balcony because Negroes were not allowed in the main sanctuary. Yes, he was born a slave in Virginia and lived in Malden after the Civil War, where a Mrs. Dickerson taught him to read and write. Yes, he left Malden at age 16 and walked 500 miles to attend Hampton Institute along Virginia's Atlantic coast. Yes, he continued his education and in 1881 became head of Tuskegee Institute, now Tuskegee University, in Macon County, Alabama.

Why would someone desecrate a statue with Washington's bust atop it? Not just deface it but pour used oil over the head and face, which soaked into the granite and mocked his blackness.

The statue had been placed in Malden beside U.S. Route 60 to recognize this great educator's time in West Virginia. It sat upon a stone base describing Washington's history and contributions to education. It was not harming any person in the unincorporated white town of Malden. Yet, someone took offense at the statue being placed there.

My first knowledge of the vandalism came through snickering in a history class I was teaching the morning after the incident occurred in the late 1960's. A group of white students were gleefully bantering about, "How black ole Booker T. was," as they entered the room. When I asked what was going on, a hush fell over the group, except for the standard noncommittal answer.

"Nothin'."

It was in the teacher's lounge later that day that I learned what had happened over the weekend to the statue. Someone, or ones, had poured used oil over the bust on Saturday night. Whoever it was, then spray painted the epithet, "Nigger," on the base of the statue. Rumors and stories began to seep through DuPont High School somewhat identifying the miscreants. Guilt never proved, a certain swagger could be seen in the attitude of a group of white seniors from Malden for several weeks after the incident. Soon after, the state moved the statue to safer, enclosed quarters away from Malden.

I pondered why this had happened. How could students who cheered black athletes at high school games, and even elected a black as senior class president, laugh about such a thing? Animosity between races was an undercurrent in the high school. It surfaced in self-segregation in the lunchroom and then subdued in plays and athletics.

DuPont High School had a diverse student body. Most were middle class, a smattering from wealthy families, and a substantial number in, or bordering on poverty. Students came from areas bounded by the Kanawha River and the hills to the north. There were two major offshoots cutting into the mountains, Campbell's Creek and Witcher's Creek. A four-lane highway ran parallel to the river. Strung between the road and the river were a series of communities and one actual town. The residential areas grouped around "Old Route 60," to the south of the new highway.

The first area to the east of the capital city of Charleston in the DuPont High School district was Malden. Campbell's Creek was perpendicular to Malden. Next to Malden, after one negotiated "deadman's curve" was the Dickerson property. The Dickersons were an old-line family with enough clout to have had the state build a road with two right angles so the road would miss cutting into their property. On the east side of the Dickerson land was

Southern Smiles and Tears

Rand. Adjacent to that was DuPont City, an unincorporated area named after the chemical plant, which dominated the sliver of flat land along the river. The chemical plant separated DuPont City from Belle, the main commercial area. Diamond was at the eastern reach of the school district. Witcher's Creek was north of the border of Belle and Diamond. With the exception of Rand, all were white communities.

Old DuPont High School was firmly ensconced in DuPont City near the old Belle Drive-In Theater. When the board of education, around 1960, decided to purchase land for a high school, it chose a section in Rand. This did not set well with many of the people in the other communities. They did not want their children going to school in Rand. Pressure applied to the proper places extended the name of DuPont City to include the soon to be built new school. Even the mailing address became that of DuPont City. Then, in perhaps the biggest insult to the minority community, the board authorized a chain link fence to be built on the western side of the school property separating it from Rand. No such fence was built on the eastern side. The school, saddled with such an auspicious beginning, was doomed to the undercurrent of tension between the races.

I believe that undercurrent led to the defacing of Booker Taliaferro Washington's statue. Just as adults had shown disrespect for the town of Rand, students believed they were free to do the same to the statue. Why they did it? I still do not understand it completely.

After all, it was just a statue of a man who overcame slavery and became an outstanding educator.

Chapter 44
Which is the Bomb?

Bomb scares in schools during the 1970's became so common that they failed to generate much excitement.

Once a telephone call came into the school, and the students were sent outside, the scene became quite festive. Students laughed and joked while waiting on the "All clear!" Those who were in the midst of an exam when the fire bell rang tended to exchange answers and pertinent information. For many, the only downside for a bomb scare was for those dressed for physical education, and the scare came in the dead of winter.

The disrespect for the bomb scares grew as the calls became more frequent, and the non-existence of the bombs became apparent. I, as a teacher in high school, became quite nonchalant to these scares.

There weren't any bombs. Were there?

I accepted the common thinking that the scares were mostly students who were either upset at the educational system or simply wanted time outside the classroom. In my ignorance, I accepted a practice instituted by Harry Douglas, the principal at DuPont High School. His idea was that it was important to return to class as quickly as possible at the end of the scare.

Volunteers from the Malden Fire Department took what the principal considered an inordinate amount of time to respond to the emergencies. The four or five firemen who responded would take at least two hours to check each locker in the school once the janitor had used his master key to open them. Mr. Douglas came up with a simple solution. Once the buildings were cleared of students and female teachers, the male teachers would begin going through the lockers. They would continue looking for bombs once the firemen arrived.

Thus students would be returned to class more quickly.

What an idea!

Like those in the *Charge of the Light Brigade*, into the valley of death we male teachers went into an area where we knew not what waited. At least the British soldiers had weapons to defend themselves. We had nothing for defense. We did not even have knowledge of our enemy.

John Williams, tall and the color of a good cup of hot chocolate, and I had our "free period" together. One day, while just the two of us were in the teachers' lounge, our conversation fell into a philosophical mode about life and death. We considered the prospect of death, as much as two men who had just turned 30 could, while debating the possibilities of life after death.

Then John dropped his bomb.

"David, what does a bomb look like?"

"Huh?"

"Would you recognize a bomb in a locker if you saw one?"

"Well. Uh. I'm not sure. Would you?"

"Not unless it had 'BOMB' written on it in red capital letters."

Silence fell upon us as we each contemplated this 500-pound gorilla that had walked into the living rooms of our minds.

Then the bell rang ending our *kaffe klatch*.

That night, as my mind walked around the edges of sleep, I revisited John's question over and over. Finally, I answered his question.

No! I would not.

Multiple doses of caffeine kept me going the next day until John and I met at our appointed time and place.

"John, I couldn't distinguish a bomb from a box of saltine crack-

ers."
"Me, neither."
"I thought all night about recognizing a bomb."
"Me, too!"
Our conversation led us into the stupidity of teachers looking for bombs in lockers. This progressed into the relative value of a female teacher to that of a male teacher. Mr. Douglas obviously believed that it was in somehow chivalrous for males to be blown into small pieces while the females outside screamed at the blast.

Then in one of those life changing moments, we decided to go down to the principal's office and ask Mr. Douglas why women and men teachers were treated differently in regards to bomb searching.

Maybe we should have contemplated a different approach.

Mr. Douglas, an ex-coach, looked at the two of us as if we did not have full complements of brain cells. We received a lecture about the responsibility of men to protect women. When he had finished, I pictured myself as a Cro-Magnon man standing at a cave opening fighting off saber-tooth tigers with a club as the women cringed behind rocks, their faces lit by flickering firelight.

Well put in our place, we dropped any further inquiries into the relative value of the genders.

Until!

The fire alarm bell was ringing as Mr. Douglas announced over the intercom that a bomb threat had been received and all students and women were to leave the buildings. All the men were to report to the office for locker search assignments. I, in perfect submission began my trek down the hall. Halfway to my destination, John fell into lockstep with me. I looked at him. He looked at me. We turned right and walked out of the building without speaking a word to each other.

As John and I stood outside awaiting the all clear bell, furtive glances were cast at us by the women teachers. It was not a glance Mr. Douglas gave us as we returned to the non-bomb holding buildings. His face was red, his eyes bulging, and his voice excruciatingly loud.

"Of all the people to embarrass me! You two!" Then the situation deteriorated.

I probably should not have said, "I have five kids, and my life is just as important as any of the women teachers!"

My retort seemed to embolden John.

"I'm not even married, and my life is as important as them. Besides, I'm a better teacher than most of them anyhow."

Southern Smiles and Tears

I don't think the words, "Get outta here, you two!" requires an explanation.

The next year I found myself teaching at a junior high school 35 miles to the west. John had decided it was an opportune moment in his life to return to graduate school. Our Mahatma Gandhi like protest did have a good result. Bomb searching was soon turned over to professionals.

I still do not believe I would recognize a bomb.

Chapter 45
Murderers Three

Teachers are supposed to have a positive influence on their students. That probably occurs in an extremely high percentage of cases. Most teachers can cite successful students. I even have had a few.

Successes do not remind me of my teaching years. The failures do. I am aware of three students I taught who murdered. How's that for success?

One murdered in war. One murdered in a threat gone awry. One murdered in a robbery. One thought murder was funny. The second had immediate remorse because his intent was to frighten, not kill. The third blamed the victim because the shot to the leg was meant to wound, not kill.

Danny was the murderer who told me about his exploits with a sense of thrill and joy. Each of his murders was sanctioned by the United States government. Danny joined the U.S. Army right after

Southern Smiles and Tears

receiving his diploma from DuPont High School. It was about 18 months later that Danny walked into my classroom. His wide-open smile was still intact. Less than six feet in height, he did not appear to have gained any weight on his lean frame. Muscles yes, weight no.

His grin covered a callousness that iced my spine. His story changed my mind about Viet Nam. Until that day I had believed the anti-war protesters of that era to be un-American. Danny revealed a side of war to me that shook my confident opinion of right and war.

"Hey, Mr. B. Are you still torturing kids?"
"You better believe it. How's it going?"
"Better than having a wild high school girl!"
"What've you been doing since I last saw you?"
"Man, I've been in Nam! It's been great!"

My curiosity piqued, I asked him if he were going to be around that afternoon. We could talk during my prep period. He said he wanted to talk to some other people but would come back fifth period.

That is when I found out how an easy going 17-year-old high school student could be changed into a ruthless killer in less than two years. Danny had never been a scholar, but he made it through school without attracting too much attention. Danny was home from his tour in Viet Nam, but he informed me that he had volunteered to go back.

I wish I had never asked him what it was like over there. He told me.

"I'm part of a team that interrogates gooks. When the grunts capture a gook, they call us in to find out what they know."
"You speak Vietnamese?"
"Nah, we got interpreters. We take them up in a helicopter and hang them outside by their feet until they tell us what we want to know."
"Are you serious?"
He replied with a smile, "Yep, we've dropped quite a few for not talkin'."
"You?"
"Of course."
"What about those who give you information?"
"Well, if they talked real fast we'll take them back to base, but if they gave us any trouble, we drop 'em anyhow."

I don't know if my face reflected my shock, but Danny soon left. My shock was based on how my brothers and brother-in-law kept their war stories to themselves. Herbie served in North Africa, Italy, France, and Germany. Never once did he relate a glorious tale of those four years. Eddie refused to talk about Korea. Carlos, my brother-in-law, did tell me once that World War II, "... was too awful to talk about." Danny may have been putting me on, but I don't think so. His service was in a different era than my three relatives.

I never saw Danny again. It was a year later I read where he had been killed after returning home from Viet Nam.

Within weeks of reading about Danny's death came the worst day in my teaching career. What began as a normal winter school day ended with a dead boy and his best friend arrested. How could such a tragedy occur to two junior high school students?

Stuart and Arthur were best friends. They were part of the class of students who often found themselves in the office of the vice-principal for a paddling. The vice-principal often used students of this group of *Untouchables* to snitch on others. One time he even bought walkie-talkies for his snitches to call him to report on smoking or other types of criminal activity. That lasted until one of the walkie-talkie snitches received a severe beating, and some teachers protested the practice.

I believe Arthur died because Stuart thought Arthur had snitched on him.

Someone, the week previous to Arthur's death, had set fire to a hallway bulletin board. The vice-principal was determined to catch and punish the perpetrator. He began to put pressure on Arthur and Stuart, trying to get them to squeal on each other. Somewhere in the interrogations Stuart must have become convinced that Arthur had identified him as the culprit.

Stuart brought a .22 pistol to school with him.

He found Arthur in the technical building of Hayes Jr. High School in St. Albans. Stuart pulled out the pistol and pointed it at Arthur. Witnesses gave different accounts, but it was clear that Stuart believed his friend had gotten him into trouble. The first shot was towards the floor. That would have killed no one, but then the gun kicked up, and with each successive time the trigger was pulled the shots became more lethal. One struck Arthur in the heart.

Stuart ran from the building. Larry Pauley, an art teacher, tried to resuscitate Arthur. Arthur died in his arms. A West Virginia State Police helicopter landed in the space between the two buildings. Students were kept in homeroom. Frantic parents flooded the school. Rumors swept the halls. Facts became apparent.

Southern Smiles and Tears

Stuart had run across the road at the front of the school and fled up a timber- covered hill. The state trooper flying the helicopter above the hill saw a message scraped out of the snow.

Arthur I'm sorry

Stuart was arrested and tried in Juvenile Court. Some objected to his only being imprisoned until he was 21 years of age. I know what he did was wrong but am not sure that he was the only guilty person.

The third murderer suffered no remorse. Carlton also fell in the subclass of students. His academic achievements were suspect but his observations held truth. One time in class he told me, "You can't make me learn that, baldy!" First, he wasn't about to learn West Virginia History, unless he wanted to do so. Second, he was the first person to let me know that my baldness was apparent to the world.

Carlton did not cause much trouble as a student and progressed through the seventh, eighth, and ninth grade with relatively little discomfiture. It was when he dropped out of high school that he made a fatal mistake.

Carlton participated in the robbery of an old man. On the way out the door, Carlton shot the man in the leg to prevent being followed. The bullet struck the femoral artery of the man's leg. He bled to death. I suspect all of the movies and television shows showing leg wounds as minor inconveniences influenced the shot to the leg. Carlton never understood why he was charged with murder as he only intended to wound the man.

I have often pondered about these three. Was there anything I did, or did not do that could have changed their paths?

I do not know. I do know I count them as my failures.

Southern Smiles and Tears

Chapter 46
Station Wagon Vacation

"We're going to go to Alabama on vacation." That was the announcement to my family that we were going to take a real vacation. We had made short trips, but this was to be a real trip with eating out and staying in motels.

I had bought a used Pontiac station wagon from Arnold Moore, a fellow teacher at Hayes Junior High School. It was blue and white, making it just perfect for visiting the blue Gulf of Mexico with waves of white foam.

Patty and I did not have any credit cards, so this was to be a cash only trip. I went to the bank and exchanged most of our dollars for American Express Traveler Cheques. The kids broke into their piggy banks, and we all prepared for our trip.

The plan was to leave on Saturday evening after I had completed my nine hours at Kroger. We packed on Friday night, and when I arrived home Saturday evening we prepared the wagon for trav-

Southern Smiles and Tears

eling. I lowered the third seat to a prone position and placed quilts and pillows in the rear of the wagon. My idea was that Penny, Cheryl, and Danny could ride in the second seat while Jeffrey and Ricky could sit on the quilts in the back. At night, while I was driving, four of them could sleep in the back and one on the seat.

The wagon had a luggage rack on top. That is where I placed our suitcases and covered them with a plastic tarpaulin. Then I tied everything down with a rope, securing the load by tying my best knots. The only things in the back with the kids were a Coleman Cooler and a bag with nonperishable bread and such. The cooler had lunchmeat, soft drinks, and assorted condiments embedded in ice. There were also two bottles of catsup, the Bice sustenance of life.

We pulled out onto Greenbriar Street in Charleston about 6:00 and headed for Kentucky. My plan was to drive about five hours to the other side of Lexington, Kentucky, take a nap for about an hour, and drive on to Mammoth Cave. About two hours into the trip, we began to notice that the people in Kentucky were extremely friendly. Drivers honked and passengers waved as they passed us. We waved back, not wanting to be thought of as being snobs. Then a car pulled up along side us and the friendly Kentuckian lowered his window. I wound down my window to find out what he needed.

"Ya'll losing all your suitcases."

Apparently my knot tying was not equal to the wind velocity generated by a vehicle traveling sixty miles per hour. It only took us an hour to reverse our trip, recover three suitcases, and retie everything.

Well, at least we made it to Morehead, Kentucky before my eyelids decided it was time to stop. I pulled onto the drive of a closed gas station and told everyone to go to sleep. It was a little after midnight.

"Dad! Dad!" A low whisper came from the middle seat.

Pulled from the land of nod, I said in the standard parental loving tone. "Go to sleep!"

"Dad!"

Again, I responded with all the loving tone of an agitated bull. "What's the matter with you. Can't you see I'm trying to get some rest."

"Dad, those men are trying to steal our suitcases."

That woke me!

Two friendly Kentuckians were busily trying to undo my triple-knotted, super duper tie job. My eyelids fully retracted, I turned the key in the ignition, pulled the gear lever into "DR", and peeled out of the lot. The only other sound than the tires trying to get a purchase on the pavement was an, "Eeyow!" One of the friendly Kentuckians had hold of the rope as the car sped away. He probably still has the rope burns on his hands.

The sun was removing the last vestiges of darkness as we drove around the outskirts of Lexington on Interstate 64. We stopped at the entrance of the Bluegrass Parkway and had a picnic breakfast. Refreshed, we continued on our journey. Not far along the Parkway, Penny made an observation that her sister and brothers taunt her with to this day.

"Look at those rocks growing out of those rocks!"

The cuts the road builders had made though the limestone rocks in Kentucky horse country left protrusions of jagged rocks along the walls. They did have the appearance of "growing out" of the cuts. Quickly forgetting that it was she who saved us from losing all of our clothing, Penny's siblings still tease her 30 years later about "growing rocks."

Outside Mammoth Cave, we were getting ready to stop and eat lunch when a whine came from the back of the station wagon.

"Dad! The quilt's wet." I still try to figure out why the word "Dad" seemed to have been used more than "Mom!" on that trip.

"It is not."

"Yes, it is!"

I pulled to the side of the rode, while explaining that the quilt had better be wet or somebody's behind was going to be red.

It was wet!

Somebody, I choose not to tell who, had failed to close the drain plug on the Coleman Cooler. The ice had melted, and the quilts had absorbed the resulting change from a solid into a liquid. We spent an hour wringing out the quilts, but they didn't really dry completely until we hit the beaches of Alabama.

I used all the wiles of parenthood by not admitting that there was chance that the error was mine. This distraction was accomplished by diverting everyone's attention to how it was so, "...exciting to be at Mammoth Cave." We toured the caves, but I believe the kids knew the culprit with the wet quilts. They did, however, have enough sense to realize that it is not a good idea to lay blame on the person driving the vehicle on their "great" vacation.

Our next stop was at the Redstone Arsenal in Huntsville, Alabama. In the 1970's the arsenal was not the glitzy, touristy, Space Center later developed in the best tradition of Walt Disney. There were picnic tables around some spring seats that astronauts

Southern Smiles and Tears

had used to become acclimated to weightlessness.

It was a glorious day.

The sun glowed as all five of our children bounced in 180-degree arcs. They laughed. They giggled. They learned. In the late 1990's, Jeffrey and Roberta brought Josiah and Caleb to Alabama. We met them in Huntsville and visited, "the new and improved" Space Center. Our grandsons enjoyed and learned about space travel, but I did not hear one giggle from them. Later, we all took a bus tour around Redstone Arsenal and saw the prototype of the Space Station. It was educational, but the highlight for me was when, from the window of the bus, Jeffrey spotted the old spring chairs and gleefully said, "There they are! Those are the weightless simulators we rode." They may sit outside rusting, but I am positive they will not rust in the memories of five Bices.

We drove on to Mobile, Alabama to a Holiday Inn. We saw my sister Martha, and I got a chance to see Johnny, for what was to be our last encounter. Our excursion then moved to another Holiday Inn on Dauphin Island. Hurricane Frederick later destroyed this motel on September 12, 1979. Bellingrath Gardens, Gulf Shores, and Fort Morgan were all included in our itinerary. I wanted to make sure the kids got to see what fascinated me as a child about the area surrounding the coast of Alabama.

A week passed quickly. It was time to head back to the hills of West Virginia. Not one to, "chew my cud twice," I selected a different route to return home. We drove through Pensacola, stopped to swim once or twice at Florida Panhandle beaches, reached Interstate 75, and turned north toward Atlanta. Upon entering the capital city of Georgia, we searched for an economical place to stay. We had one more one hundred dollar Traveler Cheque and about $30.00 in folding money.

A Day's Inn beckoned us for $19.88 for one night. It was next to the Atlanta Airport. That constituted one good point and one bad point. All of us went outside the motel and watched the multitude of giant jet airplanes. More airplanes took off and landed in one hour than in a whole day at the Charleston, West Virginia airport. The drawback was that this entrance and egress into Hartsfield continued late into the night and began early in the predawn.

Night landings were not bad at first because we went to see the Atlanta Braves play baseball. I had called the ticket office, on the off chance that we could get seats. When I asked if seats were available for the ball game that night, the agent actually laughed. Not a gentle snicker, but a full-blown side-splitter. Her reaction explained itself when the seven of us arrived at the ball field. We were able to park within a hundred feet of the stadium. That had never happened when we went to see the Cincinnati Reds play. Our seats were great. Seven places just behind the box seats. There were no more than 2,000 people in the entire stadium. The Atlanta Braves were deeply ensconced in their pre-glory days. They stunk.

The next morning, we entered the last leg of our Odyssey. I thought, *Sixty dollars should be just enough to get home.* Twenty-five dollars filled the large gas tank leaving thirty-five to reach Charleston. We ate breakfast for $11.00 and left the city of Scarlet O'Hara with the princely sum of 24 one-dollar bills and some uncounted change. We reached Chattanooga at noon with growls emitting from our collective stomachs, especially the five in the rear of the station wagon. I had erred in my calculations. We had enough to fill the fuel tank once more but did not have enough to fill our stomachs.

We held a family council. "Who had any money?" Pennies, nickels, dimes, quarters, fifty cent pieces. Anything. Pockets emptied, we came up with $1.27. The kids scoured the back of the station wagon and found thirty-one cents. The glove compartment held two quarters. That was it. We had a grand total of $2.08 for food. This had to take us the remaining seven hours.

Then we saw it. North of Chattanooga appeared, not a desert mirage, but a Burger Boy Fooderama. Hamburgers were a dime each at this fine establishment better known as BBF. We were saved! We bought 14 hamburgers and two large drinks. Duncan Hines, the restaurant gourmet, had never eaten better.

Our home welcomed us at 7:00 that evening. I ran up the 25 steps, unlocked the door, took four silver dollars from Patty's collection, ran back down the steps, and headed for a place to eat.

You guessed it. BBF.

Southern Smiles and Tears

Chapter 47
Redcoat Mary

It was s simple note. A girl in my first period class had handed me a folded sheet of paper that had been torn from a spiral notebook.

I unfolded the page and felt a smile cross my face as I read the contents.

Mr Bice,
I am doing pritty good in high school. Sarah and me are still friends but some other peeple like me. How are you? Do you remember me? I hope you do. I still remember the constitusion.
Redcoat Mary

Mary had been in my social studies classes at Hayes Junior High School for her three years there. She was part of a special program for students who progressed together through the three years of junior high school. Some had emotional problems, some lacked learning skills, and others simply had been dealt a bad hand in

Southern Smiles and Tears

family life. All were classified as having behavioral problems.

Ruth Hill, the school counselor, had asked Jack Wymer and me to come to her office at the end of the 1975 school year.

"I want to try something new with some of our incoming students who have been classified as problems. Most of them have been in special education in elementary school. I think you two can play a part in this program. It is well known that you both are strict and expect students to achieve, not only to their abilities, but to exceed them. What I would like to try is to have the students continue in their reading program but have them take classes from teachers such as you two. You will have no more than 15 students in this group. My plan is to have them come to you Jack for earth science and David for geography in the seventh grade. Because the two subjects are closely related it should help them understand better."

Ruth went on explaining that she believed that it would help these students to be better accepted and have them better prepared for high school. At the end of the year, the three of us would evaluate what had happened. If it were successful, Ruth would add other core subjects to the program. The most different aspect of the program was that the students would stay with us for all three years of junior high unless the three of us agreed that a particular student would be better off if moved into a regular program.

Jack and I were not only to teach these students the course content, but life skills. When teaching geography, I was to add a component of how to read a road map. Jack was to incorporate landscaping and gardening into his science class. We even got into the cost of planning trips and how to maintain a checking account.

Mary and her friend Sarah were part of this group. Thin with unkempt hair and non-stylish clothes Mary came into my class and headed for the back row. Mary would not speak out loud in class. Everything she said was through Sarah. Asked a question, Mary would either write a note or whisper to Sarah, who in turn would give the answer. On a written exam, Mary's answers often were illegible and unintelligible. Many were the times, I allowed Mary to tell Sarah her answers, and Sarah performed her duty as Mary's secretary.

This tandem worked together through seventh grade geography, eighth grade West Virginia History, and the first nine weeks of ninth grade American History.

Then an event occurred, which has stayed with me for almost 30 years.

Our class was studying the Battle of Bunker Hill. I divided the class into two parts. One-half of the students were to be American

Southern Smiles and Tears

rebels defending the hill. The other half was to be British soldiers walking up the hill in the attempt to take it from the Americans. The groups were to be 100 yards apart at the beginning of the battle. Each group was to write down what they believed the soldiers were thinking as the British drew closer. They were to write down seven thoughts from each point of view. Then the groups would alternate reading thoughts. Volunteers would read aloud. Mary and Sarah were to be British Redcoats.

The exercise went beyond my wildest expectations. Thoughts of sweethearts back home, fear of death, and of becoming a hero permeated the readings.

It all paled in significance when a low voice read, "I don't hate nobody." Mary had spoken aloud, and my eyes had misted. Later, I found out that Mary had not only spoken those words, but the words were her own.

About a month later, we were studying the Constitution. I offered 100 extra points to each student who would memorize the Preamble to the Constitution and recite it in front of the class. Each student was allowed to have another student serve as a coach. The coach was allowed to help the person reciting five times during the recitation. Should more help be needed, five points would be deducted for each additional prod.

Sarah was Mary's coach, and Mary was Sarah's coach.

Fourteen students recited on Monday and Tuesday. Sarah recited without help. Mary gave no indication of standing before the class and speaking. I was disappointed but not surprised. Wednesday and Thursday, I moved on to new material.

Class had just begun on Friday morning when Sarah raised her hand.

"Mr. Bice. Is it too late for Mary to say the Constitution?"

Taken aback for a moment, I responded, "Not if she wants to."

In perhaps the longest journey in her life, Mary slowly walked to the front of the room holding firmly onto Sarah's hand. Sarah pulled her hand free and sat in the front row. Mary turned sideways to the class and began.

"We the people of the...."

She completed her performance, grabbed Sarah's hand, and rushed to the back of the room. A burst of applause from her classmates and teacher followed her.

That morning was the high point in my teaching career. Until I unfolded a note from a young lady signed:

Redcoat Mary

Southern Smiles and Tears

Chapter 48
Sweet Alice Moore

It started quite simply.

Alice Moore, the wife of a Church of Christ minister, had run for and been elected to the Kanawha County Board of Education. Petite, dark-haired, with classical 1940's and 1950's movie star beauty; she was loved by conservatives and hated by liberals. The latter affixed the nickname of "Sweet" to be in a sense of derision. It became honorable, at least to me.

Sweet Alice Moore was just that as she took her seat on the board. Then the liberals began to think of other names to call her. The change occurred the evening of April 11, 1974. Sweet Alice had the audacity to question the contents of the recently adopted Language-Arts textbooks. To that date, board members had rubber-stamped recommendations of textbooks made by various committees, usually without dissenting votes. Sweet Alice upset everything. She read some of the books and calmly reported them to be anti-American, anti-religious, and discriminatory. That was the last calm moment in Kanawha County Schools for the next six months.

Until Alice awakened the people of the county, school board meetings maybe had an attendance of about 20 people at the monthly conclaves. An estimated 1,000 citizens attended the June 27, 1974 meeting. The room meant to hold 50 filled early, and the crowd spilled out into the halls, spread like water across the lawn, and onto Elizabeth Street in Charleston. Supporters of Sweet Alice and those supporting the textbook committee testified for over three hours. Board members, in shock because in the preceding five years they had not been confronted by a total of 1,000 people, tried to compromise. They voted three to two to adopt the books but agreed to delete eight supplemental reading books, deemed most objectionable.

Whew!

That sound of relief lasted only one month. The dog days of August saw the protest escalate. The anti-textbook group, Christian American Parents, began to picket and boycott a local discount chain with stores in a three-state area. Russell Isaacs, one of the three board members to vote in favor of the textbooks, was the owner of Heck's, Inc. Some thought the boycott unfair because Isaacs was performing a civic duty by serving on the school board while also chairman of Heck's. Others endorsed and supported this American expression of dissatisfaction.

As August drew to a close, a new protest group formed. The Concerned Citizens decided to expand the boycott of Hecks' to the schools until the Language-Arts textbooks were totally removed from classrooms. September 3, 1974 scared the bejabbers out of the educational establishment. Almost 12,000 of the counties 45,000 students did not report for school the first day of the new school year. Now, some may think the concern by educators was over the harm done to students' education.

Not quite.

The State of West Virginia allocated funds to the counties based on the Average Daily Attendance, or ADA, of students. This portended a financial disaster for Kanawha County Schools. Before the school board could react to the absenteeism, 3,500 coal miners went on strike in support of the school boycott. Financial concerns escalated. Coal was the linchpin of eastern Kanawha County's economy.

The power of government was unleashed upon the protesters. Injunctions and restraining orders flew from the courts on

Southern Smiles and Tears

September 5. School protesters and miners were enjoined from disrupting the schools and mines. At least that is what supposedly was to have happened. United States Marshals did arrest two women for protesting on September 10, but the protesters reacted by shutting down the countywide bus system. This left as many as 11,000 people trying to find a way to work.

Governor Arch Moore, later disgraced and sent to federal prison, called for calmer heads to prevail and seek some form of compromise. In a Keystone Cops atmosphere, law enforcement agencies argued over whom was in charge of keeping the peace. Jurisdiction and manpower disputes abounded. Many of the officers were neighbors and friends of the protesters, and they surely did not want to be perceived as taking sides.

The board tried a compromise by appointing a citizens committee to review the disputed textbooks. The compromise included removing the books from classroom, beginning September 12, pending the review. The board canceled classes and all extracurricular activities. The school board's public relations director told me that the hope was that the absence of football would bring the protesters to their senses. School was one thing, football was another. Besides, the all-important Kanawha Valley Majorette Festival was included in the cancellation. How would anyone survive without the opportunity to see the skimpily clad young ladies strut their stuff at Laidley Field?

On the same day of the compromise, a trucking company employee shot at protesters, slightly wounding one. He was severely beaten for his marksmanship. School closures spread to the mining counties of Boone and Fayette. Then the pickets at schools, mines, and some chemical plants in Kanawha County began to dissipate over the next few days, allowing the schools to reopen.

Hopes of peace surfaced, only to be severely squelched.

Several ministers took up the torch of leadership. Pastors Ezra Graley, Marvin Horan, Avis Hill, and Charles Quigley, leaders of fundamentalist churches, opposed the textbooks. Horan and Hill urged an end to the boycotts, but many thought that to be disingenuous. The Reverend James Lewis, an Episcopalian priest led the anti-boycott forces. September 17 saw a lawsuit in federal courts to prevent the use of the books. Then 11 men, including Graley, were arrested for contempt of court. Immediately, the picketing at the mines increased. Anti-textbook rallies were held at Watt Powell Park, the Charleston minor league baseball park.

The protesters on several occasions threw tacks in school driveways to deter teachers from going to work. Many teachers took the

Southern Smiles and Tears

hint and stayed home. I was one of the few who went to work. There were only seven teachers at Hayes Jr. High one day. Over 20 were not. On September 26, I received a telephone call from Sweet Alice. The night before the board had voted to establish a new textbook selection committee to review more than 300 books being used in Kanawha County.

"Mr. Bice, this is Alice Moore. Do you know who I am?"

That had to be redundant, but I answered anyhow.

"Yes, ma'am."

"The board voted last night to have a committee review all the textbooks."

"Yes, ma'am. I read about it in the *Gazette* this morning."

"Would you answer a question for me?"

"If I can."

"Why did you go to school when many teachers did not?"

I do not know what question I had expected, but that was not it. I surely paused before responding.

"Ma'am, I am a teacher under contract to teach and believe to do otherwise demeans me and my profession."

"I thought so, from everything I have heard about you."

I didn't know she knew I existed, as I was one of 1,500 county teachers.

"You resigned as president of the county teacher's association. Why?"

I explained to her that when I had attended some workshops given by national representatives of the National Education Association, I realized that the formerly professional association was turning toward unionism. I explained to her that I was a member of Food Store Employee's Union and proud of it, but that I was a professional teacher.

"Thank you for being candid. I would like to ask you a favor. Would you serve as my appointee to the review committee?"

I agreed, but establishing the committee did not stop the protests. Instead they turned violent. On October 6, over 3,000 protesters rallied urging a massive boycott. Pastors Graley and Hill, along with 17 others were arrested for violating a court order. Cabin Creek, the birthplace of basketball great Jerry West, was the sight of an elementary school being dynamited. Midway Elementary School on Campbell's Creek was firebombed.

In the midst of this increased violence, Albert Anson resigned as School Board President. David Anson, his son, had been a classmate of mine at St. Albans High School. I vaguely knew Mr. Anson. He was a quiet professional truly interested in education. His life had been threatened, but he resigned to protect his family, not himself. He also hoped his resignation would appease the protesters.

It did not.

Things worsened during October, November, and December. Several more schools were firebombed, shots were fired at school buses, another school was dynamited, and school administrators were assaulted. Hill and Horan went to Washington, DC in an attempt to get President Ford to intervene in the situation. Six members of the new review committee even resigned to form an ad hoc committee.

Ultimately, the protesters ran out of steam. The end to the protest came with the Reverend Horan and five others being indicted by a federal grand jury for conspiring to dynamite two elementary schools. Horan was later sentenced to three years in a federal prison.

Through it all, Alice Moore maintained her dignity. Many, especially *Charleston Gazette* columnist, L.T. Anderson, lampooned her. In 1994, years after she had moved to Columbus, Ohio, Anderson wrote a satirical column in *The Charleston Daily Mail* about Sweet Alice.

Her stand did influence me. I read over 100 textbooks, many out of my field. It became my first serious look into how textbooks made the trek from authors to classrooms. The route is a weaving one fraught with watering down to reach the lowest common denominator. Sweet Alice gave me courage to write my first textbook and endure the endless bureaucratic hoops one must go through to have a textbook allowed into classrooms.

I found out many things.

State textbook administrators are wined and dined by huge textbook corporations. Trips to the Mardi Gras, cruises on the Tennessee River in Nashville, water rafting in Idaho, free banquets, and shortened meetings to correspond with tee times are all part of the textbook approval system. One Texas textbook administrator at an annual meeting on Kiowa Island, Georgia had the temerity to suggest that his colleagues should meet in less auspicious surroundings. A South Carolina colleague rapidly countered with, "We work hard. Maybe you would like to meet in a Motel 6." Textbook houses even have staffs, not individual authors, who write books with the main goal to get though the adoption process, rather than to educate.

I believe Sweet Alice knew something was wrong, she just did not know the depth of the problem. The Charleston newspaper spent their ink on the result of the Great Textbook War Sweet Alice start-

Southern Smiles and Tears

ed, and not the root cause.
 Alice Moore was an easy target, textbook companies were not.

Southern Smiles and Tears

Chapter 49
A Career Change

I had always wanted to teach.

That desire lasted 17 years and ended abruptly. Two things caused me to leave teaching.

The school intercom and a book.

The school intercom is the bane of teachers. Its purpose is to inform. Its employ is to annoy. Administrators must get lonely in their offices. That or fear that if they do not broadcast regularly, rumors will begin that they do not exist. The intercom has also been used to surreptitiously listen in on teachers, though most administrators deny that usage.

I do confess that good things have happened due to the installation of school intercoms. I can remember in high school, when the World Series was still important to many people, listening to baseball games. That was truly an educational experience. It was through the intercom I learned of Kennedy's death. A teacher in

Southern Smiles and Tears

Maplesville, Alabama told me that, although irritating, the two-way ability of the intercom does allow him to immediately contact the office in the event of an emergency. In this day of non-existent discipline that could save a life.

Especially, that of the teacher.

During the seven years I taught at Hayes Junior High School, there was a vice-principal who loved the intercom. The memory of his, "Lissenup," to introduce a communication from on high still grates on my nerves. My least favorite, "Lissenup," helped me in making a decision to leave teaching and further a writing career.

"Lissenup! At the beginning of next period, I'm going to make an important announcement. I want everyone to pay attention."

An announcement of a forthcoming announcement. This must really be important!

Foolish me!

The bell rang, dismissing the interrupted class. What followed can be traced to a fault I had about teaching. It was my fervent belief that the good people of Kanawha County paid me $30.00 per teaching hour in the expectation that I would do just that. Teach. I required that students be in their seats and that I began speaking as soon as the tardy bell finished ringing.

At the beginning of the period of the forthcoming announcement, I started talking about the rigors pioneers encountered in the 1700's Appalachian Mountains. A full five minutes after the tardy bell the voice of Edward R. Murrow of the intercom came though the wires.

"Lissenup! Before you begin classes I want you to tell you something."

Before I begin class. What does he think I've been doing for five minutes?

"Tomorrow at noon the majorettes will be having a bake sale. Be sure and bring your money to help the young ladies out."

I took my penknife out of my pocket and cut the intercom wire. The students cheered.

A parent-teacher conference was the other event that finalized my decision to leave the teaching field. I had written my first textbook, *A Panorama of West Virginia*, in 1977. School systems throughout the state, in 1978, had adopted the book as the standard text for West Virginia History classes for the next five years. I now was not only teaching West Virginia History, I was using a book I had written.

That was not a problem until the parents of a student, who was not progressing to their expectations, came to their allotted 15-

minute first quarter conference with me. To make it worse, they brought the young man with them.

We got through the niceties of introductions without serious injuries, except to the psyche of the student. The father was a chemical engineer at Union Carbide. The mother taught school at St. Albans High School. The young male was busy trying to figure out why girls had suddenly become interesting and what was wrong with his voice.

"We have told Harold that there is no excuse for him to have made just a 'C' in this subject."

I pondered for a few moments about how to defend Harold, I knew him as Harry, in his parent's eyes.

"Well, it is just the first nine-weeks. Harold has plenty of time to improve."

"That is unacceptable to us?"

"I don't have a problem with him. He listens, asks question, and causes absolutely zero problems."

"He will never be accepted into a good college with that type grade. Besides, we told him that you wrote the book. There is no reason not to learn from the author."

That was the moment I knew I could no longer teach. The teacher should never be an obstacle to the students. Surely, if this pair thought that my being an author somehow imputed ability and interest to their child, other parents harbored the same expectations.

That was unfair to Harry, and all the other Harry's I would encounter should I remain. I was well aware that I only had to teach three more years to lock in my retirement with the West Virginia Retirement System.

The next morning I walked into the principal's office and told him that I was not going to return the next year. He did not believe me. The following May he talked to me about the classes I was scheduled to teach in the fall.

"Randy, I am leaving teaching. I will miss the students, but it is time for me to go."

There have been times when nostalgia for teaching overcomes me. Then I hear those fateful words.

"Lissenup!"

> # Part Four
> # 1979-2003

Southern Smiles and Tears

Southern Smiles and Tears

Chapter 50
An Angel on My Shoulder

I had written a textbook but did not have the foggiest idea about the printing process. My idea was to have a textbook that was appealing to eighth grade West Virginia History students, not only in content but also in format and color.

The two West Virginia History books available in 1977, for eighth graders were scaled down college textbooks devoid of color photographs. *How could that be in a state filled with such scenic beauty?*

Simple, I was soon to find out. Color printing costs money. Color in textbooks required the print runs be in large quantities to be cost effective. West Virginia, with a maximum of 60,000 students in the eighth grade at that time, did not appear to be a sufficient market to justify color for books. Almost every county board of education would have to approve and purchase the same textbook for a publisher to risk a West Virginia History textbook, which was equivalent to those in the national market.

I did not know that when I set about writing and publishing my first textbook. In deference to Dr. Canady, ignorance sometimes may have a good result. If I had known the cost beforehand, I may have decided to allow my dream to write a textbook remain just that.

Not a typist, I hand wrote the entire book and paid to have it typed. Then my sister Caroline, along with her daughter Tina, reviewed the manuscript and made it reading level appropriate. It was ready to become a textbook. Then money reared its ugly head.

Previous to the textbook, I had written and self-published a children's book, *The Pringle Tree*, about pre-revolution western Virginia. Harless Printing, a small independent company, had typeset and printed it before sending the pages to Cincinnati, Ohio to be hard bound. He had given me a price and handled all of the details for me.

"Mr. Harless, I have a textbook I would like you to print for me."

"A textbook?"

"Yes, and I want it to have color pictures in it."

"How many pages?"

"I guess about 320."

"What size?"

"I want it to be eight inches by ten inches."

"I can't print a book that big. My presses are too small." He paused and continued, "You will have to go somewhere like Kingsport Press."

"Where's that?"

"Kingsport, Tennessee. Let me get hold of a man I know down there and have him call you."

Thus, I came to know Darrell Jessie, a salesman for Kingsport Press. Later I was to find out that the company he represented was one of the largest printers of books in the country.

Once again, ignorance won out. Here I was a teacher in West Virginia, one of the smallest textbook markets in the United States, about to engage in a conversation with one of the best salesmen of one of the largest printers in the country. Mr. Jessie, as I then addressed him, telephoned our house about a week later. He was on his way to make sales calls in Pennsylvania but would stop and talk with me on his way back through West Virginia on Friday. I gave him directions to Hayes Junior High School and told him the time I would have my preparation period.

I am not sure what Mr. Jessie's thoughts were that Friday afternoon as I showed him my manuscript, but helpful he was. I suspect

he was astounded by my lack of knowledge about printing books.
"How many half-tones and four-colors do you have?"
"What?"
"Half-tones and four colors?"
Oh, no! This is almost the same as when the Prichard Baptist preacher gave me two chances at a correct answer for something I had no idea about.

Probably saved by the complete look of befuddlement on my face, Mr. Jessie rephrased the question.

"You know, how many black and white and color pictures?"

Here was a completely new language. Printer's talk. Over the next few years, I would become more aware of the phenomenon of "profession specific vocabulary." Words used within specific professions can be almost a foreign language to outsiders. Printers speak not only as above but with terms and phrases such as, "signatures", "perfect bound", "saddle-stitched", "case bound", "duotone", and others that are completely comprehensible to them. However, non-printing industry people, such as I was at that time, can be totally confused by the usage. There is a deeper problem than just not understanding. Knowledge is power. Lack of knowledge can be costly. Not knowing the proper terms, in which to discuss printing, new customers will often be overcharged by not asking the correct questions to find out the "hidden" charges.

Darrell Jessie, in his thirties, dark wavy hair, and impeccably dressed, switched languages for me. He began to speak with me and not to me.

"Black and white photographs have to be made into shades of dots in order to print and need one negative. Color photographs need four negatives to print. That is why they cost more."

He went on to explain several other things during our forty-five minute conversation. It became apparent to both of us that I needed much more schooling in printing before proceeding with my book. Darrell, he had requested I change my manner of addressing him, decided to get a motel in Charleston. He invited me to eat supper with him and further discuss printing.

I found out that it would cost over $30,000.00 to print the 500 books needed "to give" to school systems for evaluation. Darrell explained that textbooks had to be printed and bound to higher specifications than other books. It would also be necessary to post a bond with the State of West Virginia. Once the book was approved by the board, the bond would be security for the state that we would print the large number of needed books if counties wanted them.

Southern Smiles and Tears

Boy, was I in over my head.

Darrell, who had perused the manuscript, then gave me encouragement, for which I will always be grateful.

"We print textbooks for almost every large company. This book is as good as most of them."

He then told me, that if I had not contacted him as the possible printer of the book, he would invest in it. He explained it would not be ethical of him to do so at that point. Then he solved my money problem.

"You already have a small company. Use it to raise funds through investors."

I had told him, earlier in the day, about "Jalamap". When I had begun writing and publishing a monthly current event newspaper at Harless Printing for West Virginia History classes, a name was needed for our company. Penny, our older daughter came up with a name that reflected that everyone in the family helped in folding and mailing the paper each month.

Penny took the first letter of the middle name of each family member in order of age and created an acronym. The "J" in Patty Jo, the "A" in David Allen, the "L" in Penny Lynn, the "A" in Cheryl Ann, the "M" in Daniel Mark, the "A" in Jeffrey Alan, and the "P" in Richard Paul came to be the name of the company, which produced *A Panorama of West Virginia*. That book became the best selling textbook for eighth graders in the history of the state. It remained so, with revisions, for 15 years. The format of the book served as the model for textbooks in Florida, Georgia, Idaho, Oklahoma, and Tennessee.

I was to work with Darrell on books for several years. The last time I saw him was early one Monday morning. West Virginia had instituted a new fourth grade West Virginia Studies course, but had only given a year for textbook companies to have books ready for presentation to the state board of education to be evaluated. I had written the book in a few months. Then everyone in our small company, we now had five people working for us, jumped in to help get the book to press. We had a "drop-dead" date and time to get the book to Kingsport Press in order to have a printed book to present to the textbook reviewers. We all worked long hours the week before the Monday deadline but did not have the book ready. Everyone volunteered to work the weekend to finish the book. Meals were brought in and people took naps in chairs or on the floor. No one left from Friday morning at 8:00 A.M. until Monday morning at 4:00 A.M.

Manuscript edited and proofed with photos identified, I showered, shaved, changed clothes, and tore off for Kingsport, Tennessee at five o'clock. Two hundred fifty miles later, right before the nine o'clock deadline, I pulled up to the security gate of the press to see a pacing Darrell Jessie.

I was seven minutes early for the deadline!

Darrell called me later that year to inform me that he had terminal cancer. That was a shock, but it was not the main reason he had called.

Unbelievably, Darrell wanted to thank me.

"David, I often told people at the press that when I met you there must have been an angel on my shoulder that told me that something good was going to come from our time together. I not only enjoyed our friendship but made my best commissions from your books."

I let him know that without his guidance my writing and publishing career may have died in the womb of my mind. We talked a few more minutes, said our good byes, and disconnected.

It was our final goodbye.

Southern Smiles and Tears

Chapter 51
Boston Pops

Revenue from my first textbook expanded our family's horizons. We were able to travel more and not just by station wagon.

There was to be a National Council of Social Studies Convention and Exhibit in Boston, Massachusetts over the Thanksgiving weekend. This was two years after *A Panorama of West Virginia* became the textbook to be used in 54 of West Virginia's 55 counties. I asked our three boys, Penny was working and Cheryl was in college, if they would like to miss school the three days before the Thanksgiving school break and fly to Boston.

Stupid question.

We packed on Friday night in preparation for our short drive to Kanawha County Airport and an awaiting jet plane on Saturday morning. We flew to Pittsburgh, Pennsylvania, changed planes, and landed in Boston that afternoon. The convention was to be downtown at the Sheraton Hotel, and we had made our reserva-

Southern Smiles and Tears

tions to stay there. We now had four days to explore Boston before going to the exhibit hall to try to impress educators with our book.

The weather could not have been more cooperative. We explored downtown, walked the commons, visited Paul Revere's house, went to the harbor to see "Old Ironsides", and trekked to the site of the Battle of Bunker Hill. The diminutive size of all was a surprise. Large in our history and textbooks, they each did not match the pictures we held in our minds. Bunker, correctly Breed's, Hill was the shocker for five tourists from "The Mountain State" of West Virginia. It hardly qualified as a knoll.

We spent one complete day and evening at Harvard University and its environs. All three boys enjoyed that day, but I believe it changed Danny. He loved the campus and smell of education. The University Bookstore was his Nirvana. He probably would have been content to sequester himself there for our remaining Boston days. Danny came away with intentions of attending Harvard. Never to achieve that goal, he later did become a graduate of The University of Chicago, the "Harvard" of the Midwest.

Boston offered restaurants and food previously unknown to us in Charleston, West Virginia. A meal at Legal Seafood set the future standard for my judging meal quality at restaurants. The free Thanksgiving dinner for 2,000 people, provided by the Scholastic Company in the Sheraton banquet room, ensured that I would never eat a non-home cooked Thanksgiving dinner again. One particular item though was an embarrassment to me and a disappointment to the boys. A frappé! Just as we exited Harvard's hallowed grounds, we passed an ice cream store with a sign having that intriguing word painted in its window. None of us had any idea what a " frappé" might be.

I went up to the young man at the window to ask, ""What is a frappé?" but paused a moment for culture shock. He had two earrings. He not only had them, they were actually attached to his ears. I knew he wasn't from West Virginia. I was not totally unaware of the changing accessories used by young males, but this was my first time to see ear rings on one of my own gender. What is common in the year 2003, gave me pause that day.

Composing myself, I asked, "What exactly is a frappé"

I think he realized I wasn't from Boston.

"What?"

"I think I want to have one, but what is a frappé"

I would not say he thought I was stupid, but his facial expression appeared to place me at a low I.Q. and an even lower cultural range. In his eyes I should have been barefoot and chewing on a

Southern Smiles and Tears

straw. He did, though, attempt to answer me in his John F. Kennedy accent

"Well, you put ice cream in a cup, add flavoring and milk, and stir them together."

Frappé, my eye! You're talking about a milkshake.

I ordered five chocolate milkshakes but paid the frappé price.

Forever curious about words, on Thursday I went over to the Houghton Mifflin Company exhibit booth. I wanted a dictionary. That company published *The American Heritage Dictionary*, and it would give me the meaning of the word "frappé" for my own edification.

Ha! That milkshake wasn't a frappé.

You had to read down to the third usage of that word to find it associated with being a milkshake. First, it was a sherbert-like appetizer or dessert. Second, it was a beverage with liqueur poured over shaved ice. The word was the past participle of the French *frapper* meaning to chill.

I ought to go back and let him know that he's selling good old American milkshakes.

I did not go back, however, because I wasn't quite sure how to argue with a male wearing earrings without snickering.

The highlight of the whole trip occurred on Saturday night before we were to fly home. The five of us were taking an evening stroll when we passed a ticket window. The signboard beside the window announced the Boston Pops Orchestra was performing that night. Danny and Jeffrey begged me to see if we could go to the performance. I went to the window and asked if five seats were available. There were, but I did not have enough cash on me. For some reason, I had left my credit card back at the hotel in my suit. The lady at the window told me that the performance would begin in 20 minutes. If we wanted to see the orchestra perform, we would have to be in our seats before then.

I took off running for the hotel, which was several blocks away from the concert hall. I caught the elevator, opened our room door, grabbed my credit card, reversed my field, and walked up to the ticket window panting for breath. We were able to get five seats, but they were not together. Patty, Ricky, and I sat in the balcony on the left side, while Danny and Jeffrey had balcony seats facing the orchestra. It was an unforgettable experience.

As idyllic as life could have become for our family, it was not to be. A few years after our return from Boston, Patty and I began to view life differently. We had celebrated our 25th wedding anniversary when our marriage began to fall apart. Penny was working for

Southern Smiles and Tears

a law firm in Charleston; Cheryl was studying photography in Houston; Texas; Danny was at Bryan College in Tennessee; Jeffrey was attending Wheaton University in Illinois; Ricky was in high school; and Patty and I were arguing.

I am positive our divorce caused trauma to our five children. I regret that.

Southern Smiles and Tears

Chapter 52
Peanut Butter and Jelly

Prentice-Hall, a well-established textbook company, had plucked a honey-blond, maybe natural maybe not, extremely winsome lass out of a classroom to be a textbook representative. Her first assignment, in the early 1980's, was to travel across Tennessee presenting the company's textbooks to social studies textbook review committees.

The Tennessee Department of Education, in an effort to make it efficient for every committee to meet all the textbook representatives, had organized a caravan. Meetings were to begin in western Tennessee in Memphis and move eastward culminating in Bristol. The representatives provided their own transportation but had to be at a new location each day Monday through Friday over a three-week period. Even with discord on the home front, I did not look forward to being away from home for that long.

Many of us stayed in the same motels and would eat breakfast

Southern Smiles and Tears

and supper together for three weeks. The Prentice-Hall representative was the only female in the caravan. She also was the only person in the group on the sunny side of 30. Most of us had even seen the sun set on 40 revolutions of the earth, and a couple would never see 60 years of age again. The age factor did not stop some of the representatives from taking Miss Prentice-Hall out to eat in the evening. This is not to infer any improprieties; most of the men simply wanted company, and their employers generally allowed them excellent expense accounts. Given a choice between a bland motel room with a television and an evening with a young lady at a fine restaurant, several men chose the latter.

I seem to remember her as having come from Mississippi and am certain that she had not traveled far and wide as a teacher. She had never been to Nashville, and as the gods of entertainment would have it, the caravan ended there on a Friday. That night she was escorted to the Opry Hotel to eat and the next night was entertained with a visit to the Grand Ole Opry. The accountants must have been thrilled with this new employee. Three weeks on the road and hardly a dollar to be turned in for meals.

The beginning of the second week we zigged south and zagged north at the end of the week. We completed the week with meetings in Knoxville. By this time many of the group were beginning to wonder exactly which town, city, or county was receiving our well-honed presentations. Our only constant was the morning bet as to whom Miss P-H, as we now referred to her out of earshot, would grace with her presence that night.

That week our thoughts were jerked to something else. Two murderers, at Brushy Mountain Prison in Morgan County to the northwest of Knoxville, had escaped. Television reports and rumors had them headed eastward. The same direction as our weary band was to resume beginning Monday. I don't remember whether we were more afraid of being murdered by the escaped killers that weekend or more ecstatic that our journey would end Friday so we could travel to our own beds on Saturday.

Tuesday morning the former prevailed. The motel we had all checked into the previous evening had been robbed at gun point during the night. You probably can guess who held the guns. Two escaped convicts. Not a soul that morning at breakfast could have cared less if Clint Eastwood had shown up to ask Miss P-H out to eat that evening. It would have been nice, however, if he had appeared the night before to snarl, "Make my day!"

Without Clint to protect us, we did caravan in the true since of the word to our meetings the next two days. Twenty some cars hud-

203

Southern Smiles and Tears

dled together with none trying to arrive at the next destination earlier than anyone else. Tennessee State Trooper cars were a ubiquitous blessing along our route.

The others may have slept well Tuesday night, but I did not. Coffee became my staple food Wednesday, which may have helped me to toss and turn for my eight hours on the Serta mattress. Thursday night was much better. When we arrived at the Bristol Holiday Inn on I-81, the news brought relief. The murderers had been captured. Hallelujah! Not only did we have just one more day of meetings, our risk of being murdered had been substantially lowered.

The Friday night meal was upbeat. A couple of the representatives, who lived in Tennessee, left for home immediately after their last presentation that afternoon. The remnant met at six o'clock to eat in the motel restaurant. Almost immediately, one of the Don Juan's told Miss P-H he had been happy to make her acquaintance and would be honored to buy her meal that final evening in Tennessee.

"Will you buy me whatever I want to eat?

Taken slightly aback, he responded with, "Of course!" What did he care. Someone in Boston, Massachusetts would be paying for his largesse.

The waiter arrived at our table, gave out menus, and returned a few minutes for our orders. "Ma'am, what would you like this evening? We have a wonderful New York steak."

Miss P-H opened her mouth, spoke, and shocked all of her colleagues. "These gentlemen have taken me to eat at some great places this past three weeks," she paused here as she reverted to her Mississippi roots, " but could you fix me a peanut butter and jelly sandwich with a glass of milk."

The look on the face of the representative, who had offered to pay, was worth the travail of the previous weeks.

The waiter responded with, "I think so, but let me ask the chef."

He did not wait to take the rest of our orders, but turned and headed for the kitchen. Just as the waiter reached the double doors, a feminine voice sounded.

"On toast!"

Chapter 53
"Swave and Deboner"

Some of my mother's sophistication may have rubbed off on me, but not all. That was probably apparent to others, but it did not become clear to me until one evening as I sat alone eating my meal at Pitty Pat's Porch in Atlanta, Georgia. Expensive for my budget, I had chosen the restaurant to reward myself for what I considered a productive meeting with the Georgia State Department of Education that afternoon.

I had asked the taxi driver on my way back to the hotel if he knew a good place to eat. He asked if I knew about Pitty Pat's Porch. Answering him in the negative, he told me that it was an experience I needed to enjoy before leaving Atlanta.

I rocked in the lobby chairs and enjoyed the hors d'oeuvres for 45 minutes while waiting on a table to become empty for me. Once seated, I decided to partake of a new treat before my main meal. I had long enjoyed deep fried shrimp, but the menu specified, "Boiled

Southern Smiles and Tears

Shrimp." A platter full of pink half-crescents in front of me, I picked one up by the tail and dipped it in a seafood sauce that was laced with just the right proportion of horseradish.

Umm! This is delicious. Just a little crunchy though.

For the next fifteen minutes, I properly picked up a shrimp, dipped it, and delighted in the complementing flavors of tangy sauce and cool seafood.

They must not have boiled them enough.

Until that point, I had eaten paying scant attention to my fellow diners. Then, partially satiated, I leaned back in my chair and surveyed the room. Several people were consuming boiled shrimp as an appetizer. Something was curious. Each person had a bowl beside the platter of shrimp. I had such a bowl but thought it to be for my salad, which was I was going to get after my shrimp. The only thing was that each of the bowls on the other tables had translucent material attached to what appeared to shrimp tails.

Deciding to investigate this phenomenon, I arose with my purported salad bowl in hand and strolled over to the immense salad bar. Curiouser and curiouser. There was an ample supply of salad plates at the bar. I glanced to the left. I glanced to the right.

Oh, no!

Each person, with boiled shrimp, carefully detached the shells from the shrimp, discarded the translucent outside covering in the provided bowl, dipped the denuded shrimp, and devoured the delicacy.

How could I be so stupid?

I returned to my table trying to appear invisible.

Everybody here must be laughing at me.

I had six shrimp left. With the aplomb of a gourmand, I carefully extracted the shrimp from their encasements. I dropped each shell in the bowl from ample enough height that any of those seated nearby could tell that I knew exactly how to eat boiled shrimp. Surprisingly, these did not taste much different from those previously consumed. They were just quite a bit more tender.

I concluded that night, when back in my hotel room, that I had a great deal to learn about life outside of my former restricted awareness of life from inside a classroom. I dressed well in suits and ties but was far from "suave and debonair." I had already learned that it was one thing to receive "money from heaven" that the government sent me for teaching and trying to maintain a cash flow in one's own company. Now I had to learn proper etiquette. Whenever I found myself in a new circumstance, I would observe those around me for pointers about presenting myself properly. I

Southern Smiles and Tears

believed, with extensive travel and association with refined people, over the years that I had reached a point of acceptable sophistication.

Maybe not as "swave and deboner" as I thought I had become.

A few years later, I was at dinner with a new sales representative and two other guests. The young sales representative had not traveled much outside of West Virginia. He was a fast food aficionado and was not too pleased about having to wear a tie to a restaurant. Boots Randolph's place on Printers Alley in Nashville wasn't exactly exclusive, but it was the nicest place this salesman had ever eaten.

Aware of his discomfort, I told him, "Just watch me and do exactly what I do."

This worked fine until the meal was coming to an end and the stage was being prepared for Boots Randolph to perform. I enjoy a cup of coffee at the end of a meal and had ordered one. The waitress brought my coffee and cream before proceeding to clean the table prior to the performance. I had whitened my coffee and was reaching with my spoon toward the sugar bowl, when she returned and started to take my cup of caffeine. I shook my spoon up and down in jest.

"Don't take that, I want to drink it during the show."

She laughed at my exaggerated admonishment for stealing my untouched coffee and turned to another table. I was still holding the spoon and shaking it. All of sudden the utensil flew out of my hand, made an arc over my head. We heard a kerplkunk as the wayward spoon landed on a table three rows behind us. We all tried to look as if we were unaware of the origin of the flying missile.

We probably would have remained undetected, if my protégé had not spoken causing his three table mates to begin snickering, and then burst into guffaws.

"I'm not going to do that!"

Chapter 54
The Peabody

Business travelers soon realize that hotel life can be monotonous. One hotel room is generally just like another, no matter the name attached to it. I enjoy the Motel 6 advertisement where the announcer tells you to close your eyes in your expensive motel. Then he says that is the same way your Motel 6 room looks while you are sleeping, except his motel is less expensive.

A tremendous exception to the cookie cutter hotels and motels is in Memphis, Tennessee — the original Peabody Hotel. Once down on its luck when the big band era died after World War II and motels begin to pop up like crabgrass across the country, new owners restored the majesty and traditions of this grand building.

The stately Peabody continues one famous tradition. The duck walk every morning and afternoon. In the morning several female mallard ducks come down the elevator, walk across the red carpet spread especially for them, and jump in the fountain in the center

Southern Smiles and Tears

of the hotel lobby. At five o'clock in the afternoon, the process reverses. Hundreds of people line up beside the cordoned off red carpet to watch and photograph the royal reception and egress of these pampered fowls.

That is only part of the duck story. When we were there two sets of ducks, rotated to keep their stress down. They lived in a penthouse on the roof of the Peabody attended by a former elephant trainer for the Barnum and Bailey Circus.

The original ducks in the fountain arrived as a practical a joke. Firemen were holding a convention at the hotel in the 1930's. Several of the firemen took time off to go drinking, camping, and hunting. That is probably the proper sequence. At some point during the hunting part of the adventure, a drinker/hunter shot at a duck. It fell to the ground. The shooter walked into the marsh to recover his prize only to be surprised that the duck was alive, although wounded in the wing.

It is not known if the alcohol had made the fireman maudlin, or if he just simply could not kill the duck face to face. He picked it up and carried the downed bird back to the campsite. Here the story becomes even murkier. Sometime during the evening and night the group sitting around the campfire decided it would be funny to take the duck with the broken wing back to the Peabody and put her in the fountain. They broke camp early the next morning, sneaked the duck into the hotel, and let her loose in the fountain. They, in all probability, then returned to their rooms laughing about what they had done.

It backfired as a joke.

The next morning everyone was enthralled at the duck primly swimming around in the base of the fountain as water cascaded into the pool. And thus it has been since, except the ducks are not shot out of the air before becoming candidates for the red carpet treatment.

Alice and I have had the opportunity to stay at this grand hotel twice. The first time was with a young salesman and his wife. I was there as a guest of the hotel to write a travel story to be published in *The Charleston Daily Mail*. The hotel publicity person arranged for Alice and I to have a suite, and the other couple to have a nice room. Alice and I looked forward to a romantic evening. Here we were in a large suite with a claw foot tub, king size four poster bed, and other amenities. Just as we began to snuggle and appreciate the atmosphere the telephone rang. It was the husband half of the of the other couple.

"Hey, what's going on?"

I lied. "Nothing."

"Good. We are on our way down and thought we could play some cards See ya'll in a minute."

Playing was on my mind, but not cards.

Barely was that thought out of my mind when a knock sounded at the door. That was fast. So fast that Alice had to make a run to the bedroom to put on something appropriate for card playing. I believe she had been appropriately attired for the evening I had envisioned.

I opened the door. There stood the two of them. I could hardly believe what came out of his mouth.

"We got bored watching TV, and I went downstairs and bought a deck of cards. Look, they even have ducks on them."

Later that night, much later that night, when Alice and I were finally alone, we pondered what had happened. We tried to understand how a couple in their early twenties, married for only a couple of years would exchange a free night in an exclusive hotel alone for the opportunity to play cards with a couple, one in her late 30's and him in his late 40's. We never did.

A few years later we had the opportunity to stay at The Peabody once more. This time it was at a social studies conference where we were promoting a Tennessee History book. Alice and I had brought two of my co-authors with us to the conference. Doug Little was a supervisor for Bradley County Schools in Eastern Tennessee, and Dr. Jerome Taylor was a professor at Cleveland State College north of Chattanooga. The two were quite opposite from each other. Doug was an organized bureaucrat, who today would be classified as anal-retentive. Jerome typified the absent-minded professor. Jerome's mind worked in mysterious ways. Highly intelligent, he would begin a conversation, appear to lose his thread of thought, but then somehow tie the two diametrically opposed thoughts together in a synthesis that astounded his listeners.

Jerome's genealogy was rooted deeply into the antebellum South. His politics were liberal. He liked to tell the story of the most foolish move ever made by a Taylor. His father, a Republican, had accepted the role of trying to oust Senator Estes Kefauver and his famous coonskin cap from office. It was an unspectacular failure.

The first morning of the conference Alice, Jerome, Doug, and I met in the massive lobby of The Peabody. The hotel served either coffee, or a continental breakfast, at a cost, for those who wanted to enjoy the atmosphere of the hotel before the ducks paraded. The coffee, with refills, was five dollars. I think the continental breakfast was ten dollars. Doug, Alice, and I opted for the breakfast,

Southern Smiles and Tears

while Jerome said, "Coffee will suffice."

Several servers strolled about the room with silver coffee carafes for refilling the gold-rimmed bone china cups. Others walked about with baskets of rolls, and crystal decanters filled with cold juices.

Three of us ate, drank, and conversed while one only drank coffee. Then the three of us began declining further refills and service, but Jerome continued to accept refills of coffee. We watched him drink two more cups. Doug, wanting to get to the first session early, asked if we shouldn't be going.

"I'm not finished." Replied Jerome.

"You want another cup of coffee?" I asked. "You must've had four cups already!"

"Six!"

"And you want another?" Alice asked somewhat astonished.

Doug entered the conversation.

"Jerome, I've never seen you drink more than two cups of coffee in a day."

Jerome in his convoluted thinking solved the mystery of his sudden obsession with coffee.

"That coffee cost $5.00, and I'm going to get it down to fifty cents a cup."

Later during the seminars, we noticed that Jerome fidgeted quite a bit. He also often left his chair and headed for the room exit. I often think of Jerome in this age of $4.00 a cup Starbuck's coffee.

He would have had to drink only one and one-quarter cups, and peed less often.

Chapter 55
A Christian and a Jew

As with many people being of the Christian faith, I never had much contact with those of the Jewish persuasion.

Dr. Eckman changed that for me.

Tall, with sprinklings of hair, the doctor came unannounced to my office to tell me he had a book that needed published. It was about his experiences as a doctor during World War II.

"Just read it." He instructed. Not asked, but instructed. "You will appreciate it."

I did, and I did.

The only problem was that old obstacle in publishing. If you are unknown as a writer and not famous or infamous, having your work published is a steep climb. Many times it matters not the quality of work but the fame, or infamy, the author has attained.

I explained the difficulties of unknown authors being published, and that many people self-published their first book. Dr. Eckman

Southern Smiles and Tears

would have none of that. He wanted to be published and was not going to invest in it himself. "That's for people who have nothing to say but want it out anyway." There was another possibility. Alice and I had started a weekly newspaper in South Charleston. I suggested, and Alice agreed, that one way to develop an interest in Dr. Eckman's book would be to serialize it in the newspaper.

It worked. Two weeks of events he had encountered in Europe caused people to become interested in Dr. Eckman's book. It was serious and sad, but most of all it was real. We began to consider pre-selling the book and then publishing it from the funds.

Then disaster.

Pain spread across Alice's face. Deep, heartfelt hurt. She had answered the telephone in her usual bright voice, but it cracked within moments. She placed the receiver back in its cradle and told me I had to go to the hospital to see Dr. Eckman. I have never been good at visiting people in hospitals. Normally, quite garrulous, words fail me in the face of illness. Alice told me the doctor would not have called me if he did not need me.

Reluctantly, I drove to Charleston to visit him in his room. Doctor Eckman had informed Alice that he had requested no visitors so I would have to stop at the nurses' station to let them know who I was before being allowed in his room. I followed his instructions and entered his room. Hemming and hawing, I finally asked him how he was.

He replied bluntly "I'm dying."

No one had ever said that to me before.

"I have a malignant tumor in my brain and may live six months. But that's not why I called you. I received this letter from someone of your faith and need to know what you think of it. You're the only Christian I know who will give me an honest answer."

He handed the letter to me instructing that I read it. As I unfolded it, a well-known insurance company logo became visible. My first thought was that the letter must have something to do with life insurance. How wrong I was.

A former patient of the doctor, purporting to be a Christian, had heard that Dr. Eckman was terminally ill. This man believed it was his duty as a Christian "...to lead you to Christ." the message continued "If you do not ask Jesus to forgive you of your sins, you will burn in Hell for eternity."

I was appalled. Here was a man dying from cancer being threatened in a letter with eternal damnation if he did not switch from 70 years of Judaism to Christianity.

How insensitive.

Southern Smiles and Tears

The letter continued with a request "I came to visit you but could not get in. Would you give my name to the nurses so I can lead you to the Lord?"

"He has tried to visit me here and has telephoned several times. What should I do about him and his letter?"

Solomon faced less consternating decisions.

"Doctor, you have several choices. First, ignore it. Second, get mad. Third, since he wrote it on company letterhead, you could write his company and ask if it were company policy to proselytize."

A loud laughter exploded from the hospital bed. "I knew you would put it in the proper perspective for me. What do you think of the man who wrote the letter?"

"Well, I think he is a good man who does not realize the consequences of his actions and how what he did could offend you. He probably sits in church every Sunday absorbing the necessity to evangelize the world. Like me, he probably has not had much experience with Jews. We Christians fail to comprehend the depth of Judaism. Your religion and your being are the same. It is what you have been since birth. You do not have to do anything to become a Jew. You are a Jew. In all probability this man recently became a Christian by accepting Jesus as his personal savior. His newly found faith has excited him, and he now wants to spread his happiness to others."

"Seriously, how would you react to him?"

"If I were you and wanted no further contact with him, I would write him a letter. In it, I would tell him that you are content being a Jew, and because his God and your God are the same, you see no reason to switch religions as you near death."

Dr. Eckman did as I advised and never heard from the man again.

Later that week, the doctor checked himself out of the hospital. He went home to die, undrugged and cognizant of his environment.

Dr. Eckman lived three months. During that time I visited him almost daily. He would prop himself up in bed as I sat beside him. We then would engage in a wide spectrum of subjects. Philosophy, the Holocaust, writing, history, politics. Any subject was fair game. He would tell me when he tired, and I would leave.

One afternoon near the end of Dr. Eckman's time on Earth his wife, Miriam, invited me into her kitchen. She told me the doctor was too ill to talk with me, but he had a request. He wanted me to deliver the eulogy at his funeral. Honored, I accepted the gift.

One week later, the call came that my friend had died.

Southern Smiles and Tears

I had never been in a Synagogue before. It was humbling. Throughout the Old and New Testaments, Synagogues were where God dwelt. Handed a yarmulke, I placed it on my head and entered the temple. Several people spoke before I did. As the last speaker, I rose, went to the front, and talked about Dr. Eckman. At one point I said that I had known the doctor for only six months. When the eulogy and service was complete, I walked outside.

A lady approached me. "You only knew the doctor six months?"

"Yes, ma'am."

"You're Christian, aren't you?"

"Yes, ma'am."

"That's strange. He spoke of you as if he had known you for years."

Then she paid me one of the most touching compliments I have ever received.

"He told me you were his best friend!"

Chapter 56
Old Dogs Can Learn

Some people believe that your environment makes you as you are. Others make excuses for their actions because of being born into a particular situation. Both may be true, but I know that a person, with diligent effort and awareness, can rise above his past.

I had to take a business trip from the printing plant where Alice and I worked in Marceline, Missouri to Phoenix, Arizona and Oakland, California. Tired of flying, I decided to take Amtrak, which at that time, stopped in Marceline for passengers. As Alice and I discussed my upcoming trip, we realized it was at the same time as her parents' 43rd wedding anniversary. They neither had had a honeymoon nor been west of the Mississippi River, with the exception of a trip to visit us in Marceline.

One concern arose. George Skidmore, my father-in-law, had been reared in an all-white culture on Poca River in West Virginia. His language was laced with words normal to him, his family, and his

Southern Smiles and Tears

friends but offensive to those of a culture foreign to him. He had worked at Monsanto Chemical Company from 1949 until he retired in 1983. It was the late 1970's before the company had hired "coloreds" as he called these newly hired men. In one of those ironic twists in our lives, two of the first people of African American descent hired to work with him I had taught at DuPont High School long before I married into the Skidmore family. The Bookers had been good athletes, but more important, excellent students in high school.

Alice and I were keenly aware that we would need to talk with him about how he should refer to people outside the narrow world from whence he came. He would be encountering more blacks within two weeks than he had seen in his entire lifetime. Additionally, he would be seeing and interacting with the Latinos for the first time. We decided to discuss the issue face-to-face. A month before the big trip, Alice and I went to West Virginia to help them get ready for the trip.

Alice opened with, "Dad and Mom, before we go on the train trip there is something we need to talk about with you. Some of the words you use can insult people."

A look of curiosity crossed the faces of George and Louise.

I picked up the topic. "You grew up where it was acceptable to use the words 'colored' and 'nigger.' I have never heard you say the latter but when you refer to the Bookers you say 'Those colored boys'..."

One of our daughters had observed a trait that Alice and I have a habit of completing each other's thoughts and sentences. This was one of those occasions as Alice completed my thought.

"...and that can be insulting to them and other blacks. You will have to be aware of that and change how you talk about people."

I picked up with, "When we are in Phoenix there will be many people speaking Spanish. It is common there, but you will be surprised. Oakland has more African Americans than you have ever been around. You will have to break speaking habits of over 60 years in order not to hurt people."

This was the point at which I realized the integrity and depth of the Christian lives of my parents-in law.

George responded, "We wouldn't do anything to hurt anyone. Just tell us what to say and do."

A month later George and Louise arrived by train in Marceline. We boarded and began their great adventure. Not once did either of them slip and use derogatory terms during the two weeks. When on the various trains, George spent his days in the observation car watching the landscapes. More important, he and the conductor on the route to Phoenix began to converse. At a stop in Albuquerque, New Mexico for servicing the train, I was passing through the dining care looking for Alice. Sitting at a table were two people. One black. One white. George Skidmore and the conductor seated across from each other were laughing and joking. The conversation and interchange were not strained by race but natural in mutual friendship because of common age and interests.

I was a frequent traveler and often stayed in the exclusive membership rooms at Hyatt Hotels. Alice and I decided to surprise the honeymooning couple with a suite and access to club membership at the Oakland Hyatt. As we rode the elevator to the top floor, Alice told them this was our anniversary and honeymoon present to them.

The bellhop opened the door to the room, and Alice and I entered. After depositing our luggage and receiving his tip, the bellhop left. Something curious was happening down the hall. George and Louise were still outside their door.

"Go on in." Alice told her parents as she showed them how to use the electronic key.

Then in an act of love, George picked up Louise and carried her across the threshold. Tears welled in Alice's eyes as her mother beamed like a ray of sun light.

The next morning the four of us went to have breakfast in the clubroom. Louise, who has waited on others all of her life, giggled like a schoolgirl when the room hostess kept coming to her filling her orange juice goblet and asking if Louise needed anything. More impressive was that the four of us sat there in a social setting eating, drinking, and conversing with those of ethnic and economic backgrounds heretofore unknown to George and Louise.

The two of them may have spoken with a West Virginia twang sprinkled with "reckons", "ain'ts", and "winders", but there were no more sophisticated people seated in that room than George and Louise Skidmore. They spoke to everyone with love and regard.

I suspect Alice's parents were able to accomplish their transformation out of respect for her and me. Such a great love. They made a conscious change and in the majority have maintained it. To be sure, once in a while terms will escape their lips that are inappropriate, but within the same conversation more socially acceptable terms will surface to replace the slip.

Alice and I both cringe at the slips but inwardly glow when they are self-corrected.

Chapter 57
The Blind Can See

Years of travel in those long, silver torture chambers that sat on tarmacs and dropped hundreds of feet at inopportune times, caused me to change my mode of travel to trains when possible. That is why I was in Union Station in Chicago talking to Alice on the telephone.

"Oh, by the way." Alice said, "Somebody called you from The American Printing House for the Blind in Louisville, Kentucky. He wants to talk to you." She gave me the telephone number.

At first, I did not know why someone from Louisville would be calling me. Then I remembered. Several months before I had been reading *Publisher's Weekly* and had seen an advertisement for someone with knowledge of publishing and copyrights. I wasn't looking for a job but sent my vitae on a whim.

Alice and I were happy in Marceline, Missouri working for Walsworth Publishing where I headed up the Educational

Southern Smiles and Tears

Division. Marceline was a small town of 2,000 people half way between St. Louis and Kansas City about 90 miles north of Columbia. Housing was economical. Alice and I had purchased a two-bedroom house on an acre of land for $30,000.00, and Walsworth gave me an excellent salary and bonus.

Marceline was the boyhood home of Walt Disney. He had remained a friend with the three brothers, who had founded Walsworth. Main Street in Disneyland is a replica of Kansas Avenue, the main street of Marceline. When Disney remodeled Disneyland in California, he sent several small rides to be installed at no cost in Disney Park. He also authorized the painting of Disney cartoon characters on the walls of Disney Elementary. Many schools paint the characters on their walls. However, Disney artists painted those in Disney Elementary School. They also add new characters and maintain the old.

We were working at Walsworth during its 50th anniversary. I was asked to write a book about the company. The best story related to me was about Walt Disney. He was on one of his regular visits to the small town, when one of the Walsworth brothers asked him if he wanted to go duck hunting with them. A look of incredulity appeared on Disney's face as the father of Donald Duck said, "You want me to shoot a duck!"

I did call the personnel director at the American Printing House for the Blind. He said the company was interested in interviewing two others and me, for the position as Publisher Liaison. I was to be the last to be interviewed, and APH would send me an airline ticket. I asked if Amtrak ran through Louisville and received a negative answer.

Three weeks later, I was on an airplane headed for Louisville.

The interview was strange. The president, three vice-presidents, the director of marketing, technical director, education director, Braille coordinator, and I went to lunch. We ate; they all insisted I have a local dessert called Derby Pie, and then each began asking questions from notes. Many of the questions had to do with my background. Someone noted that APH had transcribed several of the textbooks I had written into Braille and large type for blind students. Everything seemed to be going fine until the technical director, who was blind, asked me his question.

"Can you get askey files for us to use to transcribe textbooks into Braille?"

I assumed that was a legitimate question. *What are askey files?*
It was apparent that an answer was expected.
"Of course!" I said.

Southern Smiles and Tears

"Great!" Tuck Tinsley, the president retorted.

That was the end of the interview. I spent the night at the Brown Hotel, flew home, went to the computer analyst at Walsworth, and asked, "What are askey files?"

She explained that it is a number based code computers use to typeset books.

"How do you spell askey?"

"It's an acronym. American Standard Code for Information Interchange, or A-S-C-I-I for short."

A week later, Tuck Tinsley called and offered me the position. He then transferred me to the personnel director to discuss how long I had to accept or reject and the salary.

"Alice, I think this is something I would like to do, but the salary is less than half what I am making here."

We discussed for a week whether or not to accept the position. To make the move, we would live in an apartment until our house in Marceline sold. Then we would make a decision about a house in Louisville.

There was another factor in our decision. Alice had always lived close to her family. When we accepted positions 700 miles away from Poca, West Virginia, I had agreed that Alice would get to see her mother at least once every two months. The move would put us only 225 miles away. Her mother loved the idea. We also would be that close to two of our children and two grandchildren.

There was only one person who did not understand, Alice's dad. He had worked 34 years at the same chemical plant before retiring. He was incredulous that I would take such a loss in salary to do something I wanted to do. It made no sense to him. I later found out that the money is not what amazed him, it was the idea of switching companies. I finally comprehended this when he was amazed that I would leave APH to take a position in California at six figures.

We moved to Louisville and enjoyed an experience that few people from outside the blind community have. I had had a blind student while teaching at DuPont High School but to be immersed in the society was a revelation.

Larry, the technical director, was a computer programmer with great skills. He later left APH, moved to Texas and founded a computer company. My first epiphany that the blind could "see" occurred about my third day in Louisville. Gary Mudd and his guide dog Heathcliff walked by my door.

"David, I'm going to make some coffee. Would you like a cup?"

"Sure. Do you need any help?"

Southern Smiles and Tears

This was a sign of my immaturity in working in the blind community. I never would have asked that question of a sighted coworker. Gary was perfectly capable of making a pot of coffee. Later, Gary told me of an incident while he was attending The Kentucky School for the Blind in Louisville.

Gary had become blind just before the age when boys begin to believe that driving is the highest goal that could be achieved in life. Gary and a friend had been out driving around Louisville late one night. His friend was taking him back to the dormitory on the school campus. They had just turned onto Frankfort Avenue, when Gary asked a question.

"Why don't you let me drive?"

"Are you crazy? You're blind!"

"I know that, but I have always wanted to drive!"

I came to find out that Gary was quite persuasive when he wanted to be. His friend acquiesced. Gary got behind the steering wheel and following his friend's verbal directions as the car slowly progressed down Frankfort Avenue. Everything was going well, and Gary was ecstatic.

Then a problem occurred.

Gary did not know about the problem until his friend told him he had better stop.

"Why?"

"There's a police car behind us, flashing its lights!"

The policeman had pulled them over because the vehicle had been traveling astride the line marking the middle of the street. Additionally, Gary was speeding at an astounding 10 miles per hour.

Asked for his driver's license, Gary responded, "I don't have any, I'm blind."

I have no idea of the look on the officer's face but suspect it was one of incredulity. The upshot was that the policeman told the two to switch places and go home. Gary told me that he believed the policeman just could not bring himself to go back to the station and report he had arrested a blind man for driving too slowly down Frankfort Avenue.

As Alice and I got to know Gary better, we found out that he had a wide interest in the world around him. He was an avid University of Kentucky basketball fan, even attending games. Once on a trip to Washington, DC, we toured the city after our meetings ended. We were at the Lincoln Memorial, and Gary asked us to describe it to him. Alice did the request one better. She went to the guard and asked him if Gary and Heathcliff could go up to

Southern Smiles and Tears

the monument for Gary to touch the statue. The guard dropped the barrier rope, and Gary and Heathcliff went up and met Mr. Lincoln.

I still picture in my mind Gary and Heathcliff playing ball together. Heathcliff spent much of his day beside Gary's desk. When his harness was on, he was a working dog. In the evening, Gary would remove the harness for playtime and to exercise his friend. Gary would throw a tennis ball across his front yard, and Heathcliff would bound over the grass, retrieve the yellow sphere, and return it. Gary would throw it once again. The game would go on until Heathcliff's panting let Gary know it was time to stop and rest.

The weather was miserable on one trip we took. Gary knew he had to exercise Heathcliff, but the rain was coming down in sheets. The two went out into the hallway on the 15th floor and proceeded to play "hall ball." Alice and I stood near the elevator to warn hotel guests before they disembarked and got whacked by a flying tennis ball or dog. The housekeepers went about their jobs but peeked out of the clean rooms before entering the "ball field."

Gary and I worked closely together to solve the problem involved in obtaining copyright permissions and computer data, ASCII files, of textbooks before publication. I went directly to the President of the Textbook Division of the Association of American Publishers, Don Eklund, with the problem. The presidents of the textbook companies, previously unaware of any problems, reacted quickly giving Braille publishers everything they needed. This allowed blind students to have their textbooks at the same time as sighted students. Previously, Braille textbooks sometimes arrived at a school after the student needing them had moved to the next grade.

Once that problem had been solved, I became bored from the lack of a challenge. Contacted by a California technology company that produced computer programs for the blind, I once again whisked Alice to a new location. With the exception of working with Jerry Kuns, this move was a catastrophe. My ego swelled. The money, prestige, and California culture blinded me to what really was important in my life.

Jerry Kuns, though, was a real treat to know. He lived in the middle of San Francisco and was a sales representative for the company. His territory covered southern California, Arizona, and New Mexico. In his 50's, Jerry had lost his sight while in his 20's. Jerry covered his territory without a guide dog. He used the white cane to travel solo in San Francisco and to make sales calls in greater Los Angeles.

Southern Smiles and Tears

Those things faded as accomplishments in comparison to the company he owned in San Francisco. Jerry led walking tours for sighted people in downtown San Francisco.

The name of the company?

Jose' Can You See?

Southern Smiles and Tears

Chapter 58
Roots of an Activist

Everette Knapper, in 1956, was the first black to become a class officer at St. Albans High School. About six-feet tall, thin, and light-skinned, Everette was graduated from West Virginia State College with a B.S. in Chemistry. He held a master's degree from West Virginia University and a doctorate degree from the University of Virginia. A public school teacher and vice-principal, Everette even taught part time at a graduate school.

He also was murdered.

Everette and I became friends at St. Albans High School. We remained so during our years at West Virginia State College and teaching careers in Kanawha County Schools. Our common ground was that both of us came from large families. His had eight children and mine nine. He never, as far as I can remember, ever called me by my given name. He always addressed me in his raspy, high-pitched voice as "Bice." I became active in the teacher's association;

he became active in rooting out racism. His effect is still felt in the county. Mine is a chimera.

I lost track of Everette when I began writing textbooks and moved away from West Virginia. We saw each other a couple of times between 1980 and 1995 on my periodic trips back to visit family. Our conversations never got beyond the mundane pleasantries, which old friends exchange when their paths have taken divergent routes. I was pleased he had earned his doctorate. In turn, he told me he was proud to know someone who wrote textbooks. We compared my multiple moves to his being rooted in the Kanawha Valley and reminisced about our favorite professors at West Virginia State.

At some point during those years, the mild-mannered Everette I had known became a thorn in the side of both the county board of education and the city government of Charleston. I am not positive what caused Everette to change directions from a meek teenage black, elected to office by his white schoolmates, into a confrontational black activist. Maybe he always was an activist, just not vociferous. He may not have had the platform or courage to show it. Perhaps, it dawned on him that, though society was supposedly integrated, a residual racism circled beneath the surface as if it were a hungry shark. I do know that as an adult he had the courage to take on the power structure within his realm of influence.

His first major confrontation with the school bureaucracy came in 1990 when he filed a complaint against a high school vice principal in Charleston with the state's Human Rights Commission. He accused the vice-principal of believing "...the stereotypical projections that have been used by white people to victimize black people for centuries." Everette's charge, in defense of what he saw as mistreatment of his nephew, was made against a fellow, black vice principal. If anything, Everette was an equal opportunity civil rights activist. He inferred that the black vice principal was hiding behind the white power structure within the board of education. The next year his strident accusations and criticisms ended with a five-day suspension without pay for him.

Minor skirmishes ensued for the next few years. Later in 1994, he attacked the Charleston City government for "...trying to put a black face on crime." He became the voice for the poor people of Westside Charleston. Many saw him as a troublemaker fighting for things that were supposed to have been solved in the 1960's. Everette was a lone voice decrying injustice and intolerance.

Then he was silenced at age 55.

Southern Smiles and Tears

Our daughter, Penny, telephoned me in Alabama.
"Dad, didn't you have a friend named Everette Knapper?"
"Yes. Why?"
"He was murdered last night."

Everette had a caring side, which reached further than just fighting for the rights of others. His compassion killed him. He invited a young man in his early twenties to live with him. He was helping the man to overcome societal and financial problems. On Monday, October 2, 1995, Everette died from head injuries when his guest beat him "...with a blunt weapon."

I remember little of the remainder of the telephone conversation.

Chapter 59
Cancer! Your Name Is Not Modesty

I never even liked changing clothes in school gym classes. Now my unclothed rear end has been seen by more people than a hooker's in Hollywood.

Alice and I had founded a publishing company in 1997 to help counties develop family history books. We thought we might even make a living at it. Alice was working at a hospital in Shelby County, Alabama sustaining the two of us while I freelanced textbooks.

We had come to Alabama as part of a six-month assignment from the Association of Christian Schools. The organizational headquarters in Colorado Springs, Colorado had hired me to work with its textbook division, which operated out of Birmingham, Alabama.

Southern Smiles and Tears

My assignment, unknown to those in Birmingham, was to go there and evaluate the division. A series of elementary books had had a serious cost overrun, and Colorado Springs was concerned. The pretext for me going there was to work on a high school textbook about dating, love, and marriage.

In probably one of the best acts of stabbing oneself in the back, I told the powers in Colorado Springs that the operation in Birmingham lacked internal financial controls. Everyone was doing good work producing excellent books. However, a relationship had been established with one printer, and books were being printed unbid. Costs were spiraling. At a meeting in Colorado Springs, I explained that one series of books, in particular, had extensive changes at final "bluelines" creating a major cost overrun. Not familiar with printing practices, the Birmingham group believed "blueline" proof changes were as inexpensive as copy and art changes in earlier proofs. To make a long story short, a decision was made to place textbook production on a hiatus. I was told that I would have to be "let go" for a couple of years until finances would allow everything to be moved to Colorado Springs and restarted. Then I would be brought back into the organization.

Alice and I discussed this. We weren't exactly positive how the people in Colorado thought we could wait two years. Perhaps, we could eliminate eating. That surely would save several hundred dollars each month.

Another factor was Alice had a strong opinion about my propensity to move to a new job and location as soon as I became bored. She pulled a Rebecca Boone on me. Many people are unaware that Becky, the wife of the itinerant wanderer Daniel, put her foot down only one time about his wandering. Daniel had gone south to British West Florida, came home, and suggested the family move there. Becky, who allowed him to wander around for years west of the Appalachians, and even moved to Kentucky with him, told Daniel in no uncertain terms she was not moving to Florida.

Alice had followed me back and forth across the country, without complaint, to a variety of positions. So it was quite a revelation when she informed me that I better choose where I wanted to live next with care. I believe she put it something like, "I will move one more time and buy one more house, but they will carry you out of that house in a pine box." I think this may have been due to the fact that we had moved so often that many boxes had not been unpacked in 10 years. Moving companies place one-inch square identifying stickers on moved items to prevent loss and items going astray. We had several boxes with stickers still attached from four

Southern Smiles and Tears

different companies.

I suggested we just stay in Alabama. It was warm most of the year. I like to visit snow but not to live in it. Alice agreed to remain in the South with one caveat. We were not to move to the coast with the possibility of a hurricane moving us involuntarily further inland. With the decision made about where to live, we discussed employment. I was to stay at home with our red dachshund, Popcorn, and tortoise cat, Mixer, establishing our fledgling company. Alice would be the main breadwinner for a year. That may seem as if it were an equitable division of labor except for the fact that Alice would come home in the evening do the bookkeeping and help me plan. Needless to say, I never went to the hospital to help her.

Several events took place at approximately the same time in the spring of 1997. As our business became more involved and complex Alice was needed more and more at our home office. We decided there was enough income for her to resign her position and work full-time, if 60 plus hours a week is considered full-time, with our company.

We decided at the end of April that it would be a good idea to purchase additional life insurance for me. It was to supplement the policy I had obtained the year before as a rider on Alice's policy at the hospital. A nurse came, gauged my blood pressure, drew blood for testing, and had me pee in a cup. Simple and efficient. Then in early May we located a 90 year-old farmhouse in the center of Alabama and decided to purchase it. Our life then became surreal.

No policy arrived in the mail but a form letter did. The letter notified me that I had been rejected for "health reasons." No explanation. No we're sorry. Nothing but a rejection. The insurance company did not know Alice. She was going to find out what was wrong. She telephoned the number on the letterhead. She was shunted from one bureaucrat to another, unable to receive satisfaction. Each person tried to wear her down by obfuscation and being placed on hold. I repeat, the insurance company did not know Alice. She was a mother grizzly protecting her cub. After an hour on the telephone, Alice wore down a clerk.

"He has a PSA of 110."

"What does that mean?" Alice asked.

"I can't tell you. It's confidential."

"What do you mean, it's confidential? You send us a letter rejecting him for health reasons and won't tell us what that means! I want to know and know now!"

I must interject here that those who know Alice or have spoken to her on the phone know she is the sweetest most tolerant person

Southern Smiles and Tears

on Earth.

Not now!

"Tell me what that means!"

There was a pause while the harried clerk gave in. Alice's face drained of blood and she placed the receiver back on the hook.

"What?"

"She said you have prostate cancer!"

That will turn your lives around.

Alice had already made an appointment the next Tuesday with a local doctor. This was to be our initial visit for him to become our family physician. Alice called the doctor's office, told the receptionist the problem, and got an appointment for Monday morning instead.

People often blame God and wonder why He allows a tragedy to intervene in an orderly life. Sometimes, though, God gets it right. Dr. Ajay Patel entered our lives. A short, dark, intelligent, classical musician, doctor from northern India, Dr. Ajay is loved in Clanton. We later found out that twice a year he gives all his patients and their families parties. The Christmas event is a catered event with the doctor and his children playing classical Indian music interspersed with local groups singing Christmas carols. Each summer we are all invited to a full-blown cookout on the lawn in front of his office with local people singing and playing Southern Gospel music.

Dr. Patel came into the examination room where Alice and I were nervously waiting. He was amazed when we repeated the 110 reading on my PSA. He told us that a person with seven to 10 had a serious problem. Alice gave him the letter from the insurance company. He took it and left the room. Within minutes we heard an uproar in the hall outside the room. A loud vice penetrated the walls demanding of an anonymous clerk on the other end of a telephone line that the "...PSA results for David Bice be faxed to me immediately."

He did not break down the bureaucracy of the insurance company. Whoever received his anger refused Dr. Patel's demand. I am fairly sure that his words still are rattling around in that bureaucrat's brain. Undeterred, the doctor ordered another PSA test for me and performed the standard "finger exam" on me. He then told us that he was going to make an appointment with an urologist for us. He left, came back, and announced that the first doctor he called could not take me for two weeks, but that he had arranged for me to go to an excellent doctor in Birmingham on Friday.

Once again, God got it right.

Dr. James Bryant entered our lives along with his nurses Carlton and Dorothy. Dr. Bryant was young, tall, thin, handsome, and had on a snappy tie. The doctor subjected me to another finger exam, and then along with Carlton performed biopsies on my grossly enlarged prostate. We returned to the doctor's office the next day for the results. It was bad. I did have cancer. Dr. Bryant sat down with us and explained that my PSA was indeed extremely high. I had two types of cancer cells, one kind was slow growing and the other was fast growing. He told us it was probable, with the high PSA, that the cancer was in my bones. He called in Dorothy and told her to get me a bone scan. Then he said, "Tell them, I don't care who has to be bumped I want this man to be scanned in the morning."

The next day, Alice and I were back in Birmingham. I went upstairs in the clinic and went through an hour scan. I watched the screen as the test occurred. When I saw the different colors I asked the technician what the colors meant. She told me that where there was yellow, it meant blood cells were gathering. Blood cells tend to surround cancerous areas. As the scan progressed, the yellow only appeared in a couple of small areas. She told me those were normal. When I got back down stairs to Alice, I cautioned her that I did not see any yellow spots in my bones, but not to get her hopes up.

We went into an examination room, and Dorothy came in for a few minutes. She told Alice that she had cancer that was in remission. She then told us to keep our faith. We sat there for what seemed like hours. Then the door opened. We saw a balled up fist with a thumb pointing toward heaven followed by a huge grin.

The cancer was not in my bones.

Dr. Bryant told us he wanted to operate and remove my prostate gland. We asked how soon because we were in the process of buying a house, moving, and having a family reunion. We then asked if we should cancel the house closing and not move. He told us to go ahead and buy the house and have the reunion on July 4. Dr. Bryant told us he would schedule the operation for July 7 because he knew we would not want all the family making over me while they were visiting.

We then went over to the hospital to register. The clerk asked us why I was being hospitalized. When we told her it was for prostate cancer, she said she was sorry. We laughed and told her that this was a happy day, because initially the prognosis had been for me to live four to six weeks. We went back to the clinic to see the doctor once more before my operation in two weeks. Alice told Dr. Bryant, "I will not only be praying for David but for you too!"

Southern Smiles and Tears

Dr. Bryant added, "And for God direct these hands to know what to do."

The operation was a success. One thing was memorable for Alice. Two hours into the operation, Alice received a telephone call from Dr. Bryant. Her immediate thought was that I had died. Quite the opposite. The doctor called Alice to tell her that the biopsies on my lymph glands were clear. He had taken time out from the five-hour surgery to give good news to her.

I did have a section where the cancer had metastasized and would need to have hormone shots. Fifteen months later, my PSA rose again, and I underwent radiation. During the radiation there were 35 days that I undressed and hoisted myself onto a cold, metal table where two women technicians marked my body with felt tip markers, took x-rays, and shifted my body to be in the proper position for the rays to attack the growing cancer cells. I continue to take hormone shots and pills to control my testosterone level and am subjected to regular finger exams. Many men, after prostate surgery, have problems with control of their urine. I have not. The pills and shots do cause me to be more emotional and have weakened my muscles.

The doctors, the operation, the radiation, the shots, the pills, the nakedness. All have given me a second chance at life.

Sometimes God gets it right.

Chapter 60
Celebration of Life

Fear of death for myself does not bother me anymore, but a concern for those who might be left behind inhabits my mind. Alice and I had lost our dachshund and calico cat to heart failures, and Alice wanted me to have another dog to travel with me. Mixer, our cat, had died while we were on a trip to San Antonio, Texas during the Thanksgiving holiday, 1998. I had asked Alice before my prostate operation, "If I live long enough, can we go to San Antonio to see the Christmas lights on the Riverwalk. It is something I've wanted to do."

Her answer was a simple, but comforting, "Yes."

I kept refusing to get another pet. I told her that it was unfair to have a loving dog miss me, when it was likely I would die within a few years. Nine months after I had had my operation, I realized something. God had pulled me from the hands of Satan, and He still had some reason for me to live.

Southern Smiles and Tears

"Alice. I think I would like to go look at some puppies."

I think I saw a glistening in her eyes as she asked, "When do you want to go?"

"Today."

Thus PuppaDawg came into our lives. Alice loves to tell everyone that, "PuppaDawg is David's celebration of life dog. He wouldn't consider getting another dog until he knew he was going to survive cancer."

Alice and I drove over on a Thursday to Milford Farms Nursery where the owners bred dachshunds. My intention was to pick out a red, short-hair that was similar to Popcorn. The owner put the litter out on the ground for us to choose one. We looked at the six red and one black miniatures on the ground, but I couldn't bring myself to decide. Perhaps death's nagging anguish still had hold of me. We returned home for me to think.

Our son Ricky came over on Saturday morning to visit us from his station at Warner-Robbins Air Force base in Georgia. All three of us drove to the nursery. The breeder once again placed the litter on the ground. The six red puppies, looking confused, huddled together. The black and tan scurried about, curiosity spreading with his every move. In a quick decision that ever since, I have been glad I made, I picked the black and tan bundle of energy.

Alice asked on our drive home, "What are you going to name him?"

"PuppaDawg" was my immediate response. And thus my best friend, other than Alice, entered my life.

Since that day four years ago, we have traveled to each of Alabama's 67 counties and visited 18 states together. As I travel about in our motor home on business, there are times I become depressed. It is then that my friend excels. He seems to know when something is bothering me and will climb onto my lap to give me comfort. PuppaDawg has three places that he claims as his as we go about our business in the motor home. One is on the wide dashboard where he stretches out in a great imitation of those fake dogs people put in the back window of cars, which nod their heads. Often he will crawl under the driver's seat and ride for miles. The only way I know he is there is by reaching down with my left had to feel his hiney. His favorite place though is in my lap. He stretches across my lap and sleeps with his head on the arm rest. All is then right in his world, and mine.

PuppaDawg has developed quite a fan club. Our grandchildren in Wisconsin eagerly await his arrival twice a year on our visits there. It becomes a contest as to which of the three of them will walk him first. He also is the first dog that my sister Martha has ever allowed in her house. She also buys him gifts regularly, sometimes better ones than she gives her only living brother. Our children and grandchildren in West Virginia decided one Christmas that I needed an "All Dachshund Christmas." Every gift I received had a dachshund theme, even down to a rug stating, "A Spoiled Rotten Dachshund Lives Here." Our friends Billy and Paula Ingle had an outdoor flag made with his image and name on it. Carl and Mary Puckett, two other friends, expect him to be with us when we get together to play "Mexican Train Dominoes."

He goes to church with us, usually waiting in the car until services end. Then the young people in the ask, "Can we go see PuppaDawg?" Lest anyone think that we leave him in a hot or cold vehicle, the air-conditioner runs on hot days and the heater on cold ones. When he was just a year old, I was having meetings in Linden, Alabama. One of the attendees was Charles Miller. Mr. Miller owned the largest bank in Marengo County and huge tracks of land. He came into the meeting on a hot summer day and asked, "Do you know you left your car running?"

"Yes, my dog is with me, and I leave it running for the air conditioning."

He responded with, "Oh!" and nothing further was said.

The next month when PuppaDawg and I were back in town, Mr. Miller came out to meet us as we pulled into the library parking lot.

"I brought your dog something, if you want to turn off the engine and roll down the windows. It's a cooling pad."

He handed me the pad, which had a frozen gel package inside a cloth covering. He brought the pad each meeting that summer. That fall I began driving the motor home once again to meetings because I was staying out for two weeks at a time. There was no need to run the engine as the generator powered the twin air conditioners on the vehicle. Mr. Miller no longer brought the cooling pad, but each month until age prevented him from attending our meeting, he brought PuppaDawg a box of treats.

Often people in the groups, with whom I am meeting, invite me to bring in PuppaDawg, rather than leave him "...all alone out there." Usually he will sit beside me or walk around begging to be petted. That is not what happened one evening in Marianna, Florida. He had made his rounds greeting everyone and then settled down as the group began discussing the progress on completing the county book. About 30 minutes into the meeting, we heard a crunching sound. We all looked around trying to figure out what

Southern Smiles and Tears

had made the noise. The sound was coming from underneath the table. PuppaDawg had gotten into one of the women's pocketbooks that was on the floor. He had taken out her inhaler for asthma and was busily chewing on it. He has not been invited back to meet with that group.

I believe PuppaDawg may be one of the few animals who has had a credit account. Bobbie Traywick, who works in our office, was not used to inside dogs. She and her late husband, Dewey, always had "yard dogs." PuppaDawg goes to the office each morning with me. At first, Bobbie ignored him. That was until he started going over and untying her shoes to get attention. Now, the two of them are best of friends. Bobbie takes him with her each morning to get the company mail and often takes him inside with her. It has reached the point where the postal clerks, Barbara, Don, and Emily, ask where he is if Bobbie leaves PuppaDawg in the car. His credit account came to be when Bobbie could not decide what to get him for Christmas. She went to Dr. Cox, PuppaDawg's doctor, and opened him a credit account to use for purchases.

He loves to get into women's purses. We first found that out on a trip to Texas. Alice's mother guards her pocket book as if she were a mother hen and the purse a baby chick. She always places it on the floor beside her when sitting. Once in a while she will place the purse on her left side when she sits down, instead of its proper repository on her right. When she does this while traveling we will hear, "Where's my pocket book? Oh, Lordy! I must've left it somewhere." At that juncture, we stop the vehicle and make an all out search, usually finding the missing bag calmly sitting on the floor beside her. We were just outside Abilene, Texas when Alice spotted PuppaDawg coming to the front of the motor home with a five-dollar bill in his mouth.

"Where did you get that?" she asked PuppaDawg in a voice that sounded as if she expected him to answer.

Then we heard the familiar, "Where's my pocket book? Oh, Lordy!" This was followed by, "Never mind. Here it is." Which was then followed by, "My billfold's open! Where's my money?" While Alice's mom had been napping, PuppaDawg was busy obtaining funds to purchase his next bag of Eukanuba.

I only wish that I could train him to distinguish between a five-dollar bill and a one hundred-dollar greenback.

Southern Smiles and Tears

Chapter 61
Invisible

It took almost 50 years before I truly understood how Eleanor must have felt working for our family in Prichard. She was invisible.

When members of my family talked to each other, they talked as if she were not there. An expectation existed that the things she was hired to do were to be done without a "thank you" or "well done" ever crossing our lips. After all she was a Negro.

In the early 1980s, I was in need of someone to do a reading analysis of a textbook I had written. One name kept surfacing as I inquired about someone who could help me. Alfredlene Armstong. She was an elementary teacher who had been honored by several awards from her peers, including "Teacher of the Year." It only took a few minutes for the two of us to realize that we had similar ideas about education. Our primary point of agreement was to challenge students and not teach down to them. Al and I had a professional

Southern Smiles and Tears

relationship for a couple of years as we worked together on several books. This was to change in the last part of the decade.

The summer of 1982 Al came to my office to discuss a new fourth grade history I was writing. Alice was typing the manuscript of the book. Al walked over to Alice to talk about the book. If sparks of friendship could be seen, a display of fireworks would have burst forth at that instance. The two instantly, and ever since, liked each other. Later in the mid-1980's, Al and Alice grew closer. I was accepted into the fellowship the two enjoyed. On the periphery was George, Al's husband, a chemist and physicist who traveled the world.

Al came from Eufaula, Alabama where her father, the Colonel, had been a chauffeur for rich families. This man and his wife raised seven children sending them all to college. They all were graduated, some with doctorate degrees.

Al received her bachelor's degree in Alabama and applied to enter the master's program at the University of South Carolina. She was accepted into the program. She only had one problem, Al was not white, and South Carolina's colleges and universities were still segregated. When she arrived with her letter of acceptance to register for classes, it gave the university officials pause. She exceeded the academic standards of the university but failed the social standards. Someone in the registrar's office had assumed the name was male. Further complicating Al's enrollment was her being placed in a male dormitory.

What was the university to do? The powers in charge soon found out that this was not a woman to take rejection in stride. Especially, one with an acceptance letter gripped firmly in her hand. Moments into trying to explain that there must have been some type of clerical error, Al let everyone know that she was going to attend and be graduated from that particular institution.

I am not sure what Al said. I do know she attended classes and obtained her degree. This despite that in exchange for her being allowed to attend she had to sit behind a plywood barrier so the other students would not be infected with her presence.

Petite to the nth degree, this woman whose husband makes five of her, has not stopped at any artificial societal wall of separation. She is a person and to meet her is to know that. George is a gentle giant, who overcame immeasurable odds to become a sought after chemist and physicist. His high school in Monroeville, Alabama had one microscope for the entire chemistry class.

Al and George were the first blacks to enter the house of my mother and father-in-law in Poca, West Virginia. What began as

Southern Smiles and Tears

polite acceptance of Alice's and my friends ended with heartfelt hugs and handshakes accompanied by real requests to "...come back anytime."

Throughout the years we have remained friends even with our careers taking us in different directions and to distant states. We meet sporadically, talk infrequently, but love each other.

The summer of 1999, Al, Alice, and I had the opportunity to meet in Eufaula. Alice and Al had talked a few times about my prostate cancer, and Al mentioned she would be "back home" in August for the Colonel's birthday celebration. The two worked out a time and place that we could meet in Eufaula, and Alice and I drove over to this antebellum city. We met in a shopping center parking lot. Alice jumped out of our car and ran to hug Al. Al then grabbed me and kissed my cheek. Eyes rolled at this spectacle. We talked for a few minutes and found out that Al was there for her father's 90th birthday. We then followed Al's car through a maze of streets past mansions to a neighborhood of medium-sized, kempt houses. Once inside her father's house, the four of us raced through an hour catching up and laughing.

About 1:30 in the afternoon, several friends and neighbors of "the Colonel" filtered in to begin preparing the decorations, hors d'eourves, desserts, and birthday cake. It became obvious that the preparers were also to be guests, so Alice and I motioned Al aside.

"Al why don't you let David and me do the serving while you and your dad's friends celebrate his birthday?"

Al demurred at first and then acquiesced.

Soon, Alice and I understood being in a crowd while being invisible. Al introduced us to the guests as they arrived, and we exchanged polite pleasantries. We returned to taking care of the refreshments. Slowly, the two of us became invisible. It was neither overt or on purpose. We simply did not fit into the conversations and remembrances. We were not shunned, we were just not seen. There was no discomfort, just enlightenment. Eleanor, in the early 1950's, must have experienced this.

Al, Alice, and I would meet in the kitchen laughing and talking as usual. It was as if there were two different worlds. The warm, friendly kitchen and the polite, distant dining room. We were victims of unshared experiences in one room, and brother and sisters in the other.

When all the guests had departed, the four of us sat down in the living room with sighs of relief. It had been fun but tiring. We reminisced some more, and then Alice and I departed to drive home. Filled with sweets and empty at the same time. Two worlds, which

Southern Smiles and Tears

had existed side by side for years still had a gulf between them.

   Al, Alice, George, and I have personally bridged the gulf but it is still there in most cases.

Chapter 62
Evil Still Exists

It has been years since Atticus first walked the pages of Harper Lee's *To Kill A Mockingbird*, but the evil he fought still exists in Monroeville, Alabama.

One of the films I used to teach with in the 1970's was Gregory Peck starring in Lee's great book. I then brought a projector and the film home to show it to my children. I always hoped it would work its way into their young minds.

It did.

In 1999, I was developing a county genealogical book in Monroe County, Alabama. Having arrived an hour before the time for the meeting to begin at the library, I went next door to a specialty gift shop. I asked where I could find copies of *To Kill A Mockingbird*. The owner of the shop told me Harper Lee always let her sell the books right there. She told me, though, that she did not have any copies left, but that a new edition would be out in two months.

Southern Smiles and Tears

"If I buy five, can I have them autographed?"

"Miss Lee," the owner replied, "will not autograph multiple copies anymore. She saw them being auctioned on the Internet for hundreds of dollars, when they only cost $20.00. Since then, she will not sign a group of books for me to sell here."

I then told her how I had used the film to teach my children as youngsters.

"What I want to do is give each one of them a copy, because I believe it will be a most special Christmas gift. I would like to have them individually signed to each child."

The lady said, "Just a minute." She went to the back of the store and telephoned someone. She returned the telephone to its cradle and walked back to where I was standing.

"Miss Lee told me she would be honored to sign five copies of her book for your children as soon as the new edition arrives."

I paid for the books and gave my telephone number so I could be notified when the books were available. Then I walked, with a skip in my gait, to my meeting. Evil was already there. It did not jump out and frighten everyone; it waited until after the meeting and whispered to me.

"This book will never be a success if you don't get rid of that black troublemaker!" whispered the female half of a white husband and wife team, as the male head nodded in assent.

"Who are you talking about?" I queried.

"That NAACP rabble rouser, Ezra Cunningham! Not one decent person in the county will send in a story as long as he is part of the committee."

"Well, I am not sure I could get rid of him, if I wanted to. You know Alice and I have a rule that says anyone is welcome to attend these book meetings."

"Either he goes, or we will not be back!"

My only reply at that point was "That is your decision."

There are many things I could, or should have said to them. Many great retorts came to mind as each door of their car shut with a metallic wallop. I have not seen them since.

Gwen Richardson, the book committee leader, came out of the library door just in time to hear the slams. She had a look of curiosity on her face that demanded I tell her what had happened. After I had completed my rendition, I asked her a question.

"What did Ezra do to create such anger?"

Gwen replied, "During the Civil Rights movement and marches Mr. Cunningham stirred up a few things here in the county."

"That gentle, caring old man?" was my astonished reply.

Southern Smiles and Tears

"You should have seen him 25 years ago. He was something!"

He still was to me. Earlier that summer our daughter-in law had been diagnosed with a particularly virulent form of leukemia. I had called Gwen and told her that Alice and I were going to Wisconsin to see her and try to be of help to Danny and the three grandchildren. Our minds were no longer functioning with an emphasis on books. This vibrant young lady of 30 was facing an unknown future, and we were at a loss of how to help other than to be there.

The next month, after returning to Alabama and resuming book committee meetings, I was back in Monroeville. No sooner had I entered the library on that Saturday morning when I remembered I had forgotten to place an ad in the local newspaper asking people to contribute family articles to the forthcoming book. As I was beginning to apologize for my forgetfulness, Mr. Cunningham looked at me through eyes rheumy with age and toil and said, "Son, we have all the time in the world to complete this book, but that girl needs help now!"

This 85-year old man, who had spent a lifetime with the all the injustices whites had pointed at him, then bowed his head and said, "Let's pray for her now."

He prayed as if he and God were on intimate speaking terms. There was no black and white in the room. Simply, people praying for a young woman in Wisconsin who needed help. The meeting became superfluous.

The next week Harper Lee's books arrived at our house, and Alice and I wrapped them. It was three months later, after Christmas, when our oldest daughter Penny told us that her book was the best gift ever.

Atticus, battles still remain to be fought, but I am thankful every day for you being part of my family.

Southern Smiles and Tears

Chapter 63
Grace

Just when I begin to lose hope that the South will ever achieve the dream of Martin Luther King something restores my faith in mankind.

I was conducting a book meeting in Selma, Alabama in 2000 when Dot DeRamus asked us to listen to a great story. Seventy-plus years of age, Dot displays her age as if she has the Grim Reaper in full retreat. This lady, and I use that word completely in its proper context, had previously worked on two other county books with me. One of the books would have been an abysmal failure without Dot cajoling, begging, and even ordering people to "...get a story in this book."

She began the story without further introduction.

The year was 1860, before the beginning of the terrible conflagration that ensnared the nation for four years. It was the constitutionally ordained year for all Americans to be counted. Census takers spread across the still physically intact United States to count everyone to determine the allocation of the House of Representatives. Well, that is not exactly correct. Each adult slave was to be counted as three-fifths of a person.

A census taker was working a section outside Selma in Dallas County, Alabama. He approached a plantation where he spied an elderly black woman in a rocking chair. He stepped onto the porch and knocked on the door.

A voice from behind him said, "Dey not here."

He inquired of the figure as to when the family would return. The lady replied that it would be several weeks. This caused the census taker a problem. He was to complete his count by the end of the next week. He sat down in a chair next to the rocking woman and began to converse with her.

The lady's name was Grace. She had been a slave in the family for many years. However, she had belonged to other families over her many years and had lived as far away as Virginia. Inquiring about her age, the census taker was taken aback. Grace told him she wasn't exactly positive about her age, but she did remember when George Washington became President.

Here was a woman born before the approval of the document stating the right to "…life, liberty, and the pursuit of happiness…" who had been denied the last two. She had spent her life owned by others, who decided whether she was to be happy or not. Grace lived during the presidential terms of John Adams and Thomas Jefferson the two prime writers of the document stating, "…all men are created equal." She was a slave as the nation expanded from a thin line of colonies along the Atlantic to a nation spreading from the Atlantic Ocean to the Pacific Ocean. The War of 1812, Henry Clay's Compromise of 1820, the death at the Alamo of Davy Crockett and his fellow seekers of freedom, the demise of the Whig Party, and the birth of the upstart Republican Party all came and went while Grace toiled as the property of others.

The census taker asked Grace about the family that owned her. He recorded the information and before he rose to leave wrote Grace's name on the census form. Thus Grace became an official witness and source of data in the 1860 census.

She was a real person!

The story does not end there. One of the people in the meeting asked about the source of the story.

"The story was sent in by the great-grand daughter of the family who owned Grace. She wanted to make sure that Grace not only be in the census records, but that Grace be remembered as a person

Southern Smiles and Tears

in a book."

The book in question allows people to submit family stories without charge for publication. This Texas descendant of white owners of slaves had not sent in a story about her ancestors. She had chosen instead to submit a story about Grace.

Some people have class.

Southern Smiles and Tears

Chapter 64
Y2K Southern Style

Three years and two New Year's celebration removed from the hoopla surrounding the change from 1999 to 2000, it is difficult to remember all of the tragedies doomsdayers were predicting.

Most of the dismal forecasts attached themselves to computers. It seems that many programmers in the early days of the computer revolution failed to foresee that the year 2000 was in the future. They had geared internal computer clocks to only recognize the prefix "19" as the century and ignored the "20" looming ahead.

Newspaper stories, Internet rumors, and talk show radio and television programs predicted grim events at the split of the years 1999 and 2000 because the control computers had come to exercise over our daily lives. Undeliverable electricity, underground gas tanks full of fuel incapable of being pumped, unusable credit cards, shortages of food, short circuited water lines, traffic lights all a flutter, were just a few of the things going to happen in the coming

Southern Smiles and Tears

cataclysm.

At the same time, people throughout the world were planning extravagant celebrations. Cities were to be showered with fireworks lighting up at the stroke of midnight. Adventurers scheduled exclusive trips to the International Dateline giving the travelers first access the new millennium.

Residents of Clanton, Alabama were no exception to the excitement, fears, and hyperbole.

A head deacon of a Southern Baptist church decided to take on the millennium face to face. He called a meeting of the men of the church, Southern Baptist women being unable to comprehend the depth of the coming disaster. The exchange of ideas began slowly, accelerated, and then became unintelligible as everyone tried to out talk each other. The rumors of the media shrunk in impact compared to the approaching disaster looming over Clanton. One participant even opined that this would be the perfect time for "...the Russians to attack." It was never discussed as to why Russian computers would work past midnight 1999, and American ones would not.

Finally, regaining some semblance of control, the head deacon began assigning committees to handle certain responsibilities. Baptists love committees second only to covered dish dinners. One committee was to handle water, another heat, a third gasoline, and one was in charge of sleeping arrangements for the congregation. Food, though, was to be the domain of the head deacon. Men were assigned to the various committees, and each withdrew aside to attempt to come up with solutions to the conundrums faced.

The water committee first decided a take a survey of the church members to ascertain who had wells. This was soon rejected when someone remembered that modern wells used electricity to run pumps. A second suggestion went further. Check to see how many people had swimming pools. The committee would buy tablets to purify the water for drinking. Then someone derailed that by asking how the water from the scattered pools would be carried to the church if there were no gasoline.

The gasoline committee chairman interjected that "We have a plan for gas, but need a couple of weeks to get it together."

Suddenly, in a stroke of genius, someone remembered that stores carried bottled water. A simple amendment to the budget could be presented to the church for vote. Problem solved.

Heat was next to be addressed. This was covered in a few minutes. The church would buy propane heaters, and each family would bring a propane tank as a contribution to the forthcoming disaster. No consideration was given to the fact that portable propane gas tanks are not supposed to be used indoors.

The gasoline committee brought forth a solution that could have wiped the church off the face of the earth, thereby negating the need for all the other committees. The first proposal was to get 50-gallon tanks, fill them with gasoline, and store them beside the church. Fortunately, sounder thinking prevailed. The solution was to have every vehicle, owned by members of the church, filled to capacity with fuel on December 30. The date was important because everyone knew there would be "...a run on gas stations on the 31st."

Here the discussion became theological. Because the word "member" had been used in the gasoline committee's recommendation, someone wanted to know about "nonmembers."

"What about those who attend, but haven't joined the church?"

Now the millennium had become serious.

"What about those under 12? They aren't accountable yet."

"What if someone in the neighborhood shows up? Do we let them in?"

Then followed an in depth review of the problem Jesus caused when he expanded the meaning of the word "neighbor." Finally, in true Baptist fashion another committee was formed to study the problem. The committee never reported back with a solution. This lack of knowing who would be allowed into the safety of the church allowed the sleeping committee to be able to postpone coming up with arrangements. I am not sure if the "neighbor" or sleeping problems have yet been resolved.

Surely food would not create any unrest. Baptists do know about food. However, food is usually under the control of the women of a Baptist church, and not one woman was part of the austere group making the millennium decisions.

Perhaps, that is why the food situation was solved as it was by the head deacon. I am positive that female input would have amended the decision.

"I'll buy Veeinnie Sausages."

That is how he pronounced the product, though, it is spelled "Vienna" on the labels. Those unfamiliar with this precooked delicacy, mainly, those from the North, would pronounce it as the city in Austria is said in English. Southerners pronounce the product differently. These two-inch long, cylindrical, mystery meats are "Veeinnie Sausages" in the South. They are also packed in their diminutive cans tighter than the canned sardines of Norway.

He not only purchased Vienna Sausage, but he did so with

Southern Smiles and Tears

resolve.

Thirty cases of 24 cans to each case.

Then the millennium did a sneaky thing. It came and passed without a bump in the lives of most people.

It passed though Clanton, "…like a thief in the night."

The only problem was that the thief failed to steal the 30 cases of "Veeinnies."

Southern Smiles and Tears

Chapter 65
West Texas Etiquette

Hats are a problem to me. Not all hats, but the plethora of baseball caps. Backwards, sideways, but mostly in restaurants at tables.

That probably makes me an old fogey.

I am okay with being one, if that is the entrance level to fogeyism. It may be stylish to wear hats askew, but I believe wearing them into and not removing them in restaurants and even churches is an "in your face" act. It was not too long ago that the removal of one's hat was an act of politeness, especially in the South. Now it is not even a consideration. Adults, who should know better, sit eating in restaurants without even thinking about the simple act of removing their hats.

Now that I have gotten that tirade out of my system, it is with some awe that I relate a High Plains story from West Texas.

Southern Smiles and Tears

I was in Brownfield, Texas, during the summer of 2000, to deliver a writing seminar about family history. It was my third trip to this West Texas town south of Lubbock. The town is windswept with beautiful brick streets. The wind velocity is memorialized in a book, *Walking Backwards to School.* Students had to walk backwards because the wind whipped the dust and sand viciously across their faces, if they walked into it. As is the case in many towns with original brick roadways, a group of politicians want to cover the bricks with asphalt. Blacktop is cheaper to repair than going to the trouble of maintaining a part of our history. The Historical Commission in Terry County has a view quite opposite from that of the city politicians. Save the bricks.

Brownfield has seen the "boom and bust" economy that has plagued many western towns. Once called "Fly Town" because of the plethora of flies that accompanied the cattle at this feeding stop on their way to market. Buzzing flies were so ubiquitous that people had to eat under tablecloths in order to avoid consuming the insects with a forkful of beef. The cattle boom ended with trains and trucks replacing the cattle drives as the way to get cattle to the slaughterhouses. Then "black gold" was found in Terry County. A county without a river or lake was awash in oil. At least for a few years. Then the oil reserves became as dry as the ancient river *arroyos.*

Now, if anything sustains the economy, it is the hardiness and fortitude of those who remain in the county. There is some cotton growing across the vast plain, but the people make do while waiting on the next boom. Through it all, though, remains the stoic, Stetson wearing westerners accepting the hard life while waiting for the good one.

I arrived for the seminar an hour before the meeting was to begin. About 30 minutes later people began arriving. With one exception, the men wore cowboy hats and boots — even the one man who had a pony tail hairdo braided down to his waist. Only one had a Texas Ranger baseball cap covering his locks. At first, because I moved back and forth from the foyer to the meeting room greeting and talking to various people, I failed to notice something. Though every man came to the foyer with a hat covering his head, not one had a hat on in the meeting room. Not one even had a hat in hand.

Where had all the *chapeaux* gone?

I walked back to the foyer. There on a table at the entrance to the meeting room were over 25 hats, including the owner of the baseball cap, placed upside down on the table. Each cowboy hat was

Southern Smiles and Tears

placed in that manner to maintain the all important brim shape. The baseball cap was also upside down, I suspect more from habit than necessity.

After I had delivered my seminar and the crowd began to dissipate, I watched as the men left the room. Each passed by the hat table, picked up his own but did not return it to the proper position. All of the men, including the owner of the baseball cap, held the head wear in their hands until they had exited the building.

The next morning I ate breakfast at a restaurant in town. The hat action of the previous night was not an anomaly. Every man in the filled restaurant was hatless. The only difference was that the hats hung from wooden pegs in the foyer of the restaurant.

A few weeks later Alice and I along with some friends were eating in the only steakhouse restaurant in Clanton. It was my first visit to a restaurant since my experience in Texas. There it was. A baseball cap atop a head. Then another and another. Men at tables covered with white cloths and actual metal utensils placed on cloth napkins sat, heads covered with caps facing North, South, East, and West. I longed to return a place of etiquette and politeness.

That was right after I fought back the urge to go around the room smacking hats to the floor.

Southern Smiles and Tears

Chapter 66
The Confederate Flag

 I often wondered how there could be such anger against and love for the Confederate flag.
 The adulation, I understood, fell into that idealized view of the antebellum period that many people in the South hold. Though far from reality, the view is maintained with a fervent belief that that period of history was idyllic. I had more trouble deciphering why blacks had such a hatred for this symbol. It only took a statement by two pre-teen girls at a 2002 Mardi Gras parade in Fairhope, Alabama for me to understand the insidious nature of this emblem and other symbols of that long ago era.
 Cheryl, our younger daughter, had flown from Michigan to visit and go with us for a weekend of parades in and around Mobile. She had never been to these festivities but had often heard of my tales about them. There was an added attraction for us. Jim Davis, my sister Martha's husband, was a member of "The Pharaohs" krewe.

Southern Smiles and Tears

He not only would be riding on a float; he had tickets for a Mardi Gras ball.

Before Jim's parade, several of us drove across Mobile Bay in our RV to the upscale town of Fairhope to view a parade being held there. It was to be a fun time.

We were enjoying ourselves until Cheryl motioned Alice and I aside. Both of us thought someone had shoved her, or said something inappropriate because of the look on her face. We moved back to the display windows of the Kate Spade store and huddled close enough to hear Cheryl speak in a low, angry voice.

"Do you know what those two girls just told me?"

Without giving us time to even guess who the girls were, or what they had said, Cheryl continued.

"Do you know why they are wearing shirts with the Confederate flag on them?"

Again, we did not have time to think of an answer.

"They said, 'The flag keeps them safe by scaring away the niggers!'"

"What?" Alice and I asked simultaneously.

"How in this day and time can two girls not yet teenagers spout such garbage?" continued Cheryl, almost in a state of apoplexy.

Our enjoyment of the parade faded with this revelation of racism. The three of us left that corner and walked back toward the RV much saddened by this step back into the South of the 1950's. The incident remained the topic of conversation among the three of us the rest of the evening.

Personally, I began to consider my reactions about South Carolina and the debate about flying the Confederate flag above the capitol in Columbia and other disputes about the display of the banner throughout the South. Had I thought it was the Shakespearean, "Much ado about nothing," or had I thought of how offensive and divisive this cloth had become? I concluded that, quite cowardly, I had not taken any stand.

My mind then plumbed deep into my brain to retrieve any other instances of my not understanding the pervasive nature of racism. Instantly, I ran into the assertion used by many Confederate flag defenders that it is "Heritage, not hate." Whose heritage? Surely, not those of darker skin who see the flag as a symbol of the "peculiar institution." Many of the defenders of the flag contest that the War Between the States was about State's Rights and not slavery. Ergo, the flag is not offensive. One might argue that slavery was not the "root" of the war but surely it was the trunk of the tree that grew from whatever root cause deemed to have caused that terri-

Southern Smiles and Tears

ble conflict. It has become a symbol, to many, of a culture that enslaved people of color. To others it is a symbol of a glorious war to defend the *Gone With The Wind* culture. Mostly, that flag has become divisive.

The reverence for the years 1861-1865 rears its head in some subtle ways. Where else but in the South would the defeated general of the cause have a holiday in his name. Even the president of the Confederate States of America is honored in Alabama with a day off for state employees. One group in the name of "heritage" even erected a statue of Nathan Bedford Forrest in Selma, Alabama. Yes, Forrest did help defend Selma near the end of the Civil War. However, he was also the founder of the Ku Klux Klan in Pulaski, Tennessee. Is it any wonder when the group placed the statue in a black neighborhood, it upset the residents?

My realization of the vast cultural divide in the state awoke in my conscious because of two birthdays. Jefferson Davis and Martin Luther King.

I was to have a meeting in Macon County home of world famous Tuskegee University. The local book group and I arrived for a three o'clock meeting at the courthouse annex only to find it closed. Why would a courthouse be closed on an everyday Monday? No one in the group seemed to know. Then a member of the group, arriving late, told us that he had the key.

"Today's a state holiday." He explained.

"What?" Questioned Lanice Middleton, who worked at Tuskegee. "We didn't have the day off."

The key holder explained, "It's Jefferson Davis birthday."

There it was. The men and women who had arrived with me were all black and had no idea it was a state holiday celebrating the birthday of the President of the Confederate States of America.

Opposing this was the reaction I received in another county where the book group was composed of white members. I informed the group that our meeting for the next month had to be moved up a week because the library would be closed the 20th of January.

"That Monday is Martin Luther King's birthday."

There were no comments, but the room was filled with looks of disdain and the shaking of heads. One person even loosed a. "Hrrmph!" Bigotry can be quiet as well as loud.

Politicians often perpetuate insensitivity to things that have racist connotations. A candidate in Crenshaw County, Alabama in 2002 proudly displayed the Confederate flag on his campaign posters advocating the county citizens elect him sheriff.

Sometimes the insensitivity can be almost humorous as to how far some elected officials will go to be disingenuous. A case in point is the symbol, required by law in Alabama to be on every vehicle license plate. When I first moved to Alabama the large heart with the motto "Heart of Dixie" inscribed within it held a prominent, visible presence in size and location. The license plates issued in 2002 still had the heart, but it has been reduced to less than one inch in diameter, and is completely unreadable. The "in your face" heart is still there, and state legislators have not voted to remove it for fear of criticism from the same people who see the Confederate flag as an important symbol of heritage.

A glimmer of light does exist in the reference to some of the symbols of the old South. Alice and I attended a film festival at the Alabama Theater in Birmingham in 1998. This grand theater has been restored and is the site of many events throughout the year. One of the enjoyable things at the theater is to hear the great Wurlitzer organ being played before and after the programs. The organ rises out of the stage with the organist filling the auditorium with music. When the film ended that summer night, a friend who was there with us went to the organist and asked him to play *Dixie*.

"I'm sorry," answered the organist, "but that particular tune has a negative connotation to many people in our audiences. I do not believe I should offend people by playing it."

Kenny, our friend, who was born and bred in the Alabama, surprised me by how he reacted to the refusal to his request. One of his favorite statements was "I am Alabamian by birth, Southern Baptist by choice, and proud of both."

I expected some type of harangue about Southern heritage but instead Kenny replied, "I understand. It would be nice to hear the song, but I don't think you should offend anyone."

My respect for Kenny rose at that point to a new height. Kenny reflected a sensitivity completely lacking by the girls in Fairhope in 2002.

The two girls, proudly and antagonistically wearing screen-printed Confederate flags over their petite breasts, have made something more clear in my mind. Many times the words "prejudiced" and "racist" have been used interchangeably. I believe that the two girls are prejudiced, but worse, they are racist. They have an innate distrust and hatred for a group of people and flaunt the attitude. They are ignorant of the Confederate flag and its "heritage." They do know the hate it engenders, and think it is cute to display it.

I pray that the belief held by some psychologists that attitudes developed by age 12 stay with a person throughout life is not true.

Southern Smiles and Tears

Surely, there must be hope for these two girls.
  Their present attitude has left a deep hole in my heart.

Southern Smiles and Tears

Chapter 67
What's in a Name

Our names may be one of our most personal and prized possessions. It is our identification in life, and one of our family connections to the past and future. Names often pass down through many generations. I love to watch those interested in genealogy read a book about families. They do so backwards by going first to the index of names and then to the text.

Names are the key to family knowledge.

In my family, my oldest brother's name, Herbert Voorhees, helped us to trace our paternal ancestry back to Holland in the 1600's. Ray, my father's name, went to one of my brothers as Edward Ray. My mother's name, Gunhild, is Swedish and passed down to my oldest sister and her daughter. My niece uses the diminutive "Gunnie", as did my mother. The Swedish connection followed through in my brother Billy's name. He received this from our grandfather as William Gustav. Martha Maria Christina Bice

Southern Smiles and Tears

received a whole load of ancestral identifications. My name has no family connections.

The inside joke in the family was that as the last of nine children all the good names were gone so I was given the non-family connected name of David Allen. More peculiar was that I was always told my middle name was spelled with an "a" as the second vowel. It wasn't until I needed a Social Security Number to go to work and sent for a copy of my Connecticut birth certificate, that I found out my middle name had an "e" in it. Those two simple letters caused me to have to give a lengthy explanation when I applied for my Social Security. A name is important.

My first wife did not particularly like either Swedish or Dutch names so the names did not pass down to our children. Voorhees, Gunhild, Christina, William, Edward, and Gustav were discarded. Both of our fathers were named Ray along with her brother and my brother Edward Ray. Patty thought the name was overused in both our families and did not want it passed forward. I am not positive where Penny Lynn came from, but Cheryl Ann was the name of a tugboat in a television series that Patty often watched. Two of our boys have names with biblical attributes, Daniel Mark and Richard Paul. Jeffrey Alan has the same mysterious origins as Penny. Danny's wife Sonya has been more particular with her French heritage. Zachary, Sophie, and Raney, their children, all have Sonya's maiden name as part of each of their given names.

I think my first awareness of how truly important a name can be to a person was revealed when our oldest daughter made a life changing decision. Penny is a career woman, who has not married, but who loves children. She is the prime "spoiler" of two of our grandsons, Josiah and Caleb. They are the sons of Jeffrey and Roberta and named directly from the Old Testament.

Penny's sister Cheryl had for years been the Big Sister for an abused little girl. The girl, a ward of the state, lived in various foster homes. When Cheryl's job took her to Michigan, Penny assumed the role of friend to the now teenage girl. One night Penny received a telephone call. It was from the girl's caseworker. The caseworker had picked up the girl from her weekly visit to her mother and was driving her back to the foster parents' house.

"You'll be home in a few minutes." Said the caseworker.

"It's not my home. I don't have a home."

"What do you mean? You've lived there for several years."

"Every time I do something they don't like, they tell me they will send me back. They say they don't have to keep me, and that if they didn't get paid they wouldn't want me no how."

Southern Smiles and Tears

The caseworker was horrified, and told the girl she would never have to go back there again. That is when Penny received the call from the caseworker. She asked Penny if the girl could spend the night with her until something more permanent could be worked out.

Something permanent did occur.

A year after that traumatic night we got a new granddaughter. Penny, stressful job and all, adopted the girl. When the two of them appeared before the family judge, after the girl's mother's parental rights had been taken away, the girl made a decision. She wanted to change her name. From that day forth she wanted to be Elaine Nicole Bice. She had become part of our family. She now had instant great-grandparents, grandparents, aunts, uncles, cousins, and most important, a new mother who loved her.

I am almost positive that I could not have taken on the responsibility Penny did at age 40. I was too busy completing a career in education and beginning one in writing. Penny has given her daughter something precious — her name.

One of the great things that happens during meetings I hold to develop family history books in the South is the spontaneous discussion of family names. People will be looking through some of our published books and emit sounds of joy upon locating a family name and connection. That is when I lose control of the meetings as everyone begins the scavenger hunt for names.

A spring 2002 meeting in York, Alabama had taken the turn into the origination of family names. Charles Walker, the chair of that particular county group, had diverted us into the era of slavery. This young man is a stay at home dad because of an illness and often brings his children to the meetings. Charles sports a shock of unruly black hair above a tall and spindly frame. He has a deep love for the history of Sumter County and its people. He is respectful of all those older than himself. Yes ma'am's, pardon me's and thank you's flow from his mouth in a slow moving molasses like tone. Even though we had become somewhat close over the two years of working on the Sumter County book, he still slips and calls me Mr. Bice.

Charles researches constantly to find out about the family roots of western Alabama. He reads incessantly. Alice and I had published 56 county books of Alabama between 1998 and 2002. Charles is the only person I know who had read every word of each of these books. He now was beside himself with excitement. He had found what appeared to be a previously unmarked slave burial plot on his family's property. Behind his house were the stubs of rocks

Southern Smiles and Tears

laid out in the shape of a cross.

"Mr. Bice, do you know how I can find out for sure this is a cemetery?"

"First, you need to talk with anyone you can find who may have heard that such a cemetery did exist. Listen to stories. You shouldn't just rely on facts and property records. Right here is a good place. Mrs. Black may have heard one of her family members telling about where one of her ancestors was buried. She may not have heard such a story, but may relay the story to someone else. I can tell you that it was not unusual for slaves to respect the cross of their adopted religion. You might also try to find people with the name Walker. Slaves sometimes took the surnames of their former owners at the time of emancipation."

Then a woman named Hazel, who I did not remember as having attended any previous meetings, spoke with evidence of pride in her voice.

"That is what happened with my grandfather's slaves. In fact, the blacks with my name had a reunion last year in Birmingham. I told them I would allow them to come out to our property and see the slave cemetery."

The meeting continued along another path after a few moments of discussion about names and their origins. I was gathering my computer and materials before heading home. Charles and I were discussing a couple of points when Hazel interrupted us. She had a question she wanted to ask me about how many words she could write about her grandfather. Charles shifted about as if he were a four-year-old in need of a bathroom while I answered Hazel. My final words were barely out of my mouth when Charles spurted forth to Hazel.

"Tell me more about that reunion."

"Well, there are about 700 descendants of a pair of my grandfather's slaves. They meet annually. Most of them live somewhere else, but last year they decided to come to Alabama. The man who organized it, I think he was from California, even invited me to come to their reunion in Birmingham."

Charles could hardly contain his excitement.

"Did you go?"

"Me! In a hotel full of 700 niggers. Of course I didn't go."

You say the least, when you identify this as an awkward moment. Hazel was aware of the three black women of our group still standing nearby, and because of that she had delivered her invective with a low, growling voice.

I said nothing, but Charles did.

Southern Smiles and Tears

"I would'a gone in a heartbeat."

Hazel emitted a "hmrff" and left the library.

Charles looked at me. I looked at him. Charles proved his integrity.

"I feel sorry for her. She could have met people descended from a couple who knew her grandparents but didn't because she saw black when she should have seen family heritage."

I am honored to know a real son of the South.

Southern Smiles and Tears

Chapter 68
Religion Versus Faith

Chaim Potok, author of *The Chosen,* in an interview on Public Radio in 1987 had an interesting observation about religion and faith. Terry Grose, the host of the program Fresh Air, asked him if in his view was there a type of religious chauvinism in many people.

He responded that many people were "infantileistic" in approaching religion. He further explained that in a childlike manner many religious people tend to believe their way is the only way. Mr. Potok completed this thought by telling of a visit to a Shinto Temple in Japan where he saw an old man in a long coat shuffle up to the shrine, kneel, and pray fervently. The man reminded the author of his growing up in an Hasidic neighborhood and seeing the older, bearded Jews in black hats and coats praying to their God. He wondered if the God of the Jews listened to the old man in Japan.

Southern Smiles and Tears

Potok's comments came back to me when Alice and I later made a visit to Japan. We worshipped on a Sunday morning in a Southern Baptist chapel on the grounds of the New Otani Hotel in Tokyo. The hotel, built for a summer Olympics, provided the chapel to serve the religious needs of Americans during the games. The chapel remains on the hotel grounds staffed by a missionary from the United States. This was not the only place of religion we visited. The wife and sister of a Japanese bookstore owner acquaintance took us to Yokohama where we visited a Shinto Shrine and a statue of Buddha.

Just as when I had delivered the eulogy in a Jewish Temple, God did not unleash His wrath upon Alice nor me because of these visits. However, when we returned to the States and told our church friends about our visits we received peculiar looks. I believe the thought crossed many of their minds of "What would a Baptist church choir leader and her husband be doing in a place like that?" I have no idea what they would think of us if they knew that while we were in Australia our host put us up in a hotel across the street from a brothel.

Alice and I are on the receiving end of the same looks when we mention that we have Catholic friends in Missouri and Mormon friends in Idaho. I find the latter to be peculiar, especially among my southern football fan friends. I can remember some of them, and their children, wearing San Francisco football jerseys emblazoned with the name and number of Steve Young, a devout, tithing, mission going Mormon. Mormons may be lost according to certain doctrines but if one of them can fling a pigskin he is okay. Infantileistic doesn't begin to cover this concept.

Though not exactly the same, this type of thinking invades many churches in the South concerning race. Alice was leading the choir in a Methodist Church and I was a good pew warmer. One morning in our Sunday School class that old problem of Jesus telling about the Good Samaritan popped up once again. The discussion became lively and soon the issue of blacks and Mexicans crept in. Mexicans soon became secondary, I suppose because they are too new in much of the South for anecdotal truths to have developed about them. One thing stood out. "They're taking our jobs!"

Blacks were another thing. Almost every contributor to the conversation opened with "I'm not prejudiced, but…." The discussion ended when one man stated the sentiment of what I had heard 50 years earlier in Prichard, "They have their own churches, let them go there." Alice and I were both uncomfortable and our class attendance became somewhat sporadic after that.

Southern Smiles and Tears

This incident was followed a couple of months later by two encounters that made me think deeply about religion. The first event was at a men's meeting. I had not become a member of the group but one evening decided to accept an invitation to attend. There was good fellowship and food. Then came a short business meeting. After business had been completed the men sat around talking. Almost immediately the flow turned to blacks. Because the pastor was there, I believed he would short-circuit this. He had often preached about the "fellowship of man" and that "we are all equal in God's eyes."

What happened caused this to be my first and last time to attend the men's meeting. The pastor didn't just join in the discussion; he topped it off with a stereotype.

"If we're not careful boys the blacks are going to take over no matter how lazy they are. They don't want equality, they want to rule over us."

The latter part of the statement left me with a serious question. How could the stereotype of "lazy blacks" fit with the fact that until slavery ended almost the entire economy of the South depended on the labor of blacks? Much of it still does.

The final incident in the church came in a private conversation between the pastor and me. We were planning a "Fifth Sunday Night Sing." Many churches in the South do not have regularly scheduled services on the months with a fifth Sunday. This evening is devoted to singing. Several Methodist churches in the county would get together at churches on a rotating basis and combine the sings.

One small Methodist church's membership was black. Several members of the church often attended the sings, usually rendering a few gospel songs a capello. It appeared the majority of the attendees enjoyed this greatly.

The pastor and I were discussing the order of appearances by various churches and groups, when he threw in a lightening bolt.

"I'm not sure I want that black group getting up there and dominating the sing."

"What?" came my erudite response.

"Most of us would just as soon they didn't come."

"I enjoy their singing and spirituality."

"Well, it just doesn't fit in this area."

"I don't come from this culture, but that doesn't seem right."

The pastor then said something, which had never been said to me before.

"Don't try to tell me that you're not prejudiced. Everybody is no matter where they're raised."

I do not recall the conversation after that point, but shortly thereafter Alice and I found another church.

Southern Smiles and Tears

Chapter 69
Fertilizer and Flour Sacks

Rosa Magee Williams was born October 3, 1895. My mother was born in 1897. One was birthed in Louisiana. The latter first cried in Texas. One black, one white, they never met nor knew each other's cultures, but they were similar. Both had a strong belief in education and the value of passing down stories to family. Each had married a handsome widower. Gunhild Bice had nine children. Rosa Williams raised 10 children.

When I entered Rosa's room in a nursing home in Franklinton, Louisiana, I was blessed with the opportunity to relive the times I listened to my mother tell stories of her early life. Another person was also in the room. Reflected in Rosa's eyes, I saw Eleanor.

Rosa Williams at 107 years of age was surrounded by three of her daughters and a granddaughter. They formed a cocoon trying to protect a full-blown butterfly. Appearing to be a weakened, bed ridden, shell, Rosa was as beautiful and strong as the Monarch butterflies that migrate thousands of miles each year to winter in Mexico.

I told her that I was preparing to write a book about the Village of Folsom, Louisiana. This was the town where she had lived most of her life.

"I was told that you remember quite a bit about the village! I would like to talk to you about Folsom, but first I would like to get to know you."

One of her twin daughters said, "Momma, he wants to interview you about Folsom."

Rosa lifted a rectangular piece of cardboard to the front of her faced and coughed a couple of times. The cardboard was for the benefit of visitors, not Rosa's. Then she spoke. Clearly and strongly.

"I know what he wants. He was talking to me."

She included the "g" at the end of the word "talking."

She turned her pink capped covered head toward me and said, "What do you want to talk about?"

We talked. We conversed. We chatted. We never engaged in an interview. Tears filled my eyes at times, not from sadness, but from just having had the opportunity to meet Rosa. We held hands as she talked about her good life and being ready to meet her Maker.

I told her, "I don't see any angels walking around your bed and besides I want to come back next month and talk to you some more. So if you see an angel walk through the door, tell him to get on out of here."

She laughed, gripped my hand tightly, and said, "I'll see you when you get back to Louisiana."

Few of the people whom I have met as I have passed through life have carried the label of "Lady" with such aplomb as Rosa. Not one recriminatory word passed from her mouth during our two-hour conversation. Born of slave parents, held down by Jim Crow, and hungered during the Depression, having to return to school at the death of her husband, she emitted happiness.

Rosa fairly sparkled when speaking of her "Papa." The Magee family had bought her grandfather Bob in New Orleans, and Mark had been born as a slave. He was too young, before emancipation, to work the fields. His job was to carry water to the field hands. The wife of Mark's owner, Gabrellen Magee, taught Mark how to read and write along with her own children. Once freed, he borrowed books to read and practiced handwriting. He became the first black teacher at the Washington Parish Colored School. His respect for learning was reflected in Rosa. She could hardly contain

Southern Smiles and Tears

herself as she asked if I would like to hear her recite a poem that she had learned even before she entered school. Rosa was positive that she had recited the poem before she began school. She remembered that, when she was five, her dress had caught fire from standing to close to the flames to warm herself. She had recited the poem to her family earlier that day.

"It's a lullaby poem when you rocked a baby. Flies liked to swarm about nursing babies."

After she had recited the poem to me, I asked if she would repeat it line by line. That way I could record the words. One of her daughters repeated what I had said to her. Once again Rosa admonished her 78-year-old offspring that, "I know what he asked. He's talking to me." Rosa was still firmly in control of her life and family.

She then spoke the words, one line at a time. She interspersed the staccato recitation with comments about how much she loved children. I was able to write the entire poem.

Baby Bye
Baby Bye, here's this fly
Let us watch him, you and I
How he crawls up the walls
Yet he never falls
If you and I had such legs,
You and I could walk on eggs
Little fly, open your eye,
A spider is nearby
Spiders do not use flies well
Then away, do not stay
Come again another day.

Rosa and her schoolmates had to cross Cat Kaw Creek to attend Crystal Spring School. Their teacher, Miss Celestine Dyson boarded at the home of Muggins and Vestie Chappel. Sometimes rain would swell the creek, and the students could not go home. When that happened, the students stayed overnight with the Chappels.

"Miz Vestie put sleeping pallets for the girls on the floor in our teacher's room. We laughed and giggled until Miz Dyson told us to hush. The boys stayed with Mr. Muggins. In the morning, the Chappels would fix up our lunch pails with bread, syrup, and eggs for our lunches. The syrup came from his syrup mill. When the creek went down, Mr. Muggins would let us cross to go home."

Rosa went to work taking care of the children of white families at the age of 11 or 12. She not only cared for the children, Rosa also

TIPS EFECTIVOS

para triunfar en sus entrevistas

Ros Jay

EDITORIAL TRILLAS
México, Argentina, España,
Colombia, Puerto Rico, Venezuela

Catalogación en la fuente

> Jay, Ros
> Tips efectivos para triunfar en sus entrevistas. --
> México : Trillas, 2014.
> 182 p. : il. ; 23 cm. -- (Tips efectivos)
> Traducción de: Brilliant interview
> Incluye índices
> ISBN 978-607-17-2048-1
>
> 1. Entrevistas. 2. Personal - Dirección. I. t.
>
> D- 650.144'J739t   LC- HF5549.5.I6'J3.8

Título original: Brilliant interview
Versión autorizada en español de la
primera edición publicada por
Pearson Education Limited.
Edinburgh Gate, Harlow, CM20 2JE,
www.pearsoned.co.uk
©Pearson Education Limited

La presentación y
disposición en conjunto de
*TIPS EFECTIVOS PARA TRIUNFAR
EN SUS ENTREVISTAS*
son propiedad del editor.
Ninguna parte de
esta obra puede ser
reproducida o trasmitida, mediante ningún
sistema o método, electrónico o mecánico
(incluyendo el fotocopiado, la grabación
o cualquier sistema de recuperación y
almacenamiento de información),
sin consentimiento
por escrito del editor

Derechos reservados en lengua española
© 2014, Editorial Trillas, S. A. de C. V.

División Administrativa,
Av. Río Churubusco 385,
Col. Gral. Pedro María Anaya,
C. P. 03340, México, D. F.
Tel. 56884233, FAX 56041364
churubusco@trillas.mx

División Logística,
Calzada de la Viga 1132,
C. P. 09439, México, D. F.
Tel. 56330995 FAX 56330870
laviga@trillas.mx

🛒 **Tienda en línea**
www.etrillas.mx

Miembro de la Cámara Nacional de
la Industria Editorial
Reg. núm. 158

Primera edición en español, septiembre 2014
ISBN 978-607-17-2048-1

Impreso en México
Printed in Mexico

TIPS EFECTIVOS
para triunfar en sus entrevistas

Traducción: **Javier Alejandro Barrientos y Olivares**

Índice de contenido

Acerca de la autora   9
Reconocimientos   11
Introducción   13

PARTE 1
Antes de la entrevista

Cap. 1. ¿Qué esperar?   17

Colóquese en los zapatos del entrevistador, 17. Los materiales básicos, 19. El formato, 21. Reasegurar al entrevistador, 22. Solicitudes internas, 24. Solicitantes graduados, 25.

Cap. 2. Cómo prepararse   27

Investigar a la organización, 30. Prepare su caso, 32. Esté preparado para la entrevista, 35.

Cap. 3. Primeras impresiones   39

Antes de la entrevista, 40. ¿Qué es lo que se va a poner?, 40. Su saludo inicial, 44.

PARTE 2
Durante la entrevista

Cap. 4. Controle los nervios   49

Raíz del problema, 50. Reducir los síntomas, 51.

Cap. 5. Proyecte la imagen correcta — 55
Reflexione y responda, 56. Lenguaje corporal, 58.

Cap. 6. La entrevista — 63
Estilo de la entrevista, 64. Responda positivamente, 65. Tipos de preguntas, 66. Diferentes tipos de entrevistas, 67. Haga la salida, 72.

Cap. 7. Las preguntas más comunes en una entrevista — 75
Las preguntas más comunes, 76. Verifique si está listo, 86.

Cap. 8. Las preguntas duras de una entrevista — 89
Preguntas acerca de su carrera, 98. Preguntas acerca de este trabajo, 102. Preguntas que lo invitan a autocriticarse, 106. Preguntas que le invitan a ser negativo, 109. Cuestiones acerca de su salario, 111. Preguntas inesperadas, 114.

Cap. 9. Sus preguntas — 117
Las preguntas, 118.

Cap. 10. Entrevistas con base en competencias — 125
¿Cuáles competencias evalúan?, 125. ¿Cuáles son las preguntas que ellos harán?, 126. ¿Cómo debe responder a estas preguntas?, 128. La entrevista, 129.

Cap. 11. Pruebas psicométricas — 131
Prepárese para las pruebas, 132. Pruebas de habilidad y de aptitud, 135. Cuestionarios sobre personalidad y motivación, 138.

Cap. 12. Centros de evaluación — 141
Un método objetivo y justo, 141. Prueba en equipo, 143.

Cap. 13. Segundas entrevistas — 147
Tome una bebida…, 149.

PARTE 3
Después de la entrevista

Cap. 14. ¿Qué hacer mientras espera escucharlos?   153

    Dé las gracias, 153. Haga notas, 154.

Cap. 15. ¿Qué hacer si consigue el trabajo?   157

    Mala sincronización, 157. Negociación del trato, 159. La carta de oferta, 167.

Cap. 16. ¿Qué pasa si pierde la oferta de trabajo?   169

    No se confíe, 172.

Índice analítico   175

Acerca de la autora

Ros Jay es una autora de éxitos editoriales sobre carreras y empresas. Entre sus muchos libros están *Fast Thinking Manager's Manual* (junto con Richard Templar), *Effective Presentation* (con Tony Jay), *Successful Candidate* y *How to Get a Pay Raise*.

La base empresarial de Ros es principalmente en mercadotecnia y comunicaciones, y es cofundadora y directora de su propia compañía editorial.

Reconocimientos

Quiero agradecer a las muchas personas y organizaciones que me han ayudado con este trabajo, especialmente:

- ASE solutions.
- Career World.
- Chartered Institute of Marketing.
- Ann Pinn, MD, Delta Consultants (www.delta-consultants.com).
- Fish6.co.uk.
- Hobsons (www.hobsons.co.uk).
- Penny Glazzard, Marketing Executive, Hill McGlynn (www.hillmcglyn.com).
- Jason Silk, Hill McGlynn.
- The Institute for Employment Studies.
- Oneclickhr.com.
- Phil Boyle, MD, Ramsay Hall Limited (www.ramseyhall.com).

También quiero reconocer la asistencia dada por el Grupo SHL plc por permitir que ciertas partes de los ejemplos de sus preguntas sean reproducidas aquí. Más detalles de sus materiales se pueden obtener en el sitio web SHL en <www.shl.com>.

Introducción

Una entrevista de trabajo es una cuestión muy seria. Ya sea que obtenga o no el trabajo que usted desea, puede influir mucho en su carrera y afectar toda su vida. Yo no estoy tratando de asustarle aquí, pero el hecho es que como se maneje en la entrevista es importante. Muy importante.

El entrevistador no se molestará en llamar a cualquiera para una entrevista a menos de que tenga alguna oferta prometedora. Entonces, los demás candidatos van a tener que ser buenos. Lo que significa que necesitará ser mucho mejor que ellos para obtener el trabajo.

Pero está bien. Usted puede hacerlo. Usted nada más necesita saber exactamente qué es lo que busca el entrevistador. *Tips efectivos para triunfar en sus entrevistas* se trata de esto. Usted encontrará todo lo que necesita saber, con plenitud de consejos y asesoría de expertos que le dirán lo que quieren ver y lo que les impresiona más, acerca de cómo presentarse como el mejor candidato

Las entrevistas son comedoras de nervios y nosotros a veces cometemos errores, o simplemente no damos lo mejor que tenemos. Así que prepárese, con la ventaja de saber qué es lo que su entrevistador busca y colóquese en la posición de suministrárselo. Aprenda cómo mostrarse a sí mismo bajo la mejor luz posible y maximice sus oportunidades para obtener el trabajo.

El desafío para obtener un trabajo empieza antes de que usted siquiera busque una entrevista y continúa a través de ésta con el entrevistador y más allá. Cuando se le ofrezca el trabajo, usted necesitará decidir si lo toma y –si lo hace– cómo obtener el mejor trato posible. Antes, durante y después de la entrevista existe una multiplicidad de pasos que puede tomar para colocarse por arriba y aparte de la competencia.

El mero acto de que usted tenga una entrevista (quizá muchas) alineadas es un gran inicio. Cada entrevista que obtenga es una pluma en su capa. Casi siempre lo colocarán dentro de una minoría de solicitantes, y significa que el entrevistador le vea, en el papel, como capaz de hacer todo lo que se necesita en el trabajo anunciado. Así que usted ya está bien encaminado para obtener el trabajo. Y una vez que haya leído este libro no tendrá ningún problema en destacar.

Por tanto, escuche a los expertos, encuentre qué es lo que quieren y en menos de lo que piensa estará en la envidiable posición de decidir si acepta o no esa oferta de trabajo.

Parte 1
Antes de la entrevista

Capítulo 1
¿Qué esperar?

¡Felicidades! usted tiene una entrevista. Ya tiene impresionado al entrevistador con su CV y su forma de solicitud de empleo para haber podido llegar hasta este punto. No es probable que ellos entrevisten a cada candidato, así que claramente ellos ya han visto algo en su solicitud que se sale de la masa.

Claro está, desde su punto de vista, es probable que esto parezca sólo una parte respecto a la entrevista que viene, pero no se preocupe. Una vez que haya leído este libro, obtener el trabajo será mucho más fácil para usted. Su preparación empieza aquí. Y la primera cosa que le ayudará a lograr una entrevista efectiva es saber justamente lo que se espera. Entre menos sorpresas, mejor. Así, ¿qué es lo que sucederá en su entrevista?

COLÓQUESE EN LOS ZAPATOS DEL ENTREVISTADOR

Necesita saber qué es lo que busca el entrevistador. ¿Por qué se llevan a cabo estas entrevistas? Ellos han empezado con una pila de solicitudes que han enviado y distribuido a las personas que están invitando a entrevistarse, incluyéndolo a usted.

El entrevistador no va a invitar a cualquiera que no le reconozca que pueda hacer el trabajo, así que la lista de entrevistados será hecha con personas que, en su opinión, deberían ser capaces de hacer el trabajo. Una vez más, debe motivarse por esto. Usted no estaría en la lista a menos de que el entrevistador pensara –con base en su solicitud y su CV– que no podría hacer el trabajo que ellos anuncian.

Pero el entrevistador tiene un problema. Ellos están autorizados para elegir. Tienen una lista de media docena o una docena de solicitudes, de candidatos, todos los cuales se consideran capaces para desempeñar el trabajo. Así que, ¿a quién se lo ofrecen? Necesitan más información antes de decidir, y para esto son las entrevistas.

Conocimiento efectivo

No en todos los países utilizan las entrevistas con tanta frecuencia como en las empresas del Reino Unido.* En otros países las organizaciones usan un rango de métodos de selección que no necesariamente incluye las entrevistas (aunque ellos las hacen a menudo), pero en el Reino Unido 99% de las organizaciones usan la entrevista para la selección de nuevo personal. Y 50% de ellas no emplean otro método adicional (nada de pruebas psicométricas, centros de evaluación y demás). Esto significa que su habilidad para ser entrevistado es vital para lograr obtener cualquier trabajo que usted solicite.

Fuente: www.oneclick.com, HR Information, Selection Interviews.

* Debido a que esta obra fue editada primero en el Reino Unido, se respeta la redacción original y sus ejemplos. No obstante en México el uso de entrevistas cómo método de selección en las empresas, es de manera igual o parecida. [N.E.].

El entrevistador tiene que decidir cuál de los candidatos es el más adecuado para el puesto. Ellos no tratan de medirlo en contra de otros, sino en contra de los estándares del propio trabajo. Uno de ustedes podría ser bastante más experimentado que otro, pero la experiencia no es la cosa más importante. Quizá encajar en el equipo sea lo más relevante, o la habilidad para usar un cierto *software* en particular.

En consecuencia, va a ser una decisión difícil. Todos los candidatos tendrán puntos débiles y fuertes, y el entrevistador tendrá que balancearlos. Ellos quieren a alguien que tenga mucha experiencia, ¿o quieren a alguien con menos, pero con experiencia más significativa? ¿Qué pasa si la persona con las calificaciones más inapropiadas parece que encaja mejor dentro de la cultura de la empresa?,

¿deberían optar por una persona que parece confiable y sólida, o por un candidato más creativo pero que parece menos confiable?

Es duro ser entrevistador. Y también es duro para usted porque sabe menos acerca de lo que ellos buscan. Sin embargo, si usted no sabe cuáles son sus prioridades, ampliamente sabe qué es lo que pretenden. Y si usted conoce dónde se encuentran sus fuerzas y debilidades, puede prepararse para promover sus puntos fuertes y encontrar la manera de hacer aparecer sus debilidades como menos débiles. Después veremos técnicas para hacer esto, mientras tanto puede empezar el proceso de identificar sus plus y sus debilidades usando el siguiente ejercicio.

> Es duro ser entrevistador.

Evalúese usted mismo para el trabajo

Marque en una escala de 1 a 10 en las siguientes áreas clave que su entrevistador analizará a fondo. Usted necesita evaluarse para el puesto en cuestión. Si tiene más de una entrevista pendiente, haga este ejercicio para cada una.

Usted tiene que compararse a sí mismo con lo que el entrevistador busque en cada caso, mucho de lo cual estará claro a partir del anuncio de reclutamiento y de la descripción del trabajo, del cual debería obtener una copia si la solicita. Marque de 1 a 10 cada área que pueda ver donde tiene que trabajar más para mejorar. Cuando se trate de la personalidad, querrá preguntarle a un buen amigo o a algún colega para que le dé una opinión honesta.

Área clave	1-10
Habilidades.	
Experiencia directa de las tareas relevantes.	
Calificaciones.	
Antecedentes.	
Personalidad (como viene a través de la entrevista).	

LOS MATERIALES BÁSICOS

Bien, al menos su entrevistador no tendrá que hacer la selección a ciegas. Inclusive antes de que conozca a los candidatos, no tiene más que unos cuatro documentos que le ayudan a tomar su decisión. Éstos caen en dos categorías: documentos que ayudan a definir el trabajo y los que le sirven para evaluar a los candidatos. Los primeros son:

- La descripción del trabajo, que les dice el objetivo general del trabajo y las responsabilidades clave en éste.
- La especificación del empleado, que describe cuáles habilidades y atributos necesitará tener el candidato exitoso.

> Muy pocos empleadores mostrarán a los solicitantes la especificación del empleo.

Debería tener una copia de la descripción para usted mismo, la cual sirve para evaluar su habilidad para realizar el trabajo. Después de todo, su autoevaluación es realmente un asunto de ver qué es lo que puede ofrecer ante lo que quieren. Sin embargo, muy pocos empleadores mostrarán a los solicitantes la especificación del empleo. Es un poco como mostrarle a alguien el examen antes de la prueba; los solicitantes prepararían las respuestas que saben que usted quiere escuchar.

Pero usted tiene otros dos documentos de trabajo que le dirán al entrevistador qué tipo de persona es:

- Su CV.
- Su forma de solicitud.

Su entrevistador pretende ajustar estos documentos con el primer par; en otras palabras, ellos tratan de encontrar al solicitante que mejor se ajuste a los requisitos del puesto. Su trabajo es demostrar que usted es el más adecuado.

Recomendación efectiva

Haga una copia de su forma de solicitud, así como de su CV, antes de enviarlo. De esta manera tendrá un registro exacto de lo que usted le ha dicho al entrevistador, y así estará seguro de que tendrá listas las respuestas ante lo que ellos le vayan a preguntar a partir de su solicitud.

El entrevistador –si es que sabe algo acerca de las entrevistas– tendrá dos listas de preguntas para usted:

- Una lista de preguntas que hacer a los candidatos, las cuales son las cuestiones acerca del trabajo que ellos generarán a partir de usar los dos primeros documentos: la descripción del trabajo y la especificación del empleo. A menos que ellos le pregunten las mismas cuestiones, será casi imposible evaluar cuál de todos ustedes se adecua mejor al trabajo.
- Después tendrá una lista de las especificaciones para usted, las cuales habrá formulado a partir de su solicitud y su CV. Podrían ser cuestiones acerca de su experiencia, habilidades, calificaciones o circunstancias acerca de su carrera, sus intereses y su estilo de trabajo.

EL FORMATO

Virtualmente cada entrevista sigue el mismo formato básico. Si usted no está acostumbrado a esto, ayuda el estar listo y saber lo que le espera. Así que esto es lo que su entrevistador hará:

1. Empezará dándole la bienvenida, y probablemente platique con usted por un par de minutos para relajarlo. Bien podría ofrecerle café o té.
2. Él empezará la entrevista propiamente dicha al preguntarle sobre la lista de las cuestiones generales que le preguntan a cada candidato. Serán sobre asuntos como "platíqueme acerca de usted mismo" o "¿cuál es su experiencia para entregar su trabajo en las fechas límite?".
3. Después, le preguntará cuestiones específicas acerca de su CV. Éstas serán cuestiones del tipo "yo veo que sólo ha estado en su actual empleo unos seis meses, ¿por qué se quiere cambiar tan pronto? o "yo veo una lista de expediciones a la Antártica entre sus pasatiempos, ¿cómo encaja esto ante un trabajo de 9 a. m. a 5 p. m.?".
4. Después de esto, regresará a los primeros puntos y probarán aún más si es que está interesado todavía (analizaremos esto en un momento).

5. Finalmente, cuando haya formulado sus preguntas, le dirá algunos detalles más acerca del trabajo y entonces le pedirá que haga sus preguntas.

📖 Conocimiento efectivo

Los entrevistadores están entrenados para asegurarse de que sólo hagan alrededor del 20 al 30 % de la plática durante la entrevista –hasta la etapa final–. Esto significa que ellos esperan que usted haga entre el 70 y el 80 % de la conversación.

REASEGURAR AL ENTREVISTADOR

Si su entrevistador tiene alguna duda acerca de algo que esté en su solicitud que le haga pensar que usted no es adecuado para el trabajo, ¿qué es lo que hará? Si conocen su trabajo, lo probarán hasta que obtengan una respuesta satisfactoria de usted. Y esto es justamente lo que quiere.

Si no le hace más preguntas, el resultado probable es que no desea ofrecerle el trabajo porque está preocupado, por ejemplo, acerca de una brecha de 18 meses en su CV. Él se preocupa de que obtenga el trabajo debido a sus pobres referencias, o a la falta de habilidad, pero de hecho usted se ha tomado 18 meses para atender a un pariente enfermo o, si es mujer, ha tenido un bebé. Si el entrevistador no le pregunta, puede asegurarle que la brecha de desempleo no es reflejo sobre su habilidad para hacer este trabajo.

Ahora bien, algunos entrevistadores encuentran muy fácil probar estas áreas de preocupación, pero otros son menos asertivos y se preocupan porque ellos puedan ofenderle o molestarle. Esto no debería ser porque usted estaría agradecido de que le den la oportunidad de explayarse y asegurárselo, pero en el caso de que su entrevistador muestre reticencia, esté pendiente de observar sus dudas y explíquele los hechos. De otra manera ni atenderá la cuestión a fondo

Esté pendiente de captar sus dudas y preséntele los hechos.

y podría terminar perdiendo el empleo por alguna preocupación infundada del entrevistador.

> ### 💬 Consejo efectivo
>
> **Por tanto, ¿qué hace sonar la alarma en los entrevistadores?**
>
> Nosotros le pedimos a varios entrevistadores profesionales que nos digan qué es lo que más les preocupa de una solicitud de empleo. Si alguna de estas cuestiones aparece en su solicitud, necesita contrarrestarlas. Los entrevistadores nos dijeron que se preocupan cuando ven alguna evidencia de:
>
> - Falta de experiencia relevante (por lo que usted necesita asegurarse de que cada pieza relevante de experiencia esté claramente indicada).
> - Falta de atributos personales, tales como: capacidad para trabajar bajo presión, por ejemplo; o bien, para motivar a otros (así que vea lo que se necesita en este trabajo y demuestre que puede con eso).
> - Lento progreso ante lo que ellos esperan de su ascenso en la escalera profesional (así que tenga una explicación convincente sobre por qué se demoró su carrera cuando su familia era muy joven, o de por qué usted por una razón válida no aceptó una buena promoción).
> - Las brechas en el empleo (explique claramente qué estaba haciendo durante dichas brechas y por qué esa experiencia le ha ayudado a ser apropiado para este trabajo).

Usted estará preguntándose qué es lo que se supone que hará si esta preocupación está bien fundada. Imagine que realmente le falta la experiencia necesaria o que se quedó un año sin trabajar porque no pudo conseguir un empleo. En este caso, lo mejor que puede hacer es estar listo para atender esta cuestión. Revise su solicitud y su CV y trabájelos donde puedan aparecerle algunas dudas al entrevistador. Después prepare sus respuestas.

En general, la manera de responder a estas cuestiones –cuando son genuinas– es ser honesto, pero dar plena confianza con factores compensatorios. Si a usted verdaderamente le falta experiencia, admítalo, pero demuestre que aprende rápido y que puede hacerlo en el trabajo. Y haga creer que sus fortalezas contrapesan a sus debilidades en cualquier caso.

SOLICITUDES INTERNAS

Si usted solicita un puesto dentro de su organización, ¿puede esperar que la entrevista siga el mismo formato? Sí, es posible. El entrevistador evalúa a todos los candidatos por igual bajo la misma base. Esto significa que a cada quien debería asignarle el mismo tiempo, darle el mismo nivel de respeto y privacidad, y hacerle las mismas preguntas, ya sean solicitantes externos o internos.

Es más, justamente porque su entrevistador ya pueda saber la respuesta a alguna de las preguntas, por ejemplo, "¿qué tan bien trabaja bajo presión?", él todavía querrá escuchar su respuesta a esta pregunta. Así que no diga "ésta es una pregunta tonta, usted ya lo sabe"; debe darle la respuesta que usted daría como si estuviese en una entrevista externa.

Conocimiento efectivo

Existe una tendencia creciente de los empleadores a anunciar las vacantes internas en lugar de simplemente ofrecer el trabajo a quienes ellos decidan que quieren contratar. Así que cada vez más, ante una promoción interna, usted necesita ir a través del proceso de una solicitud y de entrevista.

Si usted es un solicitante interno a quien ya conocen, puede esperar que el entrevistador siga el mismo formato, como si fuera un solicitante de una organización externa. Sin embargo, no debe pretender que nunca lo ha conocido antes. Él empezará con una charla de apertura de uno o dos minutos, y es probable que se comporte como lo hace normalmente, en lugar de pretender que usted es un extraño; esto ayudará para establecer el tono.

No se aproveche de su estatus interno, contando chistes o siendo personal –inclusive de manera positiva– acerca de sus colegas. No hay necesidad de que pretenda que el entrevistador no sepa acerca de lo que está hablando cuando ya lo sabe. Usted podría encontrar que esto ayuda a responder las preguntas como si estuviese en una entrevista externa, pero añada frases tales como "usted recordará…" o "como usted sabe…".

No se aproveche de su estatus interno.

SOLICITANTES GRADUADOS

Algunas compañías grandes reciben literalmente miles de solicitudes de graduados, de tal manera que éstas tienen que ir a través de un proceso de filtrado para ser capaces de seleccionar aquellos candidatos que ellos quieren reclutar. Esto significa que usted puede encontrarse haciendo evaluaciones y pruebas tales como las que se cubrirán más adelante (*véanse* caps. 10 al 13).

Encontrará que si solicita para un esquema de reclutamiento de graduados, las entrevistas serán externas (*outsourcing*), así que será entrevistado por una agencia de reclutamiento, más que por la compañía a la que le solicita. Esto puede sentirse algo desapegado, aunque las compañías están aumentando la integración del servicio de entrevistas. Una de las ventajas de esto es que si no obtiene el trabajo, la agencia puede enviar su CV a donde sea, así que es especialmente importante que los impresione.

Ya sea que usted sea entrevistado por la empresa a la que solicita o mediante una agencia, es probable que le pregunten sobre su curso. Si su área de estudio está relacionada cercanamente con el trabajo, puede esperar algunas buenas preguntas a fondo acerca de esto.

> Es probable que le pregunten sobre su curso.

Preparación efectiva

Prepárese para lo esperado

Usted puede estar listo para esta entrevista sabiendo lo que el entrevistador busca, y estar seguro para probar que usted lo tiene:

- Evalúese a usted mismo para el trabajo en las áreas clave de habilidades y demás.
- Considere las áreas clave en su solicitud y en el CV que sea probable que quiera preguntarle.
- Piense si su CV o solicitud muestra cualquier cosa que pudiera –correcta o incorrectamente– darle a su entrevistador causa de preocupación acerca de su habilidad para hacer el trabajo.

Capítulo 2
Cómo prepararse

Sería bastante tonto, como para que no tenga que decírselo, llegar directamente a una entrevista sin ninguna preparación por anticipado. Entre mejor preparado esté, hay mayores oportunidades de obtener el puesto. Desde luego, usted ya ha trabajado sobre su solicitud y su CV con el objeto de llegar hasta aquí, pero habiendo pasado a la segunda vuelta, es momento de hacer una tarea más.

Desastre efectivo

Usted ha tenido poca o ninguna preparación y está sentado en la entrevista. El entrevistador le pregunta: "¿Qué me puede decir acerca de esta compañía?" y usted se da cuenta de que aparte de saber en qué industria está, de su dirección (porque usted se encuentra ahí ahora), no puede responder a la pregunta. ¿Cómo se sentiría? ¡Uff!

Esencialmente usted se tiene que considerar como un vendedor y hacer la preparación que éste haría antes de obtener un gran contrato. Sí, aunque el trabajo para el que esté haciendo la solicitud no tenga nada que ver con las ventas. El punto es que está vendiendo sus servicios y su entrevistador está en el papel del comprador. Él verá lo que usted y sus competidores tengan que ofrecer, y entonces tomará la decisión de comprar. Su trabajo es persuadirlo de que usted es mejor oferta que sus competidores.

Un vendedor jamás se presentará ante un comprador sin haber hecho una preparación a fondo para la entrevista y usted tampoco debería hacerlo. Así que necesita:

- Establecer su objetivo.
- Investigar a la organización a la que le solicita empleo.
- Planificar su caso.
- Preparar su entrevista.

Establezca que su objetivo es un destino. Si no sabe a dónde va, es probable no que llegue ahí con eficiencia. Y después de todo, tal vez ni siquiera llegue. Usted debe pensar en su objetivo obvio: obtener el trabajo. Bien, está en lo correcto. Y equivocado. Esto le dice a dónde va, pero no le dice qué hacer para llegar ahí. Así como un viaje bien planeado necesita una ruta y un destino, un objetivo bien planeado necesita decirle no sólo a dónde va, sino cómo va a llegar allá.

> **Recomendación efectiva**
>
> Una vez que haya fijado su objetivo no variará mucho de un trabajo a otro, pero haga un repaso para refrescarlo para cada trabajo al que solicite, a fin de estar seguro de mantener su preparación enfocada exactamente en donde necesita estar.

Entonces, ¿cómo va a obtener el trabajo? Aquí está un objetivo más específico para usted: *obtener el trabajo demostrándole al entrevistador que yo soy la mejor persona para el mismo*. Bien, sí, eso está mejor, pero todavía no le dice todo. Es como decir que usted va a ir a Manchester vía Birmingham, pero no le da ninguna clave de cuáles caminos tomar para llegar a ese punto.

Muy bien, probemos otra vez: *obtener el trabajo demostrándole al entrevistador que yo soy la mejor persona para éste en términos de habilidad, experiencia y personalidad*. Y si usted tiene más información que añadir, en términos de las prioridades específicas del entrevistador, las puede adicionar a su objetivo. Quizá sabe que él realmente quiere a alguien con experiencia en la negociación con los proveedores. En ese caso, su objetivo debería reflejar esto: *obtener el trabajo demostrándole al entrevistador que yo soy la mejor persona para éste en términos de habilidad, experiencia y personalidad, en particular en la negociación ante los proveedores*. Esto es genial. Un objetivo claro y específico. Esto le será realmente útil.

Umm... ¿útil?, ¿un objetivo? Todo esto se ve muy profesional, pero ¿cómo le va a ayudar? Bien, es fácil caer en la trampa de pensar que los objetivos son una pérdida de tiempo. Así que muchas personas los formula y los ignora después bajo la percepción de que es correcto, que no hay que molestarse, pero si usted es inteligente, usará su objetivo y encontrará lo valioso que puede ser.

Usted ve que un claro y bien concebido objetivo es un parámetro contra el cual puede medir todo lo que haga. Éste le ayuda a estar enfocado. Si cualquier actividad no le favorece para conseguir su objetivo, no la haga. Use el tiempo para algo que le *haga* avanzar hacia éste. Por ejemplo, vamos a analizar la organización a la que está usted solicitando. Necesita hacer suficiente investigación para demostrar que ha hecho su tarea, pero más allá, ¿qué es lo que necesita hallar?

La respuesta es: usted necesita encontrar cualquier cosa que ayude a satisfacer su objetivo y no otra cosa. Así que tomemos nuestro ejemplo anterior: *obtener el trabajo demostrando al entrevistador que yo soy la mejor persona para éste en términos de habilidad, experiencia y personalidad, y en particular en la negociación con los proveedores.* Usted necesita enfocarse para conocer todo lo que hacen sus proveedores; cuántos son, quiénes son y demás.

En curso: ¿sí o no?

Tomando el objetivo: *obtener el trabajo demostrándole al entrevistador que yo soy la mejor persona para éste en términos de habilidad, experiencia y personalidad, y en particular para manejar las relaciones con los clientes difíciles,* ¿cuáles de las siguientes actividades necesita cumplir para satisfacer el objetivo?

Actividad	Sí	No
1. Obtener referencia para trabajo voluntario como un samaritano.		
2. Memorizar el reporte anual de la empresa y sus estados financieros.		
3. Buscar la certificación escolar de 1994.		
4. Buscar copias de las cartas de recomendación de los clientes.		
5. Listar la experiencia sobre el trato con personas en general difíciles.		

Respuestas: sí 1, 4, 5. no 2, 3.

No es imposible arribar a estas conclusiones –acerca de, por ejemplo, dónde enfocar su atención– sin un objetivo, pero tener un objetivo e ir por el proceso de generarlo le ayudará a concentrar su mente en las áreas esenciales y a volver a ellas. Esto le prevendrá de distraerse del núcleo de su objetivo.

INVESTIGAR A LA ORGANIZACIÓN

El entrevistador esperaría que usted haya investigado acerca de la organización. No es que quiera sorprenderle con preguntas difíciles; si ése fuese su objetivo, podría tener otras maneras de hacerlo. Sólo quiere saber dónde está usted.

- Si está haciendo algún esfuerzo para obtener el trabajo.
- Si está interesado en la organización.
- Si demuestra entusiasmo.

Si éste es un caso genuino, usted querrá investigar a la organización. ¿Cómo está seguro de que quiere trabajar ahí, si se le ofrece el trabajo?, a menos de que sepa algo acerca del lugar. Es probable que el entrevistador le pregunte algunas cuestiones acerca de lo que sabe de su empresa, nada más para asegurarse de que tiene entusiasmo, interés y realiza un esfuerzo.

> **Recomendación efectiva**
>
> No sólo investigue a la organización aisladamente, observe toda la industria. Vea dónde se encuentra, quiénes son sus principales competidores, y observe las tendencias de la industria y de otras también. De esta manera usted puede demostrar al entrevistador que entiende toda a la situación.

Entonces, ¿qué material puede tener para ayudarle a saber acerca de la organización? Aquí hay algunas ideas:

- Reporte anual.
- Folletos de ventas.
- Reporte a clientes.
- Revista interna.
- Artículos en los periódicos y revistas.

Usted será capaz de encontrar esta información de muchas maneras. Quizá conozca a alguien que trabaja en la organización, o tal vez haya puntos de venta donde pueda obtener los materiales, pero el método más sencillo es llamar por teléfono y solicitarlos.

El entrevistador no trata de sorprenderlo. Ellos no quieren dificultarle las cosas. Así que llámeles (a la secretaria o su asistente) y dígales: "Yo quisiera saber más acerca de la organización antes de presentarme a la entrevista. Por favor, ¿podría enviarme alguna información?". Ellos estarán contentos de hacerlo e impresionados por su iniciativa.

> El entrevistador no trata de dificultarle las cosas.

Recomendación efectiva

Seguramente cada empleador posee un sitio web. Así que un punto de partida obvio para investigarlo es en línea –vaya a un Café Internet si no tiene otra manera de acceder a la web– y cheque toda la información del empleador acerca de sí mismo en su sitio web.

Ahora, una vez que tiene en sus manos dicha información, ¿qué va a hacer con ella? La respuesta es que va a analizarla toda buscando las claves para que les demuestre que usted es la mejor persona para ese trabajo –desde luego teniendo en mente su objetivo–, por ejemplo:

- Suponga que observa que la compañía hace muchos negocios en Latinoamérica. Y que usted habla excelente español. Esto le dará una ventaja sobre la mayoría, si es que no sobre todos los demás aspirantes.
- O quizá puede observar que la compañía está creciendo muy rápido. Lo mismo sucede en la compañía en la que usted está ahora, y sabe que esto ocasiona todo tipo de problemas para el departamento de tecnología de la información (al que aspira trabajar). Usted ya ha pasado por todo esto y sabe cómo resolver las dificultades.
- Quizá la última cuestión es que el reporte interno está solicitando ayuda editorial, y usted editó la revista interna de una compañía anteriormente.

Usted debería ser capaz de encontrar buenas oportunidades para demostrar lo bien que está situado para adecuarse al trabajo conforme observe los materiales que haya adquirido.

> **Recomendación efectiva**
>
> No espere a que le pregunten qué sabe acerca de la compañía. Si encuentra oportunidades a través de la entrevista diga, por ejemplo, "Yo hablo español fluido y he observado que ustedes tienen muchos negocios con Latinoamérica, así que imagínese lo útil que les podría ser"; usted impresionará a su entrevistador con su investigación —así como con sus habilidades relevantes— conforme se desenvuelva. Entre más hechos relevantes pueda incluir en la entrevista acerca de su compañía, mejor. Ellos no le preguntarán si ha hecho alguna investigación. Eso será obvio.

PREPARE SU CASO

Si usted simplemente entra a la entrevista y responde cada cuestión como se le pregunte, sin haber hecho ninguna preparación, probablemente hará una presentación algo decente, pero si realmente quiere ese trabajo, esto no es suficiente. Usted no tiene idea de lo fuerte que es la competencia. Si la entrevista es bastante débil, tal vez consiga el empleo, pero ¿y si es fuerte? Una oportunidad perdida —algo que debería haber dicho, pero que se le olvidó mencionar— tal vez desbalancee las cosas contra usted.

> *Tenga una lista mental de todos los puntos más importantes que quiera expresar.*

Así que debemos asegurarnos de que esto no le suceda. Antes de que se presente a la entrevista, usted ya debería tener una lista mental de todos los puntos más importantes que quiera expresar; todas las cosas que impresionarán positivamente a su entrevistador de que es la mejor persona para el puesto.

Usted ya se ha evaluado a sí mismo para establecer cuáles son sus fortalezas clave. Ahora quiere dirigir éstas a casa. Si sus fortalezas se pueden medir objetivamente (calificaciones, habilidad para usar cierto equipo en particular, cierto tipo de cosas), simplemente con decirle a su entrevistador que usted las posee será suficiente. Sin embargo, algunas fortalezas, tales como experiencia o diplomacia, por ejemplo, necesitarán ser ilustradas con ejemplos.

Así que piense por adelantado sobre la entrevista. Suponga que considera la diplomacia como una de sus habilidades clave. Y su objetivo le dice que una de las cosas que tiene que hacer es persuadir a su entrevistador de que usted es bueno para el trabajo. Cuando le pregunten acerca de la diplomacia (y ellos lo harán si es un requerimiento importante para el trabajo), no se trata de asegurarles nada más que usted es bueno para esto, inclusive si era importante en su anterior trabajo, esto no prueba que era parte relevante del mismo.

No, usted necesita darle ejemplos claros. Hábleles acerca de la ocasión en que un cliente enojado entró embravecido aventando jitomates al personal, y de que usted lo calmó. O de aquella ocasión en que todo el equipo de choferes de distribución estaba a punto de irse, hasta que usted habló con ellos. Dígale ambas situaciones si tiene oportunidad.

Desastre efectivo

Uno de los requerimientos del trabajo es la habilidad para dirigir un equipo de personas. Tiene poca experiencia administrativa, pero le dice al entrevistador que ha tenido a alguien de tiempo completo y a otro de tiempo parcial trabajando para usted el último año. Después de que ha terminado la entrevista, se da cuenta de que olvidó mencionar que en su último trabajo organizó también las apariciones en una feria comercial, que implicó coordinar un equipo por una semana o dos varias veces al año.

Mientras tanto, uno de los candidatos con poca experiencia profesional como la de usted para administrar un equipo permanentemente, le ha dicho al entrevistador todo acerca de cómo en su actual trabajo requiere dirigir un equipo de proveedores de comida externos, de limpiadores y de otros auxiliares donde se requieran para llevar a cabo eventos tales como lanzamiento de productos. ¡Uff!

Usted puede ser capaz de pensar en un ejemplo para ilustrar sus fortalezas en el sitio donde se le pregunte, pero si se prepara por anticipado, no sólo proporcionará un ejemplo; usted presentará el mejor, y el más relevante para el trabajo al que está aspirando.

Así que ésa es su lista básica de fortalezas. Y usted también necesita ir a través de la descripción del trabajo de la misma manera, encontrando ejemplos para demostrar que tiene experiencia en todas las áreas clave de responsabilidad. Si usted no tiene una copia de la descripción del trabajo (que normalmente se le envía con la forma de solicitud), llame a la oficina del entrevistador y solicite que se le envíe una. Es una práctica estándar, así que no se preocupe por pedirla.

> **Recomendación efectiva**
>
> Cuando busque ejemplos de experiencias pasadas para demostrar que usted puede manejar las responsabilidades clave, no se restrinja a la experiencia laboral; usted puede demostrar sus habilidades motivacionales explicando cómo organizó un grupo de voluntarios para trabajar en una institución de beneficiencia local. Quizá pueda demostrar su habilidad para trabajar con fechas límite diciéndole al entrevistador acerca de la revista escolar que editó. O podría indicarle su automotivación y compromiso al explicar acerca de su grado en una universidad abierta.

Su entrevistador podría estar interesado en ver una evidencia para apoyar sus fortalezas y experiencia sobre las que habla. Mientras que es poco probable que espere ver algo más que una prueba de sus calificaciones, podría ser gratamente impresionado con algo más que le pueda ofrecer, tal como:

- Testimonios de clientes o proveedores satisfechos.
- Copias de reportes clave que usted haya escrito.
- Ejemplos de trabajos pasados.
- Recortes de prensa que haya generado.
- Artículos de prensa acerca de eventos que haya organizado...

... y similares. Así que encuentre todo lo que pueda ayudar a persuadirlos de que usted es tan bueno como parece, y tómelos consigo. Obviamente no es buena idea presentarse a una entrevista con una carretilla de cosas junto con usted. Tome lo que sea portátil y que quepa en un folder elegante o en un portafolio si lleva muchos diseños o trabajos artísticos. Después pregúntele al entrevistador qué más les podría enviar, o llévelo en una segunda entrevista, si ellos quieren verlo.

Tome lo que sea portátil y que quepa en un folder elegante.

> **Recomendación efectiva**
>
> El entrevistador podría desear quedarse con algunos materiales del portafolio que le haya mostrado. Quizá ellos quieren estudiarlos más a fondo después, o tal vez presentár-

selos a sus colegas. Así que lleve copias para dejárselas en lugar de sus originales, que usted, podría necesitar para una segunda entrevista. Si no puede sacar copias, márquelos claramente con su nombre y dirección para que se los puedan regresar.

ESTÉ PREPARADO PARA LA ENTREVISTA

Usted sabe ahora qué tiene que decir en la entrevista. Cualesquiera cuestiones que el entrevistador le ponga, existen ciertos puntos clave que quiere destacar y que ha preparado, pero ¿cómo le hará para decirlos? ¿Tiene que resumir sus puntos clave en 15 minutos o tener una hora para expresarlos lentamente, uno por uno?

La única manera de saber esto es preguntar a la oficina de su entrevistador. Así que usted necesita comunicarse al lugar (preferiblemente al mismo tiempo en que haga otras peguntas) y simplemente preguntar: "Por favor, ¿podría decirme cuánto tiempo ha sido asignado para mi entrevista?". Nuevamente, ésta es una pregunta totalmente razonable, y una que ellos estarán contentos por responderle.

Usted tiene ahora toda la información que necesita, y toda la preparación está en su sitio. El paso final es que esté listo para la entrevista en la fecha que le asignen. Y usted puede empezar por estar a tiempo. No importa qué tan temprano llegue; usted puede encontrar el edificio y hacer una caminata alrededor, almorzar o ver algunas tiendas; así que no llegue a la recepción mucho antes. Pero, eso sí, unos dos o tres minutos tarde puede significar mucho, especialmente si su entrevistador es muy exigente con la puntualidad.

> Llegar tarde dos o tres minutos puede significar mucho.

Desastre efectivo

Motivo de pesadillas. Usted sale a tiempo, pero el metro está cerrado o su auto se descompone. O quizá el viaje es correcto, sin embargo, no encuentra el edificio. Habiendo llegado al vecindario media hora antes, los minutos corren y no encuentra el edificio. O quizá llegó 20 minutos antes para su entrevista, a las 2, sólo para descubrir que la carta decía a las 12 y no a las 2. ¡Uff!

Desde luego que se puede imaginar escenarios donde ningún tipo de planeación anticipada podría haberlo puesto a la hora de la entrevista a tiempo, pero a menos de que la razón sea realmente dramática, su entrevistador no quiere escuchar excusas. Ellos quieren que usted esté ahí sin excusa ni pretexto. Así que hágase unos cuantos favores:

- Tómese todo el tiempo necesario para llegar ahí.
- Lleve con usted la carta de invitación a la entrevista, con la hora y la dirección que le hayan dado.
- Indague acerca de estacionamientos si va en auto y piense que esto podría causarle problemas.
- Lleve un celular o dinero para llamadas telefónicas, en caso de que llame para indicación de la dirección. Entonces, si a pesar de todas sus precauciones usted sale tarde, cuando menos puede llamar y hacerles saber lo que le está sucediendo.

Además de asegurarse de llegar a tiempo, usted necesitará llevar:

- El portafolio con su material y sus direcciones, celular y cualquier cosa más (todo bien arreglado en una maletín).
- Un cuaderno y pluma (también en el maletín) para tomar notas durante la entrevista.

Preparación efectiva

Un par de semanas antes de la entrevista llame a la oficina del entrevistador, si es necesario, para peguntar:

- Cualquier información acerca de la organización.
- La descripción del trabajo.
- Una idea de cuánto tiempo le han asignado para la entrevista.

Use también otras fuentes, incluyendo el sitio web de la compañia para investigar todo lo que pueda acerca de la empresa. Mire a través de esta información y encuentre cualquier cosa que le pueda servir para demostrar que ha hecho su investigación y que es la mejor persona para el trabajo.

Revise su lista de fortalezas y de las responsabilidades clave listadas en la descripción del trabajo, y piense en ejemplos concretos para demostrar sus fortalezas y habilidades tan bien como pueda. Junte una cartera con material útil para llevarlo a la entrevista.

Deje mucho tiempo para llegar a la entrevista y asegúrese de llevar con usted todo lo que vaya a necesitar.

Capítulo 3
Primeras impresiones

Su entrevistador se formará gran parte de su opinión sobre su persona con base en una proporción muy pequeña de tiempo dedicado a usted. De hecho, los primeros momentos le dirán mucho acerca de quién es, le guste o no. Su mejor defensa contra esto es, desde luego, asegurarse de enviarle los mensajes que usted quiere.

A partir de la forma en que se vista, la forma en que salude, se puede preparar para dar la mejor impresión que pueda. De hecho, ¿por qué empezar antes de que sea el día de la entrevista? Usted puede influir en la opinión de su entrevistador:

- Antes de la entrevista.
- En la manera de vestir.
- En la forma de saludar.

💬 Consejo efectivo

Después de encuestarlos, los entrevistadores citaron los siguientes factores clave que les impresionaron acerca de un candidato:

- Saludo fuerte.
- Estar inteligente y apropiadamente vestido.

Entre los factores que les impresionaron menos incluyeron:

- Impuntualidad.
- Apariencia descuidada.
- Mal arreglado.
- Mucho perfume o loción para después de afeitar.

ANTES DE LA ENTREVISTA

Sí, antes de que obtenga la entrevista, ya puede generar una fuerte primera impresión. Su solicitud inicial fue lo bastante buena para lograr la entrevista. Si ésta incluyó un CV y una solicitud bien presentada y profesional, su entrevistador ya está esperando a un fuerte candidato que pase por la puerta. Usted puede mejorar esta impresión aún más con:

- Una carta de presentación bien escrita cuando envió su solicitud, describiendo brevemente sus fortalezas (en relación con el trabajo en cuestión).
- Una carta más, nuevamente bien escrita y profesionalmente presentada, confirmando los arreglos para esta entrevista y diciendo qué tanto está usted esperando su confirmación.

Si ahora ya es muy tarde para todo esto, usted todavía puede dar una gran primera impresión, pero la próxima vez que solicite un trabajo tenga estos puntos en mente para que pueda causar una fuerte y positiva impresión aún antes de la entrevista.

¿QUÉ ES LO QUE SE VA A PONER?

Saber cómo vestirse para una entrevista ya no es lo que era antes. Era la época en que usted se ponía su mejor traje y corbata, o su mejor vestido de diseñador o un traje sastre y usted sabía cuál era su parte. Desafortunadamente, las cosas ya no son tan simples ahora. Un traje formal no se verá bien en una organización donde todos los trabajadores usan jeans y camisetas. El entrevistador pensará: "Muy inteligente. Ellos no encajan aquí".

📖 Conocimiento efectivo

Acorde con investigaciones, el 70 % de la rotación de empleados se debe a que el personal no encaja con la cultura corporativa, más que la incapacidad de hacer el trabajo en los términos de habilidad o experiencia. Entonces su entrevistador quiere ver si usted puede encajar en caso de que le ofrezcan el trabajo. La manera en que se viste es sólo una parte de esto, desde luego, pero forma una gran parte de la primera impresión del entrevistador para saber si usted es o no "uno de los nuestros".

Así que usted necesita saber cuál es el código de vestir de esa organización a la que solicita entrar. De esta manera podrá seleccionar el traje apropiado (como lo veremos en un minuto). Puede tener una idea perfectamente clara de cuál podría ser el código de vestir, esto es bastante consistente a lo largo de todas las industrias. Algunas compañías de diseño y medios tienden a vestir de manera casual, las firmas de contabilidad es probable que se vistan más formalmente. Si usted está cambiando de trabajo dentro de la misma industria, es muy probable que ya sepa el código de vestir.

> Usted necesita saber el código de vestir en esa organización.

Pero ¿qué pasa si es una industria sobre la que no está seguro? Existen varias opciones:

- Si usted es lo suficientemente suertudo para conocer o contactar a alguien que trabaje ahí, o que sea un proveedor o quizá a un cliente, usted les puede pedir ayuda para que lo asesoren.
- Si la organización está cerca, dé una vuelta a la hora del almuerzo u observe a la gente a la hora de la salida para ver qué es lo que usan.
- Vea en los folletos de ventas y los reportes anuales las fotos del personal y de los ejecutivos.

Si falla lo anterior, haga lo de siempre: pregunte. Cuando hable por teléfono a su contacto –el entrevistador, su asistente o su secretaria– pregunte cuál es el código de vestir de la empresa. Como siempre, ellos no se molestarán por preguntarles, al contrario, quedarán impresionados por su iniciativa.

Entonces, ¿cómo vestirse? Nada más porque ya sepa lo que usan los empleados regulares no significa que vaya a usar lo mismo también. Disculpe, pero no es tan simple. Después de todo, usted no es un empleado regular (todavía), es un entrevistado que necesita verse como que está haciendo un esfuerzo extra. Así que vístase un punto o dos más arriba que los empleados; véase como ellos se verían si estuviesen haciendo un esfuerzo por verse mejor.

Así que para los hombres:

Si ellos usan...	Usted use...
Casual.	Casual elegante.
Casual elegante.	Traje casual.
Traje casual (p. ej.: sin mangas o sin corbata).	Traje casual con saco y corbata.
Traje de vestir.	Traje de vestir.

Y para las mujeres:

Si ellas usan...	Usted use...
Casual.	Casual elegante (p. ej.: faldas, pero no jeans).
Casual elegante.	Elegante.
Elegante.	Elegante.

Esto parece que es más fácil para las mujeres, y en cierto sentido lo es porque existe una escala más deslizable. Para los hombres, puede ser correcto quitarse el saco o no, pero el punto es el mismo: vístase uno o dos puntos arriba de la gente que verá en el corredor cuando vaya a su entrevista, a menos de que ellos se vistan formalmente, en cuyo caso usted sólo necesita igualarlos (en lugar de vestirse para una noche de gala).

Recomendación efectiva

Cualquier cosa que haga, no vaya a comprarse un traje nuevo para su entrevista, a menos de que tenga bastante tiempo para aflojarlo. Usted tiene que estar cómodo y relajado, concentrado en la conversación, no en un cierre que acaba de descubrir que

> se pega dolorosamente a usted, o en la cintura que sintió bien cuando se lo probó en la tienda y ahora le aprieta cuando se sienta. Lleve ropa limpia y elegante, y relativamente nueva, pero que le quede cómoda y sin problemas.

Cuando se trate de aspectos específicos de la vestimenta que decida usar, aquí hay unos cuantos puntos que le serán útiles:

- No permita que su apariencia sobrepase su personalidad. Puede usar colores brillantes, pero no use algo tan fuera de lo común que llame mucho la atención. Usted es el que solicita el empleo, no su ropa.
- Evite modas extremas.
- Evite un perfume fuerte o loción para después de afeitarse.
- No lleve muchas joyas o joyas muy grandes.
- Evite colores brillantes, a menos que se restrinjan a un área pequeña, como una corbata o una mascada.
- Los colores oscuros dan más autoridad que los claros.
- Evite las perforaciones en el cuerpo, excepto aretes para las mujeres, a menos que esté solicitando para el tipo *funky* de los medios, donde son de rigor. Ellos todavía tienen una connotación negativa y pueden verlo como un aviso de una actitud rebelde, lo cual es algo que no quiere trasmitir.
- De igual manera, cúbrase todos sus tatuajes.

Cuando llegue a la entrevista –unos minutos antes– pregúntele a la recepcionista a dónde puede dirigirse para refrescarse. Péinese bien, revise su ropa y otra vez verifique:

- Sus dientes (especialmente si acaba de comer).
- Nariz.
- Joyería (especialmente los aretes en las mujeres).
- Cierres y botones (especialmente la bragueta en los hombres).
- Camisa o blusa.
- Maquillaje.

Esto vale la pena; si es una mujer, lleve un par de medias extra (si está usando medias). De igual manera, si usted es hombre, lleve una corbata extra en caso de que haya salpicado de bebida o de comida la que traía puesta. O mejor, no se ponga la corbata hasta que llegue al edificio.

SU SALUDO INICIAL

Esté listo para exudar entusiasmo y confianza.

Tanto la manera de vestirse, como la forma en que salude al entrevistador, puede formar parte importante de la primera impresión que proyecte. Así que esté listo para exudar entusiasmo y confianza tan pronto los vea a ellos. Los puntos clave que debe recordar son:

- Sonreír.
- Haga contacto visual con el entrevistador.
- Ofrezca la mano para saludarlo conforme se presenten a sí mismos.
- Diga "hola", "gusto en conocerle", o cualquier frase que resulte sencilla.
- Agite las manos firmemente (usted puede practicar su saludo con un amigo) con todos los entrevistadores si hay más de uno. Una mano débil o aguada puede dar muy mala impresión, así que asegúrese de que ha practicado su saludo, con amigos y familiares, hasta que esté confiado y seguro.
- Espere a que le inviten a sentarse.

Recomendación efectiva

Muchos entrevistadores quieren una segunda opinión informal sobre los candidatos de uno o más miembros de su equipo (después de todo tendrán que trabajar con quien ellos contraten). Así que podrían decirle a algún miembro del equipo que lo reciba, darle una taza de café o conducirlo de la recepción a la sala de entrevistas, y de regreso después. En otras palabras, necesita dejar muy buena primera impresión con todos los que le presenten, incluyendo a la recepcionista, debido a que usted no sabe quién tomará la decisión final en la selección.

Cuatro cosas que decir camino a la sala de entrevistas

Algunas veces usted es presentado por el entrevistador o un asistente en la recepción. Entonces tiene que hacer una conversación cortés a lo largo de lo que parecen kilómetros en un corredor hasta llegar a la sala de entrevistas. ¿Qué debe decir? He aquí unas ideas:

- Si le preguntan "¿Cómo estuvo su viaje?", dé una respuesta positiva (aunque el viaje haya sido pesado). Y que no sea en monosílabos. Usted podría decir algo como esto: "¡Oh!, estuvo bien, gracias. Mucho más rápido de lo que pensé y el estacionamiento fue fácil de encontrar".
- Si ellos no le preguntan, voluntariamente diga sobre su viaje: "Fue muy fácil llegar aquí. Ese mapa que me enviaron con el catálogo fue muy claro". O, "¿Qué están haciendo al final de la calle? Existe un atasco de tráfico y noté que están construyendo un gran edificio cuando pasé".
- Pregúnteles: "¿Cuánto tiempo tiene colaborando en esta organización?". A la gente siempre le gusta que usted muestre interés en ellos.
- Haga un comentario favorable acerca de lo que ve al pasar: "Qué bonita vista desde estas ventanas", o "Este edificio es realmente moderno y brillante. ¿Cuánto hace que la compañía ha estado aquí?".

El entrevistador generalmente conversará un minuto o dos al principio para que usted se relaje. Sea afectivo, pero recuerde que ninguno de ustedes está aquí para conversar. Incluso cuando le pregunten, por ejemplo: "¿Qué tal estuvo su viaje?", ellos no esperan que lo describa paso a paso. Una respuesta amistosa y breve es más que suficiente. Y si por alguna causa fue horrendo, exprese el hecho (si es que decide mencionarlo después de todo) con cierto humor en lugar de sonar como un lamento.

Ejemplo efectivo

Deje su marca

Antes de la entrevista cause una fuerte primera impresión con una solicitud bien escrita, bien presentada y con una carta confirmando la entrevista y diciendo que queda a la espera de ésta.

Elija un vestuario que vaya con la cultura de la organización y que sea un punto o dos arriba de la que usen los empleados regulares. Dé un caluroso, amistoso y confiable saludo a su entrevistador y a cualquiera que se le presente de esa organización.

Parte 2
Durante la entrevista

Capítulo 4
Controle los nervios

Casi todos nos sentimos nerviosos antes de una entrevista importante. Después de todo, se trata de algo que nos interesa y que necesitamos resolver correctamente. Así que tener nervios no es sólo natural, pero desde luego que existe un mundo de diferencia entre un pequeño choque de adrenalina que nos mantenga de pie y una parálisis muscular que seque la boca, haga sudar copiosamente y nos impida contestar cualquier cuestión.

De hecho, la mayoría de nosotros cae entre estos dos extremos, pero si usted es una de esas personas a la que se le atraviesan los nervios ante una entrevista, ¿qué puede hacer? Bien, estará satisfecho de saber que casi todos los casos de nervios severos pueden reducirse hasta un nivel manejable, y los casos menos severos pueden casi desaparecer. Sólo se requiere de preparación.

Consejo efectivo

Los entrevistadores no consideran un problema los nervios, en tanto que no interfieran para empeorar la entrevista. Los comentarios sobre el tema de los entrevistadores profesionales incluyen:

- "Si el candidato está nervioso, corresponde al entrevistador relajarlo".
- "Ellos están obviamente interesados en el puesto, de lo contrario no estarían nerviosos".

RAÍZ DEL PROBLEMA

La clave yace en entender las causas de un ataque de nervios. Y la causa es el miedo. Miedo a que podamos equivocarnos hasta el grado de secarnos completamente, o de irritar a nuestro entrevistador por tirar nuestra taza de café. Entre más remotas se vean estas causas y fallas, más remotos serán sus temores. Esto es porque a menudo observa un par de minutos antes que usted no está nervioso: las cosas van bien, usted piensa que no está haciendo el rídiculo y parece que, después de todo, es capaz de mantener una conversación normal.

> ### Recomendación efectiva
> ¿Qué puede hacer si algo va catastróficamente mal? Tira el agua sobre usted mismo o tumba una enorme pila de papeles en el piso. O quizá usted esté tan nervioso que no puede recordar el nombre de su actual empleador; no es probable que suceda después de que haya leído este capítulo, pero suponiendo...
> La respuesta es reírse de sí mismo y admitir que está nervioso. Decir algo como, "¡Eso es lo que a mí me hacen los nervios!. Esto demuestra el interés que tengo en este trabajo para mí". A menos de que usted esté siendo entrevistado para un puesto para dar grandes presentaciones, o entretener a famosas celebridades, no hay razón para que su entrevistador deba considerarlo en contra de usted, en tanto que pueda contestar bien y con humor.

Si usted puede minimizar la probabilidad de que las cosas vayan mal, minimizará sus temores. Desde luego existirá una pequeña parte de miedo irracional en la parte más interior de su mente, y cuando menos hasta que la entrevista se vaya llevando a cabo, pero esto no debe pasar más allá de un toque de adrenalina que simplemente le ayude a pensar rápido.

Su mejor apuesta es ensayar tanto como pueda.

Su mejor apuesta es ensayar tanto como pueda. Piense sus respuestas a las preguntas probables y a las difíciles (las encontrará más adelante en este libro), y practique sus respuestas ante un espejo. Ensaye su saludo inicial. Pruébese su ropa con antelación si no la ha usado recientemente.

Pero como usted quiere tomar todavía más precauciones, su divisa debería de ser: estoy preparado. Anticipe el desastre, considere cada posible urgencia o embrollo que pueda, y planee para esto. De esta manera no sucederá, pero si sucede, estará listo para afrontarlo. Aquí están algunos antídotos para uno o dos disparadores de adrenalina:

Café y té	Si está preocupado por derramarlos, simplemente decline la invitación a tomarlos; la cafeína no es una buena idea, sobre todo si está nervioso. Evítelos por lo menos dos horas antes (junto con cualquier tipo de alcohol). Si es propenso a temblar cuando se pone nervioso, mejor decline una bebida, ya que lo tembloroso se notará cuando lo tome.
Parecer nervioso	Realmente a nadie le importa si se ve nervioso en tanto que haga bien el trabajo, pero a menudo tememos parecer nerviosos. Si está inclinado a temblar al principio de la entrevista, doble sus manos juntas en su regazo donde se puedan mantener una con otra bajo control.
Se le seca la boca	Cuando decline el café, pida un vaso con agua. Si usted no lo necesita, está bien que lo deje (no tiene que tomarlo y preocuparse por derramarlo).
Incapaz de pensar o de decir algo	Aquí es otra ocasión en la que aparece en mano el vaso con agua. Tomar un sorbo o dos antes de que responda a una cuestión le compra algunos momentos para enderezar su cabeza.
Revolverse con el portafolio/ tirando los papeles	Lleve a la entrevista un sobre con sólo un documento. Deje el resto en la recepción.
Preguntas difíciles	Haga que alguien juegue el papel en una sesión de preguntas y respuestas con usted e infórmele de su difícil situación. De esta manera, la cosa real será una brisa en comparación.

REDUCIR LOS SÍNTOMAS

Por lo que concierne para mitigar los síntomas físicos de los nervios, trate de comer antes de la entrevista. No se recargue, pero un ligero desayuno o almuerzo le ayudarán (a menos de que honestamente crea que volverá el estómago). Los nervios son siempre peores con el estómago vacío.

Usted también encontrará útiles los ejercicios de relajación. La manera de reducir el estrés es relajarse y respirar lentamente. Como una receta rápida para esto, aquí está un ejercicio de relajación que puede llevar a cabo antes de la entrevista, cuando esté esperando en la recepción:

> **Ejercicio efectivo 1**
> 1. Siéntese si es posible, pero puede hacerlo de pie si es necesario.
> 2. Relaje sus brazos y manos; si está sentado, ponga sus manos en su regazo.
> 3. Cierre sus ojos si puede, pero nuevamente esto no es esencial.
> 4. Respire a través de su nariz, lentamente cuente hasta cinco. Respire tan lento como pueda, empujado su diafragma y su estómago.
> 5. Respire a través de su boca contando hasta siete; si está sentado, no se deje caer conforme respire.
> 6. Permita que su respiración vuelva a la normalidad y abra sus ojos.
>
> Usted puede repasar esto en intervalos, tan a menudo como lo necesite, pero siempre deje que su respiración regrese a la normalidad entre uno y otro ejercicio de relajación. Si no lo hace, se hiperventilará. Esto no le hará ningún daño, pero puede hacerle sentir un poco mareado, lo que lo podría poner más nervioso en lugar de relajarlo.

Inclusive cuando la entrevista se esté llevando a cabo, todavía existen técnicas que puede usar en el sitio para ayudarle a relajarse.

- Tome una respiración profunda mientras el entrevistador le esté haciendo una pregunta. Entre más tensos nos ponemos, más se elevarán nuestras costillas y pecho. Al liberarlos con una respiración profunda, que expanda su pecho, usted baja la tensión y ésta no se puede expandir. Esto no requiere de concentración, así que se puede enfocar en lo que el entrevistador le pregunte.
- Sonreír ayuda a relajar los músculos. Se puede sentir como un idiota si sonríe durante toda la entrevista, pero si lo hace de vez en cuando en las debidas oportunidades, podrá empezar a responder a una pregunta que le vaya a relajar. Y esto

también le ayudará a presentarse como una persona cordial y amistosa.

- Si se encuentra sentado, engarrotado, con las piernas y los brazos cruzados (no digamos los dedos), cambie a una posición más abierta y relajada. Trataremos sobre el lenguaje corporal en el siguiente capítulo, pero la cuestión importante para la relajación es justamente abrir y permitir que sus músculos se tranquilicen.

> Nada más ábrase y permita que sus músculos se relajen.

Sus músculos se pueden tensar como resultado del nerviosismo psicológico, pero usted puede dar reversa a la causa y efecto: relajar sus músculos lo hará sentirse menos nervioso.

Recomendación efectiva

¡Relájese!

Prepárese tanto como pueda para la entrevista. Entre más se haya preparado y ensayado, menos miedo tendrá. Y entre menos miedo tenga, menos nervioso estará, así que:

- Practique sus respuestas.
- Planee evitar o enfrentarse a los grandes derrames de adrenalina.
- Durante el día use simples técnicas de relajación para quitar los nervios.

Capítulo 5
Proyecte la imagen correcta

Ya hemos establecido la importancia de la primera impresión, pero esto no se queda ahí. Tiene que continuar dando la mejor impresión posible durante toda la entrevista. Muy aparte de lo que diga, la manera como lo diga tendrá un gran impacto en la opinión de su entrevistador sobre usted; inclusive aunque sea la mejor persona para ese trabajo.

Esto no quiere decir que usted deba tomar un curso intensivo sobre actuación en la escuela de drama de su localidad y transformarse en alguien completamente diferente. No hay necesidad de hacer una actuación, nada más sea usted mismo. Pero su personalidad natural tendrá muchas cualidades diferentes, y necesita estar seguro de que presentará su lado positivo y relevante durante la entrevista. Por tanto, debe proyectar la imagen correcta acerca de usted, pero usando la conducta que vaya a impresionar más a su entrevistador.

> **Comprobación al momento**
>
> Aquí esta una prueba rápida. Acorde con una encuesta de Career World, vea si puede decir cuáles cualidades tienen más influencia en una entrevista y colóquelas en orden de importancia:
>
> - Su personalidad, cómo se presenta en la entrevista.
> - Su experiencia.

- Las calificaciones que tiene para el puesto.
- Sus antecedentes y referencias.
- El entusiasmo que tiene hacia la organización y su posición.

Resulta conveniente reforzar que estas cinco cualidades son importantes y que usted necesita demostrar su adecuación en cada área, pero ¿cuál es la prioridad correcta? De hecho, la manera en la que están listados es el orden de importancia en el cual lo colocaron los entrevistadores. Si como usted se presente a una entrevista es el factor más importante para que pueda obtener el trabajo, entonces ¿qué es lo que necesita hacer?

REFLEXIONE Y RESPONDA

Hay algunas cualidades esenciales que usted debe proyectar.

Sea reflexivo en sus respuestas

Haga el esfuerzo de dar una respuesta completa (pero no laveríntica o cantinflesca) a las preguntas de su entrevistador, y voluntariamente proporcione más información relevante. No dé respuestas en monosílabos porque suenan hoscas e inútiles, aunque no sea su intención. Entonces, si ellos dicen: "Veo un entrenamiento original en mercadotecnia", responda, por ejemplo: "Sí, así es", pero en mi primer empleo de mercadotecnia yo hice mucho trabajo de relaciones públicas (RP), y particularmente disfruté el lado de la prensa, así que decidí especializarme en relaciones con la prensa".

> No dé respuestas en monosílabos porque suenan hoscas e inútiles.

Sea confiado

Usted podrá sentir lo que sea, pero sienta confianza, ya que ésta es una cualidad atractiva en un empleado, así que necesita demostrar que la posee. La investigación demuestra que a los entrevistadores no les gusta dar empleos a las personas que se denigran. Desde luego esto no quiere decir que sea creído y arrogante, pero no se disculpe de usted mismo. Si su entrevistador dice: "Así que desde hace dos años no ha hecho una venta real cara a cara", no conteste: "Me temo que sí". Diga algo como esto: "Así es, pero siempre he sentido que es una de aquellas habilidades que nunca se pierden cuando se han aprendido".

Desastre efectivo

Usted ha obtenido toda la experiencia adecuada y sus calificaciones son mejores que las de cualquiera de los otros aspirantes. Tiene brillantes referencias y ha hecho su investigación y esto se demuestra. Sin embargo, existe un problema. Da la impresión de que no cree en usted. Sigue diciendo cosas tales como "Lo siento, no he tenido mucha experiencia en el *software*. Yo sólo los he usado por unos meses (cuando usted debería haber dicho: "Seguro, yo lo sé muy bien. Yo lo he estado usando durante los últimos meses"). Al final, el entrevistador llegará a compartir la opinión que usted tiene de sí mismo, y el trabajo se lo dará a otro candidato. ¡Uff!

Sea enérgico

La gente que proyecta vida y energía pasa por ser más positiva, capaz e inclusive inspiradora que aquellos que se ven planos y lentos. Así que esté a la alza, siéntese derecho, hable claramente y haga contacto visual (con todos sus entrevistadores, si es que hay más de uno).

Sea entusiasta

Esto está cercanamente relacionado con ser enérgico. Hemos visto que el entusiasmo hacia el trabajo y el puesto es importante para los entrevistadores (sí, ya lo sé, es el punto cinco de la lista, pero todos ellos son muy importantes). La mejor manera de trasmitir este entusiasmo es parecer interesado en lo que ambos, usted y el entrevistador, están diciendo. Si usted genuinamente está interesado, no debería encontrar muy difícil hacer esto; nada más asegúrese de hacerlo saber.

LENGUAJE CORPORAL

La manera en que se presenta visualmente puede ser tan importante como la manera en que se exprese. Y de hecho, su lenguaje corporal también puede afectar su comunicación verbal. Aquí está un ejercicio interesante para usted.

Ejercicio efectivo 2

Causa y efecto

- Siéntese en una silla y cruce sus brazos.
- Cruce sus piernas.
- Acomódese en la silla.
- Ahora imagine que está en la entrevista y que el entrevistador se encuentra sentado frente a usted. No lo mire; en lugar de eso vea hacia el piso.
- No haga ninguna expresión facial.
- Ahora responda con voz fuerte a la pregunta: "¿Qué es lo que más le gusta de su presente trabajo?".

Ésa es la primera parte, ahora va la segunda:

- Relaje sus manos en su regazo.
- Ponga ambos pies en el piso.
- No se acomode, descanse ligeramente hacia delante.
- Vea directamente a su entrevistador imaginario.
- Sonría.
- Ahora responda fuerte y claro a la pregunta: "¿Qué es lo que más le gusta de su presente trabajo?".

Debe encontrar que existen marcadas diferencias tanto en su tono como en su respuesta usando estos dos enfoques. Cuando usted adopta un lenguaje corporal positivo, optimista (como el segundo, como estoy seguro de que usted lo realiza), todo su tono levanta y suena más confiado, enérgico y entusiasta –todas las cualidades que hemos establecido que usted necesita para su proyecto–.

Encontrará que, como ya hemos visto antes en el caso de relajar su cuerpo, disminuyen sus nervios; que la causa y el efecto puede trabajar en ambos sentidos. Si está positivo y optimista, su lenguaje corporal lo estará. O empiece con el lenguaje positivo, cáptelo correctamente y se volverá más positivo y optimista.

Vale la pena conocer las señales del lenguaje corporal óptimo, pero no se aferre a ellas. Si proyecta las cualidades correctas y siente las emociones apropiadas, el lenguaje corporal las seguirá naturalmente, pero si siente que está aflojando, que suena menos positivo de lo que le gustaría, puede monitorear su lenguaje corporal y adaptarlo con objeto de elevar su humor y su tono verbal.

> Si está positivo y optimista, su lenguaje corporal lo estará.

Consejo efectivo

Los entrevistadores profesionales dicen que un buen contacto visual con el candidato es esencial para darles una buena impresión.

Así que, ¿cuáles son los puntos esenciales del lenguaje corporal para proyectarlos durante la entrevista? Aquí están los más importantes que hay que mantener en mente:

- No se siente en la orilla de la silla. Siéntese bien, hasta atrás, excepto si es una silla muy profunda, tapizada, en cuyo caso existe el peligro de parecer demasiado relajado si usted se pierde en el fondo.
- Siéntese con ambos pies en el piso, algo inclinado hacia el entrevistador.
- Haga contacto visual frecuente con el entrevistador. Si es más de uno, haga contacto con todos, pero mire al que le esté dirigiendo las preguntas que tiene que responder.
- Sonría amablemente.
- No esconda su cara entre sus manos.
- No dé señales defensivas cruzando sus brazos y piernas.
- Trate de mantener sus manos tranquilas, excepto cuando esté gesticulando. No juegue con su cabello ni ponga las manos en sus bolsas.

Reflejar

Cuando sentimos empatía hacia alguien con quien estamos hablando, podemos subconscientemente reflejar sus acciones. Puede observar esto cuando conversa con algún amigo en la mesa durante una cena o descansando en el sofá. Usted a menudo se cambia de posición conforme ellos lo hacen, o cruza sus piernas o pone sus codos en la mesa cuando ellos lo hacen. Esto contribuye a la empatía.

Desde luego puede hacer que esto trabaje a su favor en una entrevista. Si refleja a su entrevistador las acciones y expresiones faciales que toma (sonreír cuando ellos lo hagan, por ejemplo), se sentirá más tranquilo y en armonía con usted. Es obvio que no es una buena idea copiar exactamente y de manera deliberada cada uno de sus movimientos, pero esté consciente del poder del subconsciente, especialmente en lo que se refiere al lenguaje corporal, y úselo para construir empatía con su entrevistador.

Su voz

Necesita practicar para asegurarse de que da la mejor impresión.

Su habla en una entrevista dirá mucho acerca de usted. Tenga la disciplina de observar las voces de los demás –especialmente de las personas que no ha conocido antes– y piense acerca de la impresión que le dan. Algunas voces suenan débiles, apáticas o inciertas. La gente que habla muy rápido o que murmura puede parecer menos segura de sí misma. Necesita practicar para asegurarse de que da la mejor impresión. No se trata de que finja su voz (eso nunca funciona), sino que use su propia voz en el mejor estilo posible. Aquí están unos puntos importantes:

- Hable con voz fuerte y confiada.
- Asegúrese de no murmurar o parlotear.
- No permita que su voz sea elevada (la ansiedad puede ocasionar esta exageración si no es cuidadoso).
- No hable con monotonía; mantenga su discurso variado evitando extremos de volumen o de tono, pero exprese entusiasmo.

- Pause momentáneamente antes de responder a una pregunta y tome una respiración. Esto le ayudará a mantener su lenguaje parejo y controlado.

Obviamente usted no puede recordar todo en una entrevista, y si piensa mucho acerca de algo tan inconsciente como el lenguaje corporal, olvidará a qué trabajo hizo la solicitud y, más aun, de lo que quiere decir. La idea es practicar por anticipado para que esto se vuelva natural. Durante la entrevista, si siente que algo va mal o que usted está ansioso o falto de confianza, esos son momentos buenos para revisar las señales de su subconsciente. Si ha practicado bien, sólo le llevará un instante pensar y ponerse en el camino nuevamente.

Candidato con actitud

Una vez que ha causado una buena primera impresión, temo que se deje ir. Necesita consolidar su buen trabajo mediante una proyección continua de una imagen positiva. Así que sea:

- Reflexivo para responder.
- Confiado.
- Enérgico.
- Entusiasta.

Y recuerde monitorear su lenguaje corporal (sin distanciarse de las respuestas a las cuestiones de la entrevista). En particular, cambie su lenguaje corporal si tiende a sonar letárgico, poco entusiasta o lúgubre.

Capítulo 6
La entrevista

Ya hemos establecido el formato que puede tener una entrevista. Nada más para recapitular:

- Después de una breve charla inicial, el entrevistador le preguntará algunas cuestiones generales de la lista, que son formuladas a todos los candidatos.
- Le preguntarán cuestiones acerca de su solicitud. Éstas, obviamente, son el cuerpo de la entrevista. Las veremos con más detalle en el siguiente par de capítulos.
- Después de esto, el entrevistador probablemente le dirá un poco más acerca de la organización y del trabajo.
- Finalmente, ellos le pedirán sus preguntas.

Saber el formato que se espera es de gran ayuda, pero usted todavía necesita saber cómo manejar profesionalmente la entrevista en términos generales. Así que echaremos una mirada a los principales puntos de su estilo para la entrevista, el tipo de cuestiones ante las que debe estar listo y cómo tratar con diferentes tipos de entrevistas, por ejemplo: en panel o por teléfono. Finalmente, hacer una buena salida es casi tan importante como hacer una buena entrada; veremos cómo concluir una entrevista limpia e inteligentemente.

> Hacer una buena salida es casi tan importante como hacer una buena entrada.

ESTILO DE LA ENTREVISTA

Aparte de responder a las preguntas tan positivamente como pueda, existen otras cuantas habilidades que le ayudarán a impresionar a su entrevistador (o evitar que lo deseche). La manera en que usted conteste puede ser tan importante como la respuesta que dé, así que necesita entregar el paquete completo.

- Asegúrese de hablar con claridad y de responder a las cuestiones sin murmurar. Un buen lenguaje corporal y contacto visual le ayudarán a hacer esto naturalmente.
- No interrumpa al entrevistador, aunque él lo interrumpa a usted.
- Aparte de solicitar clarificación de alguna cuestión si lo necesita, sólo haga cuando mucho unas cuantas preguntas en la entrevista. Éste es el tiempo del entrevistador para cuestionarlo; usted tendrá oportunidad de hacerle preguntas después.
- Adopte un tono similar al del entrevistador. Si ellos son muy formales, en consecuencia, usted debe serlo. Sea muy cuidadoso de cualquier cosa más allá de un humor gentil, a menos que su entrevistador esté inyectando mucho humor a la conversación (en cuyo caso ría cortésmente a sus chistes).
- No le pregunte a su entrevistador cuestiones acerca del salario. Esto hará que piense que sólo está interesado en el dinero. Si ellos le ofrecen el trabajo, después habrá bastante tiempo para discutir el salario (cómo negociar su paquete inicial se describe en la parte 3 de este libro).

Recomendación efectiva

Mucha gente se siente incómoda acerca de hacer sonar su trompeta. Parece arrogante decir "Yo soy brillante en esto", o "El proyecto se hubiera desecho en pedazos si no hubiera sido por mi previsión para detectar problemas". Usted no tiene que decir cualquiera de estas cosas; los entrevistadores obtendrán las conclusiones correctas por sí mismos. Dé buenos ejemplos de su trabajo sin tener que deletrearlo en un lenguaje tan grueso.

RESPONDA POSITIVAMENTE

Los siguientes capítulos tratan de cuestiones específicas, pero sólo son ciertos lineamientos generales para responder a cualquier pregunta que necesite resolver. Todos están dirigidos para darle al entrevistador una visión positiva de usted como alguien que es confiado, capaz y honesto.

- *No divague.* Trate de que sus respuestas no sean superiores a dos minutos cuando mucho, desde luego varias serán más cortas. En el otro extremo, como ya hemos visto, trate de evitar las respuestas en monosílabos, a menos que su entrevistador pregunte sólo para clarificar (por ejemplo: "Así que, ¿usted tiene 18 o 19 años?").
- *Use ejemplos.* Dé multitud de ejemplos de sus logros, desafíos y éxitos. Esté preparado para respaldar cada afirmación y demuestre cada logro o habilidad con un ejemplo concreto.
- *Recuerde la descripción del trabajo.* Mantenga sus respuestas específicas respecto a la cuestión del trabajo. Si su entrevistador le pregunta, por ejemplo, cuál es su principal fuerza, explique una que sea importante para el trabajo y agregue un ejemplo de esto.
- *Tome una pausa si la necesita.* Si quiere pensar por un momento antes de empezar a responder una cuestión, esto es correcto. Demuestra que lo considera con cuidado.
- *No mienta.* Sea tan honesto como pueda en sus respuestas. Usted puede –y debe– poner un punto positivo en la verdad, pero no cambiar los hechos. Esto incluye admitir que no sabe la respuesta a una pregunta, más que forcejear.
- *No critique a su actual empleador.* Si es nuevo en el mercado de trabajo, no denigre a su tutor o a su escuela. Esto puede hacerlo ver como negativo o difícil (el entrevistador podría preguntarse cuál es el otro lado de la historia), y ciertamente que el entrevistador se peguntará acerca de su lealtad.
- *No diga los secretos de su actual empleador.* Si es entrevistado por uno de los competidores actuales de su empleador, ellos tratarán de que diga más de lo que debe acerca de los planes y de la organización de su actual empleador. Sólo recuerde que

por mucho que deseen esa información también lo están probando. Si dice los secretos de su actual empleador a un competidor, ¿qué tan leal será con ellos si le dan el trabajo?

> **Consejo efectivo**
>
> Usted está interesado en saber cuáles son los secretos que los expertos consideran como la clave de lo que hay que hacer y de lo que no para manejar una entrevista. Entonces, aquí está la lista de los principales puntos de Career World (una consultora líder en la administración de carreras y colocaciones).
>
> **Hacer:**
> - Responda a la cuestión que le sea preguntada y no ofrezca información irrelevante.
> - Mantenga las respuestas concisas y concéntrese en los hechos, no en opiniones.
> - Hable clara y confiadamente y no permita desanimarse.
> - Constantemente recuerde que usted tiene algo que vender y enfóquese en cómo puede hacer una contribución positiva en el papel.
>
> **No hacer:**
> - Tratar de pasarse de listo.
> - Mentir, pretender o dar respuestas evasivas.
> - Salirse de sus casillas, espantarse, caer en pánico.
> - Criticar a sus empleadores anteriores.

TIPOS DE PREGUNTAS

Así como las cuestiones específicas cubiertas en el siguiente par de capítulos, existen tipos generales de asuntos que necesita saber para estar preparado. Aquí está una lista rápida:

- *Cuestiones hipotéticas.* Si preguntan: "Si pasa x, ¿usted qué haría?"; el asunto a reconocer es que no existe una única respuesta correcta. El entrevistador podría estar más interesado en qué tan capaz es usted de resolver el problema, más que en el resultado final. Es válido tomarse una pausa para pensar por un momento antes de responder.

- *Cuestiones técnicas.* Si usted será entrevistado para un puesto técnico, esté atento en las preguntas que le haga el entrevistador a fin de resolver un problema o un proceso. Esto podría ser una situación hipotética que ellos establezcan, o le pueden pedir un ejemplo de una experiencia propia y explicárselos detalladamente. Esté listo para este tipo de cuestiones, con ejemplos preparados.
- *Preguntas que causen estrés.* Algunos entrevistadores deliberadamente tratarán de retarlo o ponerlo bajo presión para sacarlo de quicio, como una prueba más. Ellos quieren saber cómo responde usted bajo presión ante este trato. Muchas personas sienten que este tipo de técnica es moralmente cuestionable, e inclusive dudan si deben trabajar para una persona que usa esta táctica, pero si aun quiere el trabajo, y siente que para el tipo de puesto que solicita este método es válido, mejor asegúrese de permanecer calmado sin importar la presión.

> Algunos entrevistadores tratarán de sacarlo de quicio.

Desastre efectivo

El entrevistador de repente gira alrededor de usted y lo acusa de mentir acerca de sus calificaciones. Usted se indigna y se pone a la defensiva. Sólo después se da cuenta de que nunca dudó de sus calificaciones, ellos sólo querían saber si es capaz de permanecer con calma, sin alterarse bajo presión. ¡Uff!

DIFERENTES TIPOS DE ENTREVISTAS

A menudo se encontrará en una entrevista uno a uno y muy probablemente sea ante su gerente de línea, si es que obtiene el trabajo. Desde luego, éste no es el único tipo de entrevista que existe. Casi todos los lineamientos de este libro se aplican a cualquier clase de entrevista, pero existen algunos puntos extra que vale la pena considerar si se encuentra en alguna de estas entrevistas.

Panel de entrevista

Usted se puede encontrar con tres o cuatro personas. Esto podría incluir al gerente de línea para el trabajo, a alguien de personal, quizá algún técnico si el puesto es para esta área, tal vez a un representante del sindicato, y probablemente hasta a un psicólogo.

Las entrevistas en panel tienden, por su naturaleza, a ser más formales que las de uno a uno, lo que puede hacerlas más estresantes, pero no hay razón por la que deban ser más duras de manejar que cualquier otro tipo de entrevista. Usted debe saber por anticipado que será entrevistado por un panel. Trate de saber sus nombres, y en caso de que vaya a conocerlos hasta que lleguen, pregúntele a la recepcionista sus nombres. Escríbalos.

Tenga en mente que los profesionales de Recursos Humanos (RH) y los gerentes de línea tienen diferentes enfoques en las entrevistas. Las personas de RH se ganan la vida haciendo entrevistas, ellos hacen muchas de éstas y saben exactamente lo que buscan. No trabajarán directamente con usted; por lo que a ellos se refiere el asunto está en blanco y negro: quieren que usted se ajuste a la especificación del empleo tanto como sea posible.

> Ajuste sus respuestas específicamente para cada persona que le haga la pregunta.

Por su parte, el gerente de línea odia hacer entrevistas por todo lo que usted ya sabe, y apreciará la ayuda que le puedan dar, así que es juguetón e interesado. Estarán preguntándose si tendrá una buena relación de trabajo con ellos y con el resto del equipo, así que déjeles saber que usted es sencillo y llevadero. Entonces sepa quién es quién y ajuste sus respuestas específicamente para cada persona que le haga la pregunta, mientras también toma en cuenta al resto del panel.

📖 Conocimiento efectivo

Las entrevistas en panel son particularmente populares en el sector público. Si usted solicita un puesto en el gobierno, pregunte si será entrevistado por un panel. Si la respuesta es afirmativa, puede conseguir sus nombres y sus puestos de trabajo por anticipado. Memorícelos para que pueda dirigirse a ellos por su nombre en la entrevista (no se pase con esto; demuestre que ha hecho su tarea, pero no siga usando sus nombres o empezará a sonar poco sincero).

Sólo recuerde:

- Salude de mano a todos los del panel. Si es grande (más de media docena) puede dirigirse de mano sólo al presidente del panel (la persona que se pone de pie y lo salude a usted). Si los otros le ofrecen la mano, entonces salúdelos.
- Haga contacto visual con cada miembro del panel, y asegúrese de que ellos se sientan incluidos en sus respuestas.
- Dé la mayor atención a la persona que le hizo la pregunta que usted está respondiendo.
- Cuando le toque hacer sus preguntas, diríjalas principalmente a la persona que encabeza la entrevista (es obvio quién es).

Entrevista secuencial

Ésta es más común en las grandes organizaciones. Usted se encuentra en una serie de entrevistas con diferentes personas –quizá el gerente de línea para el trabajo, un alto ejecutivo, un representante de personal; tal vez un técnico–. Aparte del peligro de sentirse dentro de un maratón mental, éste es un buen sistema para usted. Inicia cada entrevista fresco, así que inclusive si no se desempeñó muy bien en la anterior, todavía puede tener una recuperación impresionante en la siguiente.

Los entrevistadores, desde luego, no operan aisladamente. Ellos habrán discutido anticipadamente qué áreas van cubrir cada uno, y al final compararán sus notas antes de llegar a una decisión. También querrán charlar entre ellos durante las entrevistas. Si esto sucede, podría ser cuestionado acerca de algo que ya cubrió con otro entrevistador previamente –es posible que le hayan prevenido a otra persona que le vuelva a probar en la misma área –.

> Cada entrevistador busca un aspecto diferente en su solicitud.

Con las entrevistas secuenciales necesita tener en mente que cada entrevistador busca un aspecto diferente de su solicitud. Después de todo, no tiene caso para ellos repetir el mismo ejercicio con usted.

Emparejamiento

Vea si usted puede ajustar las siguientes cuestiones con la persona que es más probable que las haga, teniendo en mente que cada entrevistador tiene diferentes áreas de interés y experiencia.

A. Gerente de personal	1. ¿Cuál considera su principal fortaleza?
B. Gerente de línea	2. ¿Dónde se ve dentro de cinco años?
C. Gerente técnico	3. ¿Qué tipo de jugador de equipo es?
D. Alto ejecutivo	4. ¿Cómo respondería a una falla del software en ZP21?

Respuestas: A, B1, C4, D2.

Le puedo jurar que a usted nunca le preguntará estas cuestiones ningún otro entrevistador que no sea el indicado, pero el punto aquí es que necesita estar consciente de lo que cada uno de ellos busca, y darle la respuesta y ejemplos que se relacionen con su habilidad para hacer el trabajo dentro de su particular disciplina.

Entrevista telefónica

Algunos entrevistadores usan las entrevistas telefónicas como una manera rápida de reducir una larga lista de solicitudes a una más corta. Otros pueden usarlas si el trabajo requiere de muchas llamadas telefónicas, por lo que pueden evaluar sus habilidades telefónicas y de comunicación. Se usan a menudo en una entrevista inicial para los trabajos en el extranjero. El entrevistador puede arreglar una cita para una entrevista

> No necesariamente tendrá un aviso de que ellos están tratando de contactarlo.

telefónica con usted, o no. No necesariamente tendrá un aviso de que están tratando de contactarlo –lo primero que escuche de ellos puede ser la llamada telefónica–.

Así que si existe una oportunidad para una llamada de un entrevistador, por ejemplo, si solicita un trabajo que requiere mucho tiempo en el teléfono, tiene que estar preparado para lo siguiente:

- Mantenga una copia de su CV y de la solicitud cerca de su teléfono, junto con una pluma y un papel. Si está fuera y con su celular, manténgalas en sus bolsas o en su maletín.
- Tenga su agenda a la mano. Si les gusta el sonido de su voz en el teléfono, ellos arreglarán una entrevista.
- Si no está disponible cuando le llamen, haga una previsión para esto. Especifique en su CV o en la carta cubierta los mejores tiempos en que pueden contactarlo, junto con otros números de teléfono que tenga, e indique a quien vaya a contestar su teléfono que tome los mensajes claros con los nombres, teléfonos y demás.
- Si el entrevistador llama cuando esté fuera, deje lo que esté haciendo y busque el sitio más quieto donde pueda tomar la llamada. No vaya caminando en la calle, ni empujado su carrito por el supermercado.
- Si no puede tomar la llamada en ese momento, dígalo abiertamente. Deje en claro que está muy satisfecho de saber que ellos le han llamado, pero usted quiere estar en condiciones de brindarles la máxima atención sin ninguna presión de tiempo. Pregunte que si gusta que le devuelva la llamada o viceversa, y tome los números necesarios y repítalos para verificar que los ha anotado correctamente.
- Trate la entrevista con la misma importancia que le daría a una entrevista en persona. Ésta podría parecer menos formal, pero es tan importante como la otra.
- Si no está solo en casa, arrégleselas para que pueda tomar la llamada en privado. Es correcto pedirle al entrevistador que espere mientras se pasa a otra habitación.
- Si puede, siéntese durante la entrevista; recuerde usar un lenguaje del cuerpo directo (esto le afectará su tono de voz), y sonría fácilmente aunque nadie lo vea.

- Asegúrese de escribir el nombre del entrevistador y otros detalles que le proporcionen, tales como el número de su teléfono o la dirección donde lo puede encontrar en caso de que lo inviten a una entrevista.

> **Recomendación efectiva**
>
> Si le ofrecen una entrevista cara a cara después de una entrevista telefónica, tome todos los detalles. Luego llame para confirmar los datos. Todo esto para darle al entrevistador la impresión de su eficiencia y profesionalismo.

HAGA LA SALIDA

El entrevistador le señalará cuando la entrevista haya terminado. Y justamente como cualquier buen vendedor, no esperará cerrar el trato en el momento, pero cuando menos querrá saber cuál es el siguiente paso. Entonces pregunte qué sigue y cuándo. Usted desea saber si habrá una segunda vuelta de entrevistas, y si se enterará por teléfono o por correo, cuándo le llamarán, etcétera.

Sonría cordialmente y haga una salida limpia.

Aparte de eso, cuando termine la entrevista, póngase de pie, recoja sus cosas y váyase pronto. Antes de salir despídase de mano del entrevistador nuevamente si él le ofrece la suya. Agradézcale por haberlo visto, sonría cordialmente (como sea que se sienta por dentro) y haga una salida limpia.

En caso de que el entrevistador le acompañe hasta la recepción o hasta la puerta principal, converse conforme caminan, recuerde que usted está todavía en el *show*. No se descuide del final oficial de la entrevista ni haga comentarios inconvenientes.

> **Un enfoque totalmente profesional**
>
> Adopte un tono y estilo profesional a través de toda la entrevista:
>
> - Hable claro.
> - No haga muchas preguntas hasta que sea invitado a ello.

- Conforme se desenvuelva el tono de la entrevista, siga la guía del entrevistador.
- No pregunte por el salario.

Cuando le toque contestar las preguntas:

- No divague.
- Use ejemplos.
- Ajuste sus respuestas a los requerimientos específicos del trabajo.
- Tome una pausa antes de responder si la necesita.
- No mienta.
- No critique a su actual empleador.

Esté listo para las preguntas de tipo particular, tales como las hipotéticas; así que usted pueda dar el tipo de respuesta que el entrevistador espera. Y si su entrevista no es de uno a uno, tenga en mente los lineamientos para los demás tipos de entrevistas.

Capítulo 7
Las preguntas más comunes en una entrevista

Existen algunas cuestiones que puede esperar a que le sean preguntadas en la mayoría de las entrevistas, así que para algunas deberá estar realmente preparado. Hay ciertas cosas que el entrevistador desea saber acerca de usted, y esto se refleja en las preguntas, las cuales vienen en la primera parte de la entrevista, ya que son generalmente las que el entrevistador hará a todos los candidatos.

Estamos a punto de ver la lista de las preguntas más comunes en las entrevistas, para que usted pueda estar equipado para dar la mejor respuesta posible a cada una, pero desde luego existen algunos lineamientos generales que se aplican a cada repuesta que dé. Entonces empecemos primero por esto. En el capítulo anterior ya hemos ido a través de ciertos puntos clave en términos del estilo para responder; ahora veamos un poco más de cerca el contenido. Los puntos clave que debe recordar son los siguientes:

- *Mantenga su respuesta relevante.* Si le preguntan que defina sus fortalezas, no dé una lista larga. Tome una o dos áreas clave. Usted puede tener docenas de fortalezas, pero sólo seleccione la que su entrevistador necesita más para el candidato exitoso que debe tener este trabajo.
- *Escuche la pregunta y responda la cuestión que se le ha preguntado.* No se desvíe ante las preguntas difíciles; su entrevistador no es tonto, ellos notarán lo que está haciendo y no les va a gustar eso.

- *Sólo responda la pregunta que le hicieron.* No dé montones de información extraña. Mantenga sus respuestas tan breves como pueda sin omitir nada relevante.

> **Consejo efectivo**
>
> Cuando se les preguntó qué es lo que menos les impresiona de un candidato, la mayoría de los entrevistadores profesionales citaron "no escuchar la pregunta" como el principal factor. Esto incluye responder lo que el candidato quiere, en lugar de contestar lo que se le preguntó realmente.

LAS PREGUNTAS MÁS COMUNES

El siguiente capítulo es acerca de las preguntas duras de una entrevista. Usted podría pensar que algunas de las que están aquí son duras; esto es porque las preguntas más comunes están en este capítulo, incluyendo aquellas que podrían haber calificado para presentarlas en el siguiente capítulo.

Las respuestas recomendadas aquí no son un libreto; la idea es hacerle saber el tipo de respuesta que impresionará al entrevistador. Usted necesitará expresarla en sus palabras y proporcionar ejemplos propios.

Platíqueme acerca de usted

> No es una invitación para que cuente la historia de su vida.

No es una invitación para que cuente la historia de su vida. De hecho, usted necesita solicitarle al entrevistador que por favor sea más específico antes de que le pueda responder lo que él quiere escuchar. Así que pregúnteles a ellos: "¿Qué aspecto de mí le gustaría que le platicase?". Ellos probablemente le preguntarán acerca de cómo es usted para trabajar.

Deberá ser capaz de describir qué tipo de persona es en máximo dos minutos. Concéntrese en las cualidades positivas y el vínculo de ellas con las responsabilidades clave del trabajo que solicita. Por ejemplo: "Soy una persona común. Yo disfruto trabajar con la gente y ser parte de un equipo. Soy el tipo de persona que le gusta meterse a fondo en un proyecto, y realmente disfruto ver el proyecto desde su planeación inicial hasta sus etapas finales…", y así sucesivamente.

En caso de que deseen saber lo que hace fuera del trabajo, les puede dar una respuesta que signifique que usted está mandado a hacer para el trabajo que ofrecen. Entonces, nuevamente les demostrará que es un jugador en equipo; podría decirles: "Yo soy muy social, tengo muchos amigos y paso buenos ratos con ellos. Practico varios deportes, como *hockey* sobre hielo".

No le estoy sugiriendo que mienta. Usted tiene mucho tiempo para pensar acerca de esta cuestión antes de que llegue a la entrevista y esté listo con respuestas adecuadas y honestas acerca de su vida personal o de negocios. Si, por ejemplo, el trabajo requiere un buen jugador en equipo, es probable que tenga multitud de ejemplos de los cuales elegir.

Recomendación efectiva

Cinco frases que les gusta oír a los entrevistadores

1. "Dígame algo más acerca de la organización". El entrevistador quiere escuchar algo que le haya interesado a usted de la propia compañía y no nada más qué puede hacer ésta por usted.
2. "¿Cuáles son mis expectativas de promoción en este trabajo?". Esto muestra que usted es ambicioso y con ganas de hacer bien las cosas (ambos son atributos positivos).
3. "Yo realmente disfruto los desafíos". Nuevamente esto demuestra entusiasmo para el trabajo, inclusive si no todo va sobre ruedas.
4. "Yo observo que la tendencia de esta industria es…". Usted ha hecho su trabajo de investigación y ha tomado un mayor interés dentro de un contexto más amplio para el puesto que le ofrecen.
5. "¿Me puede dar un ejemplo…?". Entre más pueda ilustrar sus respuestas con anécdotas y con ejemplos de su experiencia pasada, mejor imagen podrá formarse de usted el entrevistador. Esto es exactamente lo que ellos quieren escuchar.

¿Qué es lo que más le gusta de su trabajo actual?

Puede ser una pregunta con truco. El entrevistador le está tentando a que diga las cosas que no le gustan de su actual trabajo. Si es así, presumiblemente habrá cosas acerca de este trabajo que tampoco le gustarán, lo que no es muy motivador. Así que la única respuesta que puede dar es que usted disfruta todo lo que se refiere a su trabajo.

Si cree que suena poco plausible, puede mencionar una o dos partes muy favoritas de su trabajo (asegúrese de que sean importantes también para este puesto en caso de que lo obtenga). Así que podría decir: "Yo realmente tengo suerte. No puedo pensar en nada que no me guste acerca de mi trabajo, pero supongo que lo que más me gusta es tratar con los clientes. Es por eso que he solicitado este empleo, porque yo quiero tener la oportunidad de dedicarme aún más a hacer esto".

Esto cubre la otra falla evidente al responder: "Yo disfruto todo", que conlleva la pregunta: "¿Entonces por qué está buscando trabajo en otro lugar?".

💬 Consejo efectivo

Cuando les pregunté qué aconsejarían a los candidatos para responder a las preguntas de los entrevistadores, ellos incluyeron:

- Mantenga el punto.
- Siempre use ejemplos para apoyar sus respuestas.
- Una vez que haya terminado, deje de hablar.

¿Cuál ha sido el mayor desafío que ha afrontado en su trabajo?

Necesita elegir un ejemplo que lo deje bien parado.

En tanto que esté preparado, es una gran pregunta. Usted necesita tener la respuesta lista con objeto de obtener lo mejor de ésta. La idea es que no sólo describa el desafío, sino que explique cómo lo resolvió. Así que necesita elegir un ejemplo que lo deje bien parado.

Existe algo más detrás de la pregunta anterior: el entrevistador trata de ver qué es lo que usted considera un desafío. Entonces piense bien sobre el ejemplo que desee describir. ¿Será una decisión difícil? ¿Una situación difícil? ¿Un sistema que necesita revisión mayor para mejorar los resultados? Tiene que decidir, así que, como siempre, tome algo que sea relevante para este trabajo.

Una buena regla a seguir: es peligroso seleccionar un ejemplo que presente problemas con otras personas. Esto puede dar la impresión de que usted considera tratar con otros como un gran desafío.

> **Recomendación efectiva**
>
> Aunque necesita preparar sus respuestas por adelantado, no es buena idea aprendérselas de memoria, porque dará la impresión de que las está recitando. Sólo prepare los puntos clave que quiera subrayar.

¿Por qué quiere dejar su trabajo actual?

No importa si la razón real es porque ya no aguanta a su jefe o que la compañía le paga un salario patético. El entrevistador busca una razón positiva para poder proseguir adelante, no una justificación negativa para que evite estar en el trabajo en que no está contento.

La única respuesta correcta a esto es: "Porque yo quiero ampliar mi experiencia y creo que puedo desempeñarme mejor en una nueva organización" (o las palabras para tal efecto). Si es relevante para el empleo, se puede expandir un poco. Por ejemplo, si el trabajo requiere dar muchas presentaciones puede decir: "En particular, yo disfruto las presentaciones y es algo en lo que he llegado a destacar. Desafortunadamente, no hay muchas oportunidades para desarrollar más mis habilidades en donde estoy".

El entrevistador busca una razón positiva.

> **Desastre efectivo**
>
> Usted está siendo entrevistado por alguien simpático y amistoso, quien le pregunta por qué busca otro trabajo. Decide ser completamente honesto, le dice que porque no

le asignaron la promoción que se merecía, y ahora tiene que trabajar con la persona que se quedó con su lugar, y quien no tiene ni la mitad de su experiencia. Su entrevistador sonríe simpáticamente e imagina exactamente la misma situación presentándose si ellos le ofrecieran el trabajo. ¡Uff!

¿Cómo es su jefe actual (o el más reciente)?

Siempre sea positivo, inclusive si su jefe es una verdadera molestia.

Nunca critique a ninguno de sus jefes (actuales, recientes o lo que sea). El entrevistador podría ser su próximo jefe y quiere a una persona leal ante sus jefes anteriores. Así que siempre sea positivo, inclusive si su jefe es una verdadera molestia. Nada más diga algo como esto: "Yo tengo la suerte de tener un jefe que es muy bueno en su trabajo". No diga más.

El punto no es nada más que su entrevistador quiere ver que usted sea leal, sino que es consciente de que no saben el otro lado de la historia. Así que usted puede saber que sus reclamos son justificados, pero le hacen sonar como una boca floja que hablará de ellos en los mismos términos si le llegan a dar el empleo.

💬 Consejo efectivo

He aquí una efectiva pieza de asesoría de Phil Boyle, MD de Ramsay Hall (una compañía de reclutamiento de ejecutivos): "Reexprese la pregunta como primera parte de la respuesta. Esto le dará al entrevistador la oportunidad de corregir la pregunta si usted la malinterpretó".

¿Cuál cree que es el papel de un...?
(cualquiera que sea su trabajo actual)

Ya debería haber pensado acerca de esta cuestión antes de que se la pregunten (como debería de hacerlo con todas las demás preguntas de este capítulo). Yo no le puedo decir la respuesta, ya que no sé cuál puesto está solicitando, pero necesita responderla en términos de una gran imagen:

- El objetivo general del trabajo.
- Las responsabilidades clave.

Como ya se habrá dado cuenta, usted puede tomar las grandes claves a partir de la descripción del trabajo si usted solicita un empleo dentro de su línea actual de actividades, pero también querrá aportar de su experiencia.

Esta cuestión se presenta a veces como una prueba; si esto sucede, el entrevistador lo interrumpirá si está en desacuerdo con usted. Su objetivo es ver si puede defender su caso con calma y convincentemente, así que no se inquiete por la interrupción. Pregúntele cortésmente para poder justificar su afirmación de que su descripción del papel está mal ("¿Qué le hace decir eso?"). Entonces demuestre que puede argumentar bien su caso y sin ponerse a la defensiva.

> Demuestre que puede argumentar bien su caso y sin ponerse a la defensiva.

¿Qué sabe acerca de nuestra empresa?

Es una gran oportunidad para demostrar que ha hecho su tarea. Manténgase en los puntos relevantes: tamaño, facturación, naturaleza del negocio, crecimiento del *ethos* de la compañía; por ejemplo, "Yo sé que ustedes son una empresa joven, creciente, con una reputación de desarrollo de personal". Sea conciso, pero añada una o dos cosas que sugieran que ha ido más allá de la simple lectura del reporte anual. Por ejemplo: "… observo en la prensa comercial que han firmado un par de grandes contratos en Europa del Este".

Recomendación efectiva

Si es un graduado solicitando su primer trabajo, su entrevistador querrá saber acerca de su carrera universitaria y de cómo ésta le ha ayudado a ser adecuado para este trabajo. Desde qué temas lee hasta cuáles fueron sus actividades extracurriculares; puede tener que contestar sobre los siguientes temas:

> - ¿Por qué eligió ese curso en particular?
> - ¿Cómo se relacionan sus estudios con este trabajo?
> - ¿Qué proyectos de trabajo ha hecho?
> - ¿Qué actividades extracurriculares llevó a cabo?

¿Por qué quiere este trabajo?

No hable de más acerca de los desafíos y de los prospectos. Hable en términos de beneficios para ellos, y sea específico acerca del tipo de retos que disfruta. Por ejemplo: "Yo soy un gran organizador, y estoy buscando un puesto que me dé el ámbito para planear y organizar", o "Yo obtengo mucha satisfacción al trabajar con equipos exitosos, y este trabajo parece que requiere de alguien que pueda encajar bien dentro de un equipo cerrado y bien motivado".

Ésta es también una buena oportunidad para demostrar la investigación que ha hecho sobre la compañía –nuevamente, sea breve y relevante –. Así que puede decir algo como esto: "Yo encuentro a las compañías crecientes más excitantes, con una atmósfera dinámica para trabajar, y sé que ustedes han estado creciendo un 6 % por arriba del promedio en los últimos cuatro años".

¿Qué puede aportar a este trabajo?

Ésta es otra cuestión que le da la oportunidad de brillar. Necesita vincular su experiencia pasada o sus habilidades con los requerimientos del trabajo. Por tanto, seleccione tres puntos fuertes a su favor que sean relevantes para este empleo. Por ejemplo: "Yo tengo mucha experiencia para tratar con los clientes, incluyendo a los truculentos. Me llevo muy bien con toda la gente, por lo que trabajo muy bien en equipo. Soy un organizador natural y encuentro fácil manejar los documentos de trabajo y encajo bien con cualquier sistema que necesite. Como yo lo entiendo, éstas son algunas habilidades especiales para este trabajo".

¿Cuánto tiempo espera estar en esta empresa?

El entrevistador no va a emplear a alguien que se irá nuevamente antes de que ellos obtengan todo el valor de éste. Así que indique que piensa estar por algunos años. Por ejemplo: "A mí me gustaría establecerme con esta empresa, crecer y desarrollarme dentro de ella. Yo me veo quedándome tanto como siga progresando y contribuyendo aquí".

Indique que le gustaría quedarse varios años.

> **Recomendación efectiva**
>
> Esté preparado para que el entrevistador le cuestione de diferentes maneras a las presentadas aquí, o prepárese mentalmente. Ellos pueden preguntarle: "¿Qué experiencia tiene en lidiar con clientes difíciles?". Igualmente, ellos tratarán de obtener la misma información preguntándole: "Hable acerca de los clientes difíciles con los que ha tenido que tratar, ¿qué es lo que hizo?" E inclusive: "¿Cuál cree usted que es la clave para tratar con los clientes truculentos o molestos?". Todas éstas son esencialmente formas de la misma cuestión. Tendrá que ser capaz de reconocerlas y de responderlas conforme se haya preparado.

¿Cuáles son sus principales fortalezas?

Vaya por ellas. Ésta es una pregunta perfecta; nada más enfoque sus respuestas sobre las responsabilidades clave del trabajo para asegurarse de que sus fortalezas sean relevantes para su entrevistador. E intente no divagar mucho; seleccione una o dos de sus fortalezas clave que sean realmente importantes para este trabajo.

¿Cuál es su principal debilidad?

¡Oh!, truculenta, es una de esas cuestiones que realmente pertenecen al siguiente capítulo (es dura). Se le invita para que diga algo negativo acerca de usted. Resista. La mejor defensa es el ataque; utilice una de estas:

- Humor ("¿Helado doble de chocolate?").
- Algo personal, no relacionado con el trabajo ("Soy pésimo para el trabajo del hogar; cambiar focos y arreglar goteras…").
- Algo de hace mucho, que ahora ya haya aprendido ("Hace quince años yo habría dicho el papeleo, pero ya he aprendido a dejar media hora al inicio de cada día para esto. Ahora reconozco que estoy mejor en el trabajo administrativo que el resto de mis colegas").
- Algo que su entrevistador considerará como una fortaleza ("Yo tengo terror de quedarme a la mitad algo. Me quedo hasta que termine el trabajo, aunque a veces mi familia se queja de que llego tarde a casa").

Sus respuestas deben evitar dar alguna verdadera debilidad (en caso de que tenga alguna) y evitar también quedar como un arrogante que se cree perfecto –algo que realmente les molesta a los entrevistadores–.

¿Dónde se ve dentro de algunos años?

Sea muy cuidadoso al contestar esto porque si da una meta específica y el entrevistador sabe que no puede cumplirla, no lo contratarán. Así que déjela abierta, pero recuerde que quieren saber que usted tiene empuje y desea incrementar su valor con ellos. Dígales algo como esto, "Ciertamente soy ambicioso y me gusta estar en acción y progresar, pero no puedo ajustar un trabajo a una lista de condiciones prefijadas. Yo encuentro más provechoso dejar que el trabajo me lleve hacia delante".

¿Cómo lo describen sus colegas?

Ésta es una invitación a listar sus puntos fuertes, así que aprovéchela. Concéntrese en sus mejores puntos como colega, apoyador, buen miembro de equipo y demás. Como con todas estas cuestiones, no es inteligente hacer reclamos desorbitados. Usted podría ser desmentido por sus referencias al ser checadas o cuando inicie el trabajo, si es que se lo ofrecen. Desde luego, puede poner el mejor escenario para estas cosas. Entonces, si es un solitario, pero se lleva bien con todos, su respuesta podría ser: "Ellos dicen que soy uno de los miembros más tranquilos del equipo, popular y en quien se puede confiar para jalar con el equipo cuando se presenta cualquier tipo de desafío".

> Concéntrese en sus mejores puntos como colega.

¿Cómo lo describen sus amigos?

¿Cuáles amigos? Es la respuesta incorrecta a esta pregunta. De hecho, va por las mismas líneas que: "¿Cómo lo describen sus colegas?". No sea poco realista acerca de usted mismo, pero seleccione los puntos más fuertes y relevantes. Siempre es mejor mencionar la lealtad y el apoyo.

El entrevistador trata de formarse una imagen completa acerca del tipo de persona que es, a fin de evaluarlo para ver si encaja con la gente que va a trabajar.

¿Cuáles son sus intereses externos?

Su entrevistador trata de indagar más. Sus intereses le dirán si es deportista, competitivo, disfruta pasatiempos de alto riesgo, le gustan actividades solo o en grupo, y demás. No invente pasatiempos (no le gustaría que su entrevistador le dijese, "¿salto de *bungee*? ¡Yo también! ¿Dónde está su sitio favorito por aquí para ir a saltar? ¿Qué tipo de equipo usa usted?"), seleccione esos pasatiempos o intereses que demuestren que es una persona correcta y amable, como la que está buscando su entrevistador.

¿Qué tipo de lectura ha disfrutado recientemente?

No dé una respuesta a la moda, ni nombre un libro de negocios que no haya leído realmente. Podrían hacerle preguntas al

> Seleccione uno que le demuestre al entrevistador el lado que le interesa ver.

respecto. No tiene que mencionar el libro más reciente que haya leído; hable de uno que haya disfrutado genuinamente aunque esté algo fuera de moda (usted no es uno de la masa). Podría elegir un clásico inusual, un título de avanzada o una biografía; seleccione uno que le demuestre al entrevistador el lado que le interesa ver.

VERIFIQUE SI ESTÁ LISTO

Aquí hay una lista con todas las preguntas en este capítulo. Cuando haya preparado las respuestas para cada una, marque una nota de esto sobre la respuesta correspondiente. Entonces, sobre el ejemplo en la línea de abajo haga una nota del mejor ejemplo que pueda dar al respecto con su respuesta. Asegúrese de tener la respuesta para cualquiera de las cuestiones en este capítulo.

Pregunta
Platíqueme acerca de usted
Respuesta
Ejemplo
¿Qué es lo que más disfruta de su actual trabajo?
Respuesta
Ejemplo
¿Cuál ha sido el máximo desafío que ha afrontado en el trabajo?
Respuesta
Ejemplo
¿Por qué quiere dejar su presente trabajo?
Respuesta
Ejemplo
¿Cómo es su jefe actual? (o el más reciente)
Respuesta
Ejemplo
¿Cuál cree que es el papel de…? (cualquiera que sea su actual trabajo)
Respuesta
Ejemplo

¿Qué sabe acerca de nuestra compañía?
Respuesta
Ejemplo
¿Por qué quiere este trabajo?
Respuesta
Ejemplo
¿Qué cree que pueda aportar a este trabajo?
Repuesta
Ejemplo
¿Cuánto piensa quedarse en este trabajo?
Respuesta
Ejemplo
¿Cuánto tiempo piensa quedarse en esta compañía?
Respuesta
Ejemplo
¿Cuáles son sus principales fortalezas?
Respuesta
Ejemplo
¿Cuáles son sus principales debilidades?
Respuesta
Ejemplo
¿En dónde se ve dentro de cinco años?
Respuesta
Ejemplo
¿Cómo lo describen sus colegas?
Respuesta
Ejemplo
¿Cómo lo describen sus amigos?
Respuesta
Ejemplo
¿Cuáles son sus intereses externos?
Respuesta
Ejemplo
¿Qué ha leído y disfrutado recientemente?
Respuesta
Ejemplo

Respuestas rápidas

Esté listo para las respuestas que sea más probable que deba contestar y asegúrese de:

- Escuchar la pregunta.
- Responder a la pregunta que le han hecho.
- Sea tan breve como se pueda, sin omitir nada relevante.
- Ponga sus respuestas en términos de que demuestre que es idóneo para este trabajo en particular.

Capítulo 8
Las preguntas duras de una entrevista

Bien, yo sé que casi toda pregunta puede parecer dura, pero comparadas con "¿Cuánto tiempo tiene en su actual trabajo?", estas cuestiones son *realmente* fuertes. Éstas no necesariamente tratan de hacer que se perturbe (aunque algunas lo hacen), simplemente son la mejor manera para que el entrevistador sepa lo que necesita acerca de usted.

Por lo que se refiere al entrevistador, esto no es una competencia. Ustedes dos están del mismo lado, así que no debería haber ningún elemento de sacar partido de usted, o de noquearlo de uno o dos golpes; ciertamente no si su entrevistador es un profesional. Las preguntas duras comúnmente lo son simplemente porque no está seguro de cómo responderlas bien.

Pero el punto es que, cualquiera que sea la intención del entrevistador, alguna de estas cuestiones podría hacerlo sentir incómodo si no está preparado para ellas. Bien, eso no es problema. Después de este capítulo estará preparado.

Consejo efectivo

Acorde con los entrevistadores profesionales, ellos no hacen deliberadamente preguntas duras sin una buena razón. Así que, ¿cuál es una buena razón? Principalmente:

- Ver cómo reacciona ante presión.
- Confirmar que está diciendo la verdad (en caso de duda).

Los entrevistadores probablemente quieran comprobar cómo reacciona bajo presión si ellos tienen alguna indicación (por ejemplo, a partir de las pruebas psicológicas) de que usted no maneja la presión como debería.

Ya sea que el entrevistador intente o no que la pregunta sea dura, debe seguir las mismas reglas básicas:

- Esté calmado.
- No se ponga a la defensiva.
- Si lo desea tome una pausa antes de contestar.

Las siguientes cuestiones están divididas en amplias categorías para ayudarle a encontrar su camino, entre ellas:

- Cuestiones acerca de usted.
- Cuestiones acerca de su carrera.
- Cuestiones acerca de este trabajo.
- Cuestiones que le invitan a criticarse a sí mismo.
- Cuestiones que le invitan a ser negativo.
- Cuestiones acerca de su salario.
- Cuestiones inesperadas.

Cuestiones acerca de usted

No todas las cuestiones de esta sección necesariamente se aplican a usted. Si solicita un empleo que no implica trabajar como parte de un equipo, es probable que no le pregunten acerca de sus habilidades para el trabajo en equipo. Si no está aplicando para un trabajo administrativo, no le preguntarán acerca de su estilo empresarial; sin embargo, para cualquier puesto que sea entrevistado encontrará que algunas de estas cuestiones de aquí se aplican y que necesitará prepararse para las respuestas.

¿Qué es lo que le preguntarán?

Eche una mirada a las cuestiones en esta lista y piense acerca de cuáles son probables que le pregunten para cada uno de los empleos listados. Marque las que crea que son más probables de que le hagan en cada trabajo.

	Gerente de producción	Asistente de ventas	Auxiliar de contabilidad	Supervisor de proyecto
1. ¿Es usted un líder natural?				
2. ¿Qué es lo que lo motiva?				
3. ¿Cómo trabaja en equipo?				
4. ¿Cómo opera bajo presión?				
5. ¿Qué es lo que más le disgusta en el trabajo?				
6. ¿Qué tan bien toma la dirección?				
7. ¿Disfruta las tareas rutinarias?				

Respuestas:
No hay garantía de lo que se preguntará o no a alguien, pero sus respuestas deben ser algo así.
Gerente de producción: 1, 2, 3, 5
Asistente de ventas: 2, 3, 4, 5, 6
Auxiliar de contabilidad: 2, 5, 6, 7
Supervisor de proyecto: 1, 2, 3, 4, 5

¿Qué es lo que lo motiva?

Usted necesita dar una respuesta, como siempre, que también beneficie a su empleador potencial y se vincule con las principales responsabilidades del trabajo. Así que no diga, "Mi cheque de pago". Dé una respuesta tal como: "Yo soy muy feliz cuando puedo ver un proyecto de principio a fin" o "Yo me siento motivado por dirigir un equipo que esté contento y sepa que es exitoso".

¿Qué tan bien toma la dirección?

Tenga en mente el hecho de que su entrevistador bien puede ser su próximo jefe si la entrevista va de acuerdo con un plan, así que es su dirección la que usted tendrá que tomar. La respuesta, obviamente, tiene que ser que toma la dirección bien. Usted puede agregar credibilidad a su respuesta expandiéndola y añadiendo algo como esto: "Yo no veo cómo puede funcionar un equipo efectivamente a menos de que sus miembros estén contentos de tomar la dirección de un líder del equipo".

¿Cómo toma las críticas?

Otra vez su entrevistador podría estar anticipando que puede ser su jefe e inevitablemente tendrá que criticarlo de vez en cuando. Ellos quieren saber si la tarea va a ser fácil para ellos, o si usted la va a dificultar.

Entonces, dé una respuesta como: "Yo soy feliz cuando me hacen críticas constructivas. De hecho, creo estar preparado para aceptar las críticas constructivas si es la mejor manera en que yo espero aprender de mis errores y mejorar mi desempeño".

¿Disfruta las tareas rutinarias?

No es factible que le pregunten esta cuestión a menos de que solicite un trabajo en el cual haya tareas rutinarias. Por tanto, su respuesta debe de ser "Sí". Sin embargo, las respuestas en monosílabos no son aconsejables; conllevará más peso si las elabora un poco para demostrar que usted entiende de la cuestión y ha pensado su respuesta.

Las respuestas en monosílabos no son aconsejables.

O sea, podría añadir: "Sí, yo tengo un enfoque ordenado para trabajar y obtengo satisfacción de llevar exitosamente actividades rutinarias de trabajo".

¿Cuál es su estilo administrativo?

No tiene caso mentir en estas cuestiones, así que dé una respuesta honesta; sin embargo, nuevamente, asegúrese de que sea relevante. No necesita dar una conferencia de 20 minutos sobre el tema, sólo un par de oraciones claras serán suficientes: "Yo prefiero el enfoque de la zanahoria (incentivo) sobre el del palo (castigo), además de que tengo una política de puertas abiertas", o "Creo que un gerente tiene que ser firme con su equipo y el equipo apreciar esto en tanto que sea escrupulosamente justo". Expresar una anécdota ayuda a seguir con esto, como algún ejemplo de un problema que resolvió con firmeza, pero con justicia, por ejemplo:

> **Recomendación efectiva**
>
> Nunca mencione en la entrevista nada que no esté en su CV. Usted se las habrá ingeniado para descartar aquellos cuatro meses que dedicó a acomodar estantería en el supermercado sin ninguna brecha en su CV, pero si hace referencia a esto en la entrevista, llamará la atención sobre su credibilidad de todo su CV. Así que o lo pone en el CV o se asegura de que no lo mencionará.

¿Es un buen gerente?

Esta cuestión es similar a aquella acerca de su estilo gerencial, pero es más directa. La respuesta claramente tiene que ser "Sí". Si aun no le han preguntado acerca de su estilo, puede describirlo con brevedad, como lo vimos en la respuesta de arriba. Nuevamente, es una buena idea relacionarlo con una corta anécdota ilustrativa de su enfoque para administrar personal.

¿Es un líder natural?

Ya que sólo se lo preguntarán si el empleo exige un líder, la respuesta debe ser afirmativa. Siga su respuesta con uno o dos ejemplos, teniendo en mente que éstos no tienen que ser exclusivamente de trabajo. Podría subrayar que fue jefe de grupo en la escuela, o que dirige la sociedad de teatro de aficionados local, así como dar un ejemplo de sus antecedentes de trabajo.

Después de todo, el líder natural a menudo empieza desde pequeño. Así que si ha dirigido grupos desde que estaba en la escuela, esto sugiere sus capacidades de liderazgo naturales y que la gente lo sigue por decisión.

> Los líderes naturales a menudo empiezan desde pequeños.

¿Cómo trabaja en equipo?

Esta cuestión la necesita responder honestamente, pero tome una manera relevante para expresar su estilo de trabajo en equipo. Dé una respuesta breve, tal como: "Yo disfruto ser parte de un equipo, y a mí me gusta la flexibilidad que esto demanda. Yo realmente me motivo con el triunfo colectivo". Siga su respuesta con una anécdota o con un ejemplo para demostrar lo que dice. Si el trabajo en equipo es una parte importante del trabajo solicitado, debería esperar esta pregunta (o una variante de la misma) y tener una anécdota lista.

¿Cómo se enfoca a un proyecto típico?

Si usted solicita un trabajo con base en un proyecto, debería esperar que le pregunten esta cuestión. No necesita dar una gran respuesta, pero demuestre que toma en cuenta los principales componentes de la planeación eficaz de proyectos:

- Plan del programa hacia atrás desde la fecha de terminación/entrega.
- Describa lo que necesita para llevar a cabo el trabajo eficazmente y a tiempo.
- Presupuestar los costos, tiempo y recursos.
- Prevenir contingencias.

Las tres mejores

Es una buena idea pensar en las tres características personales que más quiere demostrar al entrevistador. Más de tres diluirá su mensaje. Así que seleccione tres características (fuera de sus numerosos puntos fuertes) que:

- Sean genuinamente puntos fuertes suyos.
- Sean importantes para el trabajo que está solicitando.

Una vez que haya identificado las tres características que quiere promover, prepare los ejemplos y las anécdotas correspondientes para enfatizarlas, así como cualquier otro punto que quiera ilustrar. Y cuando le pregunten cuestiones tales como: "¿Qué diría su jefe acerca de usted?," presente estas características directamente en juego.

A continuación, le presentamos una lista para darle alguna idea de las características que podría elegir (puede exponer otras más que no estén aquí):

- Honestidad.
- Empuje.
- Energía.
- Flexibilidad.
- Paciencia.
- Confianza.
- Buena comunicación.
- Entusiasmo.
- Atención al detalle.
- Confiabilidad.
- Iniciativa.
- Liderazgo.
- Enfoque sobre objetivos.
- Buenas habilidades interpersonales.
- Dedicación.
- Integridad.
- Creatividad.
- Autoridad.
- Diplomacia.
- Determinación.
- Calma bajo presión.

¿Cómo opera bajo estrés?

Nuevamente, una cuestión que sólo le será preguntada si se aplica al trabajo. Una respuesta completa lo venderá mejor que una muy breve. Entonces diga que trabaja bien bajo presión –exprese que hasta lo disfruta si esto es cierto– y dé un ejemplo de una ocasión en la que manejó bien una situación bajo presión. También querrá añadir que aplica bien el tiempo administrativo para asegurarse de minimizar el estrés con que se opera (pero, como siempre, no diga esto si no es cierto).

¿Qué tan creativo es usted?

Otra vez, una cuestión para la gente que necesita ser creativa. Presumiblemente ya tiene ejemplos para proporcionar; entonces, esté listo con ellos. Si tiene que hacer mucho trabajo creativo, resuma una o dos técnicas que use para demostrar que también toma dicha actividad en serio.

¿Qué hace para obtener lo mejor de la gente?

Si es un gerente, esta cuestión sin duda se la preguntarán. El tipo de habilidades que los entrevistadores quieren escuchar acerca de esto incluyen:

- Buena comunicación.
- Habilidad para trabajar en equipo.
- Reconocimiento de cada persona como un individuo.
- Establecer un ejemplo inteligente.
- Alabar los buenos desempeños.

¿Cómo resuelve un conflicto en su equipo?

Siempre responda a esta pregunta honradamente y encuentre un ejemplo de un conflicto en su equipo que pueda usar a fin de demostrar sus habilidades para resolverlo. El tipo de técnicas que necesita para demostrarlo incluyen:

- Justicia.
- Atacar los problemas con los individuos en privado.
- Asegurarse de que llega a la raíz del problema.
- Encontrar la solución que la gente implicada esté dispuesta a aceptar.

Asumiendo que es verdad, también podría agregar: "Yo encuentro que si un equipo es administrado con justicia y los miembros están bien motivados, el conflicto rara vez aparecerá".

Recomendación efectiva

¿Qué puede hacer si se encuentra con un entrevistador incompetente? Bien, el peor error que hacen los entrevistadores incompetentes, de una u otra manera, es que no lo motivan a responder explícitamente. Ellos le hacen preguntas cerradas (requieren respuesta de una palabra) o nunca le preguntan por ejemplos o experiencias que apoyen sus respuestas.

El truco es hacer el trabajo por ellos. Voluntariamente dé amplias respuestas aunque las preguntas no se presten para esto. Dé ejemplos sin que se lo pidan. Y si usted tiene uno de esos entrevistadores que se desenfocan del punto o que detienen la entrevista con interrupciones, impresiónelos siempre siendo capaz de responder exactamente cuando le pregunten: "¿Dónde nos quedamos?".

¿Qué diría su jefe de usted?

Su entrevistador bien podría ser su próximo jefe, así que sea cuidadoso. Ellos quieren saber si es un trabajador eficaz, pero no quieren que se pare en sus dedos. Así que descríbase a sí mismo como su jefe quisiera verlo. Por ejemplo: "Mi jefe me describiría como que trabajo arduamente, que soy fácil de motivar y leal. Él diría que yo me desempeño bien por iniciativa propia y que soy un miembro de apoyo del equipo". Resista la tentación de decir "Yo creo que mi jefe diría...". Sea positivo y asertivo en su respuesta.

Si es probable que su entrevistador contacte a su jefe actual en alguna etapa como referencia, asegúrese de que su respuesta coincida con lo que su jefe vaya a decir acerca de usted cuando su entrevistador ponga esta respuesta particular en la prueba.

¿Qué es lo que más le molesta en un trabajo?

Usted ama el trabajo, ¿lo recuerda? Con seguridad este entrevistador puede contratarlo sabiendo que está motivado cada minuto de su vida laboral. Por tanto, puede decir todo lo que le molesta, con la única posible excepción de que si el empleo es totalmente diferente del último, en tal caso debería decir algo como: "Yo realmente disfruto mi trabajo, pero ocasionalmente me frustro en una compañía pequeña en la que no hay muchos clientes como me gusta. Ésta es una de las razones por las que este puesto me atrae tanto".

Recomendación efectiva

La honestidad es la mejor política por varias razones:

- Un entrevistador hábil puede ser capaz de saber si está mintiendo.
- Cualquier deshonestidad aparecerá cuando su entrevistador cheque sus referencias o sus calificaciones, en cuyo caso lo rechazarán.
- Si logra el empleo de manera deshonesta, su nuevo jefe lo notará tan pronto falle para estar a la altura de las circunstancias, el estilo de trabajo o los estándares que "prometió" en la entrevista. Usted habrá obtenido el puesto, pero una vez que esté ahí caerá a un inicio muy pobre.

Con un manejo inteligente de las cuestiones, y siguiendo los lineamientos de aquí, deberá ser capaz de desempeñarse excelentemente en una entrevista sin necesidad de mentir.

PREGUNTAS ACERCA DE SU CARRERA

Su entrevistador necesita saber si está en el punto correcto en la escalera de su carrera para ellos. Pero desean saber también a dónde cree usted que va. Está planeando moverse hacia arriba de la organización ¿mucho más rápido o más despacio de lo que ellos esperan en este trabajo? Así que las cuestiones en esta sección están diseñadas para decirle al entrevistador como se ajusta este trabajo a una imagen más amplia para usted a largo plazo.

Es una de esas áreas donde es importante ser honesto. No es que las entrevistas sólo funcionen sobre el principio de honestidad de todos, bastante más aparte del aspecto ético de ser honesto. Está también el hecho de que si engaña al entrevistador, podría terminar con el ofrecimiento de un trabajo que será en detrimento de su carrera. El entrevistador sabe bastante mejor que usted si este trabajo se ajusta a sus objetivos a largo plazo, pero sólo si le dice directamente cuáles son.

Ponga sus respuestas bajo la mejor luz que sea posible.

Al mismo tiempo de que usted quiere este trabajo, siempre querrá poner sus respuestas bajo la mejor luz que sea posible, pero hará esto sin engañar al entrevistador.

¿Por qué ha durado tanto con su empleador actual?

La respuesta a evitar es una que implique que se estaba quedando estancado y que se debería haber movido antes. Cualquier respuesta que contradiga esta preocupación no hablada por parte del entrevistador, es correcta. Por ejemplo: "Yo he estado ahí durante varios años, pero con una variedad de roles diferentes", o "El trabajo estaba creciendo continuamente, así que yo sentí como que estaba pasando por muchos movimientos sin cambiar realmente de empleador".

¿Por qué ha durado tan poco tiempo en su presente trabajo?

Su entrevistador no quiere contratar a una persona que se irá en seis meses. Por tanto, demuéstrele que no es un "saltatrabajos", independientemente de lo que contiene su CV. "Yo he querido establecerme en una sola empresa por muchos años, pero he encontrado hasta ahora que tengo que moverme con objeto de ampliar mi experiencia y evitar estancarme en el trabajo".

Me parece que usted es un saltatrabajos

Ésta es la misma pregunta, pero más dura. Si no se trata sólo de su reciente corto trabajo, sino de otros empleos también, su entrevistador estará, y es comprensible, bastante preocupado de que usted los deje en unos cuantos meses. En la actualidad, las personas se cambian de trabajo aproximadamente cada dos o cinco años, pero algo más frecuente que esto resulta preocupante para un empleador potencial. Y algunas industrias esperan que sea un poco más largo que eso.

> En la actualidad, las personas se cambian de trabajo aproximadamente cada dos o cinco años.

Si su CV da la impresión de que apenas se acaba de sentar en su escritorio cuando ya se va de nuevo, puede esperar esta pregunta. Por tanto, ¿cómo le hará para asegurarle al entrevistador que en esta ocasión sí se quedará? La última cosa que usted quiere hacer es lanzar una larga justificación defensiva por cada cambio de trabajo en turno. Es bastante mejor dar una razón general por la que se mueve constantemente.

Por tanto, adopte este tipo de enfoque: "Yo quiero encontrar una empresa en la que me pueda establecer y realmente dejar huella. Hasta ahora me ha sucedido que he tenido que cambiar de empleos con objeto de llegar a encontrar desafíos en mi trabajo". Entonces puede explicar brevemente sólo uno de sus cambios, y por qué éste tuvo sentido. Termine diciendo: "Lo que estoy buscando es una compañía bastante dinámica para mí y encontrar desafíos frescos, sin tener que moverme a otra organización".

¿Por qué no ha encontrado todavía un nuevo trabajo?

La implicación detrás de esta cuestión es que usted no es tan bueno si nadie quiere darle un trabajo. Entonces debe indicar que decidió invertir algún tiempo para buscar un buen empleo. Necesita dar una respuesta como: "Esto es importante, ya que sólo acepto un trabajo que sea realmente bueno para mí, y donde yo vea que puedo hacer una contribución a la compañía".

Si ha rechazado ofertas, dígalo: "Yo he tenido ofertas, pero no he sentido que los puestos eran buenos para mí, ni que yo fuese idóneo para las compañías interesadas".

¿Cuáles fueron sus principales logros en su actual (o más reciente) trabajo?

No es probable que este trabajo requiera exactamente los mismos logros que el anterior, aunque sería genial si encuentra un paralelismo claramente semejante. Lo que en realidad quiere saber el entrevistador son las cualidades que haya demostrado con objeto de obtener un logro. Esté listo con algo como esto:

- Reciente (o la implicación de que usted ha logrado poco de observarse desde entonces).
- Difícil de lograr.
- Tan relevante como sea posible para el trabajo que solicita.

Recomendación efectiva

Podría sentirse incómodo haciendo sonar su trompeta, que es precisamente lo que necesita hacer en una entrevista. Sin embargo, quiere evitar parecer arrogante, pero ser muy "gallito" es una preocupación legítima. Existe la tendencia para compensar esto prefijando las marcas con frases como "Yo siento…" o "Yo creo", por ejemplo:

- "Yo pienso que soy un buen administrador".
- "Yo siento que mis puntos más fuertes son…".
- "Yo pienso que mi principal logro en mi actual trabajo ha sido…".

Mientras dichas respuestas resolverán el problema de no parecer muy arrogante, esto crea otro problema: debilita y diluye lo que usted dice; por ejemplo, que es un buen gerente, simplemente eso piensa que es. Puede darle la vuelta a esto si sustituye con una frase más fuerte en lugar de "Yo pienso", por ejemplo:

- "Yo creo que soy un buen administrador".
- "Yo diría que mis puntos más fuertes son…".
- "Los colegas me dicen que mi principal logro ha sido…".

¿Si volviese a empezar nuevamente,
qué decisiones de su carrera cambiaría?

Usted está cayendo en una peligrosa trampa si empieza pensar en situaciones hipotéticas sobre su carrera pasada. Cualquier cosa que diga será usada en su contra, ya que sugiere que no está feliz con su situación. ¿Por qué querría alguien contratar a una persona que no sabe dónde está?

Así que la única respuesta razonable es que no cambiaría nada, que se encuentra feliz con las cosas como están ahora. Podría añadir algo como: "Yo soy de las personas que miran hacia atrás sin remordimientos. A mí me gusta invertir mi energía mirando hacia el futuro".

¿Considera que su carrera
ha sido exitosa hasta ahora?

Obviamente es mejor ser exitoso que fracasado, entonces, a menos que haya estado largos periodos sin empleo y encajonado en trabajos sin futuro, la respuesta a esta cuestión es "Sí". Para abundar (como siempre, lo debe hacer ante una respuesta de una palabra), usted puede definir el éxito en términos propios. Esto es particularmente cierto si su carrera en el papel es menos que sobresaliente, inclusive si es respetable.

Quizá no ha subido por la escalera profesional tan rápido como debiera. Por lo que podrá decir: "Lo que a mí me interesa, más que el dinero o el estatus, es tener un trabajo que sea interesante o desafiante, y yo he tenido suerte al respecto. Por tanto, hasta ahora mi carrera ha sido muy exitosa en ese sentido".

¿Y qué hay si su carrera ha tenido sus puntos bajos y quizá no lo ha llevado tan lejos como debiera? No tiene caso pretender que su CV brilla cuando claramente no lo hace, así que demuestre que es positivo y que mira hacia adelante: "En el pasado yo he tenido algunos problemas en mi carrera, pero eso ya quedó firmemente atrás. De ahora en adelante intento construir sobre buenas bases. Yo he tenido y disfruto de una carrera exitosa".

No tiene caso pretender que su CV brilla cuando claramente no lo hace.

¿Cuándo esperaría una promoción?

No dé ninguna fecha fija aquí. La respuesta es que uno debe esperar una promoción cuando se la merece. "Yo esperaría ser promovido una vez que haya demostrado mi valor en esta empresa y mostrado que lo valgo".

Y muestre por qué este trabajo es adecuado a sus objetivos a largo plazo: "Es por esto que quiero pertenecer a esta empresa que está creciendo; por tanto, habrá muchas oportunidades de promociones cuando esté listo para ir hacia arriba", o "Es por esto que quiero pertenecer a una gran empresa, porque existen múltiples oportunidades cuando uno se ha ganado la experiencia o ha desarrollado las habilidades".

> **Recomendación efectiva**
>
> Ciertas cuestiones son técnicamente ilegales o pueden serlo si no existe una razón sana o relevante para preguntarlas. Esto incluye asuntos relacionados con la raza, religión o sexo, preguntas acerca de su historia médica, de sus planes futuros o de familia y ese tipo de cosas, pero ¿qué puede hacer si se lo preguntan? Usted puede contestar que le gustaría, si lo desea, pero ¿qué pasa si no quiere?
>
> Mientras que usted está en todo su derecho de ponerse a la defensiva y demandar que el entrevistador se retracte ante esa cuestión, tal conducta no le ayudará a obtener el trabajo. Su mejor apuesta es decir cortésmente: "¿Puedo preguntarle por qué necesita saber eso?". A menos que haya una legítima razón, esto casi seguramente lo conducirá a una retracción. Si ellos persisten en peguntarle algo totalmente irrazonable, tendrá que elegir entre contestar o no, o responder con la verdad o no.

PREGUNTAS ACERCA DE ESTE TRABAJO

Su entrevistador está muy consciente de que existen miles de trabajos anunciados diariamente. Entonces, ¿por qué ha solicitado éste en particular? Ellos buscan la evidencia de que el empleo es el adecuado para usted, que se ajusta con sus aptitudes generales, encaja con sus objetivos a largo plazo e implica hacer cosas que le gustan.

Por esto ellos usarán dichas cuestiones para cavar más hondo en cómo se siente en realidad acerca de este trabajo, qué tan entusiasmado está y cómo de verdad piensa que disfrutará el empleo y será capaz de contribuir a la organización.

¿Cómo puede atender esta entrevista mientras trabaja en otro lugar?

La trampa oculta aquí es que, de alguna manera, debe evitar parecer deshonesto. Así que si le dijo a su jefe que tenía que quedarse en casa a esperar al técnico de mantenimiento de la lavadora o que tenía cita con el doctor, no diga nada de esto. De otra manera su entrevistador sabrá que, si le ofrecen el trabajo, ellos van a indagar qué sucederá cada vez que pida permiso para ir al doctor.

> Tiene que evitar parecer deshonesto.

Idealmente su jefe sabe que usted busca trabajo y está consciente de que fue a una entrevista. Sin embargo, a menudo éste no es el caso. Suponiendo que su jefe no sabe dónde se encuentra, la única justificación válida para poder ir a una entrevista es que a usted le debían unas vacaciones o tiempo y lo tomó para poder asistir a ésta.

¿Cómo encaja este trabajo en el plan de su carrera?

Es peligroso comprometerse consigo mismo precisamente a un plan de carrera. Entonces usted podría decirles algo así: "Los cambios en los negocios van tan rápido en estos días que es difícil planear de manera precisa, pero yo sé que quiero salir adelante en esta industria/en mercadotecnia/en administración y creo que las oportunidades para lograrlo en esta compañía son excelentes".

¿Qué es lo que menos le gusta de su trabajo?

Cuidado aquí. Cualquier cosa que mencione dará la impresión de que está menos del 100 % entusiasmado sobre este trabajo. Mejor mencione lo que más le gusta o, si se siente mal por dar este tipo de repuesta, vaya con una parte del trabajo que sea:

- Una pequeña parte de éste.
- Que no sea de mayor importancia.
- Universalmente impopular.

Uno de los mejores ejemplos es archivar o el papeleo en un puesto donde el trabajo administrativo no sea una parte importante del empleo (pero no si éste es parte importante del trabajo). Sin embargo, mejor debería expresarlo en términos positivos: "No le puedo decir que encuentro el papeleo muy inspirador, pero es muy importante para asegurar que se hagan las cosas, y realmente es bastante terapéutico".

Desastre efectivo

Le preguntan qué es lo que menos le gusta del trabajo. Se ríe y dice: "Probablemente tener que estar a las 8:30 de la mañana". Lo dice de chiste y el entrevistador se ríe con usted, pero privadamente piensa que ese tipo de comentario no viene de la nada. Si le ofrecen el trabajo, ellos se preocupan si se aburrirá por: ¿Tener que llegar temprano? ¿Tendrá un problema para administrar su tiempo? ¿Se tomará horas para entrar en acción una vez que se presente a trabajar en las mañanas? ¡Uff!

¿Está en pláticas con otras organizaciones así como con nosotros?

Le quiere demostrar a su entrevistador que está en demanda, lo cual lo hace un prospecto más atractivo, y si tiene otra oferta de trabajo esto le permitirá pujar por un mejor salario, si puede negociarlo. Si les dice al mismo tiempo que tiene tres ofertas más, ellos se decepcionarán de usted ya que todavía tiene un largo periodo por delante; otra ronda de entrevistas, por ejemplo. Indique que tiene varias pláticas sin decir que está a punto de tomar otro empleo. Si esto no es una mentira, déjeles saber si va bien. Por ejemplo: "Yo he llegado a la última vuelta de entrevistas con tres organizaciones".

¿A qué otro tipo de organizaciones o trabajos está solicitando también?

No hay necesidad de divulgar con exactitud ante quién ha solicitado. En ocasiones le cuestionarán directamente esto, pero puede evitar decirlo argumentando que la compañía todavía no lo anuncia y que considera que no debería divulgar información. Esto le quita el anzuelo y muestra que puede mantener la confianza.

Pero el entrevistador puede darle vuelta a esta cuestión preguntando no los nombres, sino el tipo de trabajo y la compañía. El asunto importante aquí es mostrar que quiere el puesto. Si queda claro que está solicitando para todo tipo de empleos en diferentes industrias, esto genera dudas sobre su compromiso para este trabajo. Entonces indique que sólo está solicitando trabajos dentro del mismo campo.

¿Cuánto tiempo le tomará hacer una contribución útil a esta compañía?

Podría pensar que no puede responder a esta cuestión sin más información. Correcto, ahora solicite la información que necesita:

- ¿Cuáles son mis objetivos clave para los próximos seis meses?
- ¿Hay proyectos específicos que ustedes necesitan que ya empiece a trabajar?

Puede usar las respuestas a estas indagaciones para ayudar a su respuesta, pero hablando ampliamente debería indicar (a menos que haya un proyecto urgente) que espera dedicar las primeras dos semanas para establecerse y tomar las cuerdas. Después de eso tiene previsto llevar a cabo una contribución dentro de los próximos cuatro o seis meses.

¿Podría estar sobrecalificado para este trabajo?

La preocupación del entrevistador revela aquí que si ellos le ofrecen el trabajo, se aburrirá rápidamente y se irá. También debe tener algunas reservas sobre este frente, pero en esta etapa usted todavía hace lo mejor que puede para obtener el trabajo. Si lo va a desechar, hágalo hasta que se lo ofrezcan; no lo descarte a la mitad de la entrevista.

Por el momento va a dar la mejor respuesta que pueda. Diga que las compañías poderosas, dinámicas, siempre usarán todos los talentos disponibles que tengan a la mano. Quiere estar en una compañía por un tiempo y si su experiencia y talento son lo bastante

> Va a dar la mejor respuesta que pueda.

sólidos, está seguro de que ellos encontrarán la manera de mantenerlo en desafío y dando toda su contribución.

¿Cuáles cree que son las principales tendencias de esta industria?

Si ha hecho su investigación, esta pregunta no le resultará difícil, y es lo que el entrevistador quiere comprobar. Esta cuestión es una versión avanzada de "¿Qué sabe acerca de nuestra compañía?"; lo importante aquí es asegurarse de que haya hecho su tarea e identificar las tendencias clave de la industria, listo para impresionar a su entrevistador.

Inclusive si usted ya ha solicitado un trabajo en la industria en la que trabaja, debería preparar de todos modos la respuesta a esta pregunta. No necesariamente saldrá de usted clara y sucinta bajo la presión del momento.

> **Recomendación efectiva**
>
> Una de las maneras en que los entrevistadores pueden probarle es preguntándole más de una cuestión a la vez. Por ejemplo: "¿Cómo se enfocaría a un proyecto típico, cuál es el proyecto más grande que ha llevado a cabo en el pasado y cuáles fueron las principales dificultades que encontró?".
>
> Los entrevistadores mal preparados pueden hacer esto no intencionadamente, pero los preparados es más factible que lo hagan para poner a prueba su inteligencia. Entre más cuestiones responda (y tiene que mantener cada una en la cabeza mientras conteste las demás), más efectivo supondrán que es usted; y si repite la pregunta otra vez hacia ellos, esto le ayudará a fijarla en su mente.

PREGUNTAS QUE LO INVITAN A AUTOCRITICARSE

La arrogancia es uno de los factores que la mayoría de los entrevistadores citan como irritante.

¡Vaya!, estas preguntas son trampas con las que debe tener cuidado. Usted tiene un pequeño dilema aquí: no quiere admitir ninguna falta ni errores, pero, por otra parte, la arrogancia es uno de los factores que la mayoría de los entrevistadores citan como particularmente irritante. Así que ¿cómo le va a hacer para evitar conceder errores sin aparecer como muy presumido y justamente perfecto?

Una pregunta clásica en esta categoría es: "¿Cuál es su mayor debilidad?"; cuestión tan popular que la trataremos en el último capítulo, y también el tipo de respuesta recomendada que ya vimos en lo que se refiere a esta cuestión. Aquí están las cuatro técnicas para autocriticarse sin admitir ningún daño:

1. Use el humor, pero sea cuidadoso. Éste no es el mejor enfoque si siente que su entrevistador carece de sentido del humor. Sin embargo, si parecen listos para reír, y esto va con su personalidad, hágalo, pero con humor. Si lo hace a cada rato, entonces empezará a parecer una salida (que lo es, desde luego).
2. Dé un ejemplo de su vida personal más que profesional cuando la pregunta lo permita. Por ejemplo: "Yo acostumbraba levantarme temprano como un gran reto, pero desde que saco al perro a caminar antes de desayunar, encuentro que realmente disfruto levantarme temprano".
3. Tome algo que haya pasado hace mucho, que pueda demostrar que aprendió de eso. Por ejemplo: "Las decisiones sin una fecha límite eran un problema para mí; nunca las cumplía. Después descubrí que el truco de imponerme fechas límite era una decisión que tenía que tomarse. Ahora ya no retraso las entregas innecesariamente".
4. Dé una respuesta que considere una debilidad, pero que el entrevistador la considere una fortaleza. Por ejemplo: "Yo soy un poco perfeccionista. No puedo dejar un trabajo hasta que quede bien hecho como se debe".

Consejo efectivo

Cinco frases que odian escuchar los empleadores:

1. "Lo siento, llegué tarde".
2. "Yo realmente no sé". A menos que la pregunta sea factual, los empleadores quieren que usted sea positivo y entusiasta al responder las preguntas.
3. "Yo no me llevo con mi jefe". Tal vez no, pero el entrevistador quiere escuchar públicamente que usted es leal, independientemente de sus sentimientos

privados. Ésta es una cualidad que ellos quieren en cualquiera al que le den un trabajo.
4. "¿Qué salario están ofreciendo por este puesto?". Esta pregunta sugiere que sólo le importa lo que la organización puede hacer por usted, y no lo que usted puede hacer por ella. Es lo mismo para las cuestiones acerca de las horas de trabajo y todo lo demás (habrá suficiente tiempo para discutir esto cuando le ofrezcan el trabajo).
5. "Usted está equivocado..." o cualquier otro desacuerdo abierto. Si lo ponen nervioso o lo irritan para hablar agresivamente, esto no dice mucho acerca sus habilidades para tratar a las personas. Es posible estar en desacuerdo de manera cortés. Recuerde, el entrevistador lo está poniendo a prueba para ver cómo responde.

Describa una situación difícil en la cual, con una comprensión retrospectiva, podría haberse manejado mejor

Nuevamente el truco aquí es estar listo con algo de hace mucho tiempo. Y trate de preparar un ejemplo donde realmente no fue su falta por haber actuado de esa manera. Por ejemplo: "Con retrospectiva puedo ver que hubiera sido más rápido evacuar a todos por la escalera central en lugar de haber usado la escalera de escape de fuego, pero como no contestaban los teléfonos no tuve manera de saber que la escalera principal era segura".

¿Qué tipo de decisiones se le dificultan?

Nunca se ha enfrentado a una decisión difícil en su vida, desde luego, pero el peligro de estas preguntas es que usted quede en el cruce implausible de ser perfecto o de sonar presumido y arrogante. Entonces, tiene que admitir algunas fallas menores, pero asegurarse de que ya han sido subsanadas o que son irrelevantes para el trabajo que solicita, o cualquier cosa que le haga sonar humano. Podría decirles: "El tipo de decisiones que menos me gustan son las que a cualquier otra persona no le gustan. Éstas no son difíciles, pero a mí no me gusta tomar una decisión para echar a alguien, por ejemplo". Si usted nunca ha tenido que correr a alguien, encuentre otro ejemplo de algo que a los demás tampoco les gusta hacer.

> Tiene que admitir ciertas fallas menores.

Describa una situación
en la que su trabajo fue criticado

Si toma un ejemplo en el cual su trabajo fue criticado injustamente y estuvo en lo correcto, se arriesga a que parezca que simplemente quiere la oportunidad para ventilar un antiguo agravio; quizá usted es alguien que guarda rencores (podrá pensar el entrevistador). Así que necesita recurrir a la opción del pasado distante.

Los entrevistadores bien podrían preguntarle esta cuestión, o una variación de ella, si quieren saber cómo enfrenta las preguntas duras. Por eso asegúrese de tener una respuesta lista para cada caso que la necesite. Usted debe responder en dos etapas:

1. Brevemente describa la tarea y la crítica que le hicieron.
2. Explique lo que aprendió de esto y que desde entonces no ha vuelto a repetir esos errores.

Esto no sólo lo hace sonar humano, y como no ha sido criticado nuevamente y por mucho tiempo, esto muestra que usted puede aceptar la crítica constructiva y aprender de ésta.

Recomendación efectiva

Por fuerte que sea la tentación, no discuta con el entrevistador. Si ellos lo consideran difícil y polémico, no lo contratarán. Tal vez lo estén probando para ver cómo responde ante preguntas beligerantes. Usted menciona que maneja un equipo de tres personas, y ellos dicen: "Eso no se puede llamar administrar, ¿o sí? Este trabajo requiere manejar un equipo de 10"; no se ponga a la defensiva, mejor diga algo como: "Creo que esto se ve muy diferente en la superficie, pero yo considero que los principios se aplican si uno administra a una persona o a 100".

PREGUNTAS QUE LE INVITAN A SER NEGATIVO

Estas cuestiones están dirigidas para buscar si usted es de naturaleza negativa o malévolo cuando se le da la oportunidad, o verificar si su instinto natural es positivo. Así que cualquier cosa que haga, no muerda el anzuelo. Rehúse ser crítico o negativo acerca de otras personas u organizaciones.

¿Cuál es la principal debilidad de su jefe actual?

> Recuerde, este entrevistador algún día podría ser su jefe, así que dígales lo que ellos quieren oír acerca de ellos mismos.

"¿Por dónde empiezo?". Ésa no es la respuesta adecuada a esta pregunta. En el capítulo anterior vimos la pregunta común "¿Cómo es su jefe actual (o el más reciente)?". Ésta es la versión dura de la misma cuestión; realmente le invita a caer en ella. Por favor no caiga en esta otra trampa, no importa la lista de quejas privadas que tenga contra su jefe. Recuerde, este entrevistador algún día podría ser su jefe, así que dígales lo que quieren oír acerca de ellos mismos.

Diga algo como lo siguiente: "Para ser honesto, tengo la suerte de tener un jefe muy apoyador que sabe su trabajo y es llevadero"; después haga como que trata de recordar alguna debilidad y añada, "Yo no puedo recordar nada; si así fuese sólo podría ser algo tan ínfimo que no vale la pena mencionarlo".

¿Cómo evalúa a su actual compañía?

Es una gran compañía que le ha enseñado mucho y le ha dado excelentes oportunidades. No me importa lo que le diga a sus compañeros, por lo que se refiere al entrevistador, ésta es la respuesta que le debe dar y a la que debe apegarse.

Esta respuesta podría, entendiblemente, seguir a la pregunta: "¿Entonces por qué quiere usted renunciar a su actual trabajo?". ya vimos cómo responder esto en el capítulo anterior.

¿Con qué tipo de personas se le dificulta trabajar?

Como siempre, para que su entrevista sea exitosa necesita resistirse a criticar a otras personas. No se deje llevar por la referencia sobre el compañero de trabajo que en su departamento siempre está tratando de mandar a todo el mundo a su gusto o del típico programador que eternamente se está quejando por su pesada carga de trabajo. Empiece por enfatizar que usted generalmente encuentra muy fácil el trabajar con la demás gente pero que si tuviese que elegir, ciertamente no serían aquellos quienes dejan caer su peso y que tal parece que no se preocupan por la calidad de su trabajo.

> **Ejercicio efectivo 3**
>
> **Causa y efecto**
>
> Se le harán preguntas muy duras durante la entrevista. Todos tenemos áreas sobre las cuales preferiríamos que no nos preguntasen o tópicos que encontramos escabrosos. O que quizá nos causan nervios cuando nos los ponen sobre la mesa. Por eso le presentamos aquí unas cuantas ideas para que le ayuden a prepararse ante las preguntas capciosas:
>
> - Siéntese y piense acerca de cinco o seis cuestiones sobre las que menos le gustaría que le preguntasen. Quizá estuvo mucho tiempo en un mismo trabajo sin promoción y no quiere que esto se interprete como que fue porque no daba resultados. O quizá encuentra a algunas personas escabrosas con las cuales tratar y no desea responder las cuestiones sobre cómo maneja usted a las personas difíciles. Escriba su lista sobre las preguntas "odiosas" y elabore las respuestas para todas.
> - Pregunte a algunos de sus amigos o colegas cúales han sido las preguntas más duras en una entrevista y analícelas.
> - Pregunte a algunos amigos y colegas acerca de las preguntas más difíciles que les hayan hecho en una entrevista y trabájelas después para que sepa cómo responderlas.

CUESTIONES ACERCA DE SU SALARIO

La regla general cuando se trata de las cuestiones salariales es hacer que ellos digan una cifra en lugar de que le tiren la bola en su cancha. Si menciona un salario, le puedo asegurar que nunca tendrá más que esa cifra que ha dicho. Así que aunque tenga una clara idea acerca de lo que ellos esperan pagarle, no se comprometa con una cifra específica.

No se comprometa con una cifra específica.

Las siguientes preguntas están dirigidas para saber su precio. Las respuestas recomendadas son para torear el asunto sin causar ofensas o parecer irrazonable. Una vez que le hayan ofrecido el trabajo, entonces puede empezar a negociar siguiendo los lineamientos del capítulo 15.

Desastre efectivo

Le preguntan qué salário espera, así que usted contesta la cifra que tiene en mente: "Algo alrededor de £ 22 000*". Subsecuentemente le ofrecen el trabajo con un salario de £ 22 000 que ya no puede negociar ya que usted mismo dijo el monto. Una vez que empieza a trabajar se encuentra con que sus colegas que hacen un trabajo similar están ganando £ 25 000. ¡Uff!

* Debido a que el idioma original de esta obra es el inglés británico y que fue editada en el Reino Unido, se respeta en el texto la redacción original respecto al uso de su moneda de uso corriente, la libra esterlina. El lector puede realizar la conversión correspondiente si así lo desea, o utilizar las cantidades como si fueran otra divisa de cualquier nación, sin alterar significativamente el resultado [N. E.].

¿Cuál es su salario actual?

Usted no desea responder esta pregunta. Si le ofrecen el trabajo, ellos tratarán de pagarle lo mismo y cuando menos bajará su poder de negociación. Diga algo como: "Yo pienso que los salarios pueden ser engañosos, ya que lo que cuenta es todo el paquete de remuneraciones. Desde luego, éste es difícil de cuantificar". Después pregunte si puede regresar a su comentario de que la cifra que dijo es muy elevada; esto es una parte de la táctica de negociación.

¿Cuánto espera ganar?

Usted tampoco quiere contestar esta pregunta, porque no hay oportunidad de decir más de lo que sabe y además existe riesgo de que los asuste si les pide mucho. Por lo que debe de responder con una pregunta como ésta: "¿Cuánto esperan ofrecer ustedes por el pago de este puesto?", o bien, pregunte cuál es el rango salarial asignado a este puesto. Si ellos se resisten a contestar en esta etapa, también lo podrá hacer razonablemente.

Si ellos le indican un salario y le preguntan que responda, hágales saber que creía que era un poco más alto, pero no fuera de su alcance (suponiendo que usted estaría de acuerdo con eso). Si ellos sugieren algún rango, cite un rango un poco más alto pero que se traslape. Así si ellos le dicen £20000-25000 usted podría decir que estaba pensando entre £24000-28000. Usted lo levanta pero no lo saca.

¿Cuánto cree que vale?

Todas estas cuestiones salariales son esencialmente buenas noticias. ¿Por qué se tomarían ellos la molestia de preguntarle, ya que están pensando en ofrecerle el trabajo? Esta cuestión es particularmente parecida a la anterior, pero ahora con un molesto recoveco. Se trata de que justifique lo que solicita, una vez que haya previamente iniciado el juego "lo que hace la mano hace la tras".

> Se trata de que justifique lo que solicita.

Usted ya debería de tener alguna idea del sueldo vigente para el trabajo en cuestión de la industria y en esa organización (especialmente si es un puesto interno); por tanto, solicite un poco más y explique adecuadamente, ya que ha analizado las encuestas salariales y dada su experiencia y habilidades que están por arriba del promedio para ese puesto, usted considera que amerita una paga también por arriba del promedio. Por cierto, puede esperar que el entrevistador le responda que la cifra que pretende es muy alta –pero recuerde que esto es también parte de la táctica de negociación–. Por tanto, no permita que le alteren su confianza.

Recomendación efectiva

Nunca baje la guardia en una entrevista. Los entrevistadores entrenados son muy hábiles para capturarlo detrás de la línea y ver cómo reacciona. Ellos podrán ser amistosos y relajados y dispararle de repente una pregunta muy dura, o pueden seguir una serie de preguntas fáciles, pero una con truco haciéndole caer en un falso sentido de seguridad.

Así que tome cada pregunta como un inicio, y nunca suponga que es una entrevista fácil. Si lo necesita, haga una pausa antes de contestar; así no podrá ser enredado para hacer comentarios con la guardia baja.

PREGUNTAS INESPERADAS

A algunos entrevistadores les gusta cacharlo con la guardia baja y muchas de esas preguntas están concebidas con este propósito. Ellos no tratan de molestarlo por gusto; ellos tienen una buena razón para conocer su respuesta, o quieren saber cómo afronta la presión ante una cuestión inesperada. Las reglas clave son:

- Tome una pausa antes de responder si la necesita (a los entrevistadores les gusta esto ya que pueden ver que está pensando acerca de su respuesta).
- Si no está seguro de lo que el entrevistador quiere decir con su pregunta, solicite una aclaración.
- Muéstrese fresco y sin nervios y no discuta con el entrevistador.

Véndame esta pluma

A algunos entrevistadores les gusta hacer esta pregunta inclusive si no solicita un puesto de ventas. El objetivo es ver que usted no se enfoque en las características ("es de plata sólida"), sino más bien en los beneficios de ellos ("impresionará a la gente"). Así que explique cuatro o cinco beneficios de la pluma (cuaderno, portapapeles o cualquier cosa que le hayan solicitado que les venda) y después termine, medio jocosamente, con la técnica de cierre estándar: "¿Le envío una o dos docenas?", o "¿La prefiere en negro o en rojo?".

Cuénteme un cuento

Esta pregunta es un semitruco. Se supone que tiene que demostrar si tiene suficiente enfoque mental lógico para preguntar por una cuestión más específica antes de responderla. Entonces pregúntele al entrevistador: "¿Qué tipo de cuento?", ellos probablemente le dirán que acerca de usted, y tal vez le especifiquen que quieren una historia relacionada con su trabajo o de su historia personal. Enseguida relate alguna anécdota que lo presente bajo una buena luz (así que tenga una lista).

¿Qué piensa acerca de la privatización/
calentamiento global/los Balcanes o lo que sea)?

El entrevistador trata de encontrar qué tanto es su interés general en los asuntos mundiales, y también obtener una idea de sus valores y actitudes ante la vida. Cualquiera que sea el tópico, necesita demostrar en su respuesta que puede ver ambos lados de un argumento, y que no sólo ve las cosas de manera simplista, sino que puede discutir un tema fluidamente y que es capaz de hacer juicios.

Así que no despotrique sobre sus puntos de vista particulares (si los mantiene fuertes) sin reconocer el otro lado del debate. Es muy probable que le hagan estas preguntas, especialmente en las compañías para las cuales esto es relevante. Las empresas farmacéuticas podrían preguntarle sus opiniones sobre el suministro de medicinas a precio de costo a los países en desarrollo; los bancos considerarán sus ideas sobre las tasas de interés. Así que tome en cuenta su probable punto de vista sobre el tema.

> No despotrique sobre sus puntos de vista particulares.

Charla pesada

No importa qué tan duras puedan ser las preguntas que le hagan. Si está bien preparado, debería ser capaz de tomarlas sin estridencia. Una vez que haya absorbido las reglas básicas de este capítulo (y de los dos anteriores), debería poder responder cualquier pregunta, inclusive alguna que no haya preparado específicamente. Nada más recuerde:

- Esté calmado.
- Tómese su tiempo para responder a las preguntas truculentas
- No discuta.
- No admita ni la más mínima debilidad.
- No critique a los demás.

Capítulo 9
Sus preguntas

Cuando el entrevistador le haya preguntado todo lo que quiere, lo invitará a cuestionarlo sobre cualquier pregunta que tenga. Está muy consciente de que la entrevista es un proceso en dos sentidos, y quiere asegurarse de que si decide ofrecerle el trabajo, usted querrá tomarlo. Así que quiere una oportunidad para ratificar cualquier punto que le preocupe.

Si está tentado en este momento a creer que la entrevista ha terminado y que se puede relajar, piénselo otra vez. Las preguntas que haga y las que no pueden decir mucho acerca de usted, y esto todavía puede influir en la decisión del entrevistador para ofrecerle o no el trabajo. Y no cuestionarlo en nada no le zafará del anzuelo; no tener preguntas lo hará aparecer sin entusiasmo y deslucido. En cualquier caso, realmente debería tener preguntas. Existen cosas que su entrevistador no le habrá dicho y que quiera saber; por ejemplo, si a usted le interesa en serio este trabajo.

💬 Consejo efectivo

Los entrevistadores profesionales realmente se impresionan con el entusiasmo; éste puede volcar la balanza a su favor si existe una decisión cerrada entre usted y un candidato que los haya impresionado. Así que cuando le pregunten si tiene cualquier cuestión, empiece diciendo: "Sí, tengo mucho interés en pertenecer a esta empresa y existen dos cosas que me gustarían saber…".

¿Qué tipo de cuestiones darán una buena impresión y cuáles desanimarán a los entrevistadores? Empecemos por el tipo de preguntas que debe evitar; debe ser capaz de ver el vínculo entre todas ellas. Aquí están algunos ejemplos típicos:

- ¿Cuál va a ser mi salario?
- ¿Qué derecho de vacaciones obtendré?
- ¿Cuánto tiempo hay para el almuerzo?
- Necesito dejar a los niños en la escuela en mi camino al trabajo, ¿podría empezar a las 9:30?

Como puede ver, todas estas cuestiones están enfocadas sobre lo que puede sacar de la organización, no lo que usted le puede ofrecer. Ahora, yo no sugiero que no quiera, y en algunos casos es una necesidad genuina el saber estas cosas, pero ninguna de ellas importará a menos que obtenga el empleo. Así que primero preocúpese por obtener el trabajo y la oferta; después quedará mucho tiempo para discutir estos detalles, inclusive asuntos prácticos como ajustar su trabajo alrededor de su vida hogareña.

Primero preocúpese de ganar la oferta del trabajo.

LAS PREGUNTAS

Existe una buena lista de cosas que usted no debería preguntar. Y después de todo no debe dejar de cuestionar. Si tiene algo que preguntar, ¿qué podría ser? Bien, necesita preguntar cuestiones que muestren su entusiasmo acerca de la organización y sobre el trabajo, y acerca de lo que usted puede contribuir. Quiere verse inteligente, ambicioso y comprometido.

Usted no tiene tiempo para preguntar docenas de cuestiones, pero reconoce que debe formular cuando menos dos o tres, y alrededor de media docena si éstas son razonablemente breves y el entrevistador no muestra signos de querer terminar la entrevista rápidamente. Así que mire a través de las ideas que fluyen y prepare unas cuantas preguntas relevantes.

> ### Recomendación efectiva
>
> Siempre es posible que durante el tiempo para llegar al final de la entrevista haya decidido que ya no quiere el trabajo. Tal vez porque no es el tipo de empresa. Quizá ya tenga otra oferta, pero mantuvo esta cita en caso de que ésta se viese mejor, pero no fue así. Aún así haga preguntas inteligentes, ya que se puede dañar su reputación y esto sí es importante. Quizá, un día, este entrevistador se moverá a otra organización y se acuerde de usted cuando esté buscando personal.

¿Por qué quedó vacante esta plaza?

Es una pregunta sensible y quizá nadie la haya hecho antes en la entrevista, pero si no ha sido así, usted pregúntelo. Si sucede que no hay nada grave de por medio, probablemente puede obtener claves a partir de la respuesta. La mayoría de las vacantes son enteramente razonables, pero algunas personas las dejan porque el empleo es frustrante o debido a que con cierto colega o superior es imposible trabajar. Si este es el caso, usted querrá saber. Si recibe una respuesta sin compromiso a su pregunta, tal como "La persona que está haciendo ahora el trabajo se está yendo", querrá saber un poco más a fondo.

Existen dos maneras de saber esto. Una es preguntar directamente: "¿Se está yendo por alguna razón que yo necesito saber?"; si hay algo que usted deba saber, va a ser difícil para el entrevistador evitar decirle. Si ellos evaden la cuestión nuevamente, esto en sí mismo debe ser una clave de que las cosas no están bien. Si su entrevistador se pone a la defensiva y usted no quiere parecer que presiona, siempre puede dejar el asunto por ahora. Si le ofrecen el trabajo, sin embargo, prosiga más sobre esta etapa.

El otro enfoque, menos directo, para indagar por qué el empleado actual se está yendo es simplemente preguntar cuánto tiempo ha estado en el trabajo. Si sólo ha permanecido unos meses, es razonable preguntar por qué se va tan pronto. Si ha estado por varios años, la razón es que ya estaba listo para el cambio. Sin embargo, si detecta cualquier defensiva en su entrevistador, debería insistir todavía más en esta cuestión, si es que le ofrecen el trabajo.

¿Usted promueve internamente
cuando es posible?

Si hace estas preguntas acerca de la promoción, muestra que ha hecho bien su plan para ingresar a la organización. Ademas, puede también peguntar si la compañía o la división se está expandiendo en este momento.

¿Qué oportunidades hay de ganar
calificaciones extra o experiencia?

> Usted quiere ser cuidadoso con las cuestiones acerca de la capacitación.

Usted quiere ser cuidadoso con las cuestiones acerca de la capacitación, si ha solicitado el trabajo estableciéndose como experto en su campo, pero si no es el caso, o si es un profesional, tal como contador o especialista legal que espera aumentar sus calificaciones, entonces sí pregunte. Nuevamente, eso demuestra que quiere mejorar sus prospectos de carrera e incrementar su valor a la compañía.

Recomendación efectiva

Lleve en mente que si usted empieza a hacer preguntas, los entrevistadores sentirán que trata de ganar el control desde el inicio; en efecto, los quiere entrevistar. Así que permanezca con diferencia y asegúrese de no tomar el control inadvertidamente. Para esto ayuda, por ejemplo, lanzar las preguntas con frases como "¿Puedo preguntar"?, en lugar de lanzar una interrogante "Dígame…"; estilo de enfoque.

¿Cuál es la máxima prioridad en este
trabajo para los próximos seis meses?

Es extremadamente útil saber la respuesta a esta pregunta, y también demuestra que se enfoca en los objetivos generales del trabajo, así que es menos factible que se enrede en los asuntos de la rutina diaria y falle en el logro de sus metas. Además, tiene la ventaja psicológica de proyectarse hacia el futuro e invitar a su entrevistador a visualizarlo en el trabajo.

Si tiene una segunda entrevista con alguien más, vale la pena hacerle nuevamente dicha pregunta. Es útil ver si usted tiene una visión consistente acerca de lo que deberían ser sus objetivos clave.

¿Si se me ofreciese el trabajo, dónde me ve dentro de cinco años?

Nuevamente le está preguntando al entrevistador que lo imagine en el trabajo. Usted demuestra un compromiso a largo plazo con la compañía e indica que quiere progresar. La respuesta también va a ser importante. ¿Qué tan rápido se mueven las carreras en esta organización y en qué dirección? Usted necesita esta información si le ofrecen el empleo.

¿Dónde quiere estar la compañía dentro de cinco años?

Los entrevistadores se impresionan particularmente con las preguntas acerca de su organización y muestran que usted tiene un amplio interés, más que la simple obtención de un trabajo. Así que es una gran pregunta para impresionar al entrevistador; también es porque realmente quiere saber la respuesta.

Nadie espera a la Santa Inquisición

Si algunas de estas preguntas suenan un poco fuertes para usted, recuerde que es el tipo de frase lo que hace la diferencia. Ciertamente puede preguntar: "¿Tiene algunas reservas acerca de mi habilidad para hacer este trabajo?", de una manera firme, inclusive un poco agresiva. Si usted es una persona confiada con un entrevistador serio, probablemente esto no le molestará, pero si se siente incómodo al cuestionar de frente, también es posible hacerlo de manera gentil y sin confrontar.

Trate de hacer las siguientes preguntas en voz alta y cambie las palabras si eso ayuda. Encuentre variedad en las frases y variaciones de tono que le permitan sentirse cómodo con las preguntas:

- ¿Por qué quedó vacante esta plaza?
- ¿Si se me ofreciese el trabajo, dónde me ve dentro de cinco años?
- ¿Tiene algunas reservas sobre mi habilidad para este trabajo?

> Usted necesitará encontrar un estilo propio, pero frases como "¿Podría preguntar...?" y "Yo estaba preguntándome...", pueden ayudar a suavizar una cuestión sin cambiar su significado. Sólo asegúrese de no sonar apologético o subestimado; entonces evite por ejemplo: "Yo espero que no se moleste si le pregunto...".

¿Tiene algunas reservas sobre mi habilidad para este trabajo?

Esta cuestión puede tener una frase de confianza a lo largo de líneas tales como: "Estoy muy interesado en este trabajo y creo que yo podría hacerlo muy bien". Puede parecer una pregunta que empuje pero, de hecho, es perfectamente razonable. Usted está vendiendo sus servicios como empleado ideal para este puesto, y necesita saber si su comprador tiene un objetivo de ventas sobresaliente. Entonces ¿por qué no preguntarle?

> Si ellos tienen reservas tendrán que expresarlas.

Si ellos dicen que no hay ninguna, expresan que no tienen razón para no ofrecerle el trabajo; una admisión que es bueno conseguir de ellos. Si existen reservas tendrán que expresarlas, y tendrá otra oportunidad para reasegurarles que no.

¿Cuándo puedo esperar saber de ustedes?

Esta cuestión ya se debería haber cubierto, pero si aun no, entonces debe formularla y hacerla su última pregunta. Aparte del hecho de que necesita saber esto, le da otra ventaja potencial. Si ellos fallan en comunicarse en la fecha que le dijeron, le da el legítimo derecho de contactarlos y llamarles.

No sólo esto le detiene de hacer tentativas por mucho tiempo; también puede tener un uso práctico. ¿Qué tal si le ofrecen otro trabajo en el ínterin? Y se supone que usted tiene que darles una respuesta pronto. Si le prometieron respuesta a esta entrevista para cierta fecha, hace más fácil poner una suave presión en el entrevistador para cumplir con esa fecha límite.

Cuestión de tiempo

Trate de llevar preguntas de las que genuinamente desea saber las respuestas; las sugeridas en este capítulo no son definitivas, éstas son meramente guías y opciones. Evite las cuestiones prácticas acerca de horarios y todo eso hasta que se le ofrezca el trabajo (el entrevistador le dirá esto de todas maneras, sin que se lo pregunte). Reconozca que hacer preguntas tiene un doble propósito:

- Adquirir cualquier información extra que usted necesita.
- Impresionar a su entrevistador con su enfoque incisivo e inteligente.

Prepare sus preguntas por adelantado y después practíquelas en voz alta, si es posible con un amigo o con un colega que juegue el papel de entrevistador, hasta que encuentre la manera de sentirse relajado.

Capítulo 10
Entrevistas con base en competencias

Puede esperar que le hablen de una entrevista de evaluación con base en competencias. O encontrar al entrevistador empleando tal tipo de entrevista sin describirle al respecto; es decir, se puede incorporar en una entrevista estándar.

¿Qué significa lo anterior? Bien, es una técnica de entrevista para evaluar la conducta hábil o "competencias", que son centrales para el trabajo que solicita. En otras palabras, examina sus habilidades en lugar de sus calificaciones técnicas. El entrevistador usará este método para juzgar, a fondo, competencias tales como:

- Trabajo en equipo.
- Habilidad para planear.
- Afrontar el cambio.
- Automotivación.
- Habilidades para la presentación.
- Servicio al cliente.
- Solución de problemas.

¿CUÁLES COMPETENCIAS EVALÚAN?

No hay necesidad de entrar en pánico porque su entrevistador le sujetará a un astringente examen transversal sobre un tópico para el cual no esté preparado, porque usted debería saber qué es lo que le van a preguntar. ¿Cómo? Ellos usarán las técnicas de entrevista basadas en competencias para evaluar habilidades que son centrales para el trabajo; y ellos le habrán dicho esto en el anuncio de reclutamiento, la forma de aplicación y cualquier paquete de información que le hayan enviado con la forma de la solicitud.

Los anuncios están llenos de frases, por ejemplo: "El candidato exitoso demostrará buenas habilidades interpersonales/calma bajo presión/la habilidad para multitareas/determinación/excelentes habilidades para influir…". Éstas son sus claves; y grandes claves también. Significan las "competencias" sobre las que se le interrogará a profundidad en la entrevista.

¿CUÁLES SON LAS PREGUNTAS QUE ELLOS HARÁN?

La entrevista basada en las competencias no es nueva ni una técnica espeluznante.

La entrevista basada en competencias no es nueva, ni una técnica espeluznante que lo tirará de su sitio (no si está preparado). Es una técnica que muchos entrevistadores han usado de alguna manera por años. Sólo que ahora que ha obtenido un nombre llamativo y ha llegado a estar más formalizada y estandarizada.

La premisa que existe detrás de la entrevista con base en las competencias es que resulta el mejor indicador de cómo se desenvolverá en un futuro, actitud generada en cómo se ha comportado en el pasado. Entonces todas las preguntas que le van a hacer están diseñadas para saber cómo ha manejado situaciones previas en las cuales se requirieron dichas competencias.

Algunos entrevistadores pueden basarse por completo en competencias, mientras que otros la usan como un avance bien estructurado, que significa que a cada quien se le hace exactamente la misma pregunta que a usted. La entrevista con base en la competencia es considerada en extremo justa por la siguiente razón: todos los candidatos son evaluados de igual manera respecto a las mismas competencias, usando las mismas preguntas. Su trabajo consiste en asegurarse de que sus respuestas sean más impresionantes que las de todos los demás.

🔵 Ejemplo efectivo

Tomemos, por ejemplo, el trabajo en equipo y veamos qué tipo de preguntas puede tener que responder. Para establecer si es un buen trabajador en equipo, su entrevistador le hará preguntas alrededor de varias competencias, tales como:

- Describa un momento cuando haya tenido que trabajar como parte de un equipo para lograr un resultado específico.
- ¿Ha sido testigo de un conflicto en un equipo del que usted formase parte? Dígame acerca de eso, y cómo lo manejó.
- ¿Ha sido alguna vez irritado o frustrado por alguien de su equipo? ¿Qué hizo al respecto?
- ¿Qué papel tiende a tomar dentro del equipo?
- ¿Ha trabajado alguna vez en un equipo pobremente motivado? ¿Dígame qué hizo para mejorar la moral del equipo?

Se puede apreciar que las respuestas a estas cuestiones le dicen al entrevistador bastante acerca de usted y de su comportamiento pasado como miembro de un equipo, lo cual en su momento indicará la manera en que trabajará como parte de un equipo si ellos le ofrecen el puesto. Tal cuestionamiento a fondo para cada competencia les da una sólida impresión de sus habilidades.

El entrevistador puede probarlo para más información acerca de estas cuestiones, y le pueden sugerir que discuta sus respuestas.

🔵 Ejemplo efectivo

Aquí está otro ejemplo; esta vez las preguntas que puede esperar que le hagan es acerca de sus habilidades para el servicio a clientes:

- ¿Qué es lo que menos le gusta acerca de tratar con los clientes?
- ¿Alguna vez algún cliente lo criticó personalmente? ¿Cómo trató esto?
- Dígame acerca de la ocasión en que usted excedió las expectativas de su cliente.
- Describa el mayor reclamo de un cliente que haya recibido. ¿Cómo trató el asunto?

> **Haga su investigación**
>
> Vaya a través de la literatura que ha recibido acerca del trabajo que solicita y anote cada competencia que sea mencionada como si fuera un requisito para el empleo. Observe en:
>
> - El anuncio de reclutamiento.
> - La forma de solicitud.
> - La descripción del trabajo.
> - Cualquier otra información que el empleador le haya enviado.
>
> A veces la información será descriptiva, por ejemplo: "El candidato exitoso será capaz de..."; sin embargo, debe extrapolar la información a partir de la descripción del empleo. Esto no debería ser difícil, ya que está claro que el puesto requiere particularmente del trabajo en equipo, habilidad organizativa, facilidad para aprender rápido, proyectar habilidades administrativas y demás.

¿CÓMO DEBE RESPONDER A ESTAS PREGUNTAS?

Para empezar, no necesita preparar sus respuestas antes de que llegue con su entrevistador. Usted ya ha identificado las competencias sobre las que probablemente se le interrogará. Para cada una de éstas necesita lo siguiente:

- Trabaje con el tipo de cuestiones que es probable que le pregunten (junto con las líneas de los ejemplos de arriba).
- Llegue con *más de un* ejemplo de su experiencia pasada para ilustrar cada competencia. Esto mostrará al entrevistador que tiene amplia habilidad en este tipo de cosas. Un ejemplo que repita constantemente esa cuestión le dará la impresión de que no tiene mucha experiencia. Si cada conjunto de cuestiones da pie a ejemplos de un par de trabajos o más, y quizá también alguno que no sea de trabajo, el entrevistador se quedará con la idea de que usted es un "lobo de mar" para demostrar su competencia.
- Prepare anécdotas reales de sus experiencias pasadas para ilustrar cualquier cuestión acerca de cada competencia que es probable que se presente. Para tomar el ejemplo de arri-

ba, del servicio al consumidor, necesita pensar en el cliente más difícil, cuando fue criticado personalmente; la vez que fue dejado por sus proveedores y haya tenido que resolver el problema; cuando una queja estuvo totalmente justificada y demás; listo para cualquier cuestión que se le pregunte.

> Prepare anécdotas reales de su experiencia pasada.

Lo que usted *no* quiere es que el entrevistador exprese: "Dígame acerca del momento cuando..." y que tenga que responder, "Umm, bien, déjeme pensar. Yo estoy seguro que esto me pasó a mí...".

Recomendación efectiva

Recuerde que puede usar ejemplos de fuera del trabajo. Ellos pueden ser tan buenos como un indicador de cómo se comporta y qué habilidades tiene. Si ha estado muy nervioso antes de ir a escena en su teatro local en cualquier presentación que haya dado; o si tuvo un truculento bulto de gente para tratar el fideicomiso de su comité local de conservación, traiga estos ejemplos a la entrevista.

Una vez que haya pasado a través del proceso de identificar la probabilidad de las preguntas y preparar ejemplos y anécdotas para ilustrar cómo las manejó, necesita practicar dando estas respuestas en voz alta. Puede hacer esto en privado o con un amigo que actúe como entrevistador. Lo importante es que no sólo identifique los ejemplos que planea usar, sino que piense también en cómo decirlos en sus palabras.

LA ENTREVISTA

Bien, está listo para la entrevista. Ha hecho todos sus preparativos, sabe qué decir y cómo decirlo con objeto de demostrar que está idealmente calificado en todas las competencias y que es la mejor persona para el trabajo sobre cualquier medida basada en competencias.

Todo lo que necesita una vez que haya llegado a la entrevista es seleccionar el ejemplo más relevante con el cual pueda responder a cada pregunta. Tenga en mente que el entrevistador desea saber lo que usted hizo personalmente en la situación que describe, no lo que el equipo hizo; o lo que piensa que debió hacer. Ellos quieren saber acerca de usted y de lo que realmente pasó.

El entrevistador quiere saber las respuestas a las preguntas, y querrá que usted sea tan específico como sea posible. No desean un amplio "Teníamos algunos clientes truculentos..."; ellos quieren escuchar: "Hubo una vez cuando un cliente en particular se presentó en la oficina, realmente molesto...". Usted puede esperar que le pregunten más cuestiones alrededor de cada respuesta y que las pruebe al detalle. Esto no significa que estén molestos con su primera respuesta; es normal para este tipo de preguntas.

<u>Todo se trata de estar listo con ejemplos específicos y relevantes.</u>

Si ha hecho bien su preparación, entonces debería hacerlo extremadamente bien en este tipo de entrevista. Se trata de estar listo con las respuestas específicas y ejemplos relevantes para demostrar su habilidad en las áreas que son importantes para el trabajo.

No se sorprenda a usted mismo criticando

Muchas de las preguntas en una entrevista con base en competencias serán acerca de situaciones truculentas. Después de todo, éstas son las que realmente prueban su habilidad. Y muchas serán truculentas por la gente implicada; si le piden que describa alguna ocasión en la que haya tenido que enfrentarse con un cliente difícil, colega o jefe, es fácil encontrarse a usted mismo criticando a la persona concerniente: "Yo tenía que tener a ese bastardo como jefe", o "Teníamos a este gruñón e irritante cliente que acostumbraba sacarnos de nuestras casillas".

Sin embargo, ofender y criticar no lo pone bajo una buena voz, como ya hemos visto, y necesita evitar esto en las respuestas que dé. La manera en como puede lograrlo es no hacer juicios de valor; si su jefe tenía mal carácter en esa época, lo puede decir, pero no diga que era un jefe malhumorado, difícil. Tiene la ventaja de que habla acerca de situaciones individuales específicas, así que no tiene que comentar sobre el comportamiento a largo plazo de las personas. Simplemente puede decir: "Mi jefe tenía un pequeño malestar ese día" o "El cliente estaba muy enojado", y dejarlo hasta ahí.

Si quiere ir un poco más allá también puede, donde sea apropiado, excusar con brevedad a la otra persona enfatizando con sutileza su comportamiento, pero no quede como crítico. Por ejemplo: "Mi jefe estaba de mal carácter ese día y compresiblemente tenía poca paciencia" o "El cliente estaba justificadamente molesto".

Capítulo 11
Pruebas psicométricas

Si en alguna ocasión afrontó pruebas psicométricas, sabe que pueden asustar un poco. De hecho, si las ha presentado antes, todavía resultan ser intimidantes, pero éstas no lo son una vez que entiende cómo funcionan y para qué sirven. Si usted es la mejor persona para el trabajo, una prueba psicométrica reforzará su posición, más que minarla.

Conocimiento efectivo

Un creciente número de organizaciones usan las pruebas psicométricas para respaldar otros procedimientos de selección (tales como las entrevistas). Éstas son más comunes como parte del proceso de selección para graduados y gerentes en todos los niveles, donde es más probable que le soliciten llenar un cuestionario personalmente.

¿Qué es exactamente una prueba psicométrica? Se clasifican en cuatro categorías:

1. *Pruebas de habilidad,* que muestran su habilidad general en amplias capacidades, como numéricas. Las pruebas del CI caen en esta categoría.
2. *Pruebas de aptitud*, que se relacionan con las calificaciones específicas para el trabajo, como ventas o administración.

3. *Pruebas de personalidad*, que evalúan su tipo de personalidad.
4. *Cuestionarios de motivación*, que evalúan lo que le guía y cuáles son sus actitudes relevantes.

Aunque en dichas "pruebas" no hay calificaciones para pasarlas o reprobarlas. Son simplemente para dar una indicación de su habilidad o personalidad; en especial en el caso de la prueba de personalidad, no hay respuestas correctas o incorrectas. Los entrevistadores profesionales no usan las pruebas psicométricas de manera aislada, sino como un respaldo para otros métodos de selección.

> Los entrevistadores profesionales no usan las pruebas psicométricas aisladamente.

PREPÁRESE PARA LAS PRUEBAS

Es muy raro que se siente a resolver una prueba psicométrica de cualquier tipo sin ningún aviso. Casi invariablemente usted será avisado cuando haya sido invitado a una entrevista, y también de que tendrá que presentar una prueba, a menudo un poco más tarde ese mismo día. O le dirán al final que al entrevistador le gustaría que presentara una prueba (o posiblemente una serie de pruebas).

El entrevistador deberá explicarle totalmente para lo que pretende usar la prueba, y cómo encaja ésta con el resto del proceso de contratación. Además de esto, ellos deberían asegurarse de que entiende de qué trata la prueba y qué es lo que se supone que debe hacer, cuánto durará y todo tipo de cosas.

✹ Recomendación efectiva

Si tiene cualquier condición médica que pudiera inhibir su capacidad para hacer la prueba (como dislexia o ceguera parcial, por ejemplo), explique esto al entrevistador. Ellos deberán ser capaces de solucionar esto fácilmente, en tanto se los manifieste.

Es menos probable que los gerentes no acostumbrados a entrevistar usen las pruebas, pero desde luego que podría encontrarse con uno de ellos y con una prueba que no le han explicado apropiadamente. Entonces siéntase libre para hacer preguntas tan pronto le soliciten resolver una prueba psicométrica. Inclusive los entrevistadores experimentados podrían no decirle todo lo que necesita saber. Así que éstas son las cosas aceptables que les puede preguntar:

- ¿Qué tipo de pruebas va a resolver: habilidad, aptitud, personalidad, motivación?
- ¿Cómo le será preguntada la prueba: verbalmente, escrita o por Internet?
- ¿Cómo encaja la prueba dentro del proceso de selección como un todo?
- ¿Cuáles pruebas tomará? Existe gran variedad, todas con sus nombres, y ellos estarán contentos de decirle cuáles usarán.
- ¿Existen algunas guías que pueda analizar? Las guías de las pruebas dan ejemplos de lo que puede esperar. Si no las hay, solicite al entrevistador unas muestras. Es como hacer prácticas de los exámenes antes de tomar su TOEFL, GCSE o niveles A; viendo ejemplos comparativos se considera una preparación prudente y no un engaño.
- ¿Qué retroalimentación puede esperar después de la prueba? Al final de ésta y una vez que los resultados hayan sido evaluados, le deberían dar una retroalimentación por parte del entrevistador o alguno de sus colegas capacitados en estas cosas.

Una vez que tenga esta información puede sentirse mejor acerca de las pruebas. Puede usar Internet para encontrar más acerca de las pruebas que le dijeron va a resolver, ya sea que se conecte al sitio web del diseñador de las pruebas o por medio de un motor de búsqueda. Muchos de estos diseñadores dan ejemplos en sus sitios web para practicar (por el servicio algunos cobran y otros no).

Desastre efectivo

¿Se quedó sin tiempo? Si no se ha sentado a resolver una prueba y está un poco oxidado, practique haciendo cualquier tipo de ejercicio durante un periodo específico de tiempo. De otra manera podría estar resolviendo efectivamente el examen y cuando vaya apenas a la mitad, le digan que el tiempo ya se terminó. ¡Uff!

Cuando llegue el momento de la prueba, asegúrese de estar listo para ésta, y no olvide sus anteojos ni nada que vaya a necesitar. Los expertos en evaluación de ASE[1] recomiendan seguir estos diez puntos principales cuando se resuelve una prueba psicométrica de cualquier tipo:

1. Trate de permanecer en calma y lea las instrucciones cuidadosamente.
2. No se salte la lectura de ninguna de las instrucciones. Es importante tener claro cómo va a responder a las preguntas.
3. Siempre complete las preguntas de práctica al inicio de cualquier evaluación. Pregunte al administrador de la prueba cualquier cosa que no entienda antes de que empiece la prueba.
4. Planee su tiempo para responder tantas preguntas como sea posible.
5. No gaste mucho tiempo en una sola pregunta; siempre podrá regresar al final.
6. Verifique que el número completado coincida con el de la hoja de respuestas.
7. Cuando evalúe preguntas difíciles de elección múltiple deseche las que sean más improbables de responderlas correctamente.
8. Si cambia una respuesta, asegúrese de que esto quede claro.
9. Si tiene duda, dé su mejor estimación.
10. Si termina pronto, regrese y revise sus respuestas.

Desastre efectivo

¿Qué puede pasar si no sigue las instrucciones cuidadosamente? La mayoría de las pruebas son perfectamente directas, pero unas cuantas pueden tener trampas ocultas. En una prueba notoria, a los candidatos se les indica que lean todo un documento antes de responder las preguntas; obviamente casi nadie se da cuenta de esto, pero cuando terminan el documento, usted se encuentra que la letra pequeña al final dice que no escriba ninguna de sus respuestas. ¡Uff!

---

[1] Reproducido con permiso de ASE.

PRUEBAS DE HABILIDAD Y DE APTITUD

Miden habilidades específicas y dan un puntaje que le dice a su empleador potencial cuál es su nivel de habilidad, o cuáles son sus potenciales para aprender nuevos conocimientos. La investigación ha mostrado que las pruebas de habilidad y aptitud son una guía excelente para el desempeño futuro, por lo que ya no es ninguna sorpresa que los empleadores las usen cada vez con mayor frecuencia.

No son pruebas de conocimientos generales, pero están dirigidas a evaluar su habilidad para razonar o pensar lógicamente. Unas cuantas pruebas son de amplio alcance, pero muchas se enfocan en habilidades específicas, por ejemplo: habilidad verbal, numérica, interpretación de datos y demás. Las más populares son las pruebas verbales y las numéricas.

Encontrará que las pruebas de habilidad y aptitud se sienten un poco como exámenes. Usted puede durar una hora y media para resolver el cuestionario, que a menudo es de opción múltiple. Frecuentemente son más difíciles conforme avance en la prueba, y bien puede haber más preguntas que las que pueda contestar. Si esto sucede, no se asuste. La proporción de las preguntas que sean correctas es más importante que el número de preguntas que conteste por completo.

> Encontrará que las pruebas de habilidad y aptitud se sienten un poco como exámenes.

📖 Conocimiento efectivo

Los puntos para las pruebas de aptitudes y habilidades están relacionados con el desempeño pasado de otras personas. Así que si todo mundo encuentra difícil la prueba, usted será evaluado en relación con todos los demás; no simplemente se le dará un puntaje bajo. Igualmente, si unas cuantas personas tienen tiempo de completar todas las preguntas, esto se tomará en cuenta en su puntuación.

Por tanto, ¿qué tan importantes son las pruebas de habilidad y aptitud en relación con el resto del proceso de selección? Puede medir esto cuando en el proceso de selección haga la prueba. Generalmente, entre más pronto la resuelva, más importante es. Si es la primera cosa que le preguntan, inclusive antes de la entrevista, es probable que sea un proceso de sondeo; a usted le darán la entrevista sólo si alcanza cierto nivel de puntaje. Entre más posterior venga la prueba, será considerada como una más de las partes del proceso de selección de personal.

Prepárese para resolver las pruebas de aptitud y habilidad

Ya hemos visto que es muy útil prepararse para estas pruebas si realiza prácticas con ejemplos de estos exámenes, pero ¿qué más puede hacer?

> ### Recomendación efectiva
>
> - Practique no sólo con muestras de estos exámenes, sino también con otros recursos, como ejercicios mentales y acertijos.
> - Para las pruebas de aptitud en particular, haga juegos de palabras y acertijos matemáticos.
> - Practique su aritmética mental y cosas como grandes multiplicaciones y divisiones.
> - Para las pruebas numéricas pregunte si le permitirán usar calculadora. Si es así (si es necesaria), sepa usar la calculadora para algunos ejercicios, por ejemplo porcentajes.

Si le solicitan resolver cualquier prueba de aptitud o habilidad, querrá practicar como ya lo hemos establecido. Aquí hay unas cuantas preguntas como muestra para que se dé una idea del tipo de preguntas que encontrará. Fueron establecidas por uno de los principales productores de este tipo de pruebas, SHL, Group Ltd., quienes tienen muchos ejemplos en su sitio web (www.shldirec.com) junto con largas pruebas de práctica en nueve idiomas. Una vez que las pruebas hayan sido resueltas, un reporte de retroalimentación gratis le será proporcionado (aplican términos y condiciones).

Ejemplo de cuestionario verbal

En esta prueba usted es requerido para evaluar cada frase en el pasaje. Lea a través del pasaje y evalúe las frases de acuerdo con las reglas:

Verdadero	Si la frase sigue lógicamente de la información o de las opiniones contenidas en el pasaje.	Responda A
Falso	Si la frase es obviamente falsa a partir de la información o de las opiniones contenidas en el pasaje.	Responda B
No puedo decirlo	Si no puede decir si la frase es verdadera o falsa sin más información.	Responda C

Muchas organizaciones encuentran benéfico emplear estudiantes durante el verano. El personal permanente a menudo desea tomar sus vacaciones durante este periodo.
Además, no es poco común para las compañías experimentar demandas pico en verano, por lo que se requiere personal extra. El empleo de verano atrae también a estudiantes que posteriormente pueden volver como candidatos calificados a una organización cuando ellos hayan completado su educación. Asegurándose de que los alumnos aprendan tanto como sea posible acerca de la organización, motiva su interés para trabajar con una base permanente. Las organizaciones les pagan a los estudiantes una tarifa fija sin los derechos usuales de pagar vacaciones o ausencia por enfermedad.

Es posible que dentro del personal permanente quienes están de vacaciones puedan dejar su trabajo para que lo lleven a cabo los estudiantes.	A B C
A los estudiantes empleados en el verano se les dan las mismas vacaciones pagadas como beneficio al del personal permanente.	A B C
Algunas compañías tienen más trabajo que hacer en el verano cuando los estudiantes están disponibles para el trabajo en vacaciones.	A B C

© SHL Grupo Ltd. Este texto ha sido reproducido con el permiso de SHL Group Ltd.

Cuestionario de habilidad numérica

El cuestionario numérico a continuación es de elección múltiple; a usted le presentan varias respuestas posibles. Cuando haya seleccionado su respuesta, circule la letra apropiada.

Lectura de periódicos				
Periódicos Diarios	Lectores (millones)		Porcentaje de adultos que leen el periódico en el año 3	
	Año 1	Año 2	Hombres	Mujeres
The Daily Chronicle	3.6	2.9	7	6
Daily News	13.8	9.3	24	18
The Tribune	1.1	1.4	4	3
The Herald	8.5	12.7	30	23
Daily Echo	4.8	4.9	10	12

1. ¿Cuál periódico fue leído por un mayor porcentaje de mujeres que de hombres en el año 3?				
A The Tribune	B The Herald	C Daily News	D Daily Echo	E The Daily Chronicle
2. ¿Cuál fue el número de lectores combinado del *Daily Chronicle*, *Echo* y *Tribune* en el año 1?				
A 10.6	B 8.4	C 9.5	D 12.2	E 7.8

© SHL Grupo Ltd. Este texto ha sido reproducido con el permiso de SHL Group Ltd.

Ejemplo de cuestionario de razonamiento inductivo

Las preguntas sobre el razonamiento inductivo que siguen son de elección múltiple. Para cada una usted tiene varias respuestas posibles. Cada problema en esta prueba consiste en una serie de diagramas, a la izquierda de la página, que siguen una secuencia lógica. Usted tiene que elegir el siguiente diagrama de una serie de cinco opciones en la derecha. Después indique su respuesta con un círculo en ella.

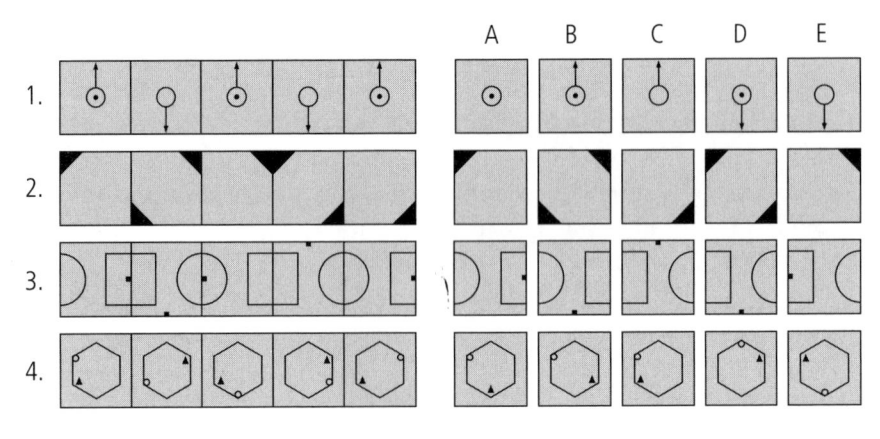

CUESTIONARIOS SOBRE PERSONALIDAD Y MOTIVACIÓN

Estas pruebas son muy diferentes de las de habilidad y de aptitud, porque no existen respuestas correctas o incorrectas (usted estará satisfecho por saberlo) y generalmente no son contra reloj. Las pruebas simplemente buscan evaluar qué tan bien se ajusta a los requerimientos del puesto y de la organización. El punto es tratar de ver qué tan adecuado es para el tipo de trabajo que va a hacer, cómo encaja en la cultura de la empresa y qué tan bien se puede llevar con el equipo del que podría llegar a formar parte.

> Las pruebas simplemente buscan evaluar qué tipo de persona es usted.

Como usted no tiene absolutamente ninguna idea de cuáles son los términos que busca la organización para el trabajo, no tiene mayor caso que dar respuestas verdaderas a estas preguntas. De cualquier manera, estas pruebas también le benefician. Si realmente no encaja en la cultura corporativa o el tipo de trabajo que va a hacer, probablemente no querría ese trabajo. El tipo de cosas que estas pruebas buscan identificar incluyen:

- Qué es lo que lo motiva.
- Su actitud ante la vida y el trabajo.
- Cómo se relaciona con otras personas.
- Cómo maneja sus emociones.
- Cómo se enfoca ante los problemas.

Los cuestionarios motivacionales son similares a los de las pruebas de personalidad, pero aquéllos se enfocan más específicamente en lo que lo motiva a usted, cuánto tiempo puede mantener sus niveles de energía para una tarea en particular, qué situaciones lo motivan más o menos, y demás. Éstos son usados más a menudo para el desarrollo personal (una vez que esté en el trabajo) más que para el reclutamiento, pero también podría encontrarlos durante el proceso de selección.

A continuación presentamos un ejemplo breve del tipo de cuestiones que podría encontrar en un cuestionario de personal.

Valoración de oraciones

En este ejemplo le piden que se autoevalúe sobre un número de frases u oraciones. Después de leer cada frase usted mismo deberá calificarse acorde con las siguientes reglas:

Seleccione (1) Si está totalmente en desacuerdo con esta frase.
Seleccione (2) Si está en desacuerdo con la frase.
Seleccione (3) Si no está seguro.
Seleccione (4) Si está de acuerdo con la frase.
Seleccione (5) Si está totalmente de acuerdo con la frase.

	Fuerte desacuerdo	Desacuerdo	Inseguro	Acuerdo	Fuerte acuerdo
Disfruto conocer gente nueva	(1)	(2)	(3)	(4)	(5)
Me gusta ayudar a las personas	(1)	(2)	(3)	(4)	(5)
A veces cometo errores	(1)	(2)	(3)	(4)	(5)

© SHL Grupo Ltd. Este texto ha sido reproducido con el permiso de SHL Group Ltd.

Pruebas, pruebas

Las pruebas psicométricas son muy directas, una vez que sepa lo que espera. Usted debe recibir un aviso si le van a aplicar una prueba, y le deben dar las explicaciones correspondientes, cuestionarios de práctica y demás.

Asegúrese de practicar lo suficiente sobre el tipo de prueba que va a presentar (solicite los nombres) en el sitio web del productor de la prueba. Existen también muchos libros que le darán todos los detalles sobre las más populares en el mercado. ¿Qué hacer cuando llega el momento de presentar las pruebas?:

- Esté tranquilo.
- Lea las preguntas e instrucciones cuidadosamente.
- Planee su tiempo para responder tantas preguntas como sea posible

Respuestas:
Verbal: C, B, B, A.
Numérica: D, C.
Razonamiento inductivo: E, B, D.

Capítulo 12
Centros de evaluación

Los centros de evaluación son otros recursos que usan a veces los empleadores (junto con las entrevistas y las pruebas psicométricas) para evaluar a los candidatos. Ahí se hacen otras pruebas, pero en esta ocasión a un nivel más práctico. Usted lleva a cabo algún tipo de ejercicio, o quizá varios, como prácticas de discusión en grupo, jugar papeles o ejercicios de proyecto en equipo. (Si está tomando pruebas psicométricas, éstas se pueden realizar en un centro de evaluación). Un asesor o un equipo de asesores lo observará durante el ejercicio.

Conocimiento efectivo

El término "centro de evaluación" es erróneo, ya que no es un lugar físico, sino un proceso. Bien se puede realizar en las instalaciones del empleador, aunque también se puede llevar a cabo en una localización externa.

UN MÉTODO OBJETIVO Y JUSTO

Como las pruebas de habilidad y aptitud, los centros de evaluación son uno de los más exactos pronosticadores del desempeño futuro. Ellos son también –estará contento de saberlo– un método reconocido por ser extremadamente justo y objetivo para evaluar a los candidatos. Así que nuevamente, si de verdad es la mejor persona para el trabajo, puede estar confiado de que dicho centro lo demostrará.

Existen varios ejercicios que usted llevará a cabo. El asunto clave es recordar que inclusive cuando el ejercicio sea diseñado hacia un objetivo final, tal como tomar una decisión, la manera en que realice el ejercicio generalmente será tan importante como el resultado final. Esto significa que deberá estar seguro de que:

- Los asesores puedan ver la preparación que ha hecho al hacerles tomar notas donde es apropiado.
- Indique cómo ha llegado a cualesquiera conclusiones.

Ejercicios de los centros de evaluación

Existen incontables ejercicios que podría llevar a cabo, pero aquí está una guía rápida de los principales tipos que podría encontrar.

En la charola

Es justamente lo que dice. A usted le dan una charola hipotética de la persona a la que sustituirá. Tiene que hacer todo lo que está en ella y marcar cada pieza de correspondencia de cómo la manejaría y que acción tomaría a partir de ésta. Ya que las anotaciones son todo lo que los asesores tienen para proseguir, necesita estar seguro de marcar todo lo que sea útil y relevante.

Estudio de caso

Aquí a usted le dan mucha información con datos acerca de una cuestión de negocios sobre la que tiene que tomar una decisión. La información puede no ser clara en algunos aspectos. Entonces tendrá que evaluarla y llegar a una decisión que presentará a los asesores, ya sea en un breve reporte escrito o como una corta presentación. Aunque es importante tomar una decisión si se le solicita, su enfoque sobre la cuestión es tan importante como su conclusión.

Grupo de discusión

Es muy similar al estudio de caso, excepto que usted tendrá que tomar una decisión o hacer una recomendación, o quizá varias, en un grupo junto con otros candidatos. A veces a cada uno de los candidatos se les da un papel particular que jugar, pero a todos se les dará la misma información.

Jugar el papel de la entrevista

En este ejercicio se le da un resumen sobre una junta que usted está a punto de llevar a cabo con un rol que jugar. Deberá usar el resumen para planear la reunión; la manera en que haga esto será parte significativa para su evaluación general. (Se le darán hasta 30 minutos para prepararse). La junta, como lo dirá en su minuta, implicará ya sea la discusión de una cuestión con un rol que jugar, o usarla para ayudar a conseguir información acerca del asunto. De cualquier manera, usted deberá usar la información, o los resultados de la discusión para tomar una decisión acerca de la cuestión.

> **Recomendación efectiva**
>
> Todas las pruebas y ejercicios son esencialmente otra manera para tratar de saber más acerca de usted al igual que la propia entrevista. El objetivo no es torturarle, engañarle o ponerlo contra la pared, sino que son simplemente para comprobar si es el mejor candidato para ese puesto. Por tanto, su mejor enfoque es tomárselo con calma, sea usted mismo y lleve a cabo los ejercicios lo mejor y tan honestamente como pueda.

PRUEBA EN EQUIPO

Si el empleador está particularmente interesado en saber cómo encaja usted en un equipo, ellos le solicitarán que tome parte en algún tipo de prueba en equipo; generalmente dura todo el día o inclusive hasta un par de días. Esto implicará cualquier cosa, desde una excursión a los páramos, hasta construir un modelo de la Torre Eiffel como portapapeles. Usted será observado y evaluado durante toda la prueba.

> **Recomendación efectiva**
>
> Un punto positivo para tener en mente es que las pruebas son costosas y su empleador prospectivo no estaría gastando tanto dinero a menos que ellos sientan que el trabajo lo vale y de que usted sea una buena inversión. Entonces, el ser invitado a tomar parte en una prueba es una motivación para su confianza.

A menos que solicite un trabajo como guardia de un parque, no es probable que su empleador prospectivo le dé dos gritos para indicarle a dónde puede ir de excursión a los páramos. Tampoco lo es que ellos necesiten un modelo de la Torre Eiffel como portapapeles. No, lo que quieren es saber cómo trabaja en equipo. Usted no quiere gastar su tiempo tratando de ser alguien que no es –y si obtiene el trabajo sobre esa base no estaría feliz de todas maneras–. En cualquier caso, tal vez usted sea puesto bajo suficiente presión y se lleve un buen tiempo para llevar a cabo un acto de duración completa.

Su trabajo en equipo es lo que cuenta, no tanto el proyecto que le han presentado.

Por tanto, esté pendiente de que su trabajo en equipo es lo que cuenta, no el proyecto que le han presentado. Sea usted mismo, pero evite los extremos que puedan disuadir a los evaluadores para que lo recomienden.

- No se la tome muy oficiosamente y se vuelva muy mandón (aunque si el equipo genuinamente lo considera como su líder, eso está bien).
- No sea tan quieto y reservado que parezca que no se involucra. Asegúrese de que hace suficientes contribuciones para que lo puedan evaluar.
- No discuta con los demás miembros del equipo. Si aparece el conflicto, juegue el papel de diplomático para ser visto como que trata de mejorar la situación.
- No opte por salirse y rehusarse a participar en el juego diciendo: "De todas maneras esto es una estupidez. ¿Cuál es el punto de hacer un modelo de la Torre Eiffel?".

- Si hay otros equipos compitiendo con el suyo, es bueno demostrar actitud competitiva, pero no hasta el punto de llegar a la rudeza. Adopte un enfoque de: "Es sólo un juego, pero todo lo demás sigue igual y preferimos ganar y haremos nuestro mejor esfuerzo". No es probable que obtenga el empleo nada más porque su equipo gane en la construcción con clips. Como se desempeña en el juego es lo que cuenta.

Aparte de ser el diplomático, los papeles más útiles que puede jugar en el equipo para impresionar a sus evaluadores, son:

- Mantener enfocado al equipo sobre el objetivo: "Hey, muchachos, ¿realmente importa cómo juntamos los portapapeles? Mejor nos concentramos en la construcción de la torre. Cada uno puede juntarlos como guste".
- Resumir cómo avanza el equipo de tiempo en tiempo: "Hemos resuelto cómo construir la cosa, pero hemos decidido no tratar de incorporar un elevador. Esto significa que necesitamos pensar acerca de cómo asignar las siguientes tareas".

Buen ejercicio

Los centros de evaluación son un buen método para juzgar su habilidad para hacer bien y objetivamente el trabajo. La manera en que se enfoque en los ejercicios puede ser tan importante como la conclusión final que haga. Algunos ejercicios son individuales, mientras que en otros se juega un papel en un grupo con otros candidatos.

Si le solicitan tomar parte en una prueba en equipo, es probable que usted sea evaluado por su capacidad para trabajar en equipo, especialmente si el ejercicio en sí mismo no es relevante para el trabajo que solicita. Entonces, relativamente poco importa que el equipo complete el ejercicio, sino que importa más la manera en cómo interactúa con los demás miembros de su equipo. Por tanto, siga estos lineamientos:

- No rechace participar ni permanezca sin involucrarse.
- No inicie discusiones, ayude a resolverlas.
- Mantenga al equipo enfocado en el objetivo.
- Resuma el avance del equipo cuando parezca que es necesario hacerlo.

Capítulo 13
Segundas entrevistas

Los entrevistadores no dan segundas entrevistas simplemente porque no pueden decidir a quién ofrecerle el trabajo y desean echar otra mirada a los candidatos. La segunda ocasión es una oportunidad para conocerlos más, o permitir una entrevista con un alto ejecutivo a una lista más pequeña de candidatos. O quizá usted fue reclutado por una agencia que lo entrevistó inicialmente, así que es la primera vez que conoce a su empleador. Cualquiera que sea el caso, no va a ser una repetición igual a la primera entrevista.

Recomendación efectiva

No olvide lo básico cuando vaya a su segunda entrevista, así como seguir todos los lineamientos de las primeras entrevistas; usted también deberá:

- Usar un traje diferente al de la primera ocasión. Esto da la impresión de que ser inteligente es parte de su segunda naturaleza, en lugar de que nada más tenga un solo traje para las entrevistas.
- Recuerde y use los nombres de todas las personas que conoció la vez anterior. Asegúrese de reconocerlos a todos ellos y saludarlos con: "Qué gusto verlos nuevamente".
- Recuerde llevar los documentos correctos y sus muestras en un portafolio.

Puede encontrarse con que debe presentar pruebas psicométricas, ejercicios del centro de evaluación o una entrevista técnica junto con su segunda entrevista. Todo bastante formal. Por otra parte, una entrevista con un colega o un gerente de alto nivel ya debidamente informados por su entrevistador inicial puede ser algo menos formal, ya que ellos sólo quieren comprobar lo que el primer entrevistador les reportó y si fue exacta su evaluación acerca de usted.

> Los entrevistadores a veces tienen un candidato "comodín" en una lista corta, y usted podría serlo.

Si existe alguna seria preocupación a partir de su primera entrevista, es factible que sea ventilada en la segunda. Sus entrevistadores pueden estar preocupados sobre si cuenta con menos experiencia que la de otros candidatos, o de alguna manera es muy diferente de la de todos ellos. O quizá ellos se preocupan porque esté sobrecalificado. Los entrevistadores a veces tienen un candidato "comodín" en una lista corta, y usted podría serlo.

Por tanto, ellos quieren reasegurarse de que sea la persona adecuada para el trabajo y de que cualesquiera características preocupantes en su solicitud sean realmente fortalezas.

Es muy posible que en su segunda entrevista le pregunten sobre estas dudas directamente, pero si ellos no lo hacen es obvio que sólo necesitan reasegurarse. Recuerde, lo llamaron por segunda vez, o sea que no consideran que le falta experiencia –o cualquier cosa que les moleste– para borrarlo. Y quizá pensaron que tiene suficientes fuerzas para considerarlo en una lista corta a pesar de sus dudas. En otras palabras, ellos quieren reasegurarse de que usted quiere hacer el trabajo.

Es probable que le hagan muchas preguntas relacionadas directamente con su desempeño en la segunda entrevista, así que esté listo para cuestiones como:

- ¿Qué mejoras ha introducido en su trabajo actual?
- ¿Qué ha hecho para mejorar la productividad?
- ¿Y su principal error?
- ¿Cómo ha mejorado la lucratividad de su departamento?

Si tiene experiencia administrativa, es probable que también le pregunten acerca de esto, incluyendo cuestiones tales como si usted ha hecho su propia capacitación, sobre reclutamiento y demás. Si el trabajo va a requerir relocalizarlo, es factible que lo interroguen acerca de cómo se siente al respecto y de cómo afectará esto a su familia.

TOME UNA BEBIDA...

Muchas segundas entrevistas se llevan a cabo de manera muy informal en un almuerzo o cena, e inclusive con unos tragos en un bar. En este caso, su entrevistador (o puede haber varios) verá qué tan bien encaja y qué tan fácil se lleva con los demás.

Sin embargo, no importa qué tan relajada sea la atmósfera, nunca olvide que usted está siendo evaluado. Asegúrese de comportarse bien y que es de fácil conversación, pero no caiga en la tentación de decir algo que no haría en una entrevista formal. No es correcto dejar a sus anfitriones con la idea de que su último éxito fue en realidad una farsa, o de lo chistoso que usted cree que es burlarse de los empleados menores pretendiendo ser un Doctor en administración estando de mal humor.

Desastre efectivo

Usted se ha tomado uno o dos tragos, o muchos más; sus anfitriones empiezan a hablar de los grandes desastres de sus carreras. Entonces ellos le preguntan acerca de los suyos. Ellos parecen muy amistosos, compañías divertidas, así que usted les dice... ¡Uff!

Y lo más importante de todo, no beba mucho. Demuestre que bebe con moderación, pero no llegue al punto que le afecte su conducta (o su volumen) de ninguna manera. Si es abstemio obviamente no querrá beber, pero no le dé la impresión a su entrevistador de que es un alcohólico reformado; esto no avanzará bien sin importar que hace mucho haya dejado el vicio.

> Muestre que bebe con moderación.

Segunda oportunidad

Una segunda entrevista no es la repetición de la primera. Es una oportunidad para que demuestre su potencial a los empleadores y para que sepan más acerca de usted, o para que alguien nuevo (y probablemente un alto funcionario superior al último entrevistador) lo conozca. Si existen serias dudas acerca de su candidatura, ellos las ventilarán en esta segunda entrevista. También puede esperar que le hagan muchas preguntas acerca de sus logros más recientes en sus trabajos.

Si es invitado a un almuerzo o cena por su entrevistador, esté relajado y amistoso, pero nunca baje la guardia. Usted está permanentemente bajo juicio, inclusive aunque no lo sienta así.

Parte 3
Después de la entrevista

Capítulo 14
¿Qué hacer mientras espera escucharlos?

Probablemente experimentará una gran sensación de alivio una vez que la entrevista haya terminado, pero no porque esto suceda quiere decir que ya no tenga nada más que hacer. Así que tan pronto como regrese a casa, necesitará hacer dos cosas:

- Escriba una carta de agradecimiento al entrevistador.
- Haga notas.

DÉ LAS GRACIAS

Yo sé que esto suena depresivo como toda esa ronda de cartas de "agradecimiento" que los padres hacen que escriban los niños en Navidad y en sus cumpleaños, pero usted necesita escribir y agradecer al entrevistador tan pronto como sea posible, ya que quiere que su carta llegue antes de que ellos tomen una decisión. Con objeto de asegurarse que esté a tiempo, siempre puede enviarla por correo electrónico, especialmente si sabe que tomarán la decisión rápido. Su carta de agradecimiento tiene dos propósitos:

1. Le permite que el entrevistador se acuerde de usted, de la misma manera que lo hacen los anuncios.
2. Le da la oportunidad de mencionar (*brevemente*) cualquier cosa importante que se le haya olvidado.

Dado que usted ciertamente sea el único candidato que le escriba después de la entrevista, esto hará mucho por traer su nombre a la atención del entrevistador, inclusive si ha sido borrado de la lista. La carta puede hacer la diferencia; por ejemplo, si estará o no en la lista corta para la entrevista final. Esto demuestra que a usted le interesa el trabajo, va en serio y es cortés en esta situación.

¿Qué es lo que va a decir en la carta? Debe decir algo como estas líneas: "Gracias por entrevistarme esta mañana. Me dio gusto conocerlo y yo quiero confirmar que todavía estoy seriamente interesado en el puesto. Espero recibir noticias de usted".

Usted quizá guste añadir una nota breve a lo largo de unas líneas, por ejemplo: "Por cierto, como discutimos la posibilidad de trabajar en el exterior, yo olvidé decirle que previamente he tomado clases nocturnas de francés e inglés". No es necesario añadir esta información a menos que sea algo importante que sienta que olvidó decírselo, y una sola frase será suficiente. Éste no es el sitio para lanzar una larga serie defensiva porque usted piense que el entrevistador tiene alguna duda acerca de su adecuación para el trabajo y sienta que deba repetirle lo que ya le ha dicho en la entrevista.

> **Recomendación efectiva**
>
> Como con su solicitud, su carta o correo electrónico necesita verse lo más profesional posible. Los estándares del correo electrónico son bastantes sencillos, pero si escribe una carta, asegúrese de que luzca inteligente y profesional, o sus efectos positivos podrían diluirse seriamente.

HAGA NOTAS

Ahora existe algo más que tiene que hacer mientras espera la respuesta: haga notas acerca de la entrevista. Cualquier punto general que anote acerca de cómo estuvo le ayudará en otras: siente que se preparó bien, estuvo confiado, discutió mucho, estuvo muy poco serio, respondió las preguntas fluidamente. Éstos son puntos útiles que anotar para que maneje aún mejor sus próximas entrevistas.

Haga notas acerca de la entrevista.

Existe otra razón para hacer notas. Podría tener una segunda entrevista. En caso de que esto suceda usted, necesita anotar:

- El nombre de su entrevistador y de quien haya conocido.
- Cualquier pregunta que sienta que podría haberla respondido mejor (para que se prepare para la próxima vez).
- Cualquier reserva que sospeche que el entrevistador se haya quedado.
- Cualquier cosa que a usted le hubiera gustado decir, pero que no lo hizo.
- Algo que los haya impresionado y que, por tanto, sea bueno reforzarlo la próxima vez.

Esté pendiente

Cause una buena impresión en su entrevistador escribiéndole una carta breve de agradecimiento por entrevistarlo. Esto lo pondrá un plus arriba de la mayoría de los otros candidatos, si no es que sobre todos. Y prepárese para causar una buena impresión la próxima vez también, escribiendo notas de cómo se sintió en su desempeño, y sobre cualquier cosa que usted necesitará recordar si es que lo vuelven a llamar para una segunda entrevista.

Capítulo 15
¿Qué hacer si consigue el trabajo?

¡Felicidades! a usted le han ofrecido el trabajo. Si gusta, acéptelo alegremente –sujeto a las negociaciones que veremos en un momento–. Si sabe que ya no lo quiere –odia la empresa o ha obtenido una oferta mejor–, eso también está bien. Decline el trabajo, pero de manera cortés. Nunca sabe cuándo se volverá a encontrar a esas personas nuevamente, y no será de gran ayuda si les dijo, no importa qué tan honestamente, que ellos podrían quedarse con su trabajo y que usted no trabajaría con ellos ni aunque le pagaran un millón de libras.

> **Recomendación efectiva**
>
> Técnicamente su nuevo trabajo no está garantizado hasta que le hayan ofrecido por escrito un contrato estipulando pago y condiciones, y usted haya contestado por escrito su aceptación. Así que no divulgue su noticia hasta que este proceso termine; de otra manera, usted tal vez podría quedarse sin el trabajo después de todo.

MALA SINCRONIZACIÓN

El problema se presenta cuando a usted le ofrecen un trabajo mientras espera saber si va a encontrar una mejor oferta de alguien más.

Usted no quiere decir "sí" y después perder un mejor empleo, pero tampoco quiere decir "no" si no le ofrecen el otro trabajo. Hmmm.

Su primera respuesta en esta situación debería ser tratar de ganar tiempo. Dígales que está feliz de que le hayan ofrecido el trabajo y, por favor, podría contestarles en, digamos, unas 24 horas. No sería razonable solicitarles más tiempo, ya que ellos supondrán qué le pasa a usted para pedir varios días para decidir. Nadie quiere ser un segundo mejor, así que no les permita saber que está esperando una mejor oferta. Si ellos le preguntan por qué necesita tiempo para decidir, les puede decir que quiere platicarlo con su familia. O simplemente dígales que aceptar un nuevo empleo es una decisión muy seria y que no le gusta andar con prisas ante las grandes decisiones. Ellos no pueden discutir con esto.

> Nadie quiere ser un segundo mejor.

Es perfectamente razonable estar en contacto con su empleador preferido en esta etapa del proceso y explicarle el problema. Estarán satisfechos de saber que ellos son su primera opción, y si piensan que todo mundo quiere emplearlo, esto lo hace parecer un mejor prospecto. No espere una respuesta al instante de ellos, pero pregúnteles si podrían llamarle mañana. Siempre podrían decirle que no.

Si esto suena como una buena técnica para obtener una mejor oferta de su primera selección de empleo, si no le han ofrecido realmente otro trabajo, no lo es. No vaya hacia eso. Si ellos le fueran a ofrecer el trabajo de todas maneras, está bien, podría persuadirles de que le ofrezcan el trabajo antes de perderlo. Y podría funcionar si ellos están titubeando entre usted y otro candidato, pero si se encuentra en el límite de su decisión, es probable que los fuerce a que le digan "no" a usted, si ellos no quieren que nadie los presione. Cuando menos un "no" en firme lo deja libre para aceptar la otra oferta, más que conjeturar si usted la acepta o no quedándose al final con nada.

Todos los tipos de circunstancias, desde luego, pueden atravesarse en el camino:

- Puede ser que su primera opción de empleo todavía no haya hecho ninguna selección.
- Quizá ni siquiera ha sido entrevistado todavía, o tal vez ellos están diseñando una lista corta para las segundas entrevistas.

- O quizá su primera selección es una promoción interna y está reticente a decirle a su jefe que ha estado solicitando trabajo en otra parte.

En cualquiera de estos casos, temo que no hay nada que pueda hacer excepto arriesgarse. Tendrá que sopesar qué tanto quiere este nuevo empleo y qué tanto le importa continuar en el trabajo donde está ahora, sus oportunidades de obtener el puesto que *realmente* quiere y demás. Pero recuerde, usted obviamente es empleable y puede dar una buena entrevista (aunque se haya esperado tanto). El hecho de que el entrevistador le haya ofrecido a usted el trabajo es una muy buena señal.

Conocimiento efectivo

La mayoría de los empleadores verifican cuando menos algunas de las calificaciones de los candidatos antes de ofrecerles el trabajo –es reconocido que cuando menos 12% de los solicitantes hacen declaraciones falsas o exageradas acerca de sus calificaciones o de su experiencia laboral–. Por tanto, usted puede esperar que casi todos los empleadores investiguen cuando menos algunas referencias y la mayoría verificará todas ellas.

NEGOCIACIÓN DEL TRATO

Debería dejar cualquier negociación –sobre el salario u otros términos y beneficios– hasta que le hayan ofrecido el trabajo. Una vez que lo hayan admitido como el candidato que ellos quieren, se encuentra en una posición de negociación más fuerte. Así

> Resista los intentos que le persuadan a hablar acerca de dinero.

que, como hemos visto anteriormente, debería resistir los intentos de persuadirlo a que hable acerca del dinero hasta este momento.

Debería esperar a negociar el contrato más que simplemente decir "sí" a cualquier cosa que le ofrezcan, lo cual muestra que usted tiene un sólido sentido de sus valores y que no es una persona fácil de convencer. Mientras, esto puede significar dar más piso del que ellos puedan querer, en términos más amplios son buenas cualidades en un empleado. En cualquier caso, ellos esperan negociar y usualmente tienen algún margen para hacerlo.

Sin embargo, no tiene caso tratar de obtener más de lo que ellos pueden ofrecer: usted terminará en un empate y podría perder el trabajo en este momento. A menos que no quiera el trabajo sin un cierto nivel de salario, asegúrese de pedir lo que ellos le puedan ofrecer. Así que, ¿cuánto le pueden ofrecer?

- Si el rango de salario ha sido mencionado –o se le menciona ahora–, puede razonablemente obtener el máximo nivel en tanto que haya demostrado que lo vale.
- Si el salario aproximado ha sido mencionado, puede suponer que existe un margen de un 10 por ciento.
- Si el trabajo es uno de aquellos donde existe una escala de pagos que es inflexible, puede negociar otros beneficios todavía.

Entre más valioso demuestre que es, mejores oportunidades tendrá de empujar al empleador hacia arriba al punto más alto del rango. Si sus calificaciones o experiencia exceden lo que ellos piden en sus anuncios de reclutamiento para el tipo de profesional que buscan, esto le da la oportunidad de mostrar que usted vale más que el promedio para ese trabajo. Necesita preparar sus justificaciones para poder solicitar el nivel máximo del rango de salarios, tales como:

- "Yo no sólo he obtenido mi 706/1 de calificación, como especificaron en su material de reclutamiento, tengo también mi 706/2 y 706/3".
- "Ustedes estuvieron buscando por dos años de experiencia en la programación de computadoras, y de hecho yo he estado programando computadoras desde que estaba en la escuela, y ahora profesionalmente por casi cuatro años".
- "En adición a la experiencia y calificaciones que ustedes solicitan, yo también hablo fluidamente francés e inglés, lo que sería una ventaja importante, ya que tienen muchos clientes extranjeros".

A usted le han ofrecido este trabajo porque puede dar mucho más que los otros candidatos, así que presumiblemente tiene habilidades por arriba del promedio. Todo lo que debe hacer es identificarlas y usarlas como una herramienta de negociación.

> **Recomendación efectiva**
>
> Antes de que empiece sus negociaciones, usted tiene que saber cuánto dinero quiere como mínimo. Podría ser lo mínimo que puede aceptar para poder vivir, o esto sería el mínimo con lo que se compensa lo que usted vale –no pudiendo tomar el trabajo por menos–. Sin embargo, si la define, tiene que ir a las negociaciones sabiendo su línea mínima; si no la conoce, es probable que la negociación quede por debajo de ésta.

Usted empieza a negociar, pero no llega a ninguna parte:

- Ha establecido su apalancamiento para solicitar un salario más alto que su oferta de apertura, porque puede demostrar que vale más, desde mayor experiencia hasta habilidades adicionales útiles.
- Sabe cuál es su línea base (salario), por lo que prefiere rechazar la oferta.

Encuentre las variables

Existe algo más que necesita hacer antes de empezar a hablar: identificar todas las variables. En otras palabras, los demás ítems que puede negociar adicionales a su salario. Si discute sólo el dinero, se queda regateando como en un mercado. Empieza unos miles por arriba de lo que ellos dicen y cada uno va dando pie hasta que se encuentran en el medio, pero una negociación salarial puede ser más sofisticada que eso, y son sus intereses lo que importa.

Las variables son todos los demás factores que puede traer en juego para equilibrarlos con su salario. Así que si le ofrecen menos de lo que quiere y se ven incapaces o sin deseos de aceptar, puede solicitar otro derecho vacacional, o una computadora suministrada por el empleador. Entre más variables tenga para jugar, más alcance tendrán ambas partes para negociar.

Eche una mirada a la lista de variables opuestas –existe capacidad para añadir más al final– en la columna de en medio puede marcar la oferta (si la conoce) y en el lado derecho escriba lo que quiere negociar. Sólo recuerde que nadie le va a dar todo. Si tiene más comisiones, tendrá que conceder algo más, como una reducción en su salario básico. Entonces llene esta lista acorde con lo que piensa que es justo, razonable y plausible, así que todavía puede completar la lista acorde con lo anterior, no de acuerdo con alguna fantasía ideal.

> Sólo recuerde que nadie la va a dar todo.

Una vez que haya establecido cuáles son las variables, no tiene que negociar todo, sino sólo aquellas que le conciernen. Sin embargo, sabe que las otras están ahí para entrar en juego en caso de que se estanque. Si ellos simplemente no se mueven más allá sobre el salario o las vacaciones, entonces podría solicitar una computadora o pensión para los niños.

La cuestión es que los empleadores pueden ser muy sensibles acerca de pagarle más de lo comparable a los demás empleados, en caso de que se hable de esto. Así que ellos estarán mucho más de acuerdo en acordar un salario que nadie va a objetar y cubrir la diferencia con otros beneficios. Igualmente, su salario es un costo directo, pero a ellos le costará bastante menos proporcionarle una computadora que lo que les costaría a usted comprársela. Juzgará el valor del aparato por el dinero que le ahorra comprar una, pero el costo actual de ellas es ahora bastante más bajo. Así que existen varias razones del por qué a menudo encontrará más fácil obtenerla a que le concedan más beneficios salariales.

Variable	Oferta actual	Objetivo
Salario		
Bonos		
Comisión		
Tiempo extra		
Participación de utilidades		
Derecho a vacaciones		
Permiso para faltar algunos días (dentista, citas, niños, enfermedad, etcétera)		
Seguro médico/otro		
Contribución a la pensión		

Opciones de acciones		
Contribución para cuidado de los niños		
Costos de relocalización		
Auto de la compañía		
Teléfono móvil		
Pensión para viajar		
Gastos de hotel		
Membrecía a un club de salud		
Fecha de inicio del trabajo		
Otros		

Técnicas para negociar

Las primeras reglas de la negociación ya han sido cubiertas:

- Establezca su apalancamiento.
- Sepa cuál es la línea de base.
- Encuentre todas las variables que pueda.

Una vez que entre en conversación, existen tres reglas más que necesitará seguir:

- Ponga todas las cartas sobre la mesa.
- Nunca dé concesiones gratis.
- Acuerde todo o nada.

Ponga todas las cartas sobre la mesa

Si está tratando con un tipo truculento, hábil para negociar el mejor trato para su compañía, existe un as que ellos pueden sacarse bajo su manga. Tiene que encontrar cuál es. Ellos podrían obtener concesiones de usted aún antes de que estén de acuerdo en hablar de un salario en particular. Ellos querrán acordar desde el principio un salario bajo, o que tome responsabilidades extra junto con las que ya han acordado originalmente. Y si tienen un trato solapado esperarán hasta el último minuto para hacérselo saber. En otras palabras, ellos esperarán hasta que usted ya haya aceptado totalmente el salario.

Y de repente: "Oh, y a mí me gustaría que usted llevase las cuentas de su colega Felipa mientras ella se encuentra en ausencia por maternidad". Ahora no es que usted no quiera tomar la oportunidad de demostrar que puede llevar las cuentas de Felipa en su trabajo, pero justamente se trata de que esto aumenta su valor aún más, y con esto el tamaño del salario inicial que se merece. Pero cuidado, ya casi ha terminado de negociar y su futuro empleador sabe que usted estaba a punto de aceptar un salario en algún momento en medio del rango advertido. Es mucho más difícil ahora echarse para atrás que cerrar un salario casi hasta el límite de su rango. Y ellos ya saben esto.

Recomendación efectiva

El principio de una buena negociación es que todos salgan sintiéndose ganadores. Una negociación junto a una oferta de trabajo debe ser menos confrontadora que la mayoría de las demás —después de todo ustedes dos están del mismo lado–, pero si está tratando con un negociador naturalmente competitivo, ellos todavía querrán sentir que encontraron a la mejor persona para el trabajo y a un precio de descuento.

La manera de prevenir esto es muy sencillo: dígales a ellos que pongan todas sus cartas sobre la mesa y haga usted lo mismo. Así puede equilibrar todas las cuestiones de uno contra otro. Todo lo que puede hacer es decir, por ejemplo: "Necesitamos hablar acerca de mi salario y también discutir mi derecho a vacaciones. ¿Existen otras cuestiones que necesitamos discutir al mismo tiempo?". Usted les ha hecho bastante difícil ponerse a hablarle sobre el tema de que tenga que cubrir las cuentas de Felipa mientras ella está afuera. Si ellos no lo mencionan y vuelven después sobre esto, tiene el derecho moral y encontrará más fácil insistir en que regresará sobre el tema una vez que los demás puntos hayan sido acordados y lo revisará bajo la luz de la nueva información.

Solicite que pongan todas sus cartas sobre la mesa.

> **Recomendación efectiva**
>
> No olvide que si no puede acordar el salario inicial que quiere, ellos podrían todavía hacer que el empleador acuerde una revisión del salario e inclusive convenir un aumento después de un periodo fijo. No es poco razonable para ellos querer asegurarse de que usted es tan bueno como lo parece. Acuerde con ellos un salario específico a revisarse si satisface las metas acordadas: "¿Qué tal ahora £ 30 000; en el entendimiento de que si incremento la productividad cuando menos en un 3 % me aumentarán a £ 32 000 en mi revisión semestral?".

Nunca dé concesiones gratuitas

Es una simple regla crucial para negociar. Todo lo que significa es que si ellos le solicitan un monto menor al que pide, o concede que esperará seis meses antes de que obtenga un aumento al salario que desea, usted no diga simplemente que sí; mejor intercambie su concesión por una de ajuste por parte de ellos.

- Si le dicen: "Yo puedo ofrecerle una revisión salarial sólo después de tres meses", no simplemente conteste "Está bien". Usted diga: "En tanto que mi salario crezca cuando menos £ 1 000 si yo completo exitosamente el periodo de prueba".
- Cuando ellos digan: "Yo sólo le puedo ofrecer un 5 % de comisión", usted conteste: "Si lo hacemos así, la comisión necesitará de ser de cuando menos 5 % del bruto".
- Cuando ellos le digan: "El derecho a vacaciones es de sólo cuatro semanas", usted responda: "En ese caso yo necesito cuando menos cinco permisos al año para ausentarme".

Ya ha captado la idea. Este principio es crucial porque significa que usted terminará con un mejor trato. Cada vez que pierda algo, debe ganar algo. Sólo asegúrese de que las concesiones que haga se ajusten con el valor de las cosas que está dando.

> Cada vez que pierda algo, también debe ganar algo.

> **Recomendación efectiva**
>
> Cuando no da concesiones gratis, su futuro empleador aprenderá pronto que usted es un negociador duro. A partir de esto ellos la pensarán dos veces antes de pedirle concesiones. Por cada concesión suya, ellos le tienen que dar algo también. Y a largo plazo es bueno que sepan que no dará algo a cambio de nada cuando se trate de negociar.

Acuerde todo o nada

La manera en como logre el acuerdo final en su negociación es mover todas las variables a su alrededor hasta llegar a un equilibrio. Por ejemplo, si el salario es más bajo de lo que usted quiere, también insista en la ayuda para cuidado de los niños. Desde luego, puede administrarse con una menor partida para el cuidado de los niños, pero sólo si obtiene más días para faltar con permiso. Y así sucesivamente. Es como si todos estos factores fuesen pesos de una balanza para llegar a un equilibrio con el que esté contento.

Lo que nunca debe perder de vista es acordar una variable antes de que acuerde todas las demás. Esto significa que uno de los pesos de su balanza faltaría y no se puede equilibrar la balanza de esta manera. Esto hace más duro acordar un trato final y usted tendrá que darle más peso del que quisiera a cada uno de esos factores para lograr un equilibrio.

> **Desastre efectivo**
>
> Usted ya ha acordado su salario inicial y su comisión. Ahora su futuro empleador le dice que el derecho de vacaciones en esta empresa es de una semana menos de lo que ha estado acostumbrado. El problema es que usted se ha quedado con muy poco con que negociar, una vez acordados casi todos los términos. ¡Uff!

Por tanto, usted quiere erradicar de la negociación cualquier comentario de ellos, tal como: "Correcto, hemos acordado el salario básico. Ahora hablemos acerca de los beneficios complementarios". No esté de acuerdo con tal cosa, y si ellos tratan de presionarlo con un comentario como éste, simplemente dígales: "No hemos finalizado el asunto del salario. Yo todavía lo estoy considerando, pero estoy muy contento de seguir adelante y discutir ahora los beneficios complementarios".

LA CARTA DE OFERTA

Una vez que el trato ha finalizado, puede esperar una carta de oferta de su nuevo empleador. Acorde con OneClickHR, ésta debería definir claramente lo siguiente:

- El puesto que se le ofrece.
- La remuneración.
- La fecha de inicio del empleo (si se acordó).
- La localización.
- Cualquier tipo de condiciones bajo las cuales esté la oferta.
- El plazo de tiempo y el procedimiento para la aceptación/rechazo de la oferta.

Suponiendo que todo esto concuerda con lo que usted acordó, está en su derecho. Responda a la oferta de la manera en que se especifica en la carta, la cual debe estar escrita en terminología jurídica, y buena suerte con su nuevo trabajo.

Adecuar el trabajo para usted

Cuando le sea ofrecido el trabajo, tendrá que decidir si lo toma. Si no está seguro, por ejemplo, si está esperando obtener una oferta mejor, puede solicitarles unas 24 horas más para decidir, pero antes o después sencillamente tendrá que tomar el reto.

Si dice que sí al trabajo, necesita negociar el mejor trato que pueda. Trabaje en lo que su empleador crea que puede y cuando se prepare para negociar:

- Establezca su apalancamiento.
- Conozca el nivel del piso.
- Encuentre todas las variables que pueda.

Una vez que las negociaciones se inicien:

- Coloque todas las cartas sobre la mesa.
- Nunca dé concesiones gratuitas.
- Acuerde todo o nada.

Capítulo 16
¿Qué pasa si pierde la oferta de trabajo?

Por más efectivo que sea en la entrevista, no siempre podrá obtener el trabajo. No todo mundo es la persona correcta para cada puesto, e inevitablemente habrá rechazo. Mientras que usted debe estar consciente de cualquier falla en su desempeño y tomar nota de ello, también puede trabajar para mejorar la próxima vez, no se debería culpar si no logra el puesto. Si ha hecho toda su preparación y seguido todos los consejos de este libro, habrá hecho todo lo que sea posible.

Bien, es correcto si tiene muchas otras entrevistas prometedoras por venir, y quizá tenga reservas acerca del trabajo que no pudo obtener, pero qué sucede si se trata de uno de esos empleos que muere por obtenerlo, ¿y siente que era el mejor candidato? ¿Es sólo mala suerte o existe algo que pueda hacer después de un rechazo?

📖 Conocimiento efectivo

Estadísticamente las entrevistas son en realidad uno de los métodos menos eficaces para seleccionar al mejor candidato (a pesar de ser lo más común). Una de las principales razones de esto es que se sustentan mucho sobre la habilidad y juicio del entrevistador, y no todos los entrevistadores están tan calificados como deberían. Acorde con Phil Boyle, director gerente de Ramsay Hall Limited, una organización exitosa para el reclutamiento de ejecutivos: "Si fue rechazado para un trabajo que sabe que puede hacer, culpe al mal entrevistador y no a alguna falla de usted".

La buena noticia es que no se sabe de los buenos candidatos que llegan al empleo después de que han sido rechazados para éste. Si llegó a la lista corta, o hasta la última vuelta de entrevistas, queda claro que es capaz de hacer el trabajo. Es justamente que su entrevistador sintió (correcta o incorrectamente) que alguno de los otros candidatos podría hacerlo aún mejor que usted.

Desastre efectivo

No obtuvo el empleo y está muy desmoralizado. Seis semanas después está todavía buscando un cambio de trabajo. Mientras tanto, el candidato que obtuvo el puesto que quería se da cuenta de que no encaja y él decide irse. El empleador se pregunta a quién ofrecerlo ahora. Ellos no han oído nada de usted desde que lo desecharon, así que entonces se lo ofrecen a otro candidato de la lista corta, quien ha estado pendiente y en contacto con ellos. ¡Uff!

No es poco común para el candidato exitoso durar poco en el nuevo trabajo. Cuando esto sucede los empleadores ya no tienden a anunciarse otra vez, sino que van de vuelta con los candidatos originales y les ofrecen el empleo si es que están disponibles todavía. A veces otra vacante similar se presenta dentro de un par de meses y nuevamente es probable que el empleador contacte a los candidatos anteriores para ver si ellos están todavía disponibles.

¿Cómo le hará para estar en el primer lugar de la lista?

Si usted fue un buen candidato y se encuentra disponible, todavía estará en su lista de personas a las que se les puede volver a ofrecer nuevamente el trabajo, pero esto no es suficientemente bueno, requiere estar en el primer sitio de la lista. Y usted necesita que ellos sepan que aún busca el empleo adecuado y que le interesa cualquier cosa que le puedan ofrecer.

¿Cómo le hará para estar en el primer lugar de la lista? Necesita escribir una respuesta a su carta de rechazo y hacerle saber al entrevistador que usted está todavía interesado en el trabajo o en cualquier otra vacante que tengan. Puede ser breve, diciéndoles algo como esto: "Muchas gracias por avisarme del resultado de mi solicitud; siento mucho que no haya sido exitoso en esta ocasión. Sin embargo, yo quedé muy gratamente impresionado de su compañía y estoy todavía interesado en trabajar con ustedes. Estaría encantado de que se comuniquen conmigo si la situación cambia, o si existe otro puesto adecuado que se presente en el futuro cercano".

> **Recomendación efectiva**
>
> Probablemente se sentirá tentado a decirle al entrevistador en su carta que ellos cometieron un error, y que usted era la mejor persona para el puesto. No lo haga. Cualquier sugerencia sobre que su decisión fue un juicio erróneo de ellos, le causará más daño que si mejor no les contesta.

Este tipo de carta no sólo le ayudará, sino que impresionará a su entrevistador. No sólo es cortés y entusiasta acerca de colaborar con su organización, sino que usted sabe cómo tragarse su ego y continuar luchando a pesar de que las probabilidades estén en su contra, el cual es un talento muy valioso que demostrar.

Sin embargo, una carta como ésta no siempre funcionará. Si un trabajo similar aparece después de unos seis meses, es casi seguro que el empleador volverá a iniciar el proceso de reclutamiento desde el inicio, en lugar de llamarlo. A menos que... usted haya estado en contacto continuo en ese lapso de tiempo.

Esto es lo que debe hacer, si genuinamente le interesa trabajar para ese empleador. Y es cierto que así es, en especial si usted labora en un puesto cómodo pero, por ejemplo, no muy demandante. En esta situación, podría estar solicitando pocos puestos y quizá hasta desechar algunos de ellos. Puede elegir ser selectivo y sólo en un par de organizaciones en las que quiere laborar y por las que desea dejar su trabajo actual.

La mejor manera es mantenerse en contacto cada dos meses más o menos con la persona que lo entrevistó. Puede telefonearle, escribirle o enviarle un correo electrónico, o variar su método de contacto en cada ocasión. Cualquier cosa que haga, sea breve, no lo irrite porque esto le causará más daño que bien. Simplemente dígale que busca todavía el trabajo adecuado y que sigue interesado con seriedad en trabajar para esa organización. Sólo hágale saber que aún tiene interés.

> No los irrite porque esto le causará más daño que bien.

Es todo lo que se necesita para mantener su nombre en su mente, y dejarles saber que todavía no ha tomado otro trabajo. Y si duda de que esto valga la pena, piense en el número de maneras con que podría obtener ese empleo.

- El candidato que se llevó el puesto no está contento y se va.
- Un puesto similar aparece en otro departamento.
- El entrevistador lo recomienda a usted con un colega en otro departamento.
- El entrevistador lo recomienda con un contacto, amigo o excolega, quien tiene un puesto relevante en otra organización.
- El entrevistador deja el trabajo para irse a otra compañía, donde ellos tienen que reclutar personal nuevo.

Ejercicio efectivo 4

1. Vaya a su agenda tan pronto sepa que ha sido rechazado para el puesto que realmente quiere, y haga una nota para contactar a su entrevistador en un par de meses, si usted no ha encontrado un trabajo mejor durante ese tiempo.
2. Decida si le llama por teléfono o le envía un correo electrónico. Si se decide por teléfono, planee lo que le va a decir por anticipado. Si se decide por el correo, piense bien acerca de las palabras de su comunicado, como si fuera una carta formal. Es muy fácil tratar los correos electrónicos de manera informal si usted no se aboca a pensar bien qué es lo que va a escribir.
3. Cada vez que les contacte, haga una nota para no repetir el mismo ejercicio dos meses después.

Las personas que entrevistan y reclutan regularmente tienden a conocer acerca de todo tipo de ofertas de trabajo, además de las propias que estén reclutando. Y si ellos no tienen un trabajo para usted, pero piensan que tiene talento, es cortés y lleno de determinación, ¿por qué no lo recomendarían con alguien más?

NO SE CONFÍE

Como regla general, no vale la pena esperar por siempre un empleo que nunca llegará. Usted ha sido informado que quedó en segundo lugar, y de que habrá un puesto dentro de unos seis meses. Obviamente necesitará mantenerse en contacto, pero siga buscando trabajo en otras partes también.

El próximo trabajo puede no aparecer o el entrevistador puede dejar la compañía, entonces usted terminará con que tiene que volver a empezar de nuevo todo el proceso sin ninguna garantía de que obtendrá el puesto al final. A menos que esté realmente contento donde se encuentra y esa organización sea la única preferencia en la que quiera trabajar, nunca ponga todos sus esfuerzos en una sola opción.

Si desea encontrarse en un trabajo nuevo, solicite a todos los que le parezcan interesantes, y cuando le sea ofrecido un puesto, piense si realmente lo disfrutará y si le ofrece un incremento en prospecto, en salario o lo que sea más importante para usted, entonces tómelo. En esta moderna era de los negocios no querrá quedarse para siempre en un lugar, y habrá otras oportunidades para solicitar ante la compañía de sus sueños; no se cuelgue indefinidamente en un empleo que nunca llegará.

> Nunca ponga todos sus esfuerzos en una sola opción.

Y mientras tanto, usted obtendrá plenitud de oportunidades para practicar lo que ha aprendido. Inclusive cuando sienta en la entrevista que éste no es el trabajo que esperaba, es todavía una oportunidad para practicar todas las habilidades que ha aprendido para que esté preparado cuando aparezca la oportunidad del trabajo que quiere, y así realice una entrevista efectiva.

💬 Consejo efectivo

Si al inicio...

No se rinda porque lo han rechazado en un trabajo. Si es realmente entusiasta, hágalo saber al entrevistador. Y manténgase en contacto con ellos de tiempo en tiempo si no encuentra algo mejor en el ínter. Tarde o temprano habrá la oportunidad de que usted consiga otro empleo. Y quién sabe, éste podría ser mejor aún que el que solicitó al inicio.

Índice analítico

Actitud
  ante la vida, 115
  competitiva, definición de, 145
Actuar en una entrevista de trabajo, 55
Adrenalina, disparadores de, definición de, 51
Agencias de contratación, reclutamiento mediante, 148
Agradecimiento, carta de, 153-154
Anécdotas, exposición de, 128-129
Argumentar, aprender a, 115
Arrogancia
  definición de, 106
  presunción de, 100
Ascensos en el trabajo, 23
Atributos personales, falta de, 23
Autoevaluación, definición de, 20

Candidato(s)
  calificaciones de los, 159
  comodín, definición de, 148
  compararse con otros, 19
  exitoso, definición de, 126
  experiencia de los, 160
  factores a favor de los, 39
  opiniones en la organización sobre los, 44
  para un trabajo, conocer a los, 82
  sondeo de, 136
Capacidad(es)
  de aprender, 107
  de despedir personal, 108
  de motivar a otros, 23
  de resolver problemas, 67
  de tomar decisiones difíciles, 108
  de trabajar
    bajo presión, 22, 24, 90
    en equipo, 76
  propias, ejemplificar, 78-79
Capacitación propia, definición de, 149

Carta(s)
    de oferta de trabajo, recibir, 167
    de presentación, redacción de una, 40
    de rechazo, definición de, 170-171
Centros de evaluación
    características de los, 141
    ejercicios para enfrentar los, 142
Choque de adrenalina, definición de, 49
Comisiones, negociar, 166
Comparase con otros candidatos, 19
Competencias
    entrevistas con base en, 130
    evaluación de, 126
    identificación de, 128
    o habilidades, definición de, 125
Competir por un trabajo, 32
Compromiso con un trabajo, 121
Concesiones gratuitas, hacer, 165-166
Confianza, sentir, 56
Conflictos, manejo de, 96
Contacto visual con el entrevistador, 59, 64
Contribuir en una compañía, 105
Conversación difícil, manejar una, 115
Conversar con el entrevistador, 45, 50, 63
Credibilidad de las respuestas, 92
Criticar a los jefes, implicaciones de, 80

Críticas
    constructivas, definición de, 92
    hacia los demás, 110
    injustas al trabajo propio, 108
    manejo de las, 130
Cualidades, proyección de, 59
Cuestionarios
    de habilidad numérica, 137
    de motivación, enfrentar, 132, 138-139
    de personal, 139
    de razonamiento inductivo, 138
    sobre personalidad, resolver, 138
    verbales, enfrentar, 136
Cultura corporativa
    conocimiento de la, 41
    vestir para satisfacer una, 43, 45
Currículum Vitae, manejo del, 20, 93

Debilidades
    del jefe actual, reconocer las, 110
    para conseguir un trabajo, 18
    reconocer las propias, 83-84
Decisiones difíciles, capacidad de tomar, 108
Derecho a comunicarse, ejercer el, 122
Descripción de uno mismo, elaborar una, 97
Despedir personal, capacidad de, 108
Diplomacia, como habilidad, 33
Discutir con el entrevistador, 109

Eficiencia, mostrar, 72
Empatía, manejar la, 60
Empleador(es)
   actual, criticar al, 65
   atribuciones de los, 20
   intereses de los, 143
   sitios web de los, 31
Empleados
   calificaciones de los, evaluación de las, 160
   cualidades de los, 160
   experiencia de los otros, 161
Enfoque
   de equipo, definición de, 145
   en las pruebas, 29, 145
   mental lógico, definición de, 114
   ordenado, definición de, 92
   profesional, definición de, 72
Entrevista(s)
   basadas en competencias, 126
   de evaluación, definición de, 125
   de trabajo
      actuar en una, 55
      agradecimiento en, 153-154
      beber en, 149
      cara a cara, definición de, 72
      características positivas en la, 95
      comportamiento correcto en, 149
      con base en competencias, 130
      con colegas, 148
      con gerentes de alto nivel, 68, 148
      con profesionales de Recursos Humanos, 68
      conclusión de una, 63, 72
      confiarse en una, 172
      definición de, 32
      desmoralización en, 170
      divagar en una, 65
      en panel, definición de, 68
      ensayar para una, 50, 143
      estructura de una, 130
      frases equivocadas en las, 107
      información para una, 35, 56
      materiales para una, 36
      mensajes en la, 39
      nervios en una, 49
      notas de una, 154-155
      pensar una, 33
      preparación de una, 27, 35-36, 130
      primera impresión en una, 40, 55
      secuenciales, definición de, 70
      segunda, implicaciones de una, 121, 147-148, 150
      sobresalir en una, 101
      solicitar tiempo en una, 158
      tipos de, 67
      vestir para una, 40
   débil, definición de, 18
   definición de, 17, 117, 169
   exteriores u outsourcing, definición de, 25
   formatos de, 21, 63
   hablar en una, 60
   observar en una, 60
   preguntas de una, 21
   secuencial, definición de, 69
   telefónicas, características de las, 70-71

Entrevistado, papel de un, 17
Entrevistador(es)
   actitudes del, 31
   apoyos de los, 96
   atribuciones del, 18
   como futuro jefe, 80, 91
   contacto visual con el, 59, 64
   conversar con el, 45, 50
   cualidades del, 17
   cuestionar al, 117
   desacuerdos con el, 108
   discutir con el, 109
   entrenamiento de los, 22, 113
   hábil, definición de, 97, 163
   impresionar al, 40, 64, 155
   incompetente, definición de, 96
   influir en el, 39, 155
   interrumpir al, 64
   mantener el contacto con el, 171
   opinión del, 39
   persuasión de un, 32
   preocupaciones de los, 23
   profesionales, 59, 117
   razones positivas para el, 79
   recomendaciones por parte del, 173
   reservas de un, 122, 155
   reticente, manejo de un, 22
Entusiasmo
   generar, 118
   manejarse con, 57
Escalar profesionalmente, aspiración de, 101
Escuchar preguntas, 75
Estrés
   preguntas que causan, 67
   reducir el, 52

Evaluación
   de competencias, definición de, 126
   de fallas, 108
   de uno mismo, 25
Experiencia
   falta de, 23
   promoción de la, 34, 57

Fortalezas personales
   lista de, 33, 83
   promoción de las, 18-19, 32-34, 56

Gobierno, solicitudes de empleo en el, 68
Grupos de discusión, participar en, 143

Habilidad(es)
   diplomacia como, 33
   ejemplificar, 65
   o competencias, definición de, 125
   por arriba el promedio, 161
   probar, 130
   vender las, 27
Hablar con claridad, 60, 64
Historia médica, exponer la, 102
Humor, manejo del, 107

Información
   para enfrentar pruebas, 133
   para una entrevista de trabajo, 35, 56
   sobre antecesores en el puesto, 120
Instinto natural positivo, definición de, 109

Intereses
  externos propios, reconocimiento de, 85
  generales, exposición de, 115

Jefe(s)
  actual, conocer las debilidades del, 110
  criticar a los, 79
  entrevistador como futuro, 80, 91

Lectura, gustos personales de, 86
Lenguaje corporal positivo
  definición de, 58, 64
  elementos del, 59
  perfeccionar el, 61

Mensajes
  de agradecimiento, 154
  en la entrevista de trabajo, manejo de los, 39
Miedo a equivocarse, control del, 50
Motivación
  personal, factores de, 91
  pruebas sobre, definición de, 138
Motivar a otros, capacidad de, 23

Negociación final, términos de una, 166
Negociar
  beneficios salariales, 162
  buenos tratos, 167
  comisiones, 166
  principios para, 164
  salario inicial, 166, 167
  técnicas para, 163

variables, 166
Nervios
  ataque de, definición de, 50
  definición de, 51
  en una entrevista de trabajo, 49
  psicológicos, control de los, 53
  síntomas físicos de los, 51

Objetivo(s)
  definición de, 29
  fijar los, 28
Observar en una entrevista, 61
Ofensas, manejo de las, 130
Ofertas
  de trabajo, rechazar, 173
  múltiples de trabajo, 104
  responder, 167
Oportunidades, tomar las, 164

Personalidad
  natural, emplear la, 55
  pruebas sobre, 138
Persuasión de un entrevistador, 33
Planeación eficaz de proyectos, 94
Portafolios, preparar un, 34
Preguntas
  clásicas, definición de, 107
  comunes, 75
  de autocrítica, manejar, 106
  de primera entrevista, 21
  de segunda entrevista, 148
  duras, manejar, 89, 106, 111, 121
  engañosas, 79
  escuchar atentamente las, 75
  evitar, 118

hipotéticas, definición de, 67, 73
inesperadas, manejo de las, 114
inteligentes, definición de, 119
negativas, manejo de las, 109
que causan estrés, 67
responder, técnicas para, 51, 56, 73
sobre el salario, 108, 111-112
técnicas, definición de, 67
Profesionalismo, mostrar, 72
Promoción
de las fortalezas, 19, 32-34, 56
en el trabajo
esperar una, 102
solicitar una, 24
Proyección personal, definición de, 84
Pruebas
de aptitud, definición de, 131, 134, 136
de conocimientos generales, definición de, 135
de habilidad, definición de, 131, 134
de personalidad, definición de, 132
en equipo, 143-145
gramaticales, 139
invitaciones a, aceptar, 144
prepararse para, 132, 134
psicométricas
afrontar, 131
definición de, 140

Razones, exposición de, 99
Reclamos, hacer, 85
Reclutamiento
de graduados, 25
mediante agencias de contratación, 147
Recursos Humanos, profesionales en, 68
Referencias débiles, problemas por, 22
Reírse de uno mismo, aprender a, 50
Relajación, ejercicios de, 52-53
Resolver problemas, capacidad de, 67
Responder
con la verdad, 102
preguntas, técnicas para, 72
Responsabilidades extra, aceptar, 163
Respuestas
credibilidad de las, 92
elaboración de, 64
inteligentes, definición de, 98
positivas, definición de, 92
ratificar, 117
recomendadas, definición de, 76
relevantes, mantener, 75
Salario
acordar el, 164
aproximado, definición de, 160
bajo, aceptar un, 163
inicial, valorar el, 166
negociar el, 159-160, 164
preguntas sobre el, 108, 111-112
revisión de, 165
solicitar mayor, 113, 162
Saludar correctamente, 44, 50

Ser
  buen gerente, 93
  creativo, virtud de, 95
  crítico, implicaciones de, 110
  diplomático, 145
  exitoso, definición de, 101
  fracasado, definición de, 101
  honesto, definición de, 98
  líder, definición de, 93
  negativo, implicaciones de, 110
  uno mismo, 144
Sitios web de los empleadores, 31
Situaciones difíciles, describir, 109
Sobrecalificación para un trabajo, 105, 120
Sobresalir en una entrevista de trabajo, 101
Solicitantes de trabajo
  actividades extracurriculares en, 81
  en ventas, 114
  filtrado de, 25
  internos, competir con, 24
  recién graduados como, 81
Solicitud(es) de trabajo
  diferente, definición de, 70
  en el gobierno, 68
  escritura de una, 45
  formatos de las, 20
  internas, presentar, 24
  presentación de una, 40
Sonreír
  cordialmente, importancia de, 72
  para relajarse, 52
Trabajar
  bajo presión, capacidad de, 22, 24, 90, 95
  con personas difíciles, 110
  en equipo, capacidad de, 77, 94, 127
Trabajo(s)
  actual, 79, 110
  administrativo, capacidades para el, 90
  amar el, 97
  cambiar de, 99
  competir por un, 31
  compromiso con un, 121
  conseguir un, 29, 118, 157
  debilidades para conseguir un, 18-19
  declinar el, 157
  desafíos de un, 82
  desagrado por un, 13
  descripción de un, 20, 33
  especificaciones de un, 21
  estándares de un, 18
  expertos para un, 120
  fortalezas para conseguir un, 18-19
  interés por el, 154
  justificar periodos sin, 101
  nuevo, 99, 170, 173
  ofertas múltiples de, 104
  personal, tasar e, 113
  prioridades al elegir un, 20
  proyectarse en el, 120
  rechazar un, 173
  sincronizar dos, 157
  sobrecalificación para un, 105, 120
  variables de un, 161-162
  y plan de carrera, 103
Trato(s)
  negociar, 167

final, condiciones del, 166
Vacaciones, derecho a, 165
Vacantes internas, solicitar, 24
Vender las habilidades, aprender a, 27
Vestirse
    para satisfacer una cultura corporativa, 41-43, 45

para una entrevista de trabajo, 40
Vida
    actitud ante la, 115
    personal, ejemplificar la, 107
Visión positiva de uno mismo, 65
Voz, manejo de la, 60

La publicación de esta obra la realizó
Editorial Trillas, S. A. de C. V.

División Administrativa, Av. Río Churubusco 385,
Col. Gral. Pedro María Anaya, C. P. 03340, México, D. F.
Tel. 56884233, FAX 56041364

División Logística, Calzada de la Viga 1132, C. P. 09439
México, D. F. Tel. 56330995; FAX 56330870

Esta obra se imprimió
el 5 de septiembre de 2014, en los talleres de
Programas Educativos, S. A. de C. V.

B 105 TW

SP
650.144 J42

Jay, Ros.
Tips efectivos :para
Floating Collection WLNF
08/15

Friends of the
Houston Public Library